CONFLICTING ETHNICITIES

CONFLICTING ETHNICITIES

Locating the Local in the Global

Edited by
KOUSAR J. AZAM

MANOHAR
2013

First published 2013

ISBN 978-81-7304-998-9

Published by
Ajay Jain *for*
Manohar Publishers & Distributors
4753/23 Ansari Road, Daryaganj
New Delhi 110002

Typeset by
Sai Graphic Design
New Delhi 110055

Printed by
Salasar Imaging Systems
Delhi 110035

To the memory of

PROFESSOR C. VIJAYASREE (1953–2012)

Director

Osmania University Centre for International Programmes

(5 June 2008–19 May 2012)

Contents

Acknowledgements

I am thankful to the Indian Council of Social Science Research for partially sponsoring the conference on Ethnicity in November 2009 at the Osmania University Centre for International Programmes (OUCIP). I extend a special word of thanks to all the paper writers and participants who contributed richly to the discussions, chaired different sessions and also provided us written reports about the conference when requested.

A very special word of thanks to Professor C. Vijaysree, the then Director OUCIP and to Professor T. Vijay Kumar, Jt. Director OUCIP for their support, cooperation and contributions making it possible for me to organize this event. I am also thankful to the entire staff of the OUCIP for shouldering the many responsibilities of organizing an international event.

The OUCIP acknowledges with thanks the permission granted by *The Hindu* to reprint the article of M.S. Prabhakara and to the Regents of the University of California, Berkeley for permitting us to reprint the article by Adeel Khan, from *The Asian Survey*. And finally I thank Dr. R.S. Sharma, former Head, Department of English and Dean, Faculty of Arts, Osmania University for his help at the various stages of this project.

A word of thanks is also due to Ramesh Jain and his team at Manohar for undertaking the publication of this work.

The Editor, Publisher and the OUCIP are not responsible for the opinions expressed by individual authors on the issues discussed in this volume.

KOUSAR J. AZAM
Advisor
Programmes and Development, OUCIP,
Osmania University, Hyderabad, AP

20 July 2012

Introduction

KOUSAR J. AZAM

The main objective of organizing a conference on Ethnicity at the end of the first decade of the twenty-first century was to review the developments during the previous decades in the multiple areas where ethnicity has made its presence felt. These include the discourses generated within and outside academia, in politics, within the legal framework of respective societies, and within the realms of Theory offering explanations for its resurgent role and relevance in the global context. As the theme of ethnicity has a never-ending relevance in contemporary societies, and has drawn the attention of activists, policy-makers and scholars cutting across disciplines during the recent decades, the purpose behind organizing an international conference on ethnicity was to look into the challenges that ethnicity poses both at the local and at the global level. Though ethnic groups have always been a historical presence in almost all the societies of the world, their assertions, and the demands for autonomy and in some cases independence, has become a difficult issue for most of the states in recent decades. A number of scholarly writings have attributed this to the failure of the respective states to contain, absorb, and to manage this conflict. In the post-colonial states of South Asia and elsewhere this has been interpreted and analysed as the unfinished business of decolonization and the ethnic unrest has been attributed to the imposition of artificial borders and setting up of artificial states. While this is true of some of the

South Asian states, not much has been written about small tribal group when they assume an ethnic identity, and get transformed into disaffected, imagined, dislocated, uprooted and transnational communities.

While this transformation appears to have taken place simultaneously with the process of state building, nation building and the adoption of democratic mechanisms to enable the functioning of participatory democracies, it has also created fresh fault-lines within the sociological orders that the institutions of state were unwilling or incapable of handling. It would not be wrong to say that ethnicity in some form or the other has accompanied the evolution and the growth of the modern nation state. While some of the states have been specifically the result of ethnic demands for autonomy and independence, the efforts of states to tackle the ethnic assertions within the parameters of their respective constitutions continues. The role of ethnicity in contemporary politics has been mostly attributed to the inherent inequalities in the evolution of traditional societies.

The continuation, manipulation and exploitation of these real and perceived inequalities have frequently created problems for policy-makers who attempt to redress the grievances arising out of this situation. In the post-colonial societies of South Asia, ethnicity remains pervasive in the political process due to the very nature of decolonization. Its resurgence in the Western world—particularly in Europe—has been attributed to the forces ushered in by the disintegration of the former Soviet Union, globalization and the new political arrangements which include the creation of new states, redrawing of the boundaries of the older states and the emergence of new political elites accompanied by the emergence of new ethnic minorities and refugees across the new international borders. The new states in Europe grapple with this comparatively recent phenomenon outside the Marxist paradigms, that were supposed to have influenced the reaction of the state to ethnicity in these societies before the end of the Cold War. On the other hand, the state in South Asia continues to be engaged with this as it threatens its very foundations. In the Indian context the problem of ethnicity in India's north-east has been perceived as a part of a wider regional problem cutting across international borders.

While these discourses create an opportunity for a rethinking of the very foundations of the post-colonial states in South Asia, the percolation of globalization in the remotest areas of the world appears to have fundamentally altered the definitions and the roles of ethnicity. But for globalization, a remote area like Tawang relevant to the policy-makers of a particular region only would not have occupied a centrestage in the global media. The fact that at the 50th anniversary of the United Nations, a plea was made to transform the UNO into a United Peoples' Organization reflects the significance and reach of the indigenous peoples in our times.

Though ethnicity poses several challenges to the contemporary state systems and their constitutional foundations, its very parameters are challenged by those state systems which provide for equal opportunity for economic development and political participation based on the secular notions of policy formulations. In between the binary of the state and ethnicity, the role of the civil society in our times also needs to be looked into. A vibrant effective civil society would question and critique the unlimited power of the state to curb, control and co-opt the ethnic assertions as much as it would blunt the sharp edges of ethnic assertions and render redundant the narrow ideologies that fan ethnic assertions and conflicts.

The present volume is a collection of select papers from a conference on 'Challenges of Ethnicity: The Local and the Global' organized in late November 2009 at the Osmania University Centre for International Programmes (OUCIP), as a part of its newly-declared Vision and Mission, i.e. to encourage inter-disciplinary and cross-disciplinary approaches to address contemporary problems across national boundaries. This event in fact marked a return to the theme of ethnicity after about a decade, when this theme was discussed at the former American Studies Research Centre (ASRC)/ Indo-American Centre for International Studies (IACIS) at a conference.

OUCIP is a young institution but with a fairly long history; variously known as the ASRC, IACIS and Inter-University Centre for International Studies (IUCIS). After Osmania University took over its administration and management in 2006 this Centre acquired an Indian Identity and became a part of the Osmania group of institutions with a name, vision and mission that opened its doors to a wide range of disciplines across Humanities and Social Sciences.

The response to the call for papers was overwhelming and the Centre was able to accommodate a sizeable number of participants from different parts of India as well as abroad. The participants/paper writers included very senior and reputed journalists, scholars, policy-makers as well as very young entrants into academia pursuing a study of the problem of ethnicity in its varied forms.

While we could not accommodate all the papers presented at the conference in this volume for reasons of relevance, repetition, continuity and coherence of theme, we do hope that the work not included herein will find a space in other academic channels.

The papers included here deal with the analysis of the multiple forms of ethnicity and its diverse expressions at the local, national and global level. However, an introductory analysis of the concept, its clarity, its use and misuse has been in order. This is provided by M.S. Prabhakara who has been involved with the theme of ethnicity and its different ramifications for over three decades now. In his paper 'Invention and Re-invention of Ethnicity' Prabhakara points out how the word 'ethnic' and 'ethnicity' moved from their origins into the realm of the political and have become a part 'of the political vocabulary of power whose defining elements in their more extreme forms of expression are exclusion and hatred for the "Other"'. Drawing mainly from his experience and exposure to the ethnic scene in India's north-east and also his experience in South Africa, he points out that there is an element of subjectivity in ethnic and identity assertions. The problem 'arises when such assertions seek to deny, diminish and if possible destroy the "Other", who is very often one's kind'. Prabhakara also refers to the plasticity of identities created out of ethnic assertions and points out that the phenomenon of invention and reinvention of identities is widespread, though particularly visible in India's north-east, where the distinctions between the self and the other are frequently blurred.

The next two papers by D.R. Sahu and V. Srilatha, tell us the story of the triumphs and tribulations of ethnic groups in India in two vastly different contexts. In the first of these analyses, 'From Conch Shell to Collective Action: A Case of Successful Ethnic Movement in Baliapal, Orissa', D.R. Sahu gives an account of the Anti-Missile Movement in Baliapal where the tribal communities triumphed using the ideology of 'home hearth' and ethnic identity against the might of the Indian state, preventing it from the establishment of the National Missile Testing Range. This was the movement that brought together political parties and ethnic groups in opposing a move of the government though for their own different reasons. The ethnic groups drew from the theme of the 'sons of the soil' and its inherent implications for political economy. Sahu analyses the historicity and the dialectics of this protest and dwells on how the play of market forces lead to an assertion of ethnic identity in the process of the crystallization of the protest. He also analyses how this micro movement received global support in realizing its objectives.

On the other hand, V. Srilatha in her paper 'Impact of Modernity on an Island Community: A Study of Andaman and Nicobar Islands' brings to our attention the sad status of the ethnic groups in the Andaman and Nicobar Islands and their neglect by the policy-makers sitting thousands of miles away in Delhi. The Andaman and Nicobar Islands that have been the home of six tribal groups for about 20,000 years are now on the verge of becoming a 'select' tourist destination as per the tourism policy envisaged for these islands. The high-value low-volume tourism potential of the region notwithstanding, experts fear that the cost of development will have to be borne by these native communities.

Srilatha points out that the government's efforts to bring the tribals into the mainstream have only resulted in the dwindling of their numbers with each passing year. The great Andamanese Tribe that was once 4,800 strong now stands at a dismal number of 46, the Onges have been reduced to 96, the Shompens have been greatly affected and by now all accept that the Jarawas are on the road to extinction. The integrationist policies of the government accompanied by protection was to tame and civilize the tribals to bring them into the mainstream. This, she feels has only resulted in further diluting their identity and security.

In the next paper entitled 'Quest for a Land of their Own: The Autonomy Argument' Ashutosh Kumar presents an analysis of the conflict situation in Kashmir while contemplating the possible pathways to conflict resolution and restoration of peace in the valley. He divides his paper into four parts. The first part deals with the dominant concerns of the states of India and Pakistan that are directly involved with the Kashmir conflict. The second part covers a discussion of the 'possible' solutions offered by specialists, the third part brings the people of Kashmir and their aspirations into focus, and the last part discusses the possibilities of granting autonomy as a solution to the problem in Kashmir.

Sajal Nag in his paper 'Resisting Nationalist Discourses: Ethnic Upsurge in Post-colonial North-East India' shifts the discussion from the hinterland to yet another periphery that has been rightly described as the laboratory of ethnic assertions, denials, mergers, within the realm of the political.

Despite his own significant contributions to the understanding of the ethnic problem in India's north-east, Nag prefers to preface his analyses by referring to a trilogy authored by Nirmal Nibedon. Introducing the three works, *Nagaland: The Night of the Guerrillas* (1979), *North East India: The Ethnic Explosion* (1981); and *Mizoram: The Dagger's Brigade* (1989), Nag traces the trajectory of ethnic assertions in India's north-east. Beginning with Nagaland, travelling through Mizoram and then engulfing the entire north-eastern India, Nag traces the roots of Indian ethnic insurgency to independence itself.

It was not just secessionist insurgency that plagued the region, there were the ethnic conflicts, autonomy movements, inter-tribal and tribal–non-tribal hostilities, violent resistance to illegal immigration, and host-refugee conflicts, in the north-eastern region that caused huge law and order problems for the new Indian state. With a population that constitutes a mere 3.9 per cent of India's population, the region has witnessed the killing of more than half its people either in mutual violence or as a result of state repression. The region remained under quasi-martial law for long periods and resentment against imposition of Armed Forces Special Powers Act still simmers, while the rest of India reaps the harvest of freedom and development. In his paper, Nag delineates the major forms of turbulence in the region and analyses the nature of the upsurge. In doing so, the reasons why the subcontinental and the sub-national movements in the north-east have to be seen as 'ethnic' rather than as 'national'.

The next analysis of the region is by P.K. Ryngnga. In her paper 'Ethnic Tensions and Community Conflicts in North-East India: A Challenge to India's Integrity and Unity', she situates the ethnic tensions and the community conflicts in the north-east in the larger context of India's national integrity and unity pointing out that in the north-east, ethnic differences have been frequently used as weapons of social mobilization usually to sharpen the conflict. 'But in most cases' she feels, 'ethnicity seems to be a mere camouflage. Beneath the so-called ethnic conflict lay social, political and economic conflicts between groups of people who happen to identify each other in ethnic terms.' She attributes the ethnic heterogeneity of the region to complexities based on distinctive historical experiences. Behind these conflicts, she suggests, lies the struggle over rights—right to land, to education, to use their own language, to political representation, to freedom of religion, to preservation of ethnic identities, and to autonomy and self-determination.

Deviating slightly from the theme, Emanuela Mangiarotti looks into the ethnic dimensions of the religion-based communalism in India with a focus on Hindu-Muslim conflict in Hyderabad city of India.

Mangiarotti focuses on the problems of defining communalism and communal conflict with respect to ethnicity. The fundamental question that she raises is, can religion-based communalism be considered a form of ethnicity? She proceeds to suggest that the discourses of Hindu-Muslim identity have features that seem to have much in common with the discourses deemed peculiar to ethnicity. She finds that religion as a source of group identity can sometimes function similarly to kinship or language, while at other times it suggests an already existing ethnic identity. In her paper she focuses on the ethnic dimension present in the discourses of religion-based communalism, rejecting a sharp distinction between communalism and ethnicity 'which risks neglecting the fundamental questions about possible common socio-political origins of the two'.

Writing on class formation within ethnic communities and its political implications. Javed Alam charters the discussion towards exploitation cutting across the divisions of caste, religion and ethnicity as the cause of conflict as also the cause of unity, among the oppressed people. He holds that this phenomena of unity of the exploited masses including caste, minority and ethnic groups has gone through a decline after the Mandal Commission recommendations. This he perceives as a decline of the communist parties, particularly in large areas of northern India. This decline of the Left and the rise of the primordial after the Mandal agitation may be understood as an additional cause for the expressions of ethnicity in recent times. He concludes by suggesting that a certain reaffirmation of Marxism may blunt the sharp edges of the divisive politics, including the ethnic politics.

Moving away from the assertions of ethnicity at the local level within the Indian context—the essays that follow provides an account of ethnicity outside India. It begins with Adeel Khan's essay on 'Renewed Ethno-Nationalist Insurgency in Balochistan, Pakistan: The Militarized State and Continuing Economic Deprivation'.

Ethnically and linguistically, Balochistan is Pakistan's most diverse province with Baloch being the largest group in the province. Territorially, the largest Pakistani province, Balochistan, has faced a military offensive from its own Federal government five times during the six decades of Pakistan's independence—first time when the Khan of Kalat declared independence on 14 August 1947 offering the new Pakistani state special relations in the areas of defense, foreign affairs and communications. Rejecting this, the newly-formed state of Pakistan launched its first military offensive in April 1948 to annex Kalat.

Khan traces the developments of over 60 years in the confrontation of the Baloch ethnics with the state and concludes with an account of the bloodiest confrontations that took place during the regime of Parvez Musharraf which culminated with the killing of the tribal Chief Nawab Akbar Bugti. He concludes, 'what lies at the heart of the Balochistan crisis is the insensitivity and the shortsightedness of successive governments starting from the inception of the Pakistani state'. The long and undisturbed hold of the military even during the brief spells of democracy that Pakistan has had, only adds to the insensitivity in understanding the needs and aspirations of ethnic groups. The Pakistani army, according to Adeel Khan, has 'earned the dubious distinction of being an army that keeps trying to conquer its own people whenever they refuse to follow its diktat'. He further recalls, 'in 1971 the military massacred Bengalis in the east wing of the country. During 1973-7 it massacred the Balochis. In 1983 it humiliated, jailed, and killed Sindhis. Today it is once again involved in killing the Balochis, Khan's is indeed a thought-provoking account about the incapacity or/and unwillingness of the state in South Asia to accept and absorb diversities honouring differences, and retaining the inherent dignity of the ethnic minorities and an insight into the extent it will use its power to co-opt, curb and control its minorities.

The next paper by K.R. Sharma is an account of 'China's Policies and Practices Towards Ethnic Uighurs in Xinjiang and the Impact of Modernization/Globalization on Ethnic Identity'. Sharma brings his expertise and experience in this field to our knowledge and understanding of the little known aspects of the status of ethnic minorities in China. Approximately 10 per cent population of China's 1.3-1.4 billion population consists of ethnic minorities numbering 55. Out of these, Sharma informs us, three have been able to resist what he terms as 'Hanization'—these three being the Tibetans of Tibet, the Mongols of Inner Mongolia and the Uighurs of Xinjiang. He finds it paradoxical that China has a Muslim population of about 22 million of which about 12 million are Chinese-speaking. The remaining 10 million include Uighurs (8 million) and Kazaks, Tajiks and Uzbeks who are of Turkish origin linguistically, and have strong Islamic ethnics roots and are resisting the official attempts to Hanize them with all their might.

Sharma discusses in detail the policy of the Chinese state to Hanize these areas by encouraging heavy migration into these areas by the non-Uighurs, and through a policy of ethnocide of the Uighurs by a systematic suppression of their cultural identities, religious rituals, belief systems and their language.

The next paper shifts the scene to Nepal, a Himalayan state that went through a radical revolution replacing its traditional monarchy with a Marxist revolutionary regime that is yet to stabilize. In his paper

'Nepal: Rise of Ethnicity and the Agenda of Inclusive Democracy', Krishna Hachhethu sees the possibilities of an accommodation of the diversities—religious, cultural and linguistic in the new state. This he hopes would be different from the earlier domination of what he calls 'the hill Hindu high caste Brahmin and Chetri groups'. In the aftermath of the April 2006 popular uprising, known as *jana andolan*, Nepali state has reset its national goal 'to achieve inclusive democracy'. He goes on to elaborate upon the paradigm shift in the nation-building project of Nepal from an assimilationist model to a model that accommodates social diversity.

The adoption of the new electoral system that ensures the participation and representation of different social segments in proportion to the sizes of their respective populations, Hachhethu suggests, would strengthen the hitherto excluded groups like the Madhesis, Dalits and women. The phenomenon of a recent hung parliament also suggests a new trend, i.e. the transformation of identity movements into political power.

R.A. Ariyaratne in his 'From Winning the Secessionist War to Addressing Ethno-Political Challenges in Sri Lanka' deals with the responsibilities of the Sri Lankan state in the aftermath of the defeat of the LTTE by the state forces. He states that at the outset war and ethnicity appears to be two different phenomena, yet they tend to influence each other. He proceeds to emphasize that at the centre of the ethnicity-war nexus lies social diversity which is the most ubiquitous feature of almost all the South Asian states.

What makes social diversity conflictual is the extreme inequality in the distribution of access to socio-economic resources, or what Robert Dahl calls 'cumulative inequality'. When groups of aggrieved ethnic communities are drawn to offer their support actively or passively to a violent struggle against a legitimately constituted government, the politics of criminalization sets in. He cites the *Wall Street Journal* 'for all those who argue that there is no military solution for terrorism we have two words "Sri Lanka".' While the Sri Lankan government occupies itself with the task of rebuilding peace and resettling their Tamil minority, what remains obvious is the fact that the state in South Asia will not allow an ethnic conflict to destroy itself.

That the ethnic groups suffer not just economic backwardness, political exploitation and societal prejudice but are also denied basic human rights—conclude B. Malini Reddy and Shilpa Deekshith in their paper, 'Ethnicity and Human Rights: A Study of the Aboriginal Australians'. They give an account of the denials and discriminations against the Aboriginal Australians who constitute about 2.4 per cent of the total population of Australia. They also describe the nature, condition, and meaning of terms like 'stolen generation' and 'stolen wages' that marked the sufferings of the Aborigines in Australia. The policy response to the existence of the Aborigines—the ethnic Australians—the original inhabitants of the country, varies and vacillates between attempts at assimilation, and a sympathetic response to their demands of self-determination. However, they suggest that without self-determination it will not be possible for them to fully overcome the legacy of colonialism and dispossession.

Writing on 'National Identity as a Factor of Effective Global Organization' Olga Potapova observes that the process of the formation of identities gives a definition of 'us' and the 'other'. Thus the concepts of 'own' and 'alien', 'we' and 'they' exclude some and include some depending upon which is the group that is giving this definition. Such assertions of national identities logically lead to demands of self-determination that sooner or later pose a problem to the territorial integrity of the states. To avoid this, she suggests that the definitions of national identity have to be more inclusive, absorbing diversities within their own specific identities. 'The only way to reconcile identities of national minorities, identities of citizenship, identities of immigrant societies, etc., is to turn to the individual identity which more or less includes all of the above.'

In her, 'The Black Heart of Brussels: The Categories of Ethnic Entrepreneurship in the African Neighbourhood of Matongé', Carmen De Michele introduces us to the intricacies of factors that lead to a consolidation and perpetuation of the ethnic practices by various ethnic groups in the countries where they migrate for economic, political or personal reasons. She begins by pointing out that almost every European city has its own specific corners that are converted by the immigrants into China Towns, Little Istanbuls and similar ethnic spaces. She focuses on the economic structure of the ethnic districts within an urban context where the business dynamics are more close to the country of their origin than those of their adoption. Also most of the immigrant communities in cities all over the world tend to be self-employed working in a range of different jobs. She probes whether it is due to discrimination or cultural heritage.

What do they say about their self-representation and how are they seen by the native population? These are some of the questions that Michele raises and explores in her analysis of the African neighbourhood in Matongé district of Brussels. Her focus is on the contributions of the ethnic entrepreneur as the backbone of the neighbourhood economy who, we might assert, defies the attempts at deprivation of his native culture in the wake of globalization and keeps it alive through conscious choices.

In his 'Coercive Semblance: Imperial Constructions of "Japaneseness" in the Early Twentieth Century' Yoshiya Makita examines the multifaceted impacts which modern international relations have exerted on the process of delineation of ethnic identity in Japan. He explains how since the Meiji Restoration of 1868, Japan had embarked upon a conscious adoption of the Western-style modernization of its social organizations. However, the eastward expansion of Japanese colonialism and the geographical proximity of these colonies resulted in large-scale migrations of diverse ethnic groups from Taiwan, Korea and north-eastern parts of China into Japan. Consequent increase in Japanese hybridity provoked intense discussions about what constituted 'Japanese' identity. While coercion was used to assimilate these groups into a single Japanese mould, attempts were also made to enlarge the ideological limit of Japanese identity and subdivide the population within the imperial hierarchy.

By appropriating the Indian expatriates from the British colonial rule, attempts were made to project a version of pan-Asianism as the basis of imperial reinterpretation of the ethnic boundaries. Departing from the previous focus on endogeneous development of 'Japanese ethnic' identity, Makita places Japanese attempts to construct a multilayered Japanese identity under the imperial order within the context of international relations.

The last paper in this collection deals with the identity crisis in Igboland in Nigeria. Victor Ukaogo in his paper 'The Dilemma of a People: Interrogating Identity Crisis in Igboland' deals with the dilemmas confronting a number of nationalities and individuals in Nigeria. There has been a practice of people selectively claiming and denying their ancestral and historical links with their kin 'in the vast terrain of their geographical inhabitation'. While this has been a general trend among most of the ethnic groups in Nigeria, it became particularly noticeable among the Igbos after the Civil War in 1970. During and after the war the Igbos across the river Niger and those 'curiously kept in Rivers state consistently and persistently denied their ancestral link with the Igbos'. Due to a number of factors, the enmity between the so-called 'core' Igbos and Igbo minorities in 'other lands' has persisted. The dilemma of categorization now confronts this community, affecting their progress and unity. Ukaogo's is a painstaking analysis of the underlying factors behind this dilemma.

The papers in this collection reflect the several challenges that ethnicity poses at the local, national and global level and how these challenges are perceived by the academia in India, South Asia and other parts of the world.

Due to the delay in publication, some papers have been published elsewhere. In particular, the papers by M.S. Prabhakara and Adeel Khan respectively were specifically written for the conference and deserved to be included here. We thank *The Hindu* and *The Asian Survey* for permitting us to reproduce them in this collection.

1

Invention and Re-invention of Ethnicity

M.S. PRABHAKARA

Many tribal communities in the north-east have reinvented themselves by assuming new nomenclatures, though the reinvention has not meant any substantial change in their social status.

The word 'ethnic' (with its derivative, 'ethnicity'), like the word 'colonial', has acquired a soft focus patina permeated with quaintness and romance, something beautiful to long for. The other side of this idealized image is its successful marketing. Thus, one finds that ethnic food, ethnic clothes and ethnic jewellery are among the most assiduously marketed and hankered after by those with the wherewithal in metropolitan areas—for, these things do not come cheap. Similar is the love and nostalgia for things colonial, especially on the part of those who have no memories of colonial rule.

Just as colonialism in action was one of the cruellest and most rapacious commercial enterprises that profoundly damaged its victims, ethnicity in action, and the uses to which it has been put to, have their ugly side too. This is certainly true of Assam and its neighbouring states where ethnicity has gone beyond being merely an idea and a word used to describe things strange and exotic, once viewed as supposedly unique to the tribal people on the margins. One nowadays speaks routinely of 'ethnic Assamese'. 'Ethnic Assamese' restaurants are a thriving business. Traditional Assamese attire worn by women is sold at 'ethnic Assamese boutiques' at very high prices which few 'ethnic Assamese' can afford.

Questions about ethnicity and ethnic identity are now a constant in any discussion of the ferment as much among different sections of the tribal and non-tribal people in Assam and its neighbourhood as among the people of the Brahmaputra Valley, the 'ethnic Assamese'. The idea as much as the word has become part of a new political vocabulary of power, whose defining elements in their more extreme forms of expression are exclusion and hatred of the 'Other'.

This is perhaps natural since underlying the present exclusionary ideologies whose other side is hatred of the 'Other' is the historic reality that those presently driving such exclusionist agendas were themselves despised, excluded and marginalized by communities that have always viewed themselves as part of our society's mainstream.

Ethnicity and ethnic consciousness are, however, a universal phenomenon. Every people possess specific identity markers, though in popular usage, ethnicity is considered a unique feature of tribal societies. The family, the home, the kinship group, gender, caste, religion, language, race, even the physical space that a people occupy—any and each one of these could be and indeed is a coordinate of a people's identity. These identity markers of their nature criss-cross, with the result that every people have multiple identities.

And yet, identity politics and ethnic, now ethno-nationalistic, assertions articulated in singular and exclusive terms have taken some of the most violent forms not merely in Assam and its neighbourhood but worldwide. There is hardly any country, from the economically most advanced to the most backward, where such ethno-nationalistic mobilizations have not taken place with a political agenda of separatism whose objective is to carve out an exclusive territorial and political space, excluding the 'Other' who has historically been part of the same territorial and political space, and has shared the same or similar ethnic identity. Often, the 'Other' is indistinguishable from the self, as in civil wars whose key component is ethnic cleansing, the other side of violent ethnic assertion.

There may be an element of subjectivity in such ethnic identity assertions. One is not merely what one is, one is also what one thinks and feels one is; and no one, certainly no 'know-all' journalist or even better qualified scholars can dismiss even the most subjectively held perceptions of a people as merely reductionism. The problem arises when such assertions seek to deny, diminish and, if possible, destroy the 'Other', who is very often of one's kind but in this process of exclusionary mobilization is cast beyond the pale.

A most curious feature of such ethnic mobilizations is the plasticity of identities in whose name such mobilizations are done, with such identities constantly invented and reinvented. When an element of fabrication enters this process of construction and invention, one has to question the very authenticity of such rigid identity assertions. One recalls that a key element in the destruction of the Federal Republic of Yugoslavia was the invention, in addition to the Serb, the Croat and Bosnian nationalities (the Montenegrins and the Slovenes were still in the making, in political and territorial terms, during those fraught years) of the Muslim as a 'nationality', virtually replacing the Bosnian, though historically there were (and are) Serbian Muslims, Croatian Muslims and Bosnian Muslims.

This phenomenon of invention and reinvention of identities is widespread in Assam and the north-east. In Assam, the process where a tribal person by going through some simple and nominal ritualistic processes would become part of the caste Hindu Assamese society, albeit at its lower levels, has been well documented. Many tribal communities have reinvented themselves by assuming new nomenclatures, though the reinvention has not meant any substantial change in their social status, but only the restoration of a nomenclature replacing the old that had pejorative connotations. There has also been a singular case of a tribal identity being 'fabricated', a creation out of airy nothing, both in name and local habitation (see 'Manufactured Identities', *Frontline*, 7 October 2005).

Manipur presents some of the most striking examples of such invention and reinvention of identities. Apart from the Meitei, thirty-two tribal communities (till recently 29), broadly classified under two heads, the Kuki and the Naga, are recognized in the state. However, the exact number of those classified under the two heads has never been clear because of an element of fluidity in this categorization. What is clear is that while there are few instances of a Naga tribe switching its identity to Kuki, traffic in the reverse direction is not uncommon. A well documented case is that of the Anal, a tribal people inhabiting Chandel district, who were once classified as Kuki and are now classified as Naga.

One of the most interesting cases of such plasticity is the Monsang, once considered a Kuki tribe and now identified as a Naga tribe. In a conversation with this author in Imphal recently, Gangmumei Kamei, a Manipuri historian, referred to Ng Mono, former MLA and leading person from the Monsang community who was at one time the general secretary of the Kuki National Assembly, and who later became a leading member of the Naga Integration Council, which demands the integration of contiguous Naga-inhabited areas under one political and administrative set-up—in short, the break up of Manipur. Kamei himself presents a most interesting transition. Once known as Gangmumei Kabui, he is now the leading ideologue of the Zeliangrong movement that seeks a homeland for the Zeliangrong community, which is literally a construct made up from the names of three Naga communities of Manipur (and Nagaland)—ZEme, LIANGmei and RONGmei. There have been similar constructs in the region.

During the Kuki-Naga clashes in parts of the state in 1993-4, the Chiru and Kom tribes who did not see themselves as part of either of the two broad categories, nevertheless chose to identify themselves as Kuki or Naga depending on the vicinity they lived in. When the clashes abated, they reverted to their original status. However, such strategies of survival have not always worked. The clashes that broke out on 24 July 1997 in Churachandpur (Lamka), headquarters of the district of the same name in south-west Manipur, and persisted for nearly a year, involved, both as perpetrators and victims, two of the major communities of the town and the district, the Thadou Kuki and the Paite, both part of the great Kuki-Chin family, and virtually indistinguishable from each other. These clashes were one of the most extreme examples of the 'Other' and the self becoming indistinguishable.

One may well ask, in the words of Shakespeare: 'Hark in thine ear. Change places and, handy-dandy, which is the justice, which is the thief?'

Who is the Self, who is the Other?

2

From Conch Shell to Collective Action

A Case of Successful Ethnic Movement in Baliapal, Orissa*

D.R. SAHU

Introduction

This paper concentrates on the people's struggle in Baliapal, (Orissa) popularly known as the Anti-Missile Movement, against the proposed National Missile Testing Range Centre in Baliapal district of Orissa. This missile testing centre was supposed to displace 55 villages covering an area of 102 sq. km and uproot more than 1,00,000 people. The significance of this protest lies in the fact that the people of Baliapal, irrespective of their caste, class, gender and political affiliations could manage to put pressure on both the Government of India and the Government of Orissa to stop this project and is considered to be one of the most successful protest movements post-Independence.

This essay attempts to locate the anti-missile movement in Baliapal in the 'new' social movement (NSM) category and tries to examine whether the sustained collective mobilization against the project can be construed in this category. According to Dhanagare, conventional movements have attracted much more attention of

* Working paper presented at the International Conference on 'Challenges of Ethnicity: The Local and the Global' from 25-7 November 2009, OUCIP, Osmania University, Hyderabad.

scholars than some of new social movements (Dhanagare 1988). The NSMs are predominantly plural in nature and their expressions range from anti-racism, anti-nuclearism, disarmament, feminism, environmentalism, regionalism and ethnicity, civil libertarianism to issues of personal autonomy, freedom and peace (Melucci 1980; Cohen 1985; Slater 1985; Touraine 1985).

Rajendra Singh has spelled out some of the characteristics of the NSMs as: (a) They raise the issue of the 'self-defense' of the community against that of the state and the consciousness of civil society, which are new phenomena of the contemporary post-modern world. (b) NSMs do not subscribe to the Marxist paradigm of explaining conflicts and contradictions in terms of 'class' and 'class conflict'. (c) NSMs generally evolve a kind of grassroot politics which often initiate micro-movements of small groups, targeting localized issues with a limited institutional base. They write their own scripts somewhat like street theatres and focus much more on the social domain of civil society rather than on the economy or state. Further, the goal of NSMs is to reorganize state, society and economy and to create a public space in which democratic discourses on autonomy and the freedom of the individual and collectives, their identities and orientations could be analysed. (d) NSMs are essentially plural in structure and generally global, non-segmental and trans-human in character such as the struggle against nuclear war arms race, movements to save the ecology and environment for peace and civil liberty, individual identity, freedom and personal dignity, etc., (Singh 2001).

Historicity and Political Economy

Balasore district is situated in the north-eastern part of Orissa bordering Midnapore district of West Bengal on the north, Mayurbhanj and Keonjhar districts on the west and Bay of Bengal in the south. Historically, the district was known as one of the Mughalbandi areas of coastal Orissa during the Maratha rule. Prior to this, during the Mughal rule, this area flourished due to overseas trade and commerce through seaports like Balasore and Pipili. European traders, particularly Portuguese, Dutch and English initially came for trading and subsequently they settled down in the area. The East India Company acquired the area in 1803 and integrated it into the Cuttack district. Finally, in 1836, Balasore became an independent coastal district along with Cuttack, Puri and Ganjam (Biswal 1987). However, the district is relatively more prosperous than the other districts of the state (Patel 1988).

During the Afghan period Baliapal was one of the Mughalbandi areas. During Aurangzeb's rule earlier, Murshid Quli Khan I governed as *subedar*, a bigger portion of Midnapore of West Bengal (adjacent to study area) was taken away from the Jaleswar *sarkar* of Orissa and in subsequent years, the river Subarnarekha was made the southern boundary of Bengal. During one of my field visits there some of the older people of Baliapal tracing the history of the area said that during Mughal period, this area was used as a military base because of the port facilities available there. Geographically, Subarnarekha River has merged with the sea. The local people had vehemently opposed the construction of a coast canal by the British in 1855, as they had to give away their agricultural land. The coast canal divides the Baliapal block and Subarnarekha River divides the Baliapal and Bhograi block. The people of Baliapal normally go to adjacent district of West Bengal for shopping purposes by simply crossing the Subarnarekha River on boats. Similarly, people from West Bengal, particularly from Contai, Midnapore and Dantan come to the weekly *haat* (market) in the villages of Baliapal, for trading purposes through this short-cut canal route.

The staple crop of this region is paddy. Productivity levels are high due to the use of HYV seeds. The area is, however, extremely vulnerable to natural calamities like landslides along the Subarnarekha and frequent changes of direction of the flow on her way to merge in the sea, cyclonic floods and entry of sea water. Other than paddy, many people of Baliapal depend upon fishing, especially the coastal villages, along with other occupations (such as) cultivators and agricultural labourers. The production of cash crops—vegetables, groundnut, betelnut, cashew nut, coconut and most importantly betel leaf have significantly enriched the economic status of the people of Baliapal.

Baliapal is situated on the crescent coastal part of north Balasore and is bordered by the river on one side and by the the sea on the other. Geographical attributes have, no doubt, hampered the growth of settled cultivation in this area. The frequent changes in the river belts and the receding aspect of the sea have forced the local people to re-locate and many times the issue of resettlement has lead to violent conflicts and legal disputes. Further, people from neighbouring areas such as Ram Nagar, Saatmaile, Contai, Midnapore in West Bengal and refugees from Bangladesh (undocumented) have migrated and settled down close to this sea coast. Their settlement pattern has led to tensions over land rights. It may be noted here that the 1934 land settlement was a dividing line for the people of Baliapal. Before this, the average landholding size was not very large.

The area is dominated by medium-sized and small-sized land-holdings with very few large holdings. Average landholdings are between 5 and 6 acres (1991 census). The PUDR report findings revealed that during the colonial rule, permanent tenancy rights were not granted to the actual cultivators by the then zamindars. According to the local people, they had only been granted rights over harvest of land termed *amal nama patta* by the zamindars, but this was not recognized as tenancy rights by Orissa land laws. Ironically, the state has been accepting land revenue from them on the basis of which the local people have been claiming their rights over the land. It was also revealed that the legal possession of government land is granted if the people have occupied it for at least 30 years and paid taxes as per the land laws of Orissa.

Other than agriculture fishing is also an important occupation for the local people. As mentioned earlier, cash crops like cashew nut, coconut, betel nut, peanut and betel leaf are the major thrust areas of Baliapal's economy, especially in the coastal areas, which has made the region relatively prosperous. The cultivation of betel leaves has made the area more prosperous. Both cultivation of cash crops and consequent prosperity of the area have much relevance to the people's resistance movement in the area (PUDR 1988). Patel argued that the major changes in the economy of this area have been caused by commercialization of existing cash crops and agriculture through introduction of groundnut in the northern parts and alternating it with *til* and rice and peanut in the southern part of Baliapal.

According to Patel, 'the introduction of *pana* was not the only factor responsible for the sudden prosperity of the poorer classes. Along with the growth of *pana*, cashew nut cultivation and fish also became an important marketable commodity' (Patel 1989). Coastal areas always depend upon sea fish which is a part of their food culture because of its easy availability. Due to the merger of Subarnarekha River with the Bay of Bengal, people of Baliapal have easy access to both sea fish as well as fresh water fish.

II

The Project and its Rationale

The missile range was to be set up as a base for research, testing and launch of India's tactical weaponry such as medium- and long-range missiles, rockets and pilotless target aircraft, by the Defence Research Development Organization (DRDO) under the Ministry of Defence, Government of India. The Department of Space, better known as Indian Space Research Organization (ISRO), was also expected to use it for firing polar satellite launch vehicles (PSLV). It was to be spread over an area of 350 km along the Orissa coast in the north up to Chilka Lake in the south. Initially, 150-200 km range missiles were to be tested and tracked with radars of the same range. The operational headquarters was to be established at the Baliapal-Bhogari blocks, and the tracking station was to be located in the Nilgiri hills, 35 km west, which was installed by the Britishers.

Defence experts had valid technical and strategic reasons for selecting this particular site. The Balasore coast is crescent-shaped with Baliapal at its tip and is ideal for the intensive monitoring required after a launch. From this very site, missiles could easily be test-fired on a horizontal trajectory into the Bay of Bengal or even further into the Indian Ocean without the possibility of collision with populated islands or sea traffic. Nestling on the east coast, it is relatively free from air surveillance of hostile neighbours.

Apart from the above, Balasore, being the district headquarters, has better infrastructural facilities and transport system, well connected with the entire country. The region has a firm soil, ideal for a launching pad. Moreover, due to silting of ports in the east coast, there is not much of sea traffic in this area. Also, there are more number of sunny and clear days (300 days out of 365 days) as compared to the Andamans (200 to 240 days out of 365 days) (Surya 1987). Besides, an abandoned aerodrome at Rasgovindpur in the neighbouring Mayurbhanj district, which was constructed during the Second World War by the British, would facilitate the project. According to Dr Arunachalam, Scientific Advisor to the Government of India, the test range would meet the long-felt need to develop and improve indigenously produced missiles and space vehicles and reduce India's dependence on other countries. Further, he stressed that this test range would enable India to develop augmented space launch vehicles (ASLV) and polar rockets.

According to the Ministry of Defence, the possible sites in the west coast suffer from major strategic problems. The Arabian Sea it feels is 'bristling with superpower presence'. The US has a permanent base at Diego Garcia and the sea traffic both local and international is quite heavy on the west coast. Moreover, Maldives, an independent country, is situated just south of Lakshadweep. The defence ministry had also surveyed a site near Dwarka in Gujarat. However, this site had more problems than those enumerated above. Its proximity to Pakistan is said to make telemetric observation very easy and the site is susceptible to air attacks. The threat posed by this site to the oil extraction installations of Mumbai High has also been taken into consideration. Similar strategic disadvantages were also found against the test range's location near Bindur in South Karnataka and the deserts of Rajasthan (PUDR 1985).

The feasibility of the Andaman and Nicobar Islands as a test range site was also rejected on the ground that locating the project in the above would be much more expensive primarily because of the transportation cost (*The Samaj*, 19 April 1985). The defence ministry also argued that the islands did not provide the required 200 clear days in a year for the experiments. Strongly, spokesperson of the same ministry revealed to the press that the islands enjoyed

200 to 240 clear days in a year. But the main reason for rejecting the island was the central government had already decided to develop this as a free trade zone for the non-resident Indians of Hong Kong after China's take over of Hong Kong (*Surya*, 13 January 1987).

The central government announced a land acquisition programme through the state government, involving 115 sq. km for the test range and 45 sq. km for its safety zone. A total area of 160 sq. km was to be claimed which would have effected a population of 70,102 comprising 11,609 families of 130 villages (*The Samaj*, 10 August 1984; *Link*, 26 October 1986; PUDR 1988). Later on the government revised the land requirement plan because of stiff resistance from all quarters that I shall discuss in the next section. The revised proposal involved a total land area of 102 sq. km—68 sq. km for the range and 34 sq. km for the safety zone. The revised plan claimed to affect only 54 villages (41 villages for the test range and 13 villages for the safety zone), 6,484 families and population of 40,793. The land to be acquired for the residential and administrative complex was claimed to involve no population displacement (*The Prajatantra*, 9 August 1986; *Link*, 6 October 1986).

The land acquisition programme of this project was conceptualized on the basis of three zones. The first was the central zone where the testing was to be done, the second was the safety zone, which was to remain as free area and the third zone of 700 acres of land was only meant for residential and administrative purposes. The test range site falls in the area south of the Subarnarekha River. In this area, land acquisition and displacement were to be almost total, and no cultivations was to be permitted. The safety zone fell in between the river Subarnarekha and the flood protection embankment known as *bhua bandha*. For this zone, 13 villages were to be displaced. While all the families in these areas had to move out to the rehabilitation centres, they would be allowed to cultivate agricultural land on lease basis even after its acquisition. However, the cultivators would have no ownership rights on the land. They could only cultivate as temporary leaseholders on the payment of a prescribed rent to the defence authorities. No private construction would be allowed in the safety zone and there would be certain restrictions on the movement of cultivators during notified periods (*India Today*, 31 August 1985; *Link*, 26 October 1986; 13 January 1987).

Besides, the government was to acquire the sea-coast as well as the Subarnarekha River mouth, which were the sources of livelihood for a large number of fishermen who inhabited the area. The fishermen families were also to be displaced (*The Prajatantra*, 17 November 1985; *The Statesman*, 29 June 1986). Despite this displacement, fishing operations in the river mouth and the sea-coast would be allowed, as per the government instruction. However, the areas falling in the safety zone including the Subarnarekha River mouth and the sea would also be kept under similar restrictions. Subsequently, the government announced a rehabilitation programme for the prospective oustees along with the revised land acquisition programmes. Under this programme, the evacuees would be resettled and occupationally rehabilitated in the proposed model villages.

III

The Protest

This movement has an ethnic character and support from all political parties due to the ideology of *bheetaa maati* (home, hearth and common identity), which has become the basis for this struggle. All the interest constellations centred on the production process and land as nature's gift as perceived by the local people, have crystallized in the form of the ideology of *bheetaa maati* (Patel 1990). This ideology is restricted to Baliapal block where 45 villages are to be acquired in the revised scheme against the 13 villages that are to be acquired in Bhograi block. The localization of the struggle in Baliapal block can be understood and explained due to the consequences of the economic, political and social processes. As already discussed, the area has excellent natural resources and cash crop economy and it is known for its growth of the market for the products such as cashew nut, coconut and especially betel vine (*pana*). The specific nature of *pana* cultivation which attracted the lower and non-cultivating castes strengthened the ideology of *bheetaa maati*. The increased demand for *pana* led to the growth of trade and market. Consequently, the market forces facilitated caste-class dynamics and the ideology of *bheetaa maati* and the crystallization of the agitation.

On the other hand, the government claimed that the project would usher in development in the region by initiating the process of much desired industrialization and modernization. An Industrial Training Institute (ITI) would be set up to train the local youth, which would enable them to find jobs in those industries. Further, the government promised to provide jobs to at least one person from each household. It also promised to implement a comprehensive rehabilitation programme which would provide a modern and developed context of living to the people of Baliapal (Department of Public Relations, Orissa).

Rejecting the government plea, the leaders of the movement argue that the area is already a developed one. The development has been initiated by the people themselves and is suitable to the local socio-cultural matrix. Unemployment and starvation are virtually unknown to the people of this area. All from children to the people, right elderly are engaged in some renumerative activity. The leaders claim that a child who clears off ground earns around Rs. 15 per day and an adult or older person, who plucks betel leaves or arranges them in the basket, earns between Rs. 20 and 25 a day. So the dependent age groups are not a liability either to the family or the community. Wage is not an issue at all, rather the scarcity of labour is. People of Baliapal revealed that the destruction of *pana* economy would destabilize all cross-sections of the community. Labourers who are specialized in setting up structure for the betel vineyard would become jobless; others engaged in plucking and arranging the betel leaves, and the artisans who make bamboo baskets for the export of betel leaves would be left without any viable means of livelihood. Even if they are provided with some jobs in any of the industries, they will not be able to cope with the new occupation.

The leaders' further stress that whatever may be the amount of compensation, there is no avenue and opportunity of investment where the people will get the same kind of returns as they are getting now. This is true even for those cultivators, agriculturalists and fishermen who are not linked with the *pana* economy. For them, the natural resources of the region give enough livelihood to make them prefer staying here rather than working as a contract labour, like many of their brethren who have migrated to other parts of country in search of jobs.

The peasant (Khandayat, Gola and Raju) caste group of the area initiated the cash crop production by encroaching upon the common property and the coastal land. *Pana* cultivation was initiated by outsiders, particularly by Bengali traders but subsequently they were eliminated and replaced by the local traders. The local peasant caste found this cultivation more profitable in a small patch of sandy land as this cultivation requires intensive care and low investment. Upper caste peasants were attracted to this production as a result of which the land consolidation process of the local people was relegated to the background. Consequently, the production process increased the demand for the agricultural labourers in the region and small cultivators and landless labourers fulfilled the demand. Gradually, they used the knowledge and started producing *pana*. Small cultivators produced *pana* in their homesteads and landless labourers produced through encroachment of the sea coast land. Subsequently, migrant Santhal tribals became *pana* cultivators too.

The increase in the demand for *pana* resulted in increased wages. This production process also attracted outside traders, particularly from Jaleswar and neighbouring areas. The spread of the market has led to a peasantization process. In a way, the market forces brought many changes in the region particularly in the people's quality of life and lifestyle choices, irrespective of their caste or class. The sustenance of cash crop, i.e. *pana* economy gained momentum due to the demand of this product in the northern and western parts of India. It empowered the local people economically and politically and their involvement in the protest became obvious. Furthermore, these groups provided resources for the mobilization process.

The economic structure and political entity facilitated the ideology of *bheeta maati*, and this ideology articulated an ethnic expression with an emotional and cultural attachment for the land, which is nature's gift to the people of Baliapal. Activists with the help of religious and mythological stories legitimized this ideology of *bheeta maati*. The mobilization process became more effective through such stories.

The struggle was for the land (*maati maa*); the *prakruti* (the symbol of nature), and the golden productive land (*sunara maati*). People of Baliapal fought against the state agency, which wanted to destroy their mother nature, and the golden productive land by setting up a missile test range centre. The slogans raised by the people of Baliapal substantiate the ideology of *bheeta maati*—we can sacrifice our life for the land but we cannot spare even an inch of our land for the project.

Similarly, the women's front too subscribed to the ideology of *bheeta maati*. For them the issue of contention was the home. Home is the symbol of love, affection, emotion, sympathy and security. For these rural women, home signifies life, security and belongingness. The women's front appealed to the womenfolk of Baliapal for active participation in the agitation. The front reinforced the role played by the Hindu goddesses Durga, Kali and Laxmi. It urged that women should preserve and protect their home and tradition actively participate in the demonstrations as well. These articulations have enabled them to come out of their private space (four walls of the house) and participate in the public realm (protest) very soon they became the frontline agitators and protestors of this movement along with students and children. Leaflets issued by the women's front contained their slogans like—'We want land, not missile centre', 'we want peace not war', 'we want creation not devastation', 'we want life not death'.

Women participated in various forms of collective action in the region. The state opposition leader, Biju Patnaik too made a special appeal to women to actively participate in the protest. Whenever faced with police repression during their various demonstrations, they were suggested to blow *sankh* (conch shells) and beat *thalis* (metal plates) to alert the people of Baliapal so that they could join the demonstrations. These means of communications acted superbly for collective action. Using *sankh* and *thali* is part of an Oriya Hindu's daily family routine. Besides, women and children actively participated as frontliners of various demonstrations, be it *rasta roko*, police repression or obstructing government officials and their vehicles to enter into Baliapal.

The fishing community, one of the major occupational communities, also subscribed to the the ideology of *bheeta maati* by creating a fishermen's front known as Matsya Jibi Gana Samukhya. More than 30,000 fishermen and women are engaged in fishing in the confluences of the Subarnarekha and Budhabalanga rivers in the sea and more than 10,000 traditional boats are engaged in fishing. It is the fishermen, and women who cater to the local weekly and nearby *haats*. More than 1,000 people from Baliapal daily go to different markets for transporting fish. Though the government had a plan to rehabilitate the fishing community in another fishing zone it could not practically accommodate such a large number of fishermen. The front was of the opinion that their skills have been acquired through experience over generations. The long acquaintance with the sea of this region has made them more comfortable with definite knowledge with regard to the movement of different fishes in different seasons and even the movement of the breeze. For them, the sea is their mother (*maa*) who protects and fulfils their basic needs. Their emotional attachment to the sea and the sea coast can be understood from the slogan they raised during protests 'The land is ours, the Sea is ours, government you go back'.

The articulation of the ideology of *bheeta maati* brought out the economic, political, social, cultural and environmental dimensions of this protest movement. At the macro level, protestors challenged not only the project but also the legitimacy of the state, especially its bureaucratic and political institutions.

IV

Post-movement Phase and Conclusion

The competitive capitalism initiated by betel vine production strengthened the local economy and it was enriched further by prawn cultivation in the area. The natural resources of the area supported both the cultivations. Here it can be argued that cash crop economy, especially *pana* economy, facilitated the anti-missile movement. On the contrary the prawn economy became the major issue of protest by the local leaders who were earlier involved in the anti-missile movement. The NSM against prawn cultivation could not garner support from the local people as it had during the anti-missile protest.

Empirical evidence spelled out the developments induced by the prawn economy in the villages under study. Coming over to the changes in the social structure, it was economic prosperity and the excellent natural resources that influenced the polity, culture and even primordial loyalties of the local people. The traditional caste-class continuum in which certain caste groups were engaged either in *pana* cultivation or fishing was broken and the higher caste groups took to *pana* and prawn cultivation because of the high profitability. If we compare both the economies, *pana* economy had high profitability and low investment whereas prawn cultivation requires huge investment and capital which led poor people to lease out their land to the moneyed people. Moreover, prawn cultivation attracted many outsiders to the area, which led to the inflow of muscle power and anti-social activities. The 'Save Baliapal' movement was launched by the local leaders, especially the educated youth and which also had significant participation of NGO, and environmentalists. Common to both the movements was the resistance of the people against state policy.

An attempt is made in this paper to understand the specific structural and organizational characterization of a contemporary social movement. Such protest movements have also been projected as critiques of contemporary social forces. This protest movement can be taken as a post-modernist expression of contemporary society, which constantly reinforces society and its people to return to the past and return to nature.

References

Biswal, B.B. (1987), *Baleshwar ra Iteebruttee*, Jaleswar: Biswabrahma Publishers.

Cohen, Jean L. (1985), 'Strategy of Identity: New Theoretical Paradigms and Contemporary Social Movements', *Social Research*, 52(4) Winter.

Dhanagare, D. and J. John (1988), 'Cyclical Movements Towards the "Eternal": Nine Theses of Social Movements: A Critique', *Economic and Political Weekly*, vol. XXIII, no. 21, 21 May, pp. 1038-92.

Frank, Andre Gunder and Marta Fuentes. (1987), 'Nine Theses on Social Movement', *Economic and Political Weekly*, vol. 22, no. 35, 29 August, pp. 1503-10.

Jena, N.R. (1991), 'Discontent, Conflict and Resistance in Baliapal', unpublished Ph.D. thesis, Chandigarh University.

Melucci, Alberto (1980), 'The New Social Movements: A Theoretical Approach', *Social Science Information*, vol. 19, no. 2, May (pp. 119-226).

Offe, Claus (1985), 'New Social Movements: Challenging the Boundaries of Institutional Politics', *Social Research*, vol. 52, no. 4, pp. 817-68.

Patel, Sujata (1989), 'Baliapal, Agitation "Socio-Economic Background"', *Economic and Political Weekly*, vol. XXIV, no. 12, 25 March.

——— (1989) 'Agni, Cyclone and Baliapal Agitation', *Economic and Political Weekly*, vol. XXIV, no. 25, 24 June.

——— (1989), 'The Baliapal Struggle and Displaced Communities', *The Times of India*, 13 December.

——— (1990), 'Baliapal Agitation: Leadership Crises', *Economic and Political Weekly*, vol. XXIV, no. 23, 9 June.

People's Union for Democratic Rights (1988), *Bheeta Maati: A Report on Baliapal Missile Base and People's Struggle*, August, Delhi.

Routledge, Paul (1988), 'Baliapal-Bhograi, India: Theater of War, Theater of Displacement', in News and Views on Missile Testing Range at Baliapal and Bhograi by the Committee to Assist the Struggle of Bhograi and Baliapal Against Missile Base.

Sahu, D.R. (2003), 'New Social Movement and Youth: A Case of Anti-missile Movement in Orissa', in V. Chandra, *Construction and Reconstruction of Indian Youth*, Lucknow: CCYRCI.

——— (2004), 'Caste, Tribe and Peasantry in the Emergence of a People's Movement', *The Eastern Anthropologist*, vol. 57, no. 1.

——— (2006), 'Social Structure, People's Movement and the Role of OBCs in Baliapal Movement', in Verma and Hasnain (eds), *Stagnation, Retrograde Change or Positive Progress?*, New Delhi: Serials Publications.

Singh, Rajendra (2001), *Social Movements, Old and New: A Post-modernist Critique*, New Delhi: Sage.

——— (2000), 'Social Movements: Old and New', in M.S. Gore (ed.), *Third Survey of Research in Sociology and Social Anthropology*, vol. 11, New Delhi: Indian Council of Social Science Research and Manas Publications.

Tilly, Charles (1978), *From Mobilization to Revolution*, Reading, Mass.: Addison-Wesley.

Touraine, Alain (1985), 'An Introduction to the Study of Social Movements', *Social Research*, vol. 52, no. 4, pp. 749-87.

3

Impact of Modernity on an Island Community

A Study of the Andaman and Nicobar Islands

VALLABU SRILATHA

The inheritance of the nation state as a model of political organization in the nature of the post-colonial states was marked by a commitment to modernity, the dominant view at the time of formation of nation states. This was based on the belief that rapid socio-economic growth and development required the creation of stable and functioning political institutions, an effective bureaucracy, and a uniform sense of national identity. Hence the overall emphasis was on, 'assimilating and acculturating minority ethnic identities into the culture of the majority or dominant community'.[1] The whole paradigm of the modern state was so committed to the principle of cultural homogeneity that ethnicity often retreated in ignominy. And yet it is precisely at the end of the twentieth century that ethnicity is at last trying to break loose from the confines of both the nation state and the inhibitions of Western civilization.[2]

In multi-ethnic India, ethnicity operates simultaneously at the local, state and all-India levels and in the context of globalization, it touches upon the political, the cultural and the social spheres. One's ethnic/racial identity may result from self-identification or from an imposition by others. Ethnicity has also been used to identify other people's ethnicity for them and has always been a powerful political tool for controlling, marginalizing, and even getting rid of them. The development of ethnic conflict in the Andaman and Nicobar

(A&N) Islands is in the initial stage. The tribals have become conscious about their ethnic boundary and have started articulating their marginal voices in favour of their better placement in the contemporary world. Since Independence, India has witnessed the rise of political movements that are mobilized along identity lines.[3] The A&N Island movement has been one such mobilization, which has integrated dispersed tribes based on their shared recognition of the forest as an integral part of their identity and livelihood. This movement has been a united struggle to safeguard tribal interests from economic exploitation that resulted from the national development programme.

For this sense of 'ethnicity' to become salient required two general conditions. The first is 'the need to distinguish one group from another'. As Thomas Eriksen has stressed, 'Ethnicity is essentially an aspect of a relationship, not a property of a group'. In other words, cultural distinctiveness in itself does not confer 'ethnicity' on a group, but only when it is contrasted with the culture of another group: 'For ethnicity to come about, the groups must have a minimum of contact with each other, and they must entertain ideas of each other as being culturally different from themselves.'[4] But for this to happen the differences must themselves be considered important. The second condition is rapid social change. As Malcolm Cross notes, 'A man living in a world where change is largely absent does not need to be reminded of his culture in order to affirm his identity.'[5] Tribals are seen as preserves of a lost way of life and therefore retain something of the 'noble savage' aura about them. Modernization led to the debate whether these tribal people should be assimilated or their culture preserved. But as acculturation is inevitable in the globalized world, there is rarely a significant degree of control over their destiny. A state policy external intervention to change these conditions would have to confront the lack of an organizational basis for the tribal values.

The Tribes of Andaman and Nicobar Islands

The A&N Islands also known as the Bay Islands or the Emerald Islands, is an archipelago of 572 islands situated in the Bay of Bengal. They are situated 1,200 km off the south-eastern coast of the Indian mainland, spreading over an area of 8,249 sq. km in a north-south direction. These historically significant islands, of which only 38 are permanently inhabited, are a treasure trove of nature's bounty, beauty and resources. Mythologically, the name Andaman is presumed to have derived from the monkey-god 'Hanuman', who was known to the Malays as Handuman. The name Nicobar seems to be a corruption of the south Indian term 'Nakkavaram' (Land of the Naked) as indicated in the great Tanjore inscription of AD 1050.[6] The A&N Islands have been inhabited for several thousand years and the earliest archaeological evidence goes back some 2,200 years; however, the indications from genetic, cultural and linguistic isolation studies point to habitation going back 30,000 to 60,000 years, well into the Middle Paleolithic era.[7]

The A&N islands have a population of around 500,000 people of which the tribals form less than 30,000. Of the tribals, the biggest group is the Nicobarese at around 20,000. The original people who lived in this island are the great Andamanese, Jarawas, Sentinelese and Onges in the Andaman group and the Nicobarese and Shompens in the Nicobar group. The tribal people of the A&N Islands belong to distinctive racial groups and have different forms of cultural and social behaviour. The tribal groups in the two respective regions have very little in common in the ethnic, linguistic or cultural sense.[8] Their lifestyles are also very different. The A&N Islands is virtually a treasure trove for ecologists as well as anthropologists. Anthropologists believe the five ancient tribes, including the Jarawas, Shompens, Onges and Sentinelese date back 70,000 years. The settlement and the time of migration of these aboriginal people to these Islands remain as a riddle. Up to the middle of the nineteenth century, purity of the tribal population remained almost unaffected. They are among the very few tribes in Asia belonging to the negrito race, having considerable ethnic affinity with two other aboriginal communities—the Semangs of Malaysia and the Aetas of the Philippines. Any ethnic relationships among them have not yet been established partly due to the fact that the latter have forgotten their own dialects, integrating the languages of their dominant neighbours.

The Great Andamanese were once the largest tribe in the Andaman region with an estimated population of 10,000 in 1789.

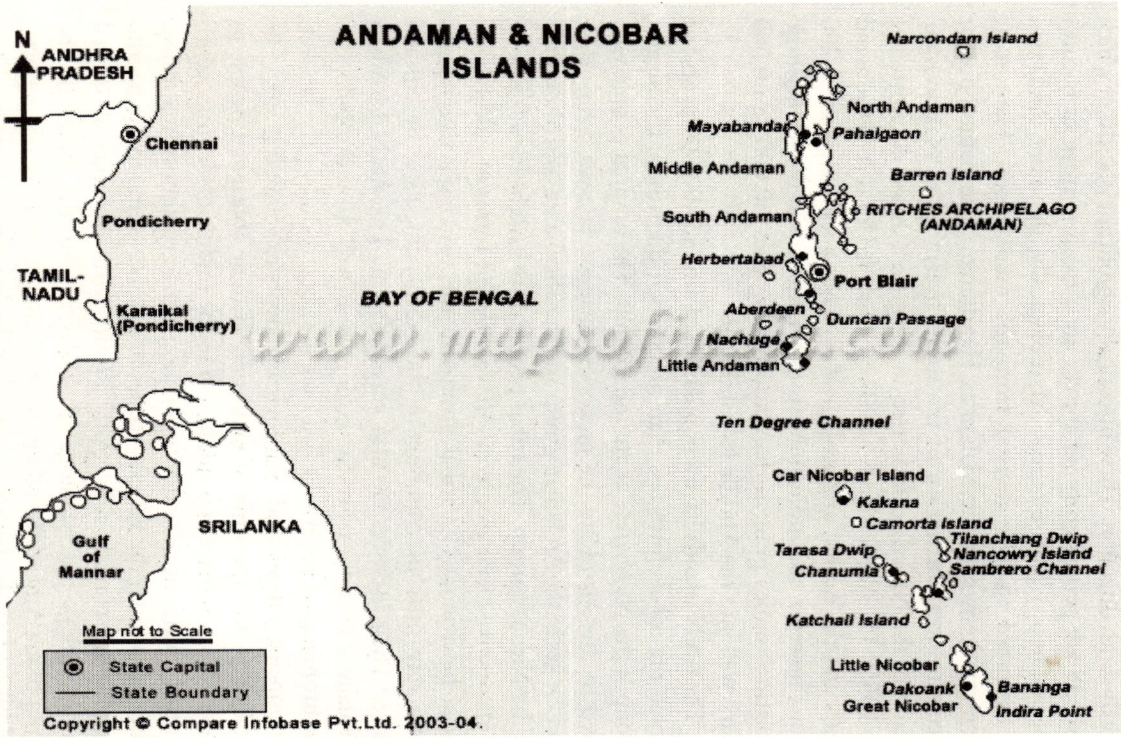
ANDAMAN & NICOBAR ISLANDS
N
ANDHRA PRADESH
Chennai
Pondicherry
TAMIL-NADU
Karaikal (Pondicherry)
BAY OF BENGAL
SRILANKA
Gulf of Mannar
Narcondam Island
North Andaman
Mayabandar
Pahalgaon
Middle Andaman
Barren Island
South Andaman
RITCHES ARCHIPELAGO (ANDAMAN)
Herbertabad
Port Blair
Aberdeen
Duncan Passage
Nachuge
Little Andaman
Ten Degree Channel
Car Nicobar Island
Kakana
Camorta Island
Tilanchang Dwip
Nancowry Island
Sambrero Channel
Tarasa Dwip
Chanumla
Katchall Island
Little Nicobar
Dakoank
Bananga
Great Nicobar
Indira Point
Map not to Scale
State Capital
State Boundary
Copyright © Compare Infobase Pvt.Ltd. 2003-04.
www.mapsofindia.com

Andamanese, who collectively represented at least ten distinct sub-groups and languages are prefixed by Aka, like Aka-Bea, -Bale, -Bo, -Cari, -Cora, -Jeru, -Juwoi, -Kede, -Kol, -Pucikwar. These tribes can be divided into two sub-divisions—a northern group and a southern group. All these different tribes were lumped together by the British administrators and outsiders in a broader group named 'Great Andamanese', later to be distinguised from the Jarawa, the Onge and the Sentinelese.[9] The Andaman tribes belong to the Negrito stock and are some of the surviving representatives of a flourishing Negrito race that once dominated the entire South-East Asia region including the A&N Islands. They speak distinctive dialects not mutually understood. In 1970 the Indian government moved the 30 surviving Great Andamanese who were scattered in various parts of south and Middle Andamans to a settlement on Strait Island. Since then they have been totally dependent on the authorities for food, clothing and shelter. Their population, however, has started to increase once again and stood at 52 individuals in January 2010.

Another Negrito group, the Jarawas also known as the Jangil's or Rutland Jarawa's inhibit the western coast of south and middle Andaman. They are mainly hunters and gatherers. The Jarawas on the Great Andaman Island suffered not only as a result of diseases introduced by outsiders but also because of the punitive expeditions carried out by the British and the Japanese who occupied the islands and built bunkers and fortifications here during Second World War. Hundreds of bow-wielding Jarawas fell victim to British bullets in 1859.[10] A reserved area was declared according to the Andaman and Nicobar Regulations, 1956, providing a Jarawa Reserve forest comprising 765 sq. km of south and middle Andamans. Indian colonization of the island and the subsequent deforestation increased the tension and conflicts followed at an accelerating scale. The construction of the Andaman Trunk Road (ATR) over Jarawa territory and the large number of Indian labourers and settlers added to the polarization. The ATR borders the Jarawa territory and at some points even cuts across it. Belatedly it has been largely agreed upon by the administration that its construction has been an error and that ATR has the potential of escalating the conflicts between Jarawas, tourists and settlers. There were regular armed clashes with authorities until the 1990s, killing several police officers who encroached on their territory.

The Onges who inhabit reservations on the Dugong Creek and the South Bay of Little Andaman Island are the most primitive of the tribes and closely related to the African pygmies. They are the most endangered, with fewer than a 100 individuals now known to exist. This is partly due to their contracting diseases like hepatitis from contact with outsiders that began under British colonial rule in 1886. The Onges are sub divided into a number of 'bands'. A 'band' is a collection of more than one family. Each band lives in one tenement known as 'Beyra'. This type of a joint family by the name *beyra* forms a social unit. The Onges have, since the Bangladesh War, been pushed back by the large number of Bengali refugees who entered their settlements. Later the resettlement in these places was done on government's initiative to protect the tribe from getting extinct.[11]

The Sentinelese, believed to be originally an offshoot of the Onges, are the sole inhabitants of the North Sentinel Island situated south-west of Port Blair. They are the most isolated of all the groups and are probably the last of the world's palaeolithic people having no contact with the outside world. The island is completely out of bounds for outsiders and they never permitted outsiders. The Sentinelese lead a life not different from what they lead thousands of years ago and are experts in using bows and arrows.[12]

Nicobar Islands

The indigenous people of the Nicobars have a similarly isolated and lengthy association with the islands. They are believed to be related to the Malays and Burmese, and speak a dialect close to the Mon-Khmer and the languages spoken in Vietnam, Malaysia, and parts of north-east India.[13] Majority of the inhabitants of the Nicobar region belong to the original tribe which consists of two main groups—the Nicobarese, or *Nicobari*, and the Shompen, restricted to the interior of Great Nicobar. The Nicobarese live throughout 12 island communities in the Islands of Car Nicobar, Chowra, Teressa, Bompoka, Katchal, Camorta, Trinkat, Nancoury, Pulo Milo, Little

Nicobar, Kondul and Great Nicobar. Even though they are known in the same generic name 'Nicobarese' each tribe that live in separate island, speaks a separate language. Moreover they are known in different names in accordance with the island where they live. The people of Choura are known as 'Som Pai' and those of Car Nicobar are known as 'Tarik', as the inhabitants of Katchal are called Kamotra and those of Trinket are known as Som Ita. As the Nicobarese are mainly fishermen, herdsman, horticulturalists and sailors, they frequently have to cross the straits between the islands for trading purposes. By the ardent efforts of the government agencies the Nicobarese have been imparted with some formal education which has enabled them to get jobs in the Police, in shipping related works, as clerks, etc. A majority of the Nicobarese have converted to Christianity.[14]

The interior tribe of Shompens, live in the river valleys of Great Nicobar on both the eastern and the western coasts along with the coastal Nicobarese community. Shompens are generally nomadic, roam in the dense forests in search of fruits, tubers, etc. The 'Kaley' and 'Keyet' both tribes found in the Great Nicobar Island come under the generic name Shompens; the former lives on the west coast of the island and the latter on the east coast.[15]

History of the Islands

Historically, the islands were well known to geographers and travellers like Ptolemy, Marcopolo and many Chinese travellers. Their maps have references to these islands and their inhabitants. Ptolemy talked of the 'Angdaman islands' (Islands of good fortune), implying thereby that these islands were being visited by the Western and later Arab merchants going to the Far East. The islands provided a temporary maritime base for ships of the Marathas in the seventeenth century. The legendary privateer and Admiral, Kanhoji Angre harassed colonial shipping routes with a base in the islands. However, it was after the British occupied that these islands gained disrepute. The British took control of the Andaman group of islands in 1790 and the Nicobar group in 1869 (which was under Dutch colonialists between 1758 and 1869). In 1788-9 the government of Bengal sought to establish in the Andamans a penal colony. The islands became more notorious as 'Kalapani', meaning island of black water. The Cellular Jail,[16] Ross Island and Viper Island were used by the British to imprison and punish the prisoners from the mainland, majority of whom were Indian freedom fighters, particularly after 1857, the year of India's First War of Independence. The primary purpose was to have an isolated penal colony for dissenters and independence fighters from the Indian subcontinent.[17] During this period the total population of the settlement, consisting of convicts, their guards, the supervising, clerical and departmental staff, with the families of the latter, also a certain number of ex-convicts and trading settlers and their families, numbered 16,106. The labouring convicts are distributed among four jails and 19 stations; the self-supporters in 38 villages. While the written accounts give the impression that these settlements were a model of progressive penal reforms; Indian accounts, state that the settlement was first and foremost a repository for political prisoners.[18]

The contact with the immigrant population caused certain diseases to spread among the tribal people, who did not possess the physiological adaptation to resist these new types of germs brought in by the immigrants. A fresh heterogeneous community belonging to different religions, castes, and ethnic groups formed and was named as 'Locals' for the sake of convenience. Some of them are the 'Bhantus' of Uttar Pradesh (considered a criminal tribe); they are further divided into about 10 sub-groups by the name 'gotor'. Further, the growing timber industry required a lot of skilled labour, not available among the tribals, hence labourers from Chota Nagpur and Jharkhand were brought. They are known as 'Ranchiwalas' or 'Sathis' which has more then dozen sub-groups—Baraiks, Chik, Lohars, Khariars, Ouaos, Kumbhars, Mundas, Gonds, etc. The Bhantus, Moplas (Mulims) and Locals are mainly agriculturists; the Ranchiwalas are mainly landless labourers. Between 1907 and 1923 people from erstwhile Burma (Myanmar) were also brought in, they are known as 'Burmese' as the former sub-groups Pallungs, Shans, Shantalokes, Kachins and Chatris Karens all lost their identities gradually.[19]

The Andaman Islands were occupied by Japan during Second World War. Thus it was here that on 30 December 1943 during the Japanese occupation, that Netaji Subhas Chandra Bose first raised the flag of Indian independence.[20] According to local historian Gouri Shankar Pandey, Japan's occupation of three and a half years (23 March 1942 to 9 October 1945) rule, killed nearly one third of the islands' then total population of 33,772. According to him, some of them were killed for their loyalty to the British and some were literally liquidated when the Japanese realized towards the end of Second World War, that they could not sustain and feed the whole population of the islands following the virtual blockade by the Allied Forces. In early 1945, the Allied Forces had regained some of their military strength in South-East Asia and did not allow any Japanese vessels carrying food, cloth, medicine and fuel to these islands. Apart from the loss of lives, Pandey says that the Japanese had literally brought the income of the islanders down to zero when they during their occupation introduced 'value-less notes' in the islands instead of their own currency of Yen. They disallowed the Indian rupee and British pound.[21] The result was that after the Japanese left their notes in the islands became counterfeit. After the end of the war they briefly returned to British control. The penal colony was closed on 15 August 1947 when India gained its freedom. It has since served as a museum to the freedom fighters.

The partition of India also had an impact in the ethnic diversification of these islands. The Hindus driven away from East Bengal had to be settled here. The Moplas from the Malabar region who had taken part in the agitation by name 'the Mopla Agitation' were deported to these islands by the British. As per the India–Sri Lanka agreement of 1987, the Tamil-speaking communities settled in Sri Lanka were to be accommodated here. Along with all these, people from all states came and got settled here adding variety to the cultural mosaic of this island.[22] While the British gained by disposing of the trouble makers into it, India supported the influx of refugees from East Pakistan and Sri Lanka. The Government of India had forbidden outsiders from interacting with the tribesmen because such contact has led in the past to alcoholism and disease among the islanders apart from sexual abuse of the local women.

But during the last few years, citizens of Myanmar, Bangladesh and Sri Lanka have permanently settled in the islands using fake

Indian ration cards, while citizens of Thailand, China, Indonesia and Malaysia have reportedly migrated temporarily to plunder the natural resources and then leave. These illegal migrants first infiltrated into India through north-eastern states or West Bengal or Tamil Nadu and then pick up ration cards and other residency documents before landing in the islands. Apparently thousands of non-tribals live illegally in the Andamans with the connivance of the officials. Retired government employees too have houses built on tribal land and are cultivating it, an activity prohibited by law. The excuse of tribal passes is used to keep out experts so that the actual functioning of the administration is not exposed. Primitive tribals of the A&N Islands are dying of disease and infection brought in by waves of colonizers from the mainlands. Available information estimates the number of foreigners in the Andamans to be about 50,000 but officials say the figure is much higher.[23]

Policies of Indian Government after Independence

In post-Independent India, the A&N Islands did not receive the due attention it deserved. First was the need for good ties with Tokyo. The Government of India had signed a Peace Treaty with Japan on 9 June 1952, which, apart from establishing 'firm and perpetual peace and amity' between the two countries, also envisaged, and this was a unique gesture, that India would not claim any war reparations from Japan. In fact, the islands are the only Indian territory which went under Japanese occupation from Britain during Second World War.[24]

Local historian Gouri Shankar Pandey, who is also the General Secretary of one Homfraygunj Martyr's Memorial Committee (HMMC), has been demanding since early 1980s not only a Japanese apology but also a compensation of a 'conservative' Rs. 2,500 crore (Rs. 1,100 crore for the loss of lives and Rs. 1,400 crore for the loss of properties). As the Japanese have paid similar compensations to South-East and East Asian countries, they should do the same to the Andamanese was contended. But the Congress party that was in power then and the then foreign minister Pranab Mukherjee tried to dissuade this group of Andamanese from persisting with this demand. However, when United Front Alliance, came to power in 1995, it asked the local administration of the A&N Islands in 1996 to furnish the details of the period under Japanese occupation. In the BJP-led NDA government in 1998, the local BJP M.P. Bishnupada Ray reportedly put further pressure on the central government to do something in favour of the petitioners. It is against this background that the final decision of the Government of India on the matter came. On 28 February 2002, the Indian Home Ministry, in a letter to Gauri Shanker Pandey stated that a Press Release was issued on 14 December 1963 quoting that the 1963 Agreement completed settlement of all claims against Japan under the peace treaty ending Second World War and India's Second World War claims against Japan have already been settled. In view of the above, it appears that the claims forwarded by HMMC cannot be forwarded to the Government of Japan. There was growing criticism that the Government of India could have better presented the case of the A&N Islands to the people of Japan before finalizing the 'Settlement of War Damages' with Japan in 1963.[25]

The second most important aspect was the fact that for many years after Independence premier school atlases of India did not even have a separate map of the area. One had to look for the map of Andaman group in one set of maps of Thailand and Myanmar while for Nicobar it was the map of Asia. Neither the Survey of India nor any other private agency has a separate map of this region, at least for public use. According to Pandey it was because of the serious lapse on independent India's part that Myanmar claimed and got some important parts of the islands, which, significantly, includes the strategic Coco Islands. Even the Muslim League pressed the British for getting the A&N Islands for Pakistan. Myanmar too, had chipped in to lay her own claim on them.[26] According to Pandey, Myanmar took possession of the Coco Islands in 1954 and illegally occupied the Narkondam Islands bordering the Cocos. It was only in early 1970s that the Indian Navy recaptured it and in 1987 that India concluded the Maritime boundaries Agreement with Myanmar. Further, the Government of India failed to ensure the territorial unity and integrity of the A&N Islands by deploying adequate forces to the nearby region, even during the India-China War in 1962 and India-Pakistan War in 1965.[27]

It was only during the late 1980s and early 1990s that the A&N Islands drew serious attention of the Indian policy makers. In August 1998, the Government of India established a 'Far Eastern Maritime Command' at Port Blair, independent of the operational control of the Eastern Naval Command at Visakhapatnam, and a 'Joint Service Command' in October 2001. Finally, there has been the realization that the geographical assets of the islands should be optimally utilized towards the generation of national wealth and employment. As an important parliamentary debate in 1997 highlighted, Port Blair could be developed as a strategic international trade centre and the islands as a whole could be converted into one of the world's best tourist attractions. The union territory is situated in such an ideal location where one can easily attract more and more trade and business on the Islands. Former Lt. Governor of A&N Nagendra Nath Jha lobbied hard with the central government for the setting up of an 'Oil Terminus and Trans-shipment Port' at Campal Bay (Great Nicobar Island) to cater to the heavy international maritime traffic across the Indian Ocean corridor, to ease the overburdened oil jetties at Singapore and Colombo. As regards the strategic concerns, the Andamans provide the key to the eventual success of the much talked about 'Look East Policy' of India (policy towards the Asia-Pacific reason) that was enunciated by the then Prime Minister Narasimha Rao in early 1990s.[28]

The A&N Islands are renowned for the serene, virgin beaches and fabulous underwater marine life. Neil Island and Havelock Island are a heaven for scuba diving, with scores of water sports centres. Havelock Beach has been rated as one of the best beaches in the world by *Time* magazine. With nearly 90 per cent of the island forested, which has been home to six tribal groups for about 20,000 years, it is proposed to become a 'selective' tourist destination as per the tourism policy envisaged for the A&N Islands. Tourism in the A&N Islands has picked up in the last 20 years. There were only 10,000 tourists visiting the islands in 1980. In 2003, the number increased almost tenfold, to 93,000. In 2004, it was expected to cross the 100,000 mark.[29] This high-value, low-volume tourism potential of the region notwithstanding, experts fear the cost of development will have to be borne by the aboriginals. Slowly and silently, the government's efforts to bring the tribals to the mainstream have only resulted in their numbers getting diminished with each passing year. The Great Andamanese tribe, once over 4,800-strong now stands at a dismal 46; the Onges have been reduced to 96; the Shompens have been gravely affected and, by now, all agree that the Jarawas are on the road to extinction.

Effect of the Tsunami

On 26 December 2004 the coastal areas of the A&N Islands were devastated by a 10 m high tsunami following the 2004 Indian Ocean earthquake. At least 7,000 people were believed to have been killed on the A&N Islands during the disaster. According to official estimates, 1,205 people have lost their lives in the A&N region in the 192 affected villages. A population of over 42,000 had been hit and 5,740 were reported missing. As many as 30 relief camps were set up housing 11,239 victims, not to take into account the thousands of illegal migrants living on the islands who are now missing. The Nicobar islanders and tribes have been the worst sufferers of these events of 26 December.[30]

On Car Nicobar Island alone, with the destruction of 80 per cent of important airbase as many as 20,000 may have perished. From an unofficial estimate of a population of 35,000, only 15,000 are still alive. Indian authorities have traditionally barred foreigners from most of the islands—partly for security reasons, because of the Indian Air Force Base in Car Nicobar, and also to protect a dwindling group of indigenous people. Even Indians need special permits to travel there. Post-tsunami a number of journalists, photographers and television crews have illegally intruded into the Tribal Reserves in gross violation of the A&N Protection of Aboriginal Tribes Regulation, 1957. Some television channels turned the aborigines into a commodity by promoting ridiculous shows like 'Janbaaz Junglees'. In an island inhabited by the Sentinelese, journalists were taken in a military helicopter and the aborginals were provoked to shoot arrows.[31] While the Great Andamanese, Sentinel, Jarawas and Onges were not hit by the Tsunami, the Great Andamanese, living in a government settlement on Strait Island, suffered serious damages. A large number of Nicobarese were also effected. As the whole concentration of national and international focus was on Car Nicobar Island, because of its airbase, other islands in the Nicobar were neglected for nearly four days before rescue missions were sent. Indian authorities have refused permission for international volunteer agencies seeking to go beyond Port Blair to carry out relief work on the ground that they do not want the aborigines to be disturbed in any way. Because the need to protect the aborigines, the A&N Islands bristles with defence installations and has, since 2001 supported a joint-service command involving elements of the army, navy, air force and coast guard under a single commander.

About 40 per cent of the densely forested area is designated as a tribal reserve where indigenous people live. The remainder is protected for wood cultivation. But there has been the violation of the tribal area when hectares of land have been taken over for rubber plantation. The plantation has also resulted in an influx of illegal non-tribals into the island. But post-tsunami, the Supreme Court of India lifted a ban on tree-felling on the islands to help rebuilding efforts. But environmentalists insist that the six-month lifting of the ban will encourage loggers and others to destroy forests which cover more than 80 per cent of the archipelago.[32] Innumerable buildings in these islands, including many government ones, have been constructed in violation of the Coastal Regulation Zone (CRZ). In the last couple of years, there were regular complaints from the construction, hotel and tourism lobby that the CRZ was obstructing the development of infrastructure and the tourism industry here. They wanted it relaxed so that buildings could come up even closer to the coastline.

Among the ten islands that are to be opened for tourism is also Little Andaman where the Onges were resettled in an attempt to segregate them from the mainstream. But the Jarawas are already in touch with the settlers around their habitation. Any further development or influx in their areas will only hasten the process of their disintegration. Further in Port Blair, the islands' capital city, administrative conception of the 'primitive' dates back to the British

Raj and the idea that these islands are somehow synonymous with backwardness is energetically promoted in today's Port Blair tourism. Although the archipelago may be a successful tourist destination but it has been possible only at the cost of the aborigines. The local NGOs[33] have been trying to secure the interest of the tribals and check illegal immigration in the islands. The immigrants who are mainly shipped from Bangladesh, Myanmar and Sri Lanka (Tamils) due to their demographic characteristics, merge with the local populace, eventually leading to socio-economic tensions, criminal activity and polarization of society on communal lines. There are also apprehensions of anti-social elements and non-state actors like ISI and terrorist organizations infiltrating these groups for subversive activities. Such a threat from human trafficking poses a daunting challenge—if such transfers are not interdicted at sea.[34]

Another important issue that has generated concern is protection of the aboriginals. Scientists believe that because of the extreme isolation of the Sentinelese, this tribe has become bio-medically valuable to geneticists. They warn that people of this tribe in the future that they could be targeted by bio-prospectors for valuable genetic traits that may have long ago vanished in other ethnic or racial groups. While few would deny the right of tribals to assert their rights to cultural survival, many agree that they were simply marginalized and spent much time in futile attempts to prevent encroachment on their traditional lands to which they rarely have legal title. Since development and acculturation are inevitable, the problem is one of retaining the most appropriate and valuable aspects of their tribal culture. The developmental changes that will enable tribal people to survive in the modern world, need to be introduced in as non-traumatic a form as possible.

Conclusion

Since Independence, India has witnessed the rise of political movements that are mobilized along identity lines to safeguard tribal interests from the economic exploitation that resulted from the national development programme. The demand to give statehood to A&N and enable tribal-people to sustain their right to self-determination, has gained momentum. The government recognizes the ethnic sentiments of some social groups and confers them with the right to preserve their distinct cultural identity. These groups have exclusive ownership of their land and resources and autonomously administers their political and judicial systems. The lack of cultural relatedness, especially of the 'tribal' culture, weakens the new political association, and the racial and cultural difference, thus, come to play a vital role in defining the self-identity. To answer the questions 'who are we?' the tribals are caught between the racial-cultural definition and the politico-administrative definition of their identity. But as a Union Territory, the A&N Islands has no legislature and thus no elected representatives with any clout apart from a single Member of Parliament. The tribals are pushed to accept a destiny that has been put beyond their control. Hence there has been growing demand for status of statehood where people are sensitized to problems and aspirations of the island communities of A&N.

Notes

1. Rajat Ganguly (1998), *Kin State Intervention in Ethnic Conflicts: Lessons from South Asia*, New Delhi: Sage; Urmila Phadnis and Rajat Ganguly, (2001), *Ethnicity and Nation-building in South Asia*, New Delhi: Sage.
2. 'Ethnicity in Bondage: Is Its Liberation Premature?' Keynote address by Ali A. Mazrui (Director, Institute of Global Cultural Studies and Albert Schweitzer Professor in the Humanities, SUNY, Binghamton), UNRISD/UNDP International Seminar on Ethnic Diversity and Public Policies (New York, 17-19 August 1994). Also see Rajat Ganguly and Ian Macduff (2003), *Ethnic Conflict and Secessionism in South & Southeast Asia: Causes, Dynamics, Solutions*, New Delhi: Sage.
3. Madhusree Mukerjee, 'Tribal Struggle: Stone Age Guardians of the Andaman Islands Fight to Survive', *Scientific American*, May 1995, pp. 10-13; Lidio Cipriani (1966) *Andaman Islanders* ed. and tr. D. Taylor Cox assisted by Linda Cole, New York: Frederick A. Praeger; Bryant S. Mason, 'An Archipelago in the Bay of Bengal', *The New York Times,* 30 October 1994; N. Iqbal Singh (1978), *The Andaman Story*, New Delhi: Vikas; B.R. Tamta (1993), *Andaman and Nicobar Islands*, New Delhi: National Book Trust.
4. T.H. Eriksen (1993), *Ethnicity and Nationalism*, London and Chicago: Pluto Press, pp. 87-8.

5. M. Cross, 'Colonialism and Ethnicity: A Theory and Comparative Case Study', *Ethnic and Racial Studies*, vol. 1, no. 1, January 1978, p. 40.
6. Prakash Nanda, 'Strategic Significance of the Andamans', *Bharat Rakshak Monitor*, vol. 5, no. 3, November-December 2002.
7. http://www.krepublishers.com/02-Journals/IJHG/IJHG-03-0-000-000-2003-Web/IJHG-03-1-001-067-2003-Abst-PDF/IJHG-03-1-005-011-2003-Kashyap/IJHG-03-1-005-011-2003-Kashyap.htm
8. Sumedha Narwa (1999) *Tribes of Andaman and Nicobar Islands*, New Delhi: Mittal Publications; E.H. Man (1883), 'On the Aboriginal Inhabitants of the Andaman Islands', *Journal of Anthropological Institute of Great Britain and Ireland*, vol. 12, Royal Anthropological Institute of Great Britain, London, 1883.
9. S.S. Sarkar (1962), 'The Origin and Migration of the Negrito in the Andaman Islands', *Man in India*, vol. 33, pp. 265-74; Nicholas Wade 'The Andamanese Negrito: An Ancient Link to Africa Lives on in Bay of Bengal', *The New York Times*, 9 January 2005.
10. Jayanta Sarkar (1990), *The Jarawa* (The ASI Andaman and Nicobar Islands Tribe Series) Calcutta: Seagull Books; 'The Descent of Isle and Man on Jarawa', *The Telegraph*, 30 October 1994.
11. Badal Kumar Basu (1990), *The Onge: Negrito Hunter-Gatherers of Little Andaman*, Calcutta, Seagull Books; M.V. Portman, 'The Exploration and Survey of the Little Andaman', *Proceedings of the Royal Geographic Society*, vol. X, 1888, pp. 567-76.
12. See T.N. Pandit (1990), *The Sentinelese* (The ASI Andaman and Nicobar Islands Tribe Series), Calcutta: Seagull Books.
13. P. Bellwood (1997), *Prehistory of the Indo-Malaysian Archipelago*, Honolulu: University of Hawai'i Press.
14. See Simronjit Singh (2003), *In the Sea of Influence: A World System Perspective of the Nicobar Islands*, Lund Studies in Human Ecology 6, Sweden: Lund University; V.S. Upadhyay, 'Changing and Disappearing Cultures in Andaman and Nicobar Islands', *Review of Ethnology*, vol. 7, 1979, pp. 50-4.
15. See T.S. Naidu, 'The Shompen Aboriginal Tribal Population and Problems of Survival in Great Nicobar Island', *Journal of Family Welfare*, vol. 44, no. 2, June 1998, pp. 59-66.
16. The Cellular Jail at Port Blair completed in 1910, included 698 cells designed to better accommodate solitary confinement; each cell measured 4.5 by 2.7 m with a single ventilation window 3 m above. The history of the Cellular Jail is rife with records of horrendous

tortures inflicted upon hapless people who had taken part in the freedom struggle.

17. Anil Raj, 'Cellular Jail, Andaman', www.sankalpindia.net/drupal/tourism/cellular-jail-andaman.
18. See M.V. Portman (1899), *A History of Our Relations with the Andamanese Compiled from Histories and Travels and from the Records of the Government of India*, Calcutta: Office of the Superintendent of Government Printing (2 vols.); Raghubir Singh, 'The Last Andaman Islanders: Arrows Speak Louder then Words', *National Geographic Magazine*, July 1975, pp. 66-91.
19. Sasi Kumar 'The People of Andaman and Nicobar Islands', 26 December 2006. http://keralaarticles.blogspot.com/2006/12/people-of-andaman-and-nicobar-islands. html#comment-26895107259694699 8.
20. Netaji Subhas Chandra Bose was the first man who had set up his provincial government in A&N Islands. It was the headquarters of the Azad Hind Fauj. When Netaji visited the islands during the war, he hoisted the Freedom Flag and named A&N Islands as Shaheed Dweep and Swaraj Dweep.
21. Prakash Nanda, op. cit.; see also Jayant Dasgupta, *Japanese in the Andaman & Nicobar Islands*, New Delhi: Manas Publications, 2002.
22. Sasi Kumar, 'The People of Andaman and Nicobar Islands', 26 December 2006. http://keralaarticles.blogspot.com/2006/12/people-of-andaman-and-nicobar-islands. html#comment-268951072596946998.
23. Prakash Nanda, 'Strategic Significance of the Andamans', *Bharat Rakshak Monitor*, vol. 5, no. 3, November-December 2002.
24. In 1942, the Japanese captured the islands from the British without a fight. Later in March 1981, a Burmese Naval Gunboat landed troops on Narkondum Island. In 1985, a community of Thai fishermen were evicted from Tillanchang Island.
25. Sasikumar, op. cit.
26. Avtar Singh Bhasin (1998) *Some Called it Partition, Some Freedom*, Delhi: Siba Exim Pvt Ltd, pp. 157-8, 165. Pakistan pleaded with the British that the A&N Islands should go to it because of geographical and strategic reasons. The Muslim League expressed the fear that with India in control of the Islands, it could refuse 'to allow any passage through India of Pakistani troops proceeding from West Pakistan to East Pakistan, or vice versa'.
27. The following observations of the former Chief of Naval Staff, Vice-Admiral V.S. Soman, recounting his experiences in 1965, are extremely significant (for details see Vice-Admiral G.M. Hiranandani (2000),

Transition to Triumph: Indian Navy 1965-1975, New Delhi: Lancer Publishers, p. 25.

28. G.S. Khurana, 'Shaping Security in India's Maritime East: Role of Andaman & Nicobar', *Strategic Analysis*, vol. 30, no. 1, January-March 2006; also see Vice-Admiral Arun Prakash, 'Evolution of the Joint Andaman and Nicobar Command (ANC) and Defence of Our Island Territories' (Part II) *USI Journal*, vol. CXXXII, 2002.
29. Subir Bhaumik, 'Considering the Silver Lining of Future Tourism', *BBC News*, 11 January 2005; *Efforts to Revive Tourism in the Andamans*, A&N Administration Press Release, 25 January 2005.
30. 'Rescue and Relief Operations Continue', Andaman and Nicobar Administration Press Release, 6 January 2005; 'A Queen is Forced to Leave', *Times of India*, 30 January 2005; Denis Giles, 'The First Relief Ship To Nan Cowry (Nicobars)', *Times of India*, 5 January 2005.
31. Kai Friese, 'Ten Little Niggers or Are they Little Indians ? The Great Andamanese Tribal Circus Continues', 24 January 2005; www.outlookindia.com/article.aspx?226308; Shailesh Shekhar, 'Tourism to Hasten Tribals Doom', April 2003 www.HindustanTimes.com.
32. See 'Go Under or Follow Coastal Regulations', *Down to Earth*, 31 January 2005.
33. Some of the institutions, NGOs and persons working for the betterment of these people are local the NGO, Society for A&N Ecology (SANE) under Samir Acharya, Manish Chandi, a researcher with the A&N Environmental Team, local-born journalist Denis Giles on early relief to the Nicobars on the extent of physical damage to the Nicobars; Amitav Ghosh, the internationally renowned novelist and Dr. Simron Jit Singh of The Andaman and Nicobar Trust Account.
34. G.S. Khurana, 'Shaping Security in India's Maritime East: Role of Andaman & Nicobar', *Strategic Analysis*, vol. 30, no. 1, January-March 2006.

4

Quest for a Land of their 'Own' in Kashmir

The Autonomy Argument*

ASHUTOSH KUMAR

Even after more than two decades of ethnic conflict, Kashmir continues to receive the attention of the whole world as the world in general and India in particular grapples with the escalation of violence in the subcontinent that is clearly linked to the non-fulfilment of the demand for what people of Kashmir call *azadi* based on the right to self-determination. The demand for *azadi* persists as the mass protest that swept the Kashmir Valley in the wake of the alleged sexual assault on two Kashmiri women or the proposed shifting of the central university from Kashmir Valley to Jammu region or 'diversion' of forest land to the Shri Amarnath Shrine Board for the Amarnath Yatra showed clearly. The present essay presents an analysis of the conflict situation in Kashmir while contemplating the possible pathways to conflict resolution and restoration of peace in the valley.

For the purpose the essay is divided into four parts. The first part addresses the dominant concerns of the both nation states of India and Pakistan who are directly involved in the conflict. It also includes an analysis of the growing concerns of the Western liberal

* This is a much revised and updated version of the essay originally published as 'Politics of Ethno-Religious Identity in Kashmir: Dominant Concerns and Possible Solutions', in *Contemporary India*, Nehru Memorial Museum & Library, vol. 3 (2), April-June 2004.

democracies led by USA. In the second part the possible 'solutions' to the Kashmir 'problem' being suggested by the Kashmir specialists are taken up with a focus on their feasibility. The third part brings in the people of Kashmir and their aspirations into the discourse. The essay suggests that any possible long-term solution to the seemingly intractable Kashmir issue would involve an understanding of the foundations on which the ethno-religious identity of the Kashmiri people has been constructed. For the purpose of analysing the foundations, one also needs to recount the tragic consequences of the failed 'Kashmir policy' of India. In the fourth part, the essay suggests that the autonomy option appears to be the only viable solution given the uniqueness of the Kashmiri identity, as the other options as discussed earlier are neither credible nor feasible.

Kashmir: Dominant Concerns

Let us first address the 'dominant' concerns of the Western liberal world led by USA over the decade. Kashmir since its accession to India has received attention of both UK and USA primarily due to its geo-strategic location. Kashmir as a region shares borders with India, Pakistan, Afghanistan, and China and also with the oil and natural gas rich Central Asian Republics. As such it is perceived as a gateway to South, South-West and Central Asia thus holding the key to the strategic balance in the region—a fact recognized even by the early Kashmir leadership.[1] The ongoing 'global war on terror' has brought other Western liberal democracies also into the picture. Second, Kashmir has been a witness to three developments that arouse the US concerns—namely the ever increasing flow of arms and drugs from across the frontiers, the growth of cross-border as well as home-grown terrorism, as well as the rise of pan-Islamic fundamentalism.[2] Third, the USA has a stake in keeping the South Asian region as a conflict-free zone as it engages Pakistan as its strategic ally in its fight against the Taliban forces in Afghanistan.[3] Four wars and a simmering war-like situation between India and Pakistan over the last six decades, notwithstanding the intermittent thaw that has once again been broken post-Mumbai carnage, has been a major source of concern for the whole world that views south Asia as one of the 'most dangerous flashpoints on earth'.[4] The fact that the conflict over Kashmir has outlasted the conflicts in Indo-China, Middle East and even the Cold War, and also that the two feuding states hold nuclear weapons underlines the critical need felt to resolve the Kashmir issue.[5] The frantic American diplomatic intervention in bringing a thaw in India-Pakistan relationship after the Pakistani terrorists attacks on Mumbai in November 2008, and the move to appoint a special envoy for South Asia by the Obama administration showed the enhanced concerns of USA. Fourth, denial of the right of Kashmiri people to self-determination by India, and the frequent incidents of the violation of the human rights both by the state agents including the state sponsored 'counter-insurgent groups' as well as the Islamist groups, has focused the attention of the global civil society on strife torn Kashmir and its helpless masses. The violation of human rights, the loss of human lives both by the state security agents and the militants during the last two decades has been colossal. Just consider the grim details: Till the date at the present writing, the death toll has been around 70,000 civilians, at least 60,000 people have been arrested and tortured, 8,000-10,000 people have been missing and there have been 33-recorded massacres. Before the mayhem started in the valley, as many as 1,25,000 Kashmiri Pandits were forced to migrate from the valley, becoming refugees in their own state.[6] As for the governmental responsibility in these deaths, an independent study conducted in 2000 showed that 80 per cent of the deaths that had occurred till then were due to cross-fire, killings by security forces, or in custody, and by renegades.[7] The major concern of the human rights groups has been to prevent custodial deaths, even if in the short-term this means accepting greater use of detention. The fact that the Indian government in the past has not allowed the human rights groups like Asia Watch and Amnesty International to visit Kashmir on their fact-finding missions raises further Western liberal eyebrows.

Kashmir has remained an obsession with Pakistan. One can broadly refer to four factors to explain as to why Kashmir runs 'in the blood of Pakistan' as a former president of Pakistan succinctly put it. First, Kashmir has always been treated by a significant section of both the classes and masses in Pakistan as the 'unfinished agenda' of the Partition, also in accordance with the two-nation theory, a Muslim majority Kashmir 'should' have been part of Pakistan. Pakistan considers Kashmir as a disputed territory as it does not accept the validity of the instrument of accession.[8] It also insists on implementation of the UN resolution regarding holding the plebiscite so that the people of Kashmir could exercise their right to self-determination as to whether they want to opt for India or for Pakistan. Second, Pakistan continues to remain what Alavi in the early 1970s described as an 'overdeveloped' post-colonial state still ruled by an oligarchy of military, bureaucracy and politicians that has thrived on a 'political economy of defense'.[9] It remains true even after the recent episode of the restoration of civilian rule. In a Pakistan torn by ethnic strife and civil war between the Islamist forces and the Pakistani Army, Kashmir has become the very basis of the process of legitimization of the idea of a militarized and increasingly authoritarian Pakistan. Third, the growing Islamicization of Pakistan since the Zia regime, has created a significant constituency of the Islamist forces not only among the masses but also more importantly, among the ruling strata including the military elite. For these forces, 'Muslim' Kashmir under a 'Hindu' India remains an anathema as they look for the creation of *Darul-e-Islam*. Fourth, even among the moderates in Pakistan the painful memory of Partition and then more recently the creation of Bangladesh continue to rankle for which they hold India responsible, citing it as the testimony to the Indian hostility to the very existence of Pakistan.

As for the Indian state, Kashmir as the sole Muslim majority constituent state in the union represents the 'shining example' or 'litmus test' of its secular credentials. In the nationalist discourse, Kashmir stands at the 'core' as its retention is considered critical for the preservation of absolute, indivisible sovereignty and political integrity of the nation state. Second is the cost factor in retaining Kashmir for India that causes the concern. The loss of human lives and resources over the period has simply been tremendous. Only the annual economic cost to combat militancy and retaining Siachin runs into more than Rs. 10,000 crore.[10] It goes without saying that this public money could have had a better utilization, for developmental purposes. Third, at a time when the economy guides the politics, it is clear that a peaceful solution to Kashmir problem would have promoted the regional cooperation mooted under the auspices of South Asian Association for Regional Cooperation (SAARC), South Asian Free Trade Association (SAFTA) and the SAARC Chambers of Commerce and Industry, located in Karachi. The success achieved by ASEAN has been instructive in this regard as its member countries have been able to resolve their bilateral issues.[11] An economically resurgent India has much to gain from the heightened economic activities in the region. Fourth, in the present globalizing world that shows immense respect for human rights, Indian democracy is embarrassingly being seen in poor light on account of its poor human rights record in the valley. Ironically India has been among the first signatories to the human rights charter, which recognizes the right of all peoples of the world to self-determination.[12]

There is no doubt that India gets a lot of flak, the world over for its bungled Kashmir issue. It has come under criticism for displaying a self-righteous rhetoric, cleverness and reluctance to compromise. At the domestic level, Kashmir's post-accession past demonstrates to some that 'the Indian government . . . listens only when people take up arms, valorises armed groups and has contempt for non-violent movements'.[13]

As the media coverage of the people's movements on the shrine board issue showed, there has been a marked reluctance to report fairly about the tragic happenings in the valley. The inadequate response of the civil society is sought to be justified on the ground that what Kashmiri people have been asking for in the name of the right to self-determination is primarily a masked communal demand being raised by the Kashmiri Muslims and that too only by those who are fundamentalists.[14] It is further argued that in the existing situation of strife and turmoil dominated by the militants, how does one gauge 'what the people really think'? In recent times, the holding of peaceful elections in the valley and large scale participation of the people in the electoral process has been put forward as the proof of peoples' desire to join the political mainstream. The fact of the matter is that there remains a groundswell of support for autonomy/*azadi* among the people that has sustained the movement till date. Then, both the state agents as well as the militants have been responsible for creating a culture of fear and silence in the valley.

Kashmir thus poses a serious question mark about the success of democracy in India. As a critical challenge to the democratic credentials of India, the ongoing movement has tended to sap the energy of the people, divert resources, encourage chauvinists, undermine democratic rights, and threaten regional stability and economic cooperation, all of which is detrimental to the country and the region's interests.[15]

Looking for Possible 'Options'

What can be the possible pathways to enduring peace in the valley? One needs to understand that the demand for *azadi*/autonomy cannot be analysed merely in the context of the militancy.[16] Even the Indian army commanders posted in the valley have long been admitting that Kashmir 'problem' is not a law and order problem but is political in nature that needs a permanent political solution.

As one understands that granting independent status to Kashmir or handing over the territory of Kashmir to Pakistan are simply out of the question, the question arises as to which are the other options left? The options being suggested by the 'Kashmir experts' fall into one of the two broad categories either as plebiscitary or partitionist in nature. The plebiscitary option would be to settle the sovereignty question by taking into consideration the will of the people expressed through the democratic method of free and impartial plebiscite held under the auspices of the UN as per the Security Council resolution. The Indian state has consistently rejected the plebiscite option as irrelevant, obsolete and unnecessary as in her opinion the people of Jammu & Kashmir have exercised their democratic rights repeatedly in the elections periodically held in the state. It also refers to the fact that the duly constituted constituent assembly of the state had accepted the accession of Kashmir to India.

The partitionist option, mooted during Simla talks in 1971 between the two states, is to convert the existing line of control into an international border and the maintenance of peace on the border with the active role of the United Nations Military Observer Group, formed in the wake of the 1949 Karachi agreement.[17] As the growing Talibanization and militarization of civil society in Pakistan rules out this option even when India seems willing to consider it, another option that is contemplated is to integrate non-Muslim dominated Jammu and Ladakh into India and having a shared sovereignty over a united valley with soft border. The idea of softening the border has been pushed forward as a humanitarian initiative that would enable the divided families and villages to reaffirm their age-old ties as well as facilitate trade on old routes.[18] This is an option, which in the recent years has been partially worked out. However, this, at the most, fulfils one of the urges of the Kashmiris on the both sides of the border, but does not meet their demands.

Another variant of the partitionist option being argued is to trifurcate the state on the basis of religion as demanded by as diverse quarters such as Rashtriya Swayamsewak Sangh (RSS), the Kashmir Study Group (KSG), and the People's Initiative for Peace and Unity over the years.[19] The idea was originally mooted by Sir Owen Dixon's 1950 proposal of 'regional plebiscites'. These groups have been asking for the creation of a separate Muslim state of Kashmir incorporating the Muslim dominated areas of Jammu regions like Doda, Poonch-Rajouri. The Hindu-dominated districts of Jammu and Buddhist-dominated district of Leh are proposed as autonomous political units.[20] Such a formulation only foregrounds religious identity and shows a disregard for the immense ethnic and linguistic variety of the state. Political trifurcation of the state can be rejected on the following grounds:

> first, trifurcation will destroy the composite identity of the state, which has existed as one unit since 1846, and send a dangerous message to the whole nation. If Hindus, Muslims and Buddhists cannot live in one state, can they do so in a larger entity? Second, it will most probably lead to a transfer of Muslims from various parts of the city but also Doda, Rajouri and Poonch, assuming that the entire province is made into a separate state. Finally, it will lead to such deep communal polarization that bloody communal riots will inevitably follow.[21]

Leaving aside the above options, can there be any *outright* solution being advocated by the popular jingoist media after every terrorist attacks on India? The strategic analysts rule out the possibility in the absence of a decisive military superiority over Pakistan as well as the nuclear power status of Pakistan.[22]

As for the role of the third party mediation, it has long been ruled out by the Indian state after the mediation of Britain and US failed in 1962-3 following the China–India war. Opposition to Obama administration's reported move to appoint a special envoy for Kashmir was the most recent illustration of India's reluctance. As for the track two and three diplomacy, advocating people to people contact or back channel discussion, it has mostly been of interest to the media and the retired civil servants.

Bringing in the Kashmiri People

The above analysis makes it clear that the Kashmir 'problem' remains intractable due to the entrenched positions as well as the antagonisms that mark the ruling class politics in both India and Pakistan. The invisibility of the people of the valley in the whole territorialized discourse on solving the issue is palpable as the national interests of the two 'nation states' overshadow them. Both states have been taking the maximalist position to serve what they consider their national interests without realizing that nationalism sometimes may become the enemy of the national interest.

The present essay would argue that there is a critical need to develop a civic political culture that can enable the civil society in the two states to transcend the 'sediments of history' that are weighing them down. Only then would it be recognized that the Kashmir 'problem' is first and foremost a problem between the people of both Indian and Pakistani parts of Kashmir who are asking for autonomy/*azadi*, and the two nation states, that refuse to listen to them with sincerity, and not as much between the two states.

To reiterate, the essay argues that in the absence of a rational analysis of the historical bases of the Kashmiri people's political alienation and political responses, their demand for democratic space and their urge to maintain their political distinctiveness remains suspect.

What follows is an exploration of the nature and bases of assertion of collective political consciousness that underlies the distinct Kashmiri ethno-regional identity.

Making of the Kashmiri Identity

In philosophical terms, the ethno-cultural identity of Kashmiri masses can be interpreted to have both cognitive as well as abstract basis.[25] In cognitive terms this distinct identity gets reflected in all those societal and cultural factors that underlay the construction of a distinctive identity of Kashmiri nation (*qaum*)—the language, the customs, and the traditions. In abstract terms, *Kashmiriat* has been historically reflected in the common philosophical underpinnings governing the vital aspects of Kashmiri life. This philosophical and cultural substance of the Kashmiri identity underlies the humanist and eclectic basis of society on the one hand, and the liberal and non-dogmatic attitude of the people towards religion, on the other.[26] *Kashmiriyat* has reflected the seminal values of the three great religious traditions, namely, Buddhism, Shaivism, and Islam that influenced the social and cultural life of the people of Kashmir at different periods. As a result, a syncretic liberal character is easily discernible in the philosophical orientation of the people of Kashmir.[27]

It follows that Islamic consciousness, which has been an integral part of Kashmir's nationalist and democratic movement, in its *Sufi* form, has been the 'preserver, consolidator and perpetuator of Kashmiri identity'.[28] Prioritizing the 'Islamic' identity of the people in the valley by the Islamist forces, has not succeeded in undermining the secular, pluralist, tolerant and accommodative nature of *Kashmiriat*.[29]

In politico-religious terms since the early twentieth century, the people of Kashmir have imagined themselves as a distinct political community and have demanded a separate territorial homeland. The geographical insularity of the valley has provided them with 'historical existence of individuality'.[30] That is the reason why people of the valley find it difficult to respond to any other wider political identity/political centre that has its nucleus outside.

The process of formation and assertion of the collective political consciousness among the people of Kashmir has been determined by a number of factors, the most important of which has been the peoples' perception of history. Kashmir has been, for a long period, under 'outsider' control. It has been ruled by the Mughals, Afghans, Sikhs and Dogras successively.[31] Long period, of outside control has left in the minds of people a memory of continued subjugation of the community and its economic oppression.

In the popular political discourse that evolved way back in the 1930s, the Dogra monarchical rule, against which the quit Kashmir movement was organized, came to be depicted as the archetype of continuous outside control and domination. The Treaty of Amritsar (1846) by which Kashmir was transferred by the British authorities to the Dogra rulers on the payment of a paltry sum of Rs. 75 lakh has always rankled in the popular memory as the symbol of the degradation and slavery of the community as a whole.[32] Hence, the lingering hope for *azadi* that is reflected in evoking the terms like *mulk* (country) and *quam* (nation).[33]

As per the early assertion of the Kashmiri identity on religious basis it was essentially a consequence of the pitiable socio-economic situation in which the community was placed at that time under the Hindu Dogra rule.[34] The landless Muslim peasants and artisans were 'taxed to the limit of the endurance and subject to an administration that . . . (was) corrupt from top to bottom, . . . vote less, unorganised and helpless in their ignorance'.[35] There was also a bias against the Muslims in terms of employment in the bureaucracy and army which heightened the sense of exclusion of an entire community by a Hindu ruler.

The substantive political and economic form of the mass politics, however, enabled the people in rising above their Muslim consciousness in the subsequent years.[36] In organizational terms, this was reflected in the conversion of the Muslim Conference, the party that led the Kashmiri uprising, into the National Conference (NC) in 1939 enabling it to succeed in transcending the narrow religious limitations. In terms of ideology the NC prioritized the radical land reforms as well as the emancipation of the people including the women from the oppressive feudal elite.[37]

The secular character of the NC was obvious as Sheikh Abdullah averred: 'my fight is for the emancipation of my country. Let us all rise above petty communal bickering and work jointly for the welfare of the masses.'[38] Thus the politics that evolved as a result of the changing process of mobilization resulted in the assertion of ethnic identity that had an overarching Kashmiri rather than an Islamic character. The political issues that emerged were the issues of political dignity, independent political space and self-rule as Kashmir came out of the feudal monarchical shackle to be part of Indian Union.

What Went Wrong: Narrating the Political Tale?

A number of interrelated developments in the post-1950 period, however, contributed to the accumulation of discontent and gradually allowed the return of the communal consciousness, now in its virulent form. These included the increasing intervention of the centre in the politics of the state; the process of constitutional integration of the state with India; the failure of the structures of articulation of democratic responses; and failure of ideology and the decline of the socially purposive politics.

While analysing the impact of the above, it is imperative to emphasize that the bases of Kashmir's negotiated relationship with India were both ideological and emotional in nature.

On ideological grounds, the political leadership had a reason for preferring India to Pakistan because of the former's commitment to the radical land reforms. Such reforms may not have been as easily accomplished in a feudal Pakistan. The secular democratic values that underpinned the nationalist movement in India also assured the Kashmiri leadership. On emotional plane there persisted a personal relationship between the Kashmiri and Indian leadership. The fact that the leaders like Gandhi and Nehru were sensitive to the Kashmiri urge for self-governance and independent political space was a satisfying matter to the Kashmiris.[39]

Unfortunately the above relationship witnessed an early setback as the Praja Parishad led movement in Jammu, supported by RSS, raised the question mark over the constitutional autonomy given to the state. Its principal slogan was *ek desh mein do vidhan, ek desh mein do pradhan nahin chalega* (meaning 'two constitutions, two flags, and two heads of state in one country are totally unacceptable').[40] It was this movement along with the rise of communalism in other parts of India that compelled Abdullah to rethink as early as in 1952 about the issue of accession.

The turning point came when a popularly elected Sheikh Abdullah, the then prime minister of the state, was arrested and kept in detention for almost two decades without any trial. This event remains etched in the memory of people of Kashmir as the mark of the denial of democracy even though in recent times the Abdullah family has lost much of its goodwill. The post-1953 period politics of Kashmir, which was constantly monitored by a hegemonic centre, added weight to such perceptions of Kashmiris.

Repeated violation of the democratic rights of the people representation who were ironically promised constitutional autonomy at the time of accession, not to mention the right to self-determination, reaffirms the contention that if at all, there has been a Kashmir policy of the Indian state all these years, it 'has been based—implicitly—on the theory that all secular and what are called pro-India forces'.[41] Working on such assumption, the centre encouraged the homogenization and hegemonization of the local politics leaving no space for opposition or dissent. The state politics, for all practical purposes, had a long stretch of one-party dominated politics till the 2002 assembly elections.

That Kashmiri people have been forced to remain mute observers to the political events taking place in the state can be clearly explained with reference to the case of the constitutional integration of the state with India. Such a constitutional integration giving way to extension of constitutional provisions beyond the original scope of Article 370 and the Delhi Agreement of 1952 has had hardly any concurrence of the people of Kashmir with the puppet governments endorsing them.[42] Most of the constitutional changes leading to the process of integration took place during 1953-75 when the governments were considered puppets of the centre. Such a dubious kind of integrationist approach naturally undermined the legitimacy of the basis of accession. In understanding the impact of politics of 'integration' on the issue of identity in Kashmir, it is important to note that it was the federal context of India that was more relevant to the Kashmiris rather than its 'nationalist' context. Having the pragmatic and functional reasons for preferring India and to Pakistan, the Kashmiri leadership was emphatic on maintaining the distinctiveness of Kashmir. Autonomy as guaranteed under Article 370 of the India's Constitution, therefore, had special significance for the people of Kashmir as endorsed by the Supreme Court ruling in 'Prem Nath Kaul *versus* state of Jammu & Kashmir'. It not merely symbolized a 'special status' but also the basis of the federal 'contract' which the state had with the Indian state.

People of Kashmir had entered into a social and political contract with Indian state that was in their views, 'sacrosanct' and 'enviable', radiating a sense of parity and negotiability. The widespread alienation among the people in Kashmir that followed emanated from the post-1953 happenings, mentioned very briefly above. The fragility of the democratic structures, especially those capable of channelling the discontent in the legitimized political space, like elections, had much to do with the emergence of extra-constitutional form of politics based on violence.[43]

Among the various factors that account for the accumulating discontent in Kashmir has been the failure of the successive regimes to pay attention to the increasing expectations and demands upon the system in the economic arena. It was in the initial period of politicization of Kashmir that their expectations were raised. Much before the transfer of power to the political elite of Kashmir, the *New Kashmir Manifesto* had promised the reorganization of the economic structure keeping in view the interests of the class of the landless peasantry and the artisans. Such a promise was given a concrete shape in the period between 1948 and 1953 when the most radical land reforms were pursued in the state by Sheikh Abdullah government.[44] There was a definite change in the socio-economic structure of Kashmir both at the levels of legislation and implementation as the landless peasantry got empowered.

The land reforms programme, however, despite its initial success soon ran into serious difficulties at the stage of implementation itself as the loopholes in the laws were exploited by the influential elements. It became a source of aggrandizing the political and other ambitions of the politicians and bureaucrats especially under the Bakshi Ghulam Mohammad government that succeeded Abdullah government. The union government's opposition to these radical measures on the ground that taking away of the surplus land from the Hindu landlords without compensation was raising communal passion in Jammu, did not help either.

Spread of education over the years has resulted in the emergence of a new generation of Kashmiris, better educated than their predecessors, more conscious of their political rights and prerogatives. It has also led to the emergence of a middle class that has thrown up a new set of political leadership different from the traditional political elite in the valley.

The growing asymmetry between the 'mobilization success' of Kashmiris on the one hand and the non- fulfilment of their aspirations, however, has come into sharp focus due to the perennial nature of crisis of governance. While modernization has exposed young Kashmiris to the possibility of alternative futures, the actual politics chokes off such opportunities.[45]

The stunted growth of agriculture as well as industry, the lack of adequate job opportunities in the administration, public and private sectors, a high level economic mismanagement and political nepotism over the years has contributed in a significant manner to the process of alienation among the youth.[46] Today there exists about 1,50,000 educated unemployed youths in the state. It is from this group that many of the today's Hurriyat leaders and the militants have come up. By one estimate about 20 per cent of the educated unemployed youth are joining the militant movement. It may be argued that the most effective strategy to combat militancy in Kashmir to create more opportunities for higher education and better employment in diverse fields for youth. As per the Economic Survey 2006-7 for Jammu & Kashmir, the unemployment rate in the state is at 4.21 per cent, which is higher than national average of 3.09 per cent.[47]

Jammu & Kashmir, being a land scarce and labour abundant state having a very low level of development, has remained one of the union's ten special category states. In fact, till the 1970s the centre funded state's five-year plan expenditure to the extent of 90 per cent. Even now it follows an aid policy of 30 per cent grants and 70 per cent loans. Such a policy of economic appeasement rather than winning the confidence of the masses has had, however, adverse implications for the beleaguered economy of the state. First, it failed to give the state an impetus to utilize its own resources for economic growth and fostered economic dependence in the form of highly subsided transfers from the centre that has been both degrading and counterproductive. At present the state's revenue covers only 25 per cent of its expenditure. The ratio of central transfers to the total revenues, which is 78.6 per cent for the state, is twice of that for all other states at 38.5 per cent. Then more than 50 per cent of the state's revenue goes towards servicing debt. Second, the policy of heavy subsidization primarily in the form of unproductive expenditure has turned Kashmir into a 'high cost economy'. Way back in December 2005, Ghulam Nabi Azad, the then chief minister claimed that 50 per cent of the 2,73,508 government employees 'had no work to do'. Ironically, the parties contesting 2008 assembly elections promised to fill vacancies running at 23,000. Third, the privileged strata of society became the sole beneficiary of centre's funding and subsidies as corruption got institutionalized. Fourth, it has failed to release the entrepreneurial initiative of people or provide sufficient benefit to the targeted groups.

The fact that as per the admission of the then chief minister of the state, by 2006 as much as two million canal or 2,50,000 acres of state land had been encroached upon by private parties can illustrate the crisis of governance. The failure of governance is also apparent when one considers that the state with identified potential of 16,200 MW of hydroelectric potential has been able to tap only 1,481 MW. The indirect way in which militancy has hit the land scarce state's economy is clear in the manner the fertile land and orchards to the tune of 170 sq km have been occupied by more than 6,00,000 armed forces (as per the government records presented in the parliament in 2003) considering that agriculture and horticulture are the main sources of income. Another critical economic sector that has been hit due to militancy is the tourism sector, which has been identified as the 'backbone of the state economy'. In this respect the successive governments have been dithering on the issue of land lease to private investors, who are non-state subjects and are interested in tourism sector, due to the fear of possible peoples' protest against 'selling out'.

It is obvious that a 'reformist long-term development strategy-to raise growth, increase employment, reduce poverty, and improve factor use efficiency' in the strife torn state is directly linked to the 'conflict resolution and prevention, and peace through economic reconstruction'.[48]

The emergent alienation in the valley fuelled the communalization process. The role of the Islamic schools, the *madrasas*, mainly set up by a Saudi financed organization, Ahl-e-Hadis, which had mushroomed in the rural Kashmir Valley in the 1970s contributed a great deal in concocting a lethal 'combination of *Kashmiriyat* and Islam'. The mosques re-emerged as 'the key political arena for the campaigns of the new Islamic groups'[49] providing outlets to the dissident population.[50] The defining moment that had 'profound impact of eliminating any major democratic outlet of Kashmiri Muslims'[51] was the arbitrary dismissal of the NC government of Farooq Abdullah in 1984 followed by an unholy electoral alliance in 1986 between same Farooq Abdullah and Rajiv Gandhi which saw the massive rigging of the assembly elections in 1987, denying electoral gains to a resurgent Muslim United Front, an umbrella organization of the Muslim groups. The elections marked a watershed in the turbulent history of the valley as people lost all the faith in Indian democracy and for a considerable period of time politics in its formal form became irrelevant in the valley. It is only now after the periodic holding of the elections since 1996 that the political parties have been able to recapture their legitimacy as well as relevance in state politics.

What Needs to be Done: The Autonomy Argument

The above account of the social, political and economic bases of the formation of the distinct ethno-regional identity in the valley also and the causes of the widespread alienation makes it clear that in order to achieve a credible and lasting peace in the valley, it is imperative that the people of Kashmir are allowed to exercise their democratic rights to participation, representation and self-government. As discussed above any other option that is statist in nature burdened by the consideration of national interest is neither feasible nor would be acceptable to the people of Kashmir.

That the basic issue in Kashmir still remains the right of the political community to determine its own political future is evident from the 2008 assembly elections in which a significant number of the Kashmiri people participated despite the call for boycott by the separatist Hurriyat Conference, the indigenous umbrella political group and threat posed by the militant organizations.

The successful holding of the recent elections also showed that the Indian state, being a democratic state unlike military dominated Pakistani state, has the ability to allow the formal as well informal structures to mobilize the disgruntled masses to articulate their grievances and aspirations. The elections in the recent years on a regular basis in a democratic manner have definitely provided an opportunity to the Indian state to come out with a comprehensive Kashmir policy that can fulfil the quest for autonomy/*azadi* of the people of Kashmir.

Notes

1. Sheikh Abdullah (1977), 'Introduction', in *New Kashmir*, New Delhi: Kashmir Bureau of Information, p. 5; Bakshi Ghulam Mohammad, (1947), *Kashmir Today Through My Eyes*, Bombay: Bombay Provincial Congress, p.1.
2. Gautam Navlakha, (2000): 'It's Never Too Late to do the Right Thing', *Economic and Political Weekly* (hereafter *EPW*), 29 July, p. 2703.
3. Morever Kashmir has also figured in the genesis of China-India boundary dispute, Amar Jasbir Kaur (1992), 'More on Kashmir Dispute', *EPW*, 18 January, pp. 94-5.
4. Pratap Bhanu Mehta (2003), 'India-Pakistan: The Enduring Stalemate', *EPW*, 24 May.
5. Jairam Ramesh (1999), 'Yankee Go Home, But Take Me with You: Yet Another Perspective on Indo-American Relations', *EPW*, 11 December, p. 3537.
6. Gautam Navlakha (2008), 'Jammu and Kashmir: Winning a Battle Only to Lose the War?', *EPW*, 8 November, p. 47.
7. Gautam Navlakha (2000), 'It's Never Too Late to do the Right Thing', *EPW*, 29 July, p. 2703.

8. Lamb has supported Pakistan's contention by arguing that the Maharaja did not sign the instrument of accession on 26 October 1947, a day before the Indian armed forces entered Kashmir to liberate it from the control of the tribals from the north-west province of Pakistan. In other words, Lamb questions the legal validity of the accession and suggests that the accession was the product of a conspiracy entered into by the Congress leadership, the Kashmiri government and the senior army officers including some British officers. [Alastair Lamb (1993), *Kashmir: A Disputed Legacy*, New Delhi: Oxford University Press.] Jha provides a direct rebuttal to Lamb's recounting of the events by quoting from counter historical material and testimonies. For Jha, however, the timing of the signing of the instrument of accession (whose wordings were the same as that of others signed by the other princely rulers at the time of their accession to India) is of no great significance (Prem Shankar Jha (1996), *Kashmir 1947: Rival Version of History*, New Delhi: Oxford University Press).
9. Hamza Alavi (1972), 'The State in Post-colonial Societies: Pakistan and Bangladesh', *New Left Review*, no. 74; see also Ayesha Jalal (1999), *Democracy and Authoritarianism in South Asia: A Comparative and Historical Perspective*, Cambridge: Cambridge University Press.
10. Gautam Navlakha (2001), 'Cease-fire in Kashmir: Some Critical Issues', *EPW*, 3 March, p. 8.
11. Rajen Harshe (1998), 'South Asian Regional Co-operation: Problems and Prospects', *EPW*, 8 May.
12. Quoted in Balraj Puri (2001), 'Sovereignty, Territorial Integrity and Right to Self-determination', *EPW*, 27 January, p. 263.
13. Gautam Navlakha (2001), 'Kashmir: Some Issues', *EPW*, 3 March, p. 726.
14. K. Balagopal (1996), 'Kashmir: Self-determination, Communalism and Democratic Rights', *EPW*, 2 November, p. 2916.
15. Sumantra Bose (1992), *The Challenge in Kashmir: Democracy, Self-Determination and a Just Peace*, New Delhi: Sage, p. 115.
16. Luv Puri (2003), 'India-Pakistan Relations: Towards a Softer Border', *EPW*, 31 May, pp. 2116.
17. Ashutosh Kumar (2001), 'Communal Trifurcation of Jammu and Kashmir', *EPW*, 21 April, p. 1359.
18. Rekha Chowdhary (2000), 'Autonomy Demand: Kashmir at Crossroads', *EPW*, 22 July, p. 2603.
19. Amitabh Mattoo (2000), 'Towards a Peace Process', *Seminar*, 496, December.

20. K. Balagopal (2003), 'What will they do to Kashmir now?', *EPW*, 21 June, p. 2468.
21. See Robert G. Wirsing (1998), *India, Pakistan and the Kashmir Dispute: On Regional Conflict and its Resolution*, New York: St. Martin Press. Another formulation for peace that can be traced to the talks between the then foreign ministers of India and Pakistan namely Sardar Swaran Singh and Z.A. Bhutto in 1965 has been that the right bank of Chenab should go to Pakistan and the left bank to India. Accepting this idea would mean that the entire valley would go to Pakistan without taking into consideration their view. It has been well argued that only a minority of the Kashmiri people would wish to join Pakistan even if the option of *azadi* is denied to them. Refer Kanti Bajpai (1995), 'India and South Asia: Community, Order, Cooperation', *Seminar*, 425, January, p. 51.
22. Pratap Bhanu Mehta (2003), 'India-Pakistan: The Enduring Stalemate', *EPW*, 24 May, p. 2014.
25. Given the regional heterogeneity of the state there is need of negotiation with credible representatives of the regions of Jammu and Ladakh also so that there can be a 'permanent institutionalization' of autonomy for the whole region. In fact, Jammu and Ladakh's discontent against the dominant Kashmiri leadership has often been used by New Delhi, to force the pace of constitutional integration of the state with Union (Balraj Puri (1992), 'Ominous Portends from Jammu', *EPW*, 19 September, p. 2020). An integral regional and inter-ethnic dialogue should precede any dialogue with Pakistan or the Kashmir militants or Kashmiri leadership. Such a grant of substantial autonomy to each region would be logical extension of the demand for restoration of original status of 'limited accession' (*State Autonomy Report* (1999): Government of Jammu and Kashmir Press). Autonomy to each region would most likely 'act as a unifying force between peoples of regions' (Balraj Puri (1999), 'How Government Scuttled Regional Autonomy', *EPW*, 5 June, p. 1400). Pertinently long ago in his address to the Constituent Assembly, Sheikh Abdullah had pledged to give 'maximum autonomy for the local organs of the state power which are the ultimate source of authority in the state while discharging obligations as a unit of the federation' (*Regional Autonomy Committee Report* (1999), Government of Jammu and Kashmir Press, p. (1)]. The formation of the autonomous development councils for Leh and Kargil has been welcome steps in this regard. Then there are ethnic groups within these regions like Gujjars, Gaddis, Paharis, and Baltis who have

their distinct identities and demands. The Kashmiri Pandits who after leaving the valley have been languishing in camps and are scattered all over India have been asking for the creation of Panun Kashmir as their separate homeland in the valley. It follows that institutional and permanent measures are to be evolved to reconcile the ethnic urges on regional basis.

26. Rekha Chowdhary and Ashutosh Kumar (2000), 'Regional Autonomy Committee Report for Jammu and Kashmir: A Critique', *Mainstream*, 12 August, p. 3.
27. G.M.D. Sufi (1949), *Kashmir: Being a History of Kashmir (From the Earliest Times to Our Own)*, Lahore: Punjab University Press; Francis Younghusband (2000), *Kashmir As It Was*, New Delhi: Rupa Paperbacks, pp. 127-75.
28. Prem Nath Bazaz (1954), *The History of Struggle for Freedom in Kashmir: Cultural and Political*, New Delhi: Kashmir Publishing Company, p. 83.
29. Balraj Puri (1995), 'The Vitality of Kashmiri Identity', *Contemporary South Asia*, vol. 4, no. 1, p. 60.
30. M.A. Stein (1979), *Kalhan's Rajatarangini: A Chronicle of the Kings of Kashmir*, Delhi: Motilal Banarsidass, p. 30.
31. Balraj Puri (2008), 'Independence, Autonomy and Freedom in Kashmir?', *EPW*, 22 March, p. 20.
32. Sheikh Mohammad Abdullah (1993), *Flames of Chinar* (tr. Khuswant Singh), Delhi: Vikas, p. 33.
33. Rekha Chowdhary, and Ashutosh Kumar (2000), 'Regional Autonomy Committee Report for Jammu and Kashmir: A Critique', *Mainstream*, 12 August, p. 13.
34. U.K. Zutshi (1986), *Emergence of Political Awakening in Kashmir*, New Delhi: Manohar; G.M.D. Sufi (1949), *Kashmir: Being a History of Kashmir* (*From the Earliest Times to our Own*), Lahore: University Press, p. 25.
35. Brailsford quoted in Bakshi Ghulam Mohammad (1947), *Kashmir Today: Through My Eyes*, Bombay: Bombay Provincial Congress Committee, p. 2.
36. P.N. Dhar (1951), 'The Kashmir Problem: Political and Economic Background', *India Quarterly*, vol. VII, no. 2, April-June, p. 143.
37. *New Kashmir: With an Introduction by Sheikh Mohammed Abdullah*, 1977, New Delhi: Kashmir Bureau of Information, pp. 28-49.
38. Ibid., p. 6.

39. In the words of Sheikh Abdullah: 'It is said that Sheikh Abdullah is a friend of Pandit Jawaharlal Nehru. Yes, I admit that I feel honoured that such a great man claims me as his friend. And he happens to belong to my own country; he is also a Kashmiri. Blood is thicker than water' [Sheikh Abdullah (1949), *Kashmir Appeal to World Conscience*, New Delhi: Government of India Press, p. 6].
39. Maroof Raza (1996), *Wars and No Peace Over Kashmir*, New Delhi: Lancer Publishers.
40. Quoted in Gautam Navlakha (1998), 'Invoking Union: Kashmir and Official Nationalism of Bharat' in T.V. Satyamurthy (ed.), *Religion, Caste, Gender and Culture in Contemporary India*, vol. 3, New Delhi: Oxford University Press, p. 95.
41. The implications of the application of Article 370 have been as follows: It extended the state within the Indian Union. Second, the Parliament's legislative power over Jammu & Kashmir was to be restricted to three subjects: defence, external affairs and communication. This was confirmed in Article 152 of the 1956 version of the Constitution where it was specified that the expression state 'does not include the state of Jammu and Kashmir'. The obvious interpretation being that the state was an autonomous polity under Indian Protection (Amar Jasbir Kaur (1992), 'More on Kashmir Dispute', *EPW*, 18 January, p. 94).
42. A.S. Anand (1998), *The Constitution of Jammu and Kashmir: Its Development and Comments*, Jammu: Jay and Kay Publishers, p. 106.
43. The constant denial to the people of the state of their fundamental right to change, choose and oppose the government and the political party in power through electoral process 'merely remind them that they are less than full citizens of India' (Balraj Puri (2000), 'The Farooq Doctrine: Kashmir's Relations with New Delhi', *EPW*, 24 June, p. 2219). The electoral manipulation evident in the form of the number of candidates 'elected unopposed' has been the highest in India: 'The number are startling: In 1951, 73 out of a total of 75 seats were won by National Conference uncontested, in the 1957 elections, 43 candidates out of 75 were elected unopposed; 70 candidates were returned unopposed in the 1962 elections. In 1967, nomination papers of 118 opposition candidates were rejected to have 39 out of 75 assembly constituencies returned candidates unopposed!' [Editorial (1999), 'Kashmir: The Negative Vote', *EPW*, 18 September, p. 2703.]
44. W.I. Ladejinsky (1952), 'Land Reform Observations in Kashmir', in

Ladejinsky (ed.), *Agrarian Reforms as Unfinished Business: The Selected Papers of Wolf Ladejinsky*, New York: Oxford University Press, p. 183.

45. Sumit Ganguly (1997), *The Crisis in Kashmir: Portents of War, Hopes of Peace*, Cambridge: Woodrow Wilson Press and Cambridge University Press, p. 30.
46. Siddhartha Prakash (2000), 'Political Economy of Kashmir since 1947', *EPW*, 10 June, p. 2051.
47. See http://indiabudget.nic.in/es2006-07/esmain.htm
48. Gautam Navlakha (2007), ' State of Jammu and Kashmir's Economy', *EPW*, 6 October, pp. 4034-8.
49. Vernon Hewitt (1995), *Reclaiming the Past? The Search for Political and Cultural Unity in Contemporary Jammu and Kashmir*, London: Portland Publishers, p. 15.
50. Tremblay, Chowdhary, Reeta (2002), 'Kashmir Conflict: Secessionist Movement, Mobilization and Political Institutions', *Pacific Affairs*, Winter 2001-2, p. 573; Sumit Ganguly (1997), *The Crisis in Kashmir: Portents of War, Hopes of Peace*, Cambridge: Woodrow Wilson Press and Cambridge University Press, p. 30; Pir Gias ud-Din (1997), *The Historical Destiny of the Kashmir Insurgency*, Jammu: Jay and Kay Publishers, p. 80.
51. Atul Kohli (1999), 'Can Democracies Accommodate Ethnic Nationalism? The Rise and Decline of Self-determination Movements in India', in Amrita Basu and Atul Kohli (eds.), *Community Conflicts and the State in India*, New Delhi: Oxford University.

5

Resisting Nationalist Discourses

Ethnic Upsurge in Post-Colonial North-East India

SAJAL NAG

The title of a book published in 1981 *North East: The Ethnic Explosion* written by a journalist Nirmal Nibedon.[1] It aptly describes the turmoil in north-east India around that period. Two more books were published earlier by the same author entitled *Nagaland: Night of the Guerillas*[2] (1979) and *Mizoram: Dagger's Brigade* (1980).[3] The titles of the books indicate the trajectory of a turmoil which originated in Nagaland and then travelled to Mizoram and finally engulfed the entire north-east India. Though it is a fact that there was turbulence in north-east India right from the days of Independence, which later intensified, magnified and proliferated, but it was not just secessionist insurgency that troubled the north-east part of India. There were ethnic conflicts, autonomy movements, inter-tribal and tribal-non-tribal hostility, violent resistance to illegal immigration, host-refugee conflict, etc., each of which resulted in a huge law and order problem for the state. In fact, north-east has seen more violence than any other part of India post-Independence. Though its population is only 3.9 per cent of the country's population yet it has accounted for more than half the people killed either through violence or state repression.[4] While other parts of India enjoyed the fruits of the new found freedom and democracy, the north-east remained under quasi-martial law for long periods. Faced with the challenge of this ethnic upsurge responded by the Indian state formulated draconian laws like the Armed Forces Special Powers Act. In this paper an attempt has been made to trace the trajectory of this upsurge and the developments that have taken place in the troubled north-east.

Defining 'Ethnicity'

Although Nibedon named his book as *Ethnic Explosion* he failed to explain the fundamental question, i.e. what was 'ethnic' about the explosion. What he actually meant was that the turbulence that unsettled north-east India was the result of the assertive movements of certain tribal communities like the Nagas and Mizos whom he referred to as 'ethnic'. In fact, this was the first time that the turmoil in north-east was described in terms of ethnic unrest. The north-east is the home of mostly tribal people. There are a total of 209 listed scheduled tribes in the region belonging to six different categories. The actual number of tribes and sub-tribes in the respective states are given later in this paper. What is a matter of theoretical concern is that if the majority of the movements in the region emanated from these tribes, then why are the secessionists and autonomy related insurgency movements emanating from some of the major tribal groups here termed ethnic? Other sources of turmoil were from inter-tribal and tribal-immigrant conflicts. Without going into the morass of theoretical debates and competing but similar and even contradictory definitions of ethnicity,[5] one could say that these movements were 'ethnic' in terms of modern development in which mobilization was on the basis of the pre-modern concept of solidarity. In other words, ethnicity can be defined as a pre-modern concept which burst into the scene in modern times; the advent of capitalism is the backdrop against which nationality formation takes place. But certain kinship groups which are not sufficiently democratized and fail to qualify as nationalities use their pre-capitalist ties to forge an identity to combat the oppression of the advanced nationalities and which fight the oppressions of the nation state, can be described as ethnic. These were part of the sub-national upsurge that the modern world experienced, but on their own they were pre-pre-modern in character. It was not national in character or theory though often the nationalist discourse was appropriated to either justify the secessionist agenda or demand autonomy, as elaborated later. Most of the conflicts are tribal in character as they are a continuation or a legacy of the primordial relationship. But they are termed 'ethnic' as the identities were based not on kinship groups but on generic entities which are more extensive than tribal. In fact, it is in this sense we find convergence of north-eastern situation with the way ethnicity is defined by eminent political thinker Rajni Kothari. He states,

> A new spectre is haunting the power elite of our time. It is the spectre of ethnicity, variously expressed as assertion of cultures, communal upsurges, revivalism of religions, voices and movement of marginalized people, regions and nationalities. It represents the affirmation of diversity, of indigenous authenticity, of organic as against televised or museumised cultures—or classical cultures as found in ancient texts.[6]

According to Kothari, ethnicity can take the form of defiance to a modern nation state and its homogenizing monotheistic thrusts. It is a revolt against majoritarianism. To quote him

> Ethnicity is a response and a reaction to the excesses of the modern project of shaping the whole humanity around the three pivots of world capitalism, the state system and world culture based on modern technology, a pervasive communication and informative order and a universalizing education system. The project of modernity entails a new mode of homogenizing and straightjacketing the whole world . . . homogenizing is colonizing, necessarily rejecting all other universals and castigating them as ahistorical and anachronistic or at best historical antecedents to this more scientific and rational and hence superior universal. It is a mode of homogenization which takes upon itself the task of fragmenting and splintering all other social and ethical cohesions, undermining all other unities and imposing its globalizing will power on all others . . . ethnicity represents a powerful rebuttal to this paranoid drive of the modern project of fashioning the world after the idea of a world as emanated from the occident following which it has almost succeeded in subjugating the immense diversity and richness of human experience.[7]

Ethnic Secessionism in North-East India

The unrest in north-east India had certain *well defined forms.* Some parts of it were secessionist right from the beginning. North-east India is inhabited by myriads of tribes who are mostly Indo-Mongoloid, speaking Tibeto-Burman languages and are either animists or Christians. Indoctrinated with separatist ideas by the British colonizers, the Naga and Mizo tribals believed that they were not basically Indians and therefore wanted to remain independent when the British left. The Mizos eventually joined India but the extremist section of the Nagas led by Angami Zaphu Phizo launched an armed struggle for sovereignty of the Nagas.[8]

North-east India poses a number of problems for the Indian government, the most serious of them being the problem of secessionist insurgency. It is serious as this is not merely a law and order problem but a threat to the unity and integrity of the entire country. It not only questions the concept of one nationhood for all the communities of India but even questions the legitimacy of the Indian state to rule over communities like the Nagas, Meiteis, Assamese, Khasis, Bodos, Tippera, etc., who demand the right to self-determination and freedom to opt out of the Indian Union as separate sovereign nation states. The Government of India has had therefore to confront serious crises from the challenges to its authority from rather small tribal communities problem. It began with the Nagas and was soon followed by the Mizos, the Meiteis, the Khasis, the Garos, the Bodos, the Kukis, Karbis, the Dimasas, the Tripuri tribes—turning the entire region into a war zone. All these tribes have an underground outfit each with the declared objective of seceding from India. Besides attacking the Indian armed forces, the major activities of these outfits generally involve massive extortion drives, kidnapping, and ethnic 'cleansing' of certain targeted communities.

In fact, north-east India was no exception to the subcontinental political processes that followed independence. Manipur, Tripura and Khasi states were princely states. The areas inhabited now by Nagas, Mizos and Arunachal Pradesh (known as North Eastern Frontier Agency) fall in the category of excluded areas. The British neither allowed any political party to enter the region nor allowed any political activity in these areas. Hence the Congress could not make its presence felt here. When the British withdrawal became imminent the tribals of this region became politically restive. They now realized the urgent need of politically organizing themselves. The Nagas formed the Naga National Council in February 1946, the Mizos, the Mizo Union in April 1946, the Manipuris, the Nikhil Manipuri Mahasabha (1934), and in Tripura there was the Tripura Rajya Gana Parishad (1939) etc. In each of these organizations there were huge debates about the uncertainties of their future, discussions on the advantages and apprehensions of remaining within the India (Union) and what would be the consequences fearful of withdrawing from India. It is interesting to note that at this juncture of history, the dominant opinion was in favour of remaining within the Indian Union. The Naga National Council (NNC) signed an agreement with the Government of India agreeing to remain in India with provisions for the safeguard of their special interests and requirements. But disagreement over the interpretation of the Ninth Clause of the Agreement led to the breakdown of the Agreement. The extremist elements in the Council depicted it as a betrayal by the Indian state and popularized the idea of 'secession' among the people. However, the hope of abolishment of the oppressive institution of chieftainship under the Indian Constitution made the Mizos opt for merger with India. The Nagas, finding that the option to move out of India incorporated in the Akbar Hydari-Naga National Council Agreement was dispensed with, also hardened their secessionist attitude. As the Indian government tried to suppress the movement, NNC went underground, announced the formation of a Revolutionary Government of Nagaland and tried to combat the Indian army. This was the beginning of the insurgency in the Naga Hills. Caught in the crossfire between the Indian army and the underground insurgents a section of the Naga leadership came to the negotiating table (1960). As a goodwill gesture the then Indian prime minister, Jawaharlal Nehru, despite opposition from his own party and the opposition, made huge concessions of granting statehood to a tiny Naga population, paradoxically under the Ministry of Foreign Affairs. But this failed to have much impact on the insurgency movement which continued. In 1975 an Accord was signed by the underground NNC and the Indian state signifying the cessation of the Naga struggle and eventual acceptance of Indian hegemony. But as in all insurgent movements, the younger section of the underground rejected the Accord and decided to continue their struggle for an independent state under a new organization called the National Socialist Council of Nagaland (NSCN) led by Th Muivah, Isac Chisi Swu and S.S. Khaplang. Subsequently the Khaplang group broke away to form another faction called NSCN (Khaplang) to fight the Thankhul-Sema supremacy in the NSCN. The two factions since then have continued parallel struggles for the same objective.

The Mizos too were dissatisfied with the Assamese hegemony. Although chieftainship was abolished, lack of basic development, and poverty had alienated the Mizo people and their earlier enthusiasm to remain within the Indian Union declined. The leadership dominated by the chiefs who wanted to opt out of the Indian Union from 1946 onwards, now capitalized on this alienation and reinforced the separatist movement. The opportunity came when the periodic famine devastated the Mizo Hills in 1959, without any aid or relief from the Assam government, and when Assamese language was sought to be forced as the official language on the tribal people, the discontent reached its peak. The voluntary organization Mizo National Famine Front (1958) was converted into a political party. Although it had a specified secessionist objective, it contested elections for two years and having gathered enough arms and ammunition, it attempted a *coup d'état* on 1 March 1966. It invited stern military measures from the Indian government with certain conciliatory measures like the separation of the Mizo Hills from Assam and the creation of a Union Territory in 1978. In 1986 the MNF chief Laldenga signed an agreement with the Indian government by which the struggle for independence was given up and Mizoram was granted full-fledged statehood. But this did not end the insurgency in Mizoram. The Hmar people demanding a separate statehood formed the Hmar Peoples' Convention and resorted to insurgent activities. The oppression of the dominant Mizos of the small Hinduized tribe called Bru (Riang) made the latter resort to insurgency under the

Bru National Army. The violent activities of the two are keeping the ruling MNF party on its toes.[9]

Although there was opposition, the princely state of Manipur and the moderate section of the Nikhil Manipuri Mahasabha had actually merged with the Indian National Congress in 1946. There were considerable debate about the final merger with India. But the rise of communist powers in China and Myanmar bordering north-east India and the growing communist activities in Manipur and Tripura prompted a panic-stricken Indian state to use unethical means to effect the accession. The people of Manipur were appalled at the way they were ignored in enforcing the merger. Hizam Irabot Singh had already tried to establish a sovereign socialist republic of Manipur through a Telengana-like communist uprising during 1946-50. The front which opposed the merger regrouped themselves to organize the United National Liberation Front (UNLF) in 1964 with the declared objective of seceding from India. A breakaway faction of the UNLF subsequently formed the Revolutionary Government of Manipur (RVG) with similar objective. As Manipur reeled under poverty, famine, unemployment and political instability, more such outfits came into existence. The most powerful was the Peoples' Liberation Army (PLA) with the active support of China. It was led by a few Maoist youths under N. Bisheswar Singh in 1975. This was followed by the formation of the Peoples' Revolutionary Party of Kanglaipak (Prepak) and the Kanglaipak Communist Party. All of them simultaneously attacked the Indian state and launched parallel struggles to achieve independence of Manipur. The counter-insurgency operations, the ambushes and the factional violence along with extortion drives, kidnappings and fratricidal murders rendered Manipur into a virtual killing field.

The PLA is the strongest insurgent group among them all. It was formed in 1976-7 under the leadership of N. Bisheswar Singh. The PLA presently has close links with NSCN and shares two camps with them—one in Myanmar and the other in Bangladesh. It has an understanding with the NSCN regarding the areas of their operation; they operate without interfering with each other. It also has some Muslims in its cadre supported by Pakistan's Inter Services

Intelligence (ISI). The PLA had been very active in Imphal, Thaubal and Bishenpur districts. It was well armed and has a strength of about 1,000. A few dissenters broke away from it and formed the People's Revolutionary Party of Kangleipak (Prepak) in October 1977. It has a strength of about 1,000.

The UNLF is the oldest Meitei extremist organization, formed in 1964 under Samarendra Singh. The approximate strength of this group is 700. It operates in eastern Imphal under the leadership of R.K. Meghan Yamiamma. The UNLF maintains links with the NSCN. The KYKL was formed in January 1994. This group has a strength of about 200 and it is expanding its recruitment base.

Tripura, formerly a princely state, secured statehood under the Indian Republic in January 1972. Large-scale influx of Bengali immigrants from East Pakistan (now Bangladesh), the growing pressure on land, acute food shortage, increasing unemployment among youths, and backwardness of tribals led to serious socio-economic tensions and ethnic conflicts. Tripura's demographic complex is very different from that of any other tribal state in this region. The tribals here are vastly outnumbered by the Bengali immigrants from neighbouring Bangladesh. In fact, the tribals here were never in the majority. Census report prepared by the then princely state in 1911 put the total population of Tripura at 2,99,613 out of which the tribals numbered 1,08,526. In 1931, Tripura's population increased to 3,82,450 out of which the tribals numbered 1,86,260 and Bengalis (both Hindu and Muslim) numbered 1,96,190. It was the Noakhali (East Bengal) communal riots in 1946, the Partition of 1947, and the communal riots of 1963 led to the rapid increase of Bengali-speaking Hindus who entered Tripura in waves. The unabated flow of immigrants from Bangladesh basically weakened the agricultural economy of the state. The one-time self-sufficient state became a chronic deficit area, depending heavily on the Government of India for food grains every year.

The main source of tension between the tribal and non-tribals was agricultural land. In the past, even in the face of a law, against the same the tribals lost their land to Bengali cultivators who in thousands of cases got the title deed of their lands changed. But now, caught between the state's insistence on preservation of forests and opposition to 'jhum' cultivation on the one hand and dispossession of land on the other, the tribals demanded the restoration of their land from the non-tribals. Tripura Upajati Juba Samiti (TUJS) took up the cause of the tribals in 1967. In 1974, the Congress government amended the Land Revenue and Land Reforms Legislations of 1960 providing for restoration of all lands transferred by tribals to non-tribals. These legislations were, however, strongly opposed by the anti-tribal organization known as 'Amra Bangali', which clashed with TUJS. Widespread violence swept Tripura in June 1980 and left death and devastation all round. The CPI(M) was active among the tribals and took up the cause of the tribals when it came to power. The Congress (I), Janata and Amra Bengali combined to oppose the CPI(M) government's proposal to give autonomy to tribal areas. This move alarmed the tribals who resorted to rioting and looting.

To arouse hatred against the non-tribals, TUJS gave a call for a bazaar boycott for a week from 1 June 1980. In fact, the trouble started from 29 May and between 29 May and 5 June 1980 at least 12 non-tribals were killed. In 1983 there were about 50 clashes between security forces and the Tripura National Volunteer Force (TNV) and about 30 persons were killed in these clashes.

In 1984 the number of clashes increased and 50 persons were killed. The TNV was receiving help from Mizo National Front (MNF) and the Bangladesh government. The beginning of the tribal militancy in Tripura can be traced to 1941. Between 1941 and 1983 as many as ten organizations, some of them operating underground, were set up to safeguard tribal interests. At one point of time there were as many as 24 'hit groups'. The political situation has sharply deteriorated ever since the dominant National Liberation Front of Tripura (NLFT), the All Tripura Tiger Force (ATTF) and the Tripura Resurrection Army (TRA) began asserting themselves increasingly.

Among several insurgent and terrorists units operating in Assam, the United Liberation Front of Assam (ULFA) is the most active. ULFA aims to liberate Assam and the people of the state from 'Indian rule'. It is engaged in the bloodiest and most treacherous attacks on non-Assamese government officials, industrialists, businessmen and politicians and non-tribals whom it considers to be foreigners and even central government institutions.

The ULFA was founded on 7 April 1979. The Preamble to the Constitution of this organization declared that independence of Assam is to be achieved through armed revolutionary struggle. It also adopted a flag depicting a rising sun against a white background. The ULFA which aims secession from India is essentially a by-product of the prolonged Assam agitation which began in 1978-9 spearheaded by the Asom Gana Parishad and the All Assam Student Union against all Bangladeshi foreign nationals residing in Assam and threatening to become a majority.

Among those assassinated by ULFA militants include: Tankeswar Dhingia, Youth Congress (I) general secretary and former rural development minister; Ranjit Barua, president of Jorhat Congress (I) unit and son of a former minister of forest development; Rajiv Rajkhoa, chairman of the United Minorities Front; Kalipada Sen, an advocate, who was critical of ULFA activities, Sourav Bora, a student leader who formed a front against the Assom Gana Parishad (AGP), the ruling party of Prafulla Mahanta, and Surendra Pal, Chairman, Assam Frontier Tea Company (AFTC) and Daulat Singh Negi, Superintendent of Police, Dibrugarh.

Kalipada Sen, an advocate and a spokesman of the Bengali-speaking community in Assam was assassinated in 1986 at his residence in Guwahati. Within the next couple of years, the toll of murders by ULFA militants was reported to be 133 and the money they collected through extortion and armed bank hold-ups was reported to be several hundred crores of rupees. Killings and kidnappings by ULFA militants were frequently reported.

But ULFA is not the only militant organization in Assam. There are others like Bodo Liberation Tigers (BLT) and National Democratic Front of Bodos (NDFB). Both emerged from the demand of a separate state for the Bodos, the largest tribal group in Assam. The initial peaceful movement subsequently turned violent and gave rise to these pro-underground militant organizations. The same was the case with the Dimachas of north Cachar which resulted in Dima Halom Daoga (DHD) and Karbis of Karbi Anglong district and subsequently, the United Peoples' Democratic Solidarity (UPDS) as well as Karbi National Volunteers (KNV). The Bodos and Khasis too joined the fray of insurgency initially under the same umbrella organization called Hynewtrep Achik National Volunteers (MALC) which later disintergrated into two—Achik National Volunteer Force (ANVF) and Hynewtrep National Liberation Council (HNLC) according to their tribal bases. While the Garo (Achik)-based organization demand separate statehood, the Khasis (Hynewtrep) demand secession from India.

Arunachal Pradesh has been the base camp of the NSCN(K) for years. Now a new organization called the Arunachal Dragon Force has surfaced with the avowed objective of secession from India.[10]

Table 1: Active Insurgent Organizations in North-East India

Active insurgent organization	Ethnic Base	State	Nature
United Liberation Front of Assam	Assamese	Assam	Secessionism
National Democratic Front of Bodoland	Bodo	Assam	Secessionism
Bodo Liberation Tiger Force	Bodo	Assam	Secessionism
Karbi National Volunteers	Karbi	Assam	Secessionism
Dima Haloa Daoga	Dimasa	Assam	Secessionism
Bengali Protection Force	Bengali immigrants	Assam	Protection
Muslim United Liberation Tigers of Assam	Immigrant Muslims	Assam	Protection
Arunachal Dragon Force renamed East India Liberation Front	Arunachalese	Arunachal Pradesh	Secessionism
Peoples' Liberation Army	Meitei	Manipur	Secessionism
United National Liberation Front	Meitei	Manipur	Secessionism
Peoples' Revolutionary Party of Kangleipak	Meitei	Manipur	Secessionism
Kangleipak Communist Party	Meitei	Manipur	Secessionism
Kanglei Kanba Lup	Meitei	Manipur	Secessionism
National Socialist Council of Nagaland (Isak Muivah)	Naga	Nagaland, Assam, Arunachal Pradesh	Secessionism
NSCN (Khaplang)	Naga	Nagaland, Arunachal Pradesh	Secessionism
All Tripura Tiger Force	Tripuri	Tripura	Secessionism

National Liberation Front of Twipera	Tripuri	Tripura	Secessionism
Bengali Tiger Force	Bengali	Tripura	Protection
Abcik National Volunteer Council	Garo	Meghalaya	Secessionism
Hynewtrep National Liberation Council	Khasi	Meghalaya	Secessionism
North East Red Army	Khasi	Meghalaya	Secessionism
Hmar National Army	Hmar	Mizoram	Protection
Bru National Liberation Front	Bru	Mizoram	Protection
Kuki National Army	Kuki	Mizoram	Protection
Mizo National Front (since settled as a political party and has warned up its secessionism agenda)	Mizo	Mizoram	Secessionism
Kamatapur Liberation Organisation	Koch Rajbanshi	West Bengal	Autonomy
Naga National Council	Naga	Nagaland	Secessionism
United Peoples' Democratic Solidarity	Karbi	Assam	Secessionism
Muslim United Liberation Force of Assam	Immigrant Muslims	Assam	Secessionism
Liberation Islamic Tiger Force	Immigrant Muslims	Assam	Secessionism
Muslim Security Council of Assam	Immigrant Muslims	Assam	Secessionism
Hynewtrep Socialist Democratic Front	Khasi	Meghalaya	Secessionism
Peoples' Liberation Front of Meghalaya	Garo	Assam, Meghalaya	Secessionism
All Meghalaya Liberation Front	Garo, Khasi	Meghalaya	Secessionism
Meghalaya-e-Sunna	Muslims	Meghalaya	Secessionism
All Meghalaya Islamic Liberation Front	Muslims	Meghalaya	Secessionism
Karbi Peoples' Front	Karbi	Assam	Secessionism
Gorkha Liberation Organisation	Gorkha	North-East	Protection
Assam Tiger Force	Assamese	Assam	Secessionism
Tripura Resurrection Army	Tripura	Tripura	Secessionism
Citizens Right Preservation Committee	Non-Karbi Plains men	Assam	Protection
Karbi Peoples' Front	Karbi	Assam	Secessionism
Kuki National Front	Kuki	Manipur, Nagaland	Secessionism

United Bengali Liberation Force	Bengali	Tripura	Protection
Adivasi Cobra Force	Adivasi	Assam	Protection
Muslim Liberation of Assam (MLA)	Muslims	Assam	Protection
United Muslim Liberation Front of Assam	Muslims	Assam	Protection
Peoples' United Liberation Front	Meiteis	Manipur	Secessionism
Hindu Liberation Army of Assam	Hindu	Assam	Protection
Assam Peoples' Liberation Army (predecessor of ULFA)	Assamese	Assam	Secessionism

A report prepared by the Institute of Conflict Management, New Delhi states that there are about 34 underground outfits in Assam, 35 in Manipur. According to this report, in the year 2000 there were a total of 800 persons killed in conflict as against 511 in 1999. The existence of such a large number of armed underground outfits are bound have an impact on the law and order situation in the region. In Manipur, 237 people lost their lives in 2000 as compared to 231 in 1999. In Tripura a total of 405 persons lost their lives in 2000 as compared to 303 in 1999. In Nagaland, despite ceasefire, a total of 13 civilians, 4 security personnel and 82 militants lost their lives in 2000 as against 26 civilians, 4 security personnel and 124 militants in 1999. Arunachal Pradesh witnessed the spill over effect of insurgencies from the neighbouring states. The first insurgent organization there, the Arunachal Dragon Force, made its official appearance in 2001 but its presence was known from 2000. The districts of Tirap and Changlang were the most affected by extortion, kidnapping and attacks.

There were fatalities also in this conflict between the Indian armed forces and the underground outfits.

Ethnic Autonomy Movements

The *second trend* was based on autonomy demands. At Independence the entire region except Manipur and Tripura comprised the state of Assam. But when the Assam government sought to impose Assamese language on non-Assamese people through the Official Language Bill of 1960 there was opposition and protest riots throughout the state.

Table 5.2: Insurgency and its Effects

States	Militant-Army encounter	Militant killed	Civilian killed	Abduction	Army killed	Militant arrested
Tripura	826	38	360	558	17	NA
Assam	536	321	419	105	76	NA
Manipur	245	102	93	32	51	NA
Nagaland	195	84	13	58	4	NA
Meghalaya	74	15	11	12	7	61
Arunachal Pradesh	73		8		3	NA
Mizoram	NA	1	4	NA	7	NA

Source: Annual Home Ministry Report, 2000-2001, Government of India.

Table 5.3: Fatalities in Insurgencies and Terrorist Conflicts in North-East India, 1992-2001

		Assam	Manipur	Meghalaya	Mizoram	Nagaland	Tripura	Arunachal Pradesh	Total	Annual CT
	C	80	84	0	0	34	59	0	257	
1992	SF	34	30	0	0	33	18	0	115	492
	M	19	51	0	0	29	21	0	120	
	C	74	266	0	0	62	148	1	551	
1993	SF	24	91	0	0	43	28	2	188	913
	M	33	66	0	0	68	7	0	174	
	C	173	189	4	0	110	206	3	685	
1994	SF	35	98	0	0	26	22	0	181	1,058
	M	63	63	0	0	56	10	0	192	
	C	170	183	7	0	80	178	3	621	
1995	SF	73	64	0	0	25	34	0	196	1,071
	M	27	74	0	0	108	45	0	254	
	C	302	117	3	0	144	140	4	710	
1996	SF	87	65	4	4	48	31	1	240	1,235
	M	62	93	0	0	112	18	0	285	
	C	285	233	3	0	104	205	9	839	
1997	SF	85	111	0	0	38	50	1	285	1,680
	M	167	151	1	0	218	19	0	556	

	C	531	87	5	0	26	214	2	865	
1998	SF	72	62	14	0	14	25	2	189	1,431
	M	180	95	1	0	72	26	3	377	
	C	214	89	5	2	26	240	2	578	
1999	SF	77	64	17	5	4	41	0	208	1,216
	M	212	78	0	0	118	22	0	430	
	C	366	93	12	4	13	453	7	907	
2000	SF	65	51	7	4	4	16	3	162	1,654
	M	327	102	17	1	84	45	24	585	
	C	2,512	1,411	62	6	624	1,989	72	6,676	
2001	SF	59	25	8	0	2	31	12	137	7,394
	M	283	161	8	0	76	42	11	581	
	C	2,459	1,371	63	6	603	2,082	31	6,245	
Total	SF	611	649	50	13	235	296	9	1,833	11,252
	M	1,373	830	27	1	882	255	31	3,174	
CT State Wise	C SF M	4,443	3,006	140	23	1,802	2,633	134	12,137	

Note: Cumulative total (all categories): M: Militants; SF: Security Force Personnel, C: Civilians

Source: Ajay Sahni, 'Survey of Conflicts & Resolution in India's Northeast', *Frontline,* vol. 12, May 2002, pp. 39-112.

The major tribes wanted to separate from Assam. They formed the Eastern India Tribal Union transformed it into a more comprehensive All Party Hill Leaders Conference in 1960 and demanded a tribal state to be carved out of Assam. The central government was compelled to create Meghalaya, Mizoram and Arunachal Pradesh out of Assam. Tripura and Manipur were upgraded into states too. But this was not the end of autonomy demands. In Manipur the Kukis want an autonomous area; the Nagas want to merge with Nagaland. In Assam the Bodos, Karbis and Dimasas wanted separate states through overground movement as well as insurgency. Karbis have been granted an autonomous state council and Dimasas have been granted autonomy under district councils while Bodos were recently given autonomous council. In addition the smaller tribes like the Rabhas, Hasong, Tiwa, Mising, Sonowal Kachari, Thangal

Kachari and Deuris have been granted autonomous district councils to satisfy their autonomy aspirations. Some of them still threaten to graduate to full-fledged statehood demands. There are demands from other groups like the Koch, Ahom, Moran, Mattock, Chutia and the various ex-tea plantation labour population for the grant of Scheduled Tribe status. The state government is making effort to grant them the desired status but it could then transform into demands for autonomy. Even immigrant settler groups like the Gorkhas are demanding an autonomous council for themselves.[11]

In Mizoram the Chakma, Paite and Hmar were also granted district councils while the Brus continue their fight. In Meghalaya the Garo and Khasi tribes want to break up Meghalaya into two separate states for each of them. Autonomy demands often led to common clamour over the same habitat resulting in conflict between two communities as happened in the case of Naga-Kuki, Kuki-Mizo, and Naga-Meitei. The Bodos frequently attacked the neighbouring Santhal and non-tribal settlers. Similar was the case with the Karbi-Dimasa, Hmar-Dimasa riots. As can be seen, unlike other parts of India, the states of north-east India are more administrative units rather than representing a sub-national area. Each of it was actually a conglomeration of ethnic groups, sometimes hostile to each other where powerful groups dominated the smaller communities. Hence smaller groups complained of injustice and demanded autonomy for themselves. As statehood for every small group becomes impossible, the communities complain of apathy and neglect. The easy availability of arms due to extensive international boundary makes them take up arms to compel the government to concede to their demands. Some of the known underground outfits which demand statehood for their tribes are the Karbi National Volunteers, United Peoples Democratic Solidarity, Dima Haloa Daoga (two factions)—Kuki National Front and Kuki National Army—Bodo Security Force, National Democratic Front of Bodoland and so on.

Ethnic Conflicts in North-East India

The *third trend* is that of ethnic conflicts. Ethnic conflict took two different forms.[12] One was inter- or intra-tribal and the other is indigenous *vs* exogenous. We shall discuss them under the following rubric.

Inter-tribal and Intra-Tribal Conflicts: Attempts at Ethnic Cleansing

Intra-tribal conflicts were a part of the pre-colonial history of north-east India. Most of the tribals were competing with each for scarce resources, land and hegemony due to which they frequently raided each others' territory and often practised head-hunting. The British rule and impact of Christianity had not only reduced the conflicts but also almost stopped the head hunting. But certain old rivalries reappeared in new forms. The most notorious of those conflicts have been the Naga-Kuki conflicts.

NAGA-KUKI

Nagas are a conglomeration of 23 tribes whereas Kuki is a generic name given to at least 37 sub-tribes. Tangkhul among the Nagas and Thadou among the Kukis are the dominant tribes. The British also settled Kuki villages in the land between the Naga and British territory which resulted in competition for scarce land. Sporadic riots often erupted between the two tribes. Colonialism with its divide and rule policy, created the feeling of 'we' and 'they'. The tribal leadership initiated a unity move, (i) first by Lunneh of Motbung and Largo—a prominent Naga leader in 1947 but it failed. The Naga armed rebellion of 1956 provided them with the opportunity to take revenge against the Kukis. During 1956-64 Nagas devastated nearly 60 villages and Tamenglong and Ukhrul districts of Manipur. The idea was to compel them to migrate so that the Nagas could utilize them. Another bone of contention was the recent attempt of the NSCN(I-M) to compel the smaller Kuki tribes like Anal, Chothe, Lamkang, Chiru, Maring, Moyon, Monsang, to identify themselves as Nagas. The Kukis resented and opposed the move which also caused bloodshed. With NSCN taking the Naga cause, the Kukis formed an organization called the Kuki National Army (KNA) to fight the armed might of the Naga underground leading to an organized bloodshed. Besides possession of each others' land, a contest brewed over the control of trade routes too. The economic mainstay of the Kukis in the region is trans-frontier trade in contraband goods which takes place along the National Highway No. 39 connecting Imphal with Moreh and Pallel on the Myanmar border. These two tiny towns are hubs of illegal activities. Since the areas along this highway are inhabited by the Kukis, they control a large chunk of the trade. In fact, the KNA is financed by the Kuki smugglers. Realizing that this road and its lucrative trade constitutes the lifeline of the Kukis, the NSCN tried to take control of these trade routes which also added fuel to the already extensive fire. In the early 1990s the riots intensified and there were armed attempts at ethnic cleansing which have continued up to the present day. As a result of the conflict, most Nagas migrated from non-Naga areas and so did the Kukis, leading to huge displacement of population.

KUKI-PAITE CONFLICT

The Kuki-Naga conflict led to a spin off conflict between the Thadou—a tribe associated with the Kukis—and the Paites who describe themselves as a sub-tribe of the Mizos. Though they are disunited, the Kuki-Chin-Mizo belong to the same ethnic stock. The hostility developed over the silence and indifference of the Paites over the Kuki-Naga conflict. The Kukis felt that since the Paites were closer to the Kukis, they should have supported them in the conflict. Instead they alleged that the Paites maintained closer links with the Nagas during the crisis. The Paites, however, insist that they were Mizos and not Kukis. They also objected to the reported move of the displaced Kukis to settle around Paite villages. The Paites feared that the Kukis would subjugate them if they were allowed to settle near them. There are about 31,000 Paites and 57,000 Kukis in Manipur. The ensuing violence killed 200 Kukis and 290 Paites in 1992-3. It also displaced 7,500 Kukis and 15,700 Paites and had about 50 Kuki and 55 Paite villages burnt. The signing of a peace accord in 1993 between the two warring tribes brought peace. The State High Level Committee headed by W. Nipamacha Singh, the then chief minister of Manipur, initiated the peace move. As per its instructions the Zomi Council (the Paite body) and Kuki Impi (a Kuki organization) pledged to forgive and forget. It was also agreed that the nomenclature and identity of each other would be respected by each other and neither would try to impose the others identity. The agreement also pledged to restore and return the land, house and property of the others occupied during the conflict and no Zomi or Kuki militant shall indulge in any forcible collection of funds, taxes from the other.

KUKI-VAIPHEI CONFLICTS

Another offshoot of the Naga-Kuki conflict was Kuki-Vaiphei hostility. Vaipheis are another tribe numbering 50,000 inhabiting the Churachandpur district of Manipur who have close affinity with the Mizos since both belong to the Chin family. Kukis considered Vaipheis like Paite, as their cousins, and expected them to come to their aid during the Naga-Kuki riots. But since it was not forthcoming, on 25 November 1997 as many as 21 innocent Vaipheis were butchered. The worst was in Phainuam village. The Kuki militants were armed to the teeth. Since then it has become a veritable hell for the Vaipheis who are scattered all over the Churachandpur district occupying isolated pockets. The Vaipheis bore the brunt of military raids leaving nearly 50 villages torched and desolate. According to figures released, the death toll was placed at 73 including a woman whose head was severed from her body on 30 July 1998. On 10 July 1997, at Mata village, four persons were brutally murdered. According to an independent probe, the bulk of the victims were males with six females among the 73 dead. On March 1998 Nianglianting (20) of Mata village was tortured to death.

On 26 March 1998, a semblance of normalcy was restored following the signing of a memorandum of understanding between the Zomi Council and the Kuki Impi. But even after that, sporadic incidences of violence and murder continued in which the minority tribe like the Vaipheis were targeted. The Vaiphei community was not sure of its generic identity as it was close to the Mizos and Kukis both of whom bear affinity with each other. It was only in mid-1994 that the community adopted a resolution to use the Zomi (Mizo) identification for themselves. On 2 September 1995, the Vaiphei National Organisation signed a 'Charter of Agreement' with the Zomi Reunification Organisation (ZRO) merging with the Zomi tribes and working towards the formation of a Greater Zoland. The agreement was also signed by the Paite National Council, Simte National Council and the Tedim Chin Union. But the new identity seemed to have created more enemies than friends for the Vaipheis.

KHASI-GARO CONFLICT

Khasis and Garos are two major tribes that compose the state of Meghalaya. Khasis, who belong to the Austric group of people speaking a language belonging to the Mon Khmer family while Garos are a Mongoloid people speaking a Tibeto-Burman language. Though ethno-linguistically distinct, they have been placed in the same state, as they countered the Assamese hegemony and fought for a tribal state. In fact, it was prominent Garo leaders like Williamson Sangma and Khasi leader like B.B. Lyngdoh who spearheaded the tribal state movement through parties like the Eastern India Tribal Council, which later metamorphosed into All Party Hill Leaders' Conference. Thus, the Garos and Khasis were clubbed together for the state of Meghalaya which was formed in 1972 and an equitable share of resources and development was assured for both. Although the Garos were numerically superior and had contributed successive chief ministers like Williamson Sangma, Purno S. Sangma, Salseng Marak, the Khasis were politically dominant and often dictated the running of the system. Shillong being the capital, which was a traditional stronghold of the Khasis, all the important institutions like the secretariat, university, medical college, market complexes were located here while Garo Hills continued to be neglected. The only compensation made was granting the office of the Meghalaya Board of Secondary Education (MBOSE) to Tura (Garo Hills). The arithmetic of employment was 40 per cent for Khasis, 40 per cent for Garos and 20 per cent for non-tribals reserved. But Garos being educationally backward fulfil not more than 20 per cent at any time which then went to the educationally advanced Khasis. The 20 per cent open category was also taken by the Khasis as non-tribals were never given employment. Thus Garo Hills virtually remained the colonial hinterland of the Khasis. Things came to a head when the Khasi Students' Union demanded that the Office of the MBOSE should be shifted to Shillong and the reservation for Khasis should be raised to 60 per cent. This was opposed by the Garos. Intimidated by the development, the Garos realized that their future was not secure with the Khasis and hence demanded a separate state for Garos. The movement was spearheaded by Garo Students Union, Garo National Council and Achik National Volunteer Force. Although it has not result in any violence so far, there have been strong currents of resentment and hostility between the two. During 2001, the situation threatened to erupt into violence. The restraint, however, has not been able to resolve the issue that has been contentious.

MIZO-BRU (REANG) CONFLICT

Although Mizoram is a state of the Mizos it has a large number of smaller tribes who arc akin to them but not necessarily Mizos, e.g. Hmar, Paite and Reang (Bru). Reang is a major tribe of Tripura but in Mizoram they are small in numbers, dispersed in various districts bordering Tripura and Assam.

The Mizo population is about 6 lakh in Mizoram as compared to 80,000 Reangs in the state. The Reangs due to their proximity to Bengalis have become more Bengalicized as well as Hinduized though they have not formally declared themselves as Hindu. Their tribal animistic form of religion has been synthesized with Hinduism and since Hinduism was the state religion of Tripura in the pre-Independence period, they identified more with Hinduism. The Reangs were also untouched by the Christian Missionary influence. The Mizo Christian missionaries have been very active among the Reangs but with little success. The Reangs consistently resisted the advances of the missionaries although they received the missionary activities relating to education, health and hygiene. In October 1997 the young Reang leadership, demanded an Autonomous Council under the Sixth Schedule so that they could resist the tyranny of the dominant Mizos. With this aim they formed a political organization called the Bru-National

Union. But this initiative let all hell loose on them. The Mizos alarmed by the demand and resistance let loose their volunteers on the Bru villages who torched the houses, attempted ethnic cleansing and terrorized the Reang minority. As a result, a huge number of Reangs left Mizoram and took shelter in the neighbouring states of Assam and Tripura. Mizoram state had to quell the violence as the RSS and VHP took up the issue as defenders of Hindu minority. The Reangs themselves formed an underground organization called Bru National Liberation Front (BNLF) to protect its people through arms.

BODO-SANTHAL

The Bodos are the single largest community in the north-east constituting 6 per cent of Assam's total population of more than 13 lakh in number, settled in the area spanning from Rangia to Kokrajhar. Deprived and disempowered under the hegemony of the caste Hindu Assamese they have begun trying to revive their culture and identity on the plank of ethnicity. Earlier the Plains Tribal Council of Assam (PTCA) and the Bodo Sahitya Sabha were the premier representative bodies of the Bodos. However, since 1986 the All Bodo Student Union (ABSU) under the leadership of Upendranath Brahma started a movement for a separate state for the Bodos. The movement became violent as two underground organizations like the Bodo Liberation Tiger (subsequently Bodo Security Force) and National Democratic Front of Bodoland (NDFB) launched an armed movement to achieve the goal. In fact, the NDFB went a step ahead and demanded sovereignty. By 1993 the centre started negotiation with the Bodos and the Bodo leadership agreed to come down from the demand of statehood to autonomy under the provision of the Bodo Accord (1993). As a result of the Accord, pending elections, an interim Bodoland Autonomous Council (BAC) was formed but without a clear-cut boundary and with a non-Bodo population. Some areas under the BAC had more than 50 per cent non-Bodo population composed of Asomiya Hindus, Asomiya Muslims, naturalized immigrant Muslims, Rabhas, Bengali Hindus, Santhals, and Nepalis. In a large part of BAC area, the

Bodos did not constitute even a simple majority. In order to create a majority for the Bodos—so that these areas do not oppose being included in the BAC area—an ethnic cleansing process had started. Initially, the Bodos started targeting the non-tribal Assamese, Bengali and Nepali settlers both Hindus and Muslims but then they shifted their attention to the Adivasi Santhal population of the area. These Santhals were settled in the area by the British, often forcibly ejecting them from Jharkhand consequent upon the Santhal rebellion of 1855-6, who number about a lakh. In an attack in May-June 1996 about 1,000 Santhals were massacred and 2,50,000 displaced according to unofficial sources. The violence against the Santhals was aimed at generating fear in order to displace them from their present living space and to recapture the space for the Bodos. In May 1998 the Bodos massacred the Santhals again killing 30 people on the spot and displacing 25,000 people. Soon after, the Santhals began to organize themselves to counter the offensive. They formed organizations like the Birsa Munda Force, Cobra Force, etc., and armed themselves to resist attempts to displace them. The offensives and counter-offensives continued well up to 2002.

NAGA-MEITEI CONFLICT

Manipur comprises hills covering an area of 20,088 sq. km and a valley comprising an area of 2,239 sq. km. The hills are the abode of various Naga, Kuki, and Chin tribes totalling 29 whereas the valley is the home of the Meiteis both Hindus and Muslims and Scheduled Castes. Being more economically stronger the Meiteis enjoy as such a political hegemony over the others. The Nagas and Kukis are, however, formidable minorities. The hill-plains divide is also reinforced by the hill tribes and Christians. After the adoption of Hinduism by the Meiteis in the eighteenth century they began to practice a strict caste system Mangba-Sangba (pure and impure) in their dealing with the tribals. Naga-Kuki tribals were thus considered impure by the Meitei Hindus and untouchability was practised on them. Hence the relationship has been filled with undercurrents of tension over the centuries and it is a miracle that it has hardly ever erupted into violence. This also explains the fact that though the

NSCN is based in the Ukhrul district of Manipur where there are a dozen Meitei underground organizations active, seldom there was any collaboration between them. But of late the relation has begun to show signs of strain and is fast turning into one of mistrust and hatred. The first development to cause this was the inclusion of the Manipuri language in the VIII Schedule, which created widespread apprehension in the tribal minds that the Meiteis were taking advantage of their political dominance, and wanted to impose it on the non-Meiteis. The second issue is the opposition of the Meiteis to the extension of the provisions of the VI Schedule on the hill areas of Manipur as they fear it would undermine their authority over the hill areas. This was also compounded by the Meitei move to extend Manipur Land Revenue and Land Reforms Act 1960 to the hill areas which the tribal viewed as a threat to the rights over their lands. If implemented this Act would enable anyone from the valley to buy lands in the hill areas also which was so far not permitted. The Meiteis were alarmed by the persistent demand of the NSCN (I-M) that the Naga areas of Manipur should be attached to Nagaland to create a Greater Nagaland. The Meiteis were opposed to any move to balkanize the state of Manipur. But this is what exactly happened when the centre signed an agreement in Bangkok on 14 June, 2000 extending the ceasefire between the NSCN and the Indian Army in the territory of Manipur. The centre's decision to bow to the NSCN demand was viewed by the Meiteis as the first sign of the realization of the Naga demand and the consequent disintegration of the Manipur territory. This resulted in a mass upheaval in the valley—there were widespread demonstrations, destruction of public property, torching of the Legislative Assembly, hunger strikes and creation of chaos in the state. Large-scale violence and police firing failed to quell the uprising. In a show of solidarity all sections of the people, politicians, intellectuals, leaders, underground, women, students and even children participated in the mass demonstration.

This created a panic among the Nagas of Manipur specially those who live in the valley. In panic about 50,000 Nagas left their houses in the valley and took shelter among their kinsmen in the hills. Seventeen Meiteis died during the demonstration. The upheaval subsided only when the centre revoked the agreement to extend ceasefire over Manipuri territory. Now it was the turn of the Nagas to launch a protest movement. The Nagas of Senapati, Ukhrul, Tamenglong and Chandel districts launched a series of protests. The Naga organizations blocked the National Highway Nos. 39 and 59 from the end of July till the first week of August and also declared a *bandh* in Naga areas. But in a remarkable show of restraint both parties prevented violent eruption. In fact, the United Committee of Manipur (UCM) comprising 14 powerful Meitei bodies appealed to the displaced Nagas to come back to their homes in the valley. Although they did come subsequently the relation was damaged permanently and a violent confrontation would not be surprising.

KONYAK-CHANG

The Konyak and Chang are two tribes who associate themselves with the generic Naga identification. They inhabit the Mon district of Nagaland which formed a district of North-East Frontier Agency (NEFA) or the present Arunachal Pradesh. Konyaks numbered 72,319 in 1971 while the Changs numbered about 16,075 in 1971 living in the Central Tuensang district. Konyaks are one of the most ferocious tribes in the sense they were practising headhunting till even recently. Changs are a relatively weaker tribe which has been hunting ground for the Konyak head-hunters. In fact, there are no specific causes of their confrontation but traditional animosity. The history of mutual war and headhunting has spilled into the present and a small event could spark off a violent confrontation mainly because of the prevalent sense of communitarianism. Personal misunderstanding is used as community problem and collective retribution.

KUKI-KARBI

In the colonial period many migrant Kukis had settled in the vicinity of the Karbi villages of Karbi-Anglong district of Assam. The frequent eruption of Naga-Kuki violence had forced many more Kukis to migrate to the Karbi areas. Initially the Karbis were sympathetic to the Kuki cause and allowed them to settle in their wastelands. In fact, Kukis were given representation even in the Karbi Autonomous Council. But emboldened by the encouragement, the Kukis demanded a Kuki District Council within the Karbi Anglong district. The political ambition of the Kukis threatened the Karbis who saw grand designs in the Kuki movement. The initial conflict between the two tribes became violent when the respective underground outfits of the Kukis and Karbis took over the fight.

DIMASA-ZEMI NAGA

The Dimasas and the Zemi Nagas are traditional neighbours who shared the land in north Cachar and lived amicably. The Zemi Nagas are generally looked down upon by other Naga subtribes for being a non-martial tribe. They were even called Kacha Nagas. But in its drive to mobilize more and more people behind its movement, the NSCN(IM) developed a base among the Zemi Nagas and through them extended its area of operation in south Assam too. Its design became clear when north Cachar was demanded in the proposed Greater Nagaland. This alarmed the Dimasas as it threatened to partition their ancestral habitat. The NSCN continued its effort by settling more and more Zemi Nagas in all the vacant areas and even sometimes by forcibly driving the Dimasas out of their villages. This led to violent retaliation by the Dimasas. The result was bloody, ethnic cleansing riots between the two tribes led by their underground outfits NSCN and DHD.

DIMASA-KARBI

Dimasa and Karbi tribes are traditional neighbours. At the same time Karbis consider the Dimasas their traditional rivals as well. Again the conflict broke out on the question of land, settlement of villages and encroachment issues. This conflict is one of the ongoing bloody riots in the region.

It is interesting that newer forms of conflict between new sets of tribes are rising with the passage of time. These are mostly manufactured and constructed as old and traditional rivalries.

Indigenous *vs.* Exogenous: Resistance to Sharing of Political Space and Economic Resources

The opposition to the presence of outsiders was quite an old issue in north-east India originating in the colonial period itself. In the post-colonial period such movements broke out in Assam and Tripura over Bengali refugees from East Pakistan, in Arunachal Pradesh over Chakma, Hajong and Tibetan refugees from Bangladesh and Tibet respectively, in Mizoram over Chakma and Riang settlers, in Meghalaya over Bengali refugees from Pakistan as well as other non-tribal settlers. These latecomers, either from India or its neighbours are seen as encroachers of scarce resources like land and potential competitors in employment opportunities and political power. The Assamese suspected that there was a huge number of illegal Bengali Muslim settlers from Bangladesh. They felt that unless these foreign nationals are detected and deported they would reduce the indigenous Assamese into a minority. Since governments failed to tackle the issue, the All Assam Students Union launched an Anti-foreign national movement in 1979 to attract the centre's attention to it. There were other economic issues too. There was widespread poverty and unemployment in Assam despite the existence of natural resources like oil, tea and coal. It was felt that these were drained out of the state without any commensurate benefit to the people. Eventually after six years of turmoil, the centre responded by signing an accord in 1985, following which the Students Union and the Asom Gana Sangram Parishad organized themselves as a regional political party called the Asom Gana Parishad (AGP). It came to power in 1985 with the promise of resolving the foreign national issue as well as to build a 'Golden Assam'. However, in the five years of its rule the AGP failed to solve either the problem of poverty or of infiltrators.

Resistance to Nationalist Discourses

The North Western Frontier formed the gateway to the Indian subcontinent for the numerous migratory waves from Central Asia while, the north-east India formed the other gateway from the opposite direction through which similar migration from East and South-East Asia took place. Different groups of the great Sino-Tibetan-speaking people who had their *nidus* near western China have come from south and west from the pre-Christian era. Most of these tribes settled along the western course of Brahmaputra. The great Bodo tribe appears to have settled in the region early and entered into north and east Bengal thereafter into north Bihar. The Abors, Akas, Daflas, Miri and Mishmi came later and settled themselves in the mountains north of the Brahmaputra Valley. Some Austric and Dravidian tribes settled here before the Mongoloid Bodos came to settle here. In the historical times we have the Siamese-Chinese section of the Mongoloids in their Thai tribe of the Ahoms migrating to the Brahmaputra Valley and ruling for six centuries. Finally we have the incursions of the Kuki-Chin tribe in the southern north-east. There are a total of 209 listed Scheduled Tribes in the region belonging to six different categories.[13] There are a total of 192 languages and dialects in the region as against the 1652 of all-India figure. They are representatives of the Austric, Tibeto-Chinese, Dravidian and the Indo-European families.

Such profusion of tribes, ethnic groups, languages and dialects is suggestive of the degree of complexity and its consequent implication in the political, economic and socio-cultural relation in the region. However, big or small each of these indigenous tribes or communities were, they had their own evolved polity. The Khasis had their *Hima*, the Jaintias, Dimasas and Tipperas had their own monarchy, the Ahoms and the Meiteis had a full-fledged state, each of the Naga and Mizo sub-tribes had their polity in the form of chieftaindom. Such numerous and petty polity formations in a relatively narrow space have been described by Stanley Thambiah in anthropological terms as the 'galactic polity', in the context of South-East Asia.[14] It was compared to a political galaxy formed by several principalities and dependencies within a small territory. The north-eastern situation in pre-colonial times could be profitably seen as a similar galactic polity—in a continuous state of migration, polity formation, and varied stages of political evolution. Such state formation remained in a fluid state for long spells of time. Each of these polities was autonomous in some form in pre-colonial times and most of them even were at war with their neighbouring tribes or plainsmen. The post-colonial situation was a continuation of this situation which has to be understood because the colonial system did not touch them much and the colonial administration did not interfere with the structure. The autonomy demand that arose in north-east India was on the basis of these pre-colonial polity formations which explains the profusion of such demands. The demands arose because the tribes/communities in question were wary of the nationalist discourses and the nation state's power of submerging smaller and marginal communities. Since the federal polity allowed them some sort of autonomy, these groups wanted autonomy on the basis of their pre-colonial status which the Indian state could not afford as it would mean virtually every village would have to be granted a province, district or autonomous council. The result was a stalemate in which there was a confrontation between these communities and the Indian state.

Although these areas were made a part of the empire, the British did not introduce any of the developmental measures such as the modern political system, modern economic activity or Western education or ideas, which even though colonial in nature, transformed Indian society. While tribals were kept 'excluded', all measures like Education, health care and ideas were left to the Christian missionaries—the only people who were allowed to function in the tribal areas. As a result, the tribals, received only those ideas or institutions which either the colonial administration or the missionaries provided. They were thus kept away from ideas such as rationalism, secularism, liberalism or cosmopolitanism which marked modernity. They were brought up amidst theocratic, exclusivist and insularist ideas and institutions and encouraged to perpetuate their pre-colonial ways of life mostly. Even when the rest of India experienced restricted self-rule, the tribals were kept outside its purview by devices like Excluded Area, Partially Excluded Area (Government of India Act 1935) and Innerline and Outerline (Bengal Frontier Regulation Act 1873). Although the tribes revolted in fierce uprisings against the colonial British rule, they were not allowed to participate in the organized national movement of the rest of India. When the British decided to quit India, the tribals found themselves politically unequipped to face the situation. The British encouraged them to move for separation but refused to retain them within the empire. To meet the crisis the emerging middle classes of the respective tribal groups formed political platforms under a generic tribal identity instead of the pre-colonial clan-based solidarity. The Nagas thus formed the Naga National Council (1946), Mizos, the Mizo Union (1946); Garos formed the Garo National Council (1946); the Karbis, the Karbi National Darbar (1946); the Jaintias, Jaintia Darbar, Khasis, Khasi National Darbar (1923) and so on. Though such organizations were conceptually modern and had features of nationalist discourse, their objective was to seek autonomy and resist absorption by the nascent Indian nation state. Not only this, they ensured that since most of them are not a united tribe as yet, all the sub-tribes that were represented in the organization also represented their collective general interests and bargained with the Indian National Congress leadership for their continuation within India. In fact, most of the tribes toyed with the idea of an independent existence outside India mainly because they had begun to consider the Indians as an alien majority who could easily subsume them. The political environment in the subcontinent marked by secessionism of the Muslim League, Akali Dal and the Congress's assurance that it would not compel any community to merge with India against their will facilitated such a thinking. The colonial administrators too constantly reminded them of being different from Indians and even conceived of plans like a crown colony to continue to retain them under colonial rule. Though the British left without implementing them, the ideas remained in circulation. Moreover, there were no well meaning assurances from the Indian leadership which was taking over power from the British. They offered to these marginal people the promise of a nation state in which they will have a constituent membership. But the offer was not negotiable. In other words, the tribes were not given any option to reject the offer. This frightened them. If at independence such was the situation what it would be like in the future? Moreover the nationalist discourse had its baggage. It brought along other discourses and developments like communalism, partition, republicanism, majoritarianism, cosmopolitanism, liberalism, secularism, federalism, modern legal system and jurisprudence, and a ruthless capitalist economy—all of which were perceived to be detrimental to the interest of these small communities. A modern nation state was foreseen to spell disaster for them. The state by nature was hegemonic, authoritarian and coercive. The Indian nation state right from its inception was demonstrative of its true character in its dealing with various constituents. The Nagas, Mizos, Meiteis, had all articulated their apprehensions of such a disaster and wanted to perpetuate their own indigenous political and economic systems in a sovereign space.[15] This they felt was the only way in which they could resist the advancement of Indian nation state and its consequent absorption of marginal communities.

The movements emerged as a part of the sub-nationalist upsurge that the Indian subcontinent experienced during the colonial rule. As capitalism in the form of British colonialism expanded to India, it initiated the modern nationality formation process.[16] The process manifested in two separate but coeval processes. One was based on a pan-Indian identity and the other its regional linguistic-cultural identity. The second was strongly subservient to the former in the colonial period which makes it the sub-national stream. The ethnic upsurge in north-east India is part of the second stream. It took an ethnic character because these movements drew from the pre-colonial ideas of kinship, solidarity and identity. There was a resistance to modern identities though they did sometimes appropriate the nationalist discourse but it was for strategic purposes. Even the movements both secessionist or for autonomy were restorative and the conflicts were often a continuation of the traditional conflicts. Ethnic identities no doubt fell short of national identities but were more than tribal. Ethnic identities could camouflage primordialism in a modern world. The tribals resisted national identities as such identities had to accommodate multiple tribes and sub-tribes and even be secular and cosmopolitan, which they did not want to do.

As has been seen above, there were massive ethnic upsurges in north-east India in the post-colonial period in different forms. A closer look will demonstrate that these are open or veiled attempts of the tribes to assert themselves either against the nascent Indian state, neighbouring tribes, traditional adversaries or against the changes that they were experiencing in their world. As has been defined earlier, ethnicity emerged as a discourse to resist the ruthless onslaught of capitalism into the innermost recesses of the world. Ethnic uprisings are the indigenous people's defense mechanism to the advancement of a capitalist system which was slowly engulfing the entire world and against whom the small indigenous people had no defense. Nationalist discourses have been a product of advancing capitalism. While capitalism invaded the remotest territory through colonialism, the post-colonial world sought to integrate cultural areas into an integrated market and link it to the world capitalist system through the concept of nationalism and nation state. The tribal and indigenous people were equally unequipped to deal with the onslaught of nationalist discourses. Hence, here too their defense against the nationalist discourses was ethnicity. While they resisted colonialism through open and violent rebellion, they resorted to ethnicity to resist integration, absorption and thereby subsuming to the slogan of nationalism and nation state. The ethnic upsurge in north-east India has to be seen in this context.

It has to be put in perspective that secessionist movements were not just restorative in the sense that the tribals involved, they were wanted to revert to their old status after British withdrawal from India, also prompted in part by the desire of the traditional chieftains to retain their hegemony over the people.[17] The new middle classes which emerged out of modern education had actually opposed this move. This was true of all the Naga and Mizo movements. In doing so they often imitated nationalist discourse stating that each of these tribes was a nation by itself. But since there was a multiplicity of tribes in each of these hills who had their own inner contradictions, there was always a move to constitute a generic tribe resembling a nation in terms of demography and political strength. The identity projected was national but since drawn from its pre-modern roots and composition, it actually was an ethnic identity—more than a tribe but less than a nation.

Moreover, post-colonial experience proved the apprehensions of the constituent communities. Nationalism had emerged to be a legitimizing ideology of a modern nation state. The imagination of Indic civilization in modern India was consolidated by differentiation with the Western civilization. Sanskritic culture and Brahmanic order were its essential features. In this imagination, Hindus were seen as a symbol of composite-culture. The communities of north-east India were to fit into the framework of the cultural imagination of India. Despite the fact that north-east India did not really figure in this imagination, any resistance to assimilation was seen as a threat to its composite cultural ethos. Hence autonomy demands were seen as threats to national integration. Force was used instead of governance. Development was not seen as an independent enterprise but was related to peace and tranquillity. Interrogating the nationhood of India and the demand for restructuring of the polity was viewed as secessionism.

Notes

1. Nirmal Nibedon (1981), *North East: The Ethnic Explosion*, Delhi: Lancer.
2. Nirmal Nibedon (1979), *Nagaland: Night of the Guerillas*, Delhi: Lancer.
3. Nirmal Nibedon (1980), *Mizoram: The Dagger Brigade*, Delhi: Lancer.
4. Sajal Nag (2000), 'The Killing Fields: Mapping Conflicts and Violence in North East India', unpublished report prepared for the Violence Mitigation and Amelioration Project, Delhi: Oxfam India, 2000.
5. John Hutchinson and Anthony D. Smith (eds) (1996), *Ethnicity*, Oxford Readers Series, Oxford; Michael Banton, 'Ethnicity, Ethnic Group', in *Macmillan Student Encyclopaedia of Sociology*, ed. Michael Mann (1983), London: Macmillan Press, rpt. 1985; E.G. Hobsbawm (1980), *Nations and Nationalism since 1780* (1983), Cambridge: Cambridge University Press; Paul Brass (1991), *Ethnicity and Nationalism*, Delhi, Newbury Park; London: Sage.
6. Rajni Kothari, 'Ethnicity', in *Illustrated Weekly of India*, 6-13 March 1988, pp. 42-5.
7. Ibid.
8. For a detailed discussion on secessionist movement in north-east India see Sajal Nag (2002), *Contesting Marginality: Ethnicity, Insurgency and Sub-Nationalism in North-East India*, Delhi: Manohar, 2002.
9. Also see Nirmal Nibedon's work on Mizoram mentioned above. Also see Lalchungnunga (1996), *Mizoram: Politics of Regionalism*, Guwahati: United Publishers; R.N. Prasad (1987), *Government and Politics in Mizoram*, Delhi: Concept.

10. For a study of secessionist and insurgency in north-east the other reading lists are: B. Pakem (ed.) (1998), *Insurgency in North East India*, Delhi: Omsons; P. Tarapot (1983), *Insurgency Movement in North East India*, Delhi: Vikas; H. Sareen (1982), *Insurgency in North East India*, Delhi: Sterling; Samir Das (1998), *ULFA: A Study*, Delhi: Ajanta; B.G. Vergese (2001), *India's North East Insurgent*, Konark.
11. For autonomy movements in north-east India see, L.S. Gassah (1997), *Autonomous District Council*, Delhi: Omsons; P.S. Dutta (1997), *Autonomy Movements in Assam*, Delhi: Omsons; R.N. Prasad (1994), *Autonomy Movements in Mizoram*, Delhi: Northern Books; Sanjib Baruah (2002), *India against Itself*, Delhi: Oxford University Press.
12. Although north-east India has been a veritable minefield of ethnic conflict, there has been very little work on them. The following provide a good account. Monirul Hussein (ed.) (2005), *Coming out of Violence: Essays on Ethnicity, Conflict Resolution and Peace Process in North east India*, Delhi: Regency; Sandhya Baruah et al. (2007), *North East India: Development, Communalism and Insurgency*, Delhi; N.C. Datta (ed.) (1997), *Politics of Identity and Nation Building in North-East India*, Delhi; P.S. Datta (ed.) (1993), *North East India and the Indian State Paradoxes of a Periphery*, Delhi: Vikas; Bimal J. Deb (ed.) (2006), *Ethnic Issues, Secularism and Conflict Resolution*, Delhi: Concept.
13. Although each of the state is known after the major tribe/ethnic group, in reality all these states are composite states and every tribe is a generic name to a conglomeration of tribes/sub-tribes. Nagas have at least 16 sub-tribes within the territory of Nagaland. They are Angami, Ao, Chakesang, Chang, Chiru, Khiamngan, Konyak, Lotha, Makware, Phom, Rengma, Sangtam, Sema, Tikhir, Yimchunger, Zeliang. Other tribes living in Nagaland are Kuki, Boro, Dimasa and Karbi.

    The major communities in Meghalaya are Khasi, Garo and Jaintia. Khasis are dispersed in Meghalaya, both Brahmaputra and Barak Valley of Assam and Tripura. They are divided into Khasi, War Khasi, Lyngam, Pnar, Jaintia, Syateng Khynrium, Bhoi Khasi, and Khasi Muslim. Besides the Khasis there are Garo, Rabha, Banai, Koch, Lalung, Hajong, Man, Dalu, Bodo and Mikir tribes also in the state.

    In Mizoram the major tribes are the Mizos which is a generic name of a number of sub-tribes, like Biate, Lusai, Mara, Pang, Riang, Tlan, Bauri, Hualngo, Paite, Pawi, Ralte, Hmar and Lakher. The other tribes living in Mizoram are Pnar, Chakma, Magh and Thadou.

    The major tribes in Tripura are the Tippera (Tripuri), Riang, Jamatia, Chakma, Halam, Magh, Noatia and Koloi. Others are Bhil,

Chakma, Garo, Kaipeng, Khasi, Kol, Lushai, Munda, Koch, Kuki, Magh, Murasing, Santhal, Tripuri-Thakur, Oraon, Ralte, Rupini and Uchai.

Arunachal Pradesh has an amazingly high number of tribes and sub-tribes—Adi-Ashing, Adi-Bori, Adi-Karko, Adi-Milang, Adi-Padam, Adi-Pangi, Adi-Ramo, Adi-Tangam, Adi-Bokar, Adi-Gallong, Adi-Komkar, Adi-Minyoung, Adi-Pailibo, Adi-pasi, Adi-Shimong, Aka, Apatani, Bangni, Chakma, Deori, Hill-Miri, Khamba, Khamiyang, Khampti, Khowa, Lisu (Yobin), Memba, Miji, Mikir, Mishing, Miri, Monpa-But, Monpa-Chug, Monpa-Dirang, Monpa-Kalaktang, Monpa-Lish, Monpa-Tawang, Mishmi-Digaru, Mishmi-Idu, Mishmi-Miju, Na, Nishi/Nishang, Sherdukpen, Sonowal Kachari, Tagin, Nocte, Singpho, Sulung, Tangsa-Havi, Tangsa-Jugli, Tangsa-Kimsing, Tangsa-Lumgchang, Tangsa-Lungphi, Tangsa-Lungri, Tangsa-Morang, Tangsa-Mosang, Tangsa-Muklam, Tangsa-Renrang, Tangsa-Sangwal, Tangsa-Sanke, Tangsa-Tikhak, Tangsa-Tonglim, Zakhring, Nocte besides the Chakmas and Tibetans.

14. Stanley Tambiah (1985), 'The Galactic Polity in South East Asia', in *Culture, Thought and Social Action:An Anthropological Perspective*, Cambridge, Mass.: Harvard University Press.
15. See Sajal Nag (2002), *Contesting Marginality: Ethnicity, Insurgency and Sub-Nationalism in North-East India,* Delhi: Manohar, for details.
16. For an elaboration of this process see Sajal Nag (2000), *Nationalism, Separatism, Secessionism*, Delhi and Jaipur: Rawat.
17. A detailed discussion on this is available in my 'A Comparative Analysis of Naga, Mizo and Meitei Insurgencies', in *Faultlines: Writings on Conflict and Resolution*, vol. 14, July 2003, pp. 67-79.

6

Ethnic Tension and Community Conflict in North-East India

A Challenge to India's Integrity and Unity

P.K. RYNGNGA

Introduction

North-east India is the home of many ethnic groups ranging from the Meitei-Pangal, Naga, Kuki and Mizo in Manipur, Mizoram and Nagaland to the Garo and Khasi in Meghalaya, the Boro, Karbi, Assamese, Tai Ahom, Rabha and Dimasa of Assam to the Aka, Adi, Nyishi and others in Arunachal and Tripura. The Brahmaputra and Barak valleys and the hill areas have distinct cultures, traditions and histories but have co-existed for many centuries marked by intermittent peace and strife. In the past conflicts revolve mostly around land and power but they have got intensified in the last one century.

Diversity becomes a problem when the inequalities are based on cultural or racial differences or when groups perceive each other as a threat to their identity. Identity assertion is often based on contesting claims over a homeland, territory or other resources. The rise of a dominant community adds to the threat and results in an atmosphere of mistrust and fear of domination. From it, grows a feeling of vengeance. In the wake of land and other shortages this threat has become even more heightened. Amidst the ensuing conflicts, groups articulate their identity in linguistic, cultural and ethnic terms.

Increasingly, the elite turn the cultural systems, values and practices into tools of competition for political or economic power. This explains why poverty, along with a weak government and a lack of effort to address the ethnic problems and developmental issues has resulted in a period of instability and armed conflicts. Thus, apart from identity, land, economic benefits, immigration and ethnic discrimination, lack of national identity and a low level of state legitimacy form the bases of the conflicts indicating the failure of the state institutions. There is a growing insecurity among the people because of the conflicts and it affects all age groups but has a greater impact on the youth. Because of the presence of fear in the society, the democratic institutions seen meaningless to the people, especially the youth. The imposition of a dominant will of one community on the other remaining communities further widens this gap.

Most ethnic conflicts emanate from an ethnic consciousness and nationalist aspirations. Many of them revolve around land which is not only an economic commodity but also the centre of the culture and identity of most communities of the region. Since identity, land and other resources are inseparable, identity assertion is central to the effort to protect the natural resources. Ethnic movements are often supported and legitimized through exclusive ethnic histories which brought about asserting one's right over the resources. Every community uses these ethnic histories as a means to protect its livelihood to declare itself as the first inhabitant of a given area. Based on it, the community demands exclusive rights over its resources and benefits. Thus, what causes conflicts is not history as such but the search for an exclusive identity, shaped by economic shortages and attacks on their culture. History only legitimizes the conflicts. This shows the need to take a fresh look at the history of the north-east India and take steps towards a composite history that moves away from this exclusive approach and underlines inter-dependence.

North-East: A Scene of Instability and Conflict

The states in the north-eastern regional system have dynamic societies and are modernizing in varying degrees of response, stress, and stability. In fact, the region is experiencing conflict situations associated with the problems of economic development, participation, representation and political change. Interaction within this system is being affected constantly by external forces and assumes dimensions that aggravate the crisis parameters in the regional system. Moreover, the states within the system are also changing their responses towards each other (as well as within) in ways that are directly related to the happenings in their respective political economies. Change in the regional system is, therefore, an issue related to the political equations within and between states on the one hand and with the centre on the other. It is also frequently associated with contests and conflicts of interests between groups and sub-groups, which reflect the intense activity over policies and institutionalization of power in a region where there already exist alternative traditional political structures operating simultaneously with the modern ones. These are of particular concern as the regional system forms one of the pillars of the territorial and political stability of the Indian state.

The most significant change in the region is associated with the problems of performance and governability. Political processes are affected by pluralistic stagnation, as performances are made difficult by aggressive and forceful articulation of conflicting and often divergent interest that are not aggregated. Besides, there is a continuous pressure to satisfy a large proportion of demands of the constituent population groups and sub-groups, and are frequently resolved through allocations. This makes the state to over extend its limited distributive resources to satisfy their respective political options, which in turn stimulates disenchantment while making long-term resolution difficult.

It, therefore, suggests that change and transformation that followed consolidation of the region laid stress on the irreversibility of the change. Divergent responses to this phenomenon accentuated dormant and latent cleavages and encouraged the rise of differences and contradictions within the regional society. It influenced the transactions and relations in the subsequent periods and became acute after the Partition of the subcontinent, Independence and the administrative reorganization of the region.

Developments in the region during the British period clearly suggest that the responses to change were more or less proportional to the degree of impact the change had brought upon the groups and sub-groups whose territories were gradually, in distinct phases, incorporated in the colonial state. However, these were considerably strengthened by the distance accessibility conditions and framework. It was only when political change involving larger territorial interests and objectives became a reality, that the consolidation-control themes extracted specific responses from the inhabitants occupying the border states of India.

However, the post-1947 situations projected an entirely different equation altogether. The constituent unit-population elements revived the themes for reversing the territorial-administrative process and they once more assume their earlier pre-colonial status. But the state's welfare measures (though limited), works of various agencies, and so on, had in fact, introduced several changes that affected the traditional societies of the region. These were in terms of relationships within as well as between groups. And, in doing so, it had established the irreversibility of change in the politico-geographical processes that drastically transformed the region. The movements towards separation and the formation of several discontented groups in the region, therefore, suggest reasons that go well beyond their present stance and lie perhaps in their respective territories or aspects that closely influenced their concerned territories. Nevertheless, these elements failed to solve their respective legitimacy problems/issues and became vulnerable. In most cases, such instances were dependent upon the availability of resources being generated within the respective territories or provided by the regional/national core.

The strife and mistrust among and between groups in the north-east heightened with every phase of development to the extent that there exists tremendous inter-group instability, insecurity and volatility row. This is discussed below.

Inter-Ethnic Conflicts

Hmar-Dimasa and Kuki-Karbi clashes in Karbi-Anglong and the consequent exodus of Khasi-Pnars from Karbi-Anglong led to further conflict and violence. Many of the insurgencies grew out of inter-ethnic conflicts. They have spread to the neighbouring states where their ethnic groups are in sizeable numbers, for example, Naga group's presence in Changlang and Tirap districts in Arunachal Pradesh. Ethnic groups based in Tripura and Manipur such as Reangs, Brus and Hmars have both physical and political presence in Mizoram. A large number of these groups have been militarized as well as politicized. Ethnic militias have become part of the civil societies because of the feeling of insecurity *vis-à-vis* other ethnic groups. They are fighting battles on two fronts—one against the other hostile ethnic groups and the other against the Indian state, though not all demand secession from the Indian Union.

The demand for a separate homeland for the Bodos has generated strong opposition from the non-Bodo groups, many of whom are no less disadvantaged than the Bodos. In this complex ethnic scenario some disadvantaged groups are demanding Schedule Tribe status for their community in order to be able to enjoy the basic citizenship rights as they feel doubly deprived and disadvantaged. Some of these groups have been living here for centuries and have no other home to go to if forced to leave from here. ULFA has started a violent campaign for the ouster of these communities from Assam. The proliferation of ethnic agenda, ethnic militias and ethnic violence are the result of misconceived short-term solutions to complex issues which demand an integrated approach for solving the problems on a long-term basis. The farce of a dialogue with the ULFA leaders through interlocutors from the civil society has only strengthened the ULFA, who after their ouster from the sanctuaries in Bhutan had been considerably weakened. It is unfortunate that the narrow political interests and not national interest continue to dictate government policies.

Another illustration of how sensitive various ethnic groups are about their ethnic identity is the Zomi-Kuki conflict. Their conflict is over the trivial issue of nomenclature. But it was no less bloody! The Paite-Zomi and Thadeu-Kuki conflicts took as many 562 lives in 1997. The situation, however, has not remained static. They keep on changing their demands and allies. The ULFA and the National Democratic Front of Bodoland (NDFB) seek protection and sanctuary in Bangladesh, a country whose people they had earlier sought to kill and deport from Assam. Religious tensions in Assam are also on the increase. The rise of the communal forces in the state does not augur well for peace and stability in the state. The attempt to mobilize the Muslims in favour of the Congress party has not worked according to the plan. Distrustful of the Congress party's motives, they have formed their own party in the hope of playing the balancing role in the tussle of power between the main contenders.

Militancy and Insurgency

The Naga insurgency was the first armed conflict in this region. It started soon after India's Independence in 1947 when the Naga leadership under Z.A. Phizo raised its banner of revolt. Since then the number of armed conflicts has multiplied. From just one Naga insurgency at the time of Independence in 1947, the number of insurgencies has multiplied to over hundred spread all over the region.

The Nagas were the first to raise the separatist flag. The British did not discourage their ambition for a separate state. In fact, there is enough evidence to show that they actively encouraged it, because they did not trust the new rulers in India, who had fought a long struggle for independence against the British. According to their assessment then, the British interests would be safer in the hands of the Naga leaders. Aware of the danger to India's integrity and security, Prime Minister Nehru took a number of steps to win their loyalty and meet their aspirations for a separate identity. The division of Assam into tiny states on ethnic lines became the main plank of his policy. In hindsight one can say that this was the beginning of trouble in the region. Once the central leadership allowed identity politics to play a free role, it was only a matter of time before the other ethnic groups started demanding their own separate states. Having started the process, the central government could not reverse it. It is still going on! Militancy and insurgency confined to the Naga area soon spread to other parts of the region. Till the end of the 1970s, insurgency was confined to a limited area and only two or three ethnic groups were involved. Today it numbers more than a hundred, for instance the insurgencies by the Nagas, Mizos, Tripura tribes, Meities, ULFA, Karbis, Khasis, Garos in the hills, and the Bodos, Kacharis, Tiwas, Rabhas, Misings, Ahoms, Chautias, Deuries, Kosch, Rajbonshis, Moran, Matak and by the Meiteis in the plains. Many of them are the outcome of inter-ethnic conflicts. These include, the conflict between Bodos and Santhals, the Kouch Rajbonshi and Bodos, the Karbis and the Kukis, the Kukis and the Nagas, the Khasis and the Jaintias and Garos, the Dimasas and the Hmars in the Barak Valley, the Tripuris and the Bengalis, the Mizos and the Reangs, the Chakmas and the Arunachalis, the Khamtis and the Mishimis), etc.

One factor that is fuelling insurgencies in the region is that most political and economic benefits are being monopolized by the dominant ethnic group. This is creating insecurity and tensions among the minority groups in a region already afflicted by scarcity of opportunities and resources. These insecurities and tensions have led to demands for secession, separate homelands, and ethnic cleansing. The smaller communities not being in a position to influence the outcome of political verdict find themselves being pushed to the margins of the political and economic system. The local elite exploits the situation for their own selfish ends. They assume the leadership to mobilize the people against the state and the rival ethnic groups and push them towards militancy. The insurgent groups have close links with mainstream politicians of their own ethnic group.

Ethnic politics could well be the flip side of the incapability of the state to guarantee security of life and property which is being provided now by their ethnic armed militias. Whatever the genesis of the insurgency, the dynamics of its persistence has acquired a momentum of its own. The collusive arrangement between the different militant factions and the various political parties and civil servants are more the norm than the exception. This nexus has helped in building a massive network of extortion and intimidation. The extremist politics have more than one component. Their demand for separate political identity and ethno-centric demands are an integral part of their political agenda. The obvious conflict of interest over land, government jobs, and cultural and ethnic identity have only further complicated and aggravated the situation. The ambitious political and economic elite manipulate these conflicts to mobilize mass movements. Many of the ethnic communities demand separation from the Indian union; they demand a separate sovereign state for their own ethnic community. They have crossed the stage of ethnicity into the stage of nation formation. It is also true that the demand for secession in the initial stages of these movements is more a bargaining tactic than a genuine demand by the insurgents. History of ethnic assertion is closely linked to the history of political evolution and the emergence of new social forces. Without the numbers and political clout, ambitious politicians, not unlike in the other parts of the country, use emotive issues and slogans to whip up public support. The movements for secession, statehood, and autonomy can be divided into various categories: discrimination by the dominant communities, concern with issues of culture and language—attempts at assimilation or ethnic cleansing through the imposition of language of the dominating community—like the Bodos and Bengalis in Assam; against outsiders, like in Tripura and Arunachal Pradesh; against other indigenous people, like in Karbi-Kuki, Dimasa-Hmar, Naga-Kuki, Kuki-Paite, Reang-Mizo and Hmar-Mizo conflict.

Before 1947 no ethnic group, except the Naga National Council (NNC) demanded secession from the Indian Union. The situation has undergone a dramatic change for the worse since then. The reasons for the division of Assam and the creation of new states were entirely political. Political expediency rather than in-depth thinking decided a very complex issue in a simplistic manner in the hope that the creation of new states will put an end to the turmoil and secessionist demands. But instead of bringing about peace and development to the region, this one step is responsible for creating more problems than any other. It has fuelled more militant demands for the creation of more autonomous units or separate states on the basis of ethnic numbers or secession from the Indian Union. With the exception of Assam, all other states are too small and lack resources to become financially self-reliant. Pumping in more funds for development, instead of leading to faster development has only bolstered 'patronage politics'. Securing maximum funds from the central government becomes the main task of the elected government. For this obvious reason, the ruling party at the centre finds it easier foist its own party government on the people in the state. It is not a coincidence that more often than not, each time there is a change in the party ruling at the centre, there is a corresponding change in the party ruling in most states of the region. The voting pattern suggests a bias in favour of the party ruling at the centre.

Ethno-National Feeling and 'Tribal' Identity

The pejorative term 'tribal' carries a denotation of primitivity and inferiority of the people for whom the name is applied. The Constitution of India also categorically equates 'Scheduled Tribe' with 'Scheduled Castes'. Consciously or unconsciously, 'tribals' are reduced to the lowest level of the socio-ritual hierarchy of the Indic cultural system. For the simple reason that they are non-Indic and remain outside the traditional Hindu *varna*, they are placed alongside the 'outcastes' of the Hindu caste system. Such a detrimental categorization is not acceptable to the proud north-east 'tribes'. At the scholarly level, there are a few attempts to understand and to explain the distinctive case of the non-Hindu 'tribals' of the north-east, but in the national majority's understanding, tribals are tribals. The attitude of the national mainstream that primitivizes and thereby inferiorizes the 'tribals' is in serious conflict with the proud self-understanding of the tribals in the north-east. Such a pride, as indicated above, is exhibited in their ethno-national feeling. The people's experience of being despised as 'untouchables' and their fear of losing their identity were the major factor that led to ethno-political movements of insurgency. In tracing the historical development of insurgency in Nagaland, Asoso Yonuo attributes the people's unpleasant experience of interaction with the 'non-tribals' to be one of the main causes of the revolution. The Naga National Council's original demand was 'some sort of regional autonomy', he says, and in the course of their interaction with the 'non-tribals' they developed the fear of 'losing their identity . . . in the midst of Hindu rule' leading to a demand for 'outright sovereign independent Nagaland state'. The people's experience was crucial in the evolution of ethno-national feeling and the spirit of separatism. The separatist tendency had evolved mainly because of the treatment meted out to them by the converted Hindus and Muslims in Assam and Manipur who regarded them as 'untouchables' or 'dirties', for their religion and food habits.

Challenge to the Nation's Integrity and Unity

The many ethnic clashes and separatist movements flourishing in the area, pose the biggest challenge to the security establishment. The area is too large and the terrain too difficult to be pacified by force alone. Only a glance at the map would show how vulnerable this region is to both external and internal subversion. Ninety-nine per cent of its borders are international borders; only 1 per cent is linked to the rest of the country through a narrow strip of land in Siliguri in the Darjeeling district of West Bengal, rightly called, the 'Chicken's Neck'. Hostile forces will always be tempted to squeeze India through the Siliguri Corridor, an area plagued with militancy and separatism. The adjacent countries have been less than friendly to India. The countries in the neighbourhood do not miss any opportunity to destabilize the situation to further their own agenda. In the political parlance of India today, the very term 'north-east' has almost come to denote a region characterized by ethno-political movements. Since India's Independence in 1947, there has not been a single decade of peace in the region. Instead, each decade saw new movements of political unrest, most of which turned to violent revolutions. One need not make a substantial argument to show that these movements have their origin in the ethno-national understanding of the identity. Insurgency, an extreme form of ethno-political upsurge, has rocked five of the seven states at one time or another, and the remaining two states are highly poised for a similar movement. Its strategic location has only created more problems for the people instead of rapid economic development. The dispersal of some ethnic groups to the neighbouring countries has created additional problems. But the problem is basically political. A number of armed conflicts have been smouldering in the region since Independence. The inward-looking self-definition of identity as an ethno-national entity now not only effects the people's relations with 'the outsiders', but also the inter-ethnic groups' relations within the region. The expectations to achieve economic and political liberation on the basis of ethnic groups have led to feuds between the people and groups within the region. Although a common enemy is still strongly felt to be 'the outsiders', in the attempts to define one's ethnonationality and in the struggle for 'autonomy' and liberation, the more powerful neighbouring ethnic groups came to be identified as obstacles. The Naga-Kuki clash in recent years is a good example. If the trend continues as it is, we may expect to see more feuds among the ethnic groups.

History and geography have combined to make the people feel isolated and alienated from the rest of the country. Deprived of even the most essential public services, they feel disgruntled and dissatisfied with the functioning of the government. Disgruntlement of the people may not be a unique feature of the north-east, but there is a big difference. When people in the rest of the country feel aggrieved and disgruntled, they vote out the incumbent government, but in the north-east they blame the central government and start demanding separation from the Indian Union. The demand might not have been raised too seriously in the beginning, but falling prey to the separatist propaganda it soon becomes serious enough to give birth to militancy and insurgency. Instead of giving special attention to economic and social development of the region, the central government followed the more convenient route since Independence, of politically empowering the dominant ethnic group by creating tiny states on ethnic lines. The policy has increased and not lessened alienation. Political and economic empowerment must go hand in hand. One without the other has little meaning. The short-sighted policy made the minority ethnic group more insecure and alienated than before. The unintended effect of this policy has been to give rise to many more demands for the division of even these tiny states and the creation of more states on ethnic lines. Division and sub-division along ethnic lines is not a solution to the problem of alienation of the people. Late Prime Minister Jawaharlal Nehru rightly understood the sensitivity of the region and its people but failed to recognize the complexity of its social structure. The various arrangements devised in an ad hoc and short-sighted manner to solve the problems have failed to achieve the desired objective. They have, in fact, created new conflicts and demands for more division and fragmentation on ethnic lines.

The government has not been able to formulate a long-term and comprehensive strategy to deal with the problem. This is the major reason why neither military/ethnic groups meant, nor peace talks or accords have been successful in bringing about peace in the north-east. The problems with each other coupled with the frustrations and discontentment of different ethnic groups, the government's attitude towards their problems compelled the communities to take the law in their own hands to the extent of operating from underground. The government's ad hoc policies to combat tension and unrest have only exacerbated the problem. An essential requirement of a successful peace dialogue is that it should manage to bring the major parties to the dispute, if not all groups, on board. This, the government failed to do in most such dialogues, including the protracted cease-fire and peace dialogues with the NSCN(IM). The ceasefire has not brought peace also because its terms have been allowed to be blatantly violated by the NSCN(IM) cadres. The government has also made efforts to accelerate the pace of development by allocating large funds to all the states in the north-east. The strategy has failed because development and security cannot be separated. Security and development are closely intertwined. They are two faces of the same coin and one cannot be separated from the other. When in large parts of the north-east the state is unable to perform its most basic functions, like maintenance of law and order, delivery of essential services and collection of taxes, it would be unreal to expect any meaningful development. To plan development policies without taking into consideration the security situation on the ground is unrealistic. It is not possible to get results unless the instruments of planning and implementing economic, political and security policies are combined in one institution of the state. The three cannot be separated; each has both short-term and long-term impact on the other. The North East Council which started with much fanfare in the 1970s has not achieved much success because of this impractical division between economic, political and security policies. It has not made much impact even on the extremely slow pace of development of the region, as no development project can take off without creating a reasonable security environment.

The so-called 'Look East Policy' announced with so much fanfare has also made no headway. There is very little trade with the neighbouring countries through the land route primarily because of conditions of insecurity on the Indian side. It also must be recognized that land routes are much more difficult and expensive than sea-routes. Most of the international trade in this region continues to be conducted through sea-routes. Nor has the strong military response or short-sighted political initiatives succeeded in controlling the situation and bringing peace to the strife-torn region. In fact, the reverse has happened. At the time of Independence India had to face only one insurgency, that from the Nagas. But since this threat has multiplied hundredfold, the number of insurgent groups operating today in this region has multiplied to well over hundred. The situation can still be managed if there is consensus among the main political parties about how to deal with it. Further illegal migration can be stopped and a solution found for the migrants who are already in the state for economic reasons. Granting work permits to them without political rights, is one such solution. Creating one or more non-territorial constituencies for all non-locals could be another solution if at all they are to be granted political rights. Article 171 of the Indian Constitution provides for doing this. Granting them legal status will not only foster regional and national solidarity but also improve the security situation. The suggestion that immigration due to economic and social distress, aggravated by natural disasters, can be countered by regulating legitimate labour movements through work permits needs serious consideration. A series of interrelated initiatives could point the way to understanding the requirements for peace and development. Any further drift and pouring funds into bottomless pit that do not reach the target group will only lead to further deterioration of the situation. The many serious issues need to be squarely faced and not evaded and swept under the carpet. The feeling of deprivation will only lead to further alienation and assertion of identity. Pandering to unreasonable demands will also worsen the situation. The policy-makers have still not learnt the lesson from past experience. Giving in to demands for separation and autonomy on ethnic lines, and thus causing further fragmentation, are remedies worse than the disease. And yet the unending process of fragmentation is still on because of narrow political considerations. The state police in the north-east needs immediate attention from the central government if they are to perform effectively their role of enforcing the rule of law and providing protection of life and property. Postings in the north-east should not be treated as punishment postings. Negotiating secretly with insurgent groups, however, strong, like with the NSCN(IM), is unlikely to bring peace in this troubled region. The demands like Nagalim (greater Nagaland) are best addressed by creating a space in which all the stakeholders in these conflicts can express their views and meet their aspirations. The people of the region must be taken into confidence, for a lasting solution to the divergent claims of various ethnic communities. Sixty years is not a long enough period for honest stock-taking and reassessment of the strategies and policies pursued so far. The fact that they have so far failed in achieving their aims and objectives cannot be denied.

In conclusion, it is suggested that a holistic view should be taken of all the security, political, economic, social, and ethnic problems of the region and their linkages with the neighbouring countries. Otherwise, it will not be possible to tackle the serious situation in the north-east. The strategy to solve the many issues should include: appropriate reforms in the Constitution, and political and legal institutions to accommodate the aspirations of the people. It should think in terms of cooperative federalism, decentralization and regional autonomy.

References

Abubakar, Carmen A. (1989), 'The Moro Ethno-nationalist Movement', in *Ethnicity: Identity, Conflict, Crisis,* ed. D. Kumar and S. Kadirgamar, Hongkong: Arena Press; quoted in Anjan Ghosh (1991), 'Ethno-nationalism: A Conceptual Clarification', in *Ethnonationalism: An Indian Experience,* ed. A. Ghosh and R. Chakrabarti, Calcutta: Chatterjee Publishers, p. 31.

Agarwal, K.S. (ed.) (1999), *Dynamics of Identity and Intergroup Relations in North East India*, Shimla: Indian Institute of Advanced Study.

Béteille, André, 'The Concept of Tribe with Special Reference to India', *Archives Européennes de Socìologie* 27 (1986): 299.

Gopalakrishnan, R. (1995), *Insurgent North-Eastern Region of India*, New Delhi: Vikas.

Marwah, Ved (1986), *Ethno Political Situation in India's Northeast*, New Delhi: Vikas.

Sarin, V.I.K. (1982), *India's North-East in Flames*, Ghaziabad: Vikas, pp. 254-5.

Srinivas, M.N. and R.D. Sanwal (1972), 'Some Aspects of Political Development in the North-Eastern Hill Areas of India', in K.S. Singh (ed), *The Tribal Situation in India*, Simla: Indian Institute of Advanced Study, p. 121.

Yonuo, Asoso (1974), *The Rising Nagas: A Historical and Political Study* Delhi: Vivek Publishing House, p. 166.

7

Communalism and Nationalism in India

A Perspective

EMANUELA MANGIAROTTI

In India, communal violence has been considered one of the most insidious challenges to the stability of the democratic state, questioning its pluralistic vocation and, ultimately, its unity.

However, because of its origins and the assumptions it entails, the validity of 'communalism' as a descriptive clincher for the variety of phenomena and situations it is normally referred to needs to be questioned. This paper contains an introductory argument to the study of interfaith relations in India. Its aim is both to propose a critique to the employment of the terminology of 'communalism' and to take a stand with respect to it.

I will introduce my argument with a brief exploration of the debate regarding the 'ethnicity' paradigm and its use in the field of conflict studies with special reference to its 'ethnic group/conflict' declensions. The analysis will mainly focus on the risk of essentializing the category of ethnicity and overlooking the processes and dynamics through which collective identities and group boundaries become relevant in socio-political relations.

Drawing from these critical strands, the paper focuses on the implications embedded in the unquestioned use of the notion of communalism. The first part challenges the analytical validity of communalism as a concept, pinpointing the risk of reifying the object of analysis in terms of 'antagonistic religious communities'. The second part analyses the ideology of communalism as a boundary-drawing narrative and discusses its role as a fundamental aspect of the phenomena it is meant to describe.

From a methodological point of view, the purpose of this analysis, as part of a larger study on narratives and practices of interfaith relations in Hyderabad (India), is to underline the importance of acknowledging the origins of such conceptualization and the possible implications deriving from their use as descriptive tools. This is mainly due to the fact that, in the case of communalism, narratives and practices configuring interfaith relations as social spaces and phenomena are grounded on the very concepts employed for their description.

In developing this perspective, I will show that these terms can become political weapons, especially in the realm of identity politics. For this purposes I will draw from the argument proposed by G. Aloysius (Aloysius 1997) on the distinction between 'power as dominance' and 'power as resistance', conceived as two intertwined and interacting levels at which power can be exerted.[1] As Aloysius frames it, 'to resist, is as much an expression of power as to dominate' (Aloysius 1997: 24). Thus, if the ascriptive, unequal distribution of power embodied by the caste system is a striking example of power as dominance (system) legitimized by an appeal to religion (ideology), the various and disparate[2] expressions of 'contra-Brahminism/caste-ism' which emerged in the subcontinent during the colonial times can be regarded as forms of resistance (Aloysius 1997: 28-9).

In the course of this analysis, I will focus on the way the concept of nationalism is used in India with respect to communalism. Reference will be made to the so-called 'Hindu nationalist' organizations, in order to highlight the way narratives and practices in the realm of identity politics can contribute to build social boundaries.[3]

As remarked by Aloysius on the concept of nationalism and the terms derived from it, '[...] as categories of crisscrossing political discourses, they are ambivalent both as weapons with their own dynamics as well as playthings at the mercy of groups and forces in conflict' (Aloysius 1997: 11).

On the Concept of Ethnicity

The concepts of 'ethnicity' and 'ethnic group' have been largely used in the academic field, especially in the study of intrastate conflicts. While different approaches concentrate on specific aspects and possible implications of this phenomenon, criticism of the very conceptual framework of ethnicity has focused on its applicability as an analytical tool.

In his seminal work on ethnic boundaries, F. Barth argues that studies of ethnicity and conflict have tended to neglect the processes through which symbols of ethnic difference become meaningfully relevant under certain circumstances (Barth 1969). According to him, attention should be paid to the processes and dynamics that generate and maintain ethnic boundaries rather than on structures and institutions of groups.

Similarly, S. Fenton maintains that the notion of 'ethnic group' implies that 'membership' and the contents of ethnic identity are 'summative *and* totalizing' (Fenton 2004: 180-1). Contrarily, he argues, awareness of ethnicity becomes relevant only in certain situations when circumstances contribute to configure it as the main markers of collective identification.

For the study of ethnic conflict, Fenton suggests an approach aimed at identifying the conditions in which this awareness of internal commonalities and external differences increases, instead of focussing solely on ethnic aspects and differences.

In analysing the Yugoslav wars of the 1990s, V. P. Gagnon (Gagnon 2004) underlines that violence did not stem from pre-modern antagonisms or hatred between different ethnic groups, but was the outcome of an elite-driven strategy to maintain power positions, facing mobilization for socio-economic and political change.[4] The use and ethnicization of violence was aimed at '*demobilizing* key parts of their population by trying to impose political homogeneity on heterogeneous social spaces'. Perceiving a threat to the existing structure of power, elites adopted the strategy of re-framing the concept of political space in order to focus the discourse on 'the question of who "owns" the space',[5] rather than on the claims around which the population was mobilizing. Gagnon maintains that violence was in at least three ways instrumental to such a reconfiguration. First, it redirected the demands for change towards an alleged threat. Second, it reformulated ethnicity as a fixed, immutable category producing ethnic groups whose interests perfectly matched those of the 'status quo elites'. Third, and consequently, they engaged in the construction of a homogeneous political space, effacing demands for new opportunities in the contemporary power structure (Gagnon 2004: 7-9).

Though Gagnon's analysis indulges excessively on an image of conflict as an elite-driven phenomenon, it allows for the possibility that ethnic antagonism may be the outcome rather than the cause of violence and for the role played by representations of conflict in generating ethnic boundaries.[6]

These examples highlight the need for studies of ethnicity and conflict that acknowledge the importance of symbols, rituals, discourses and more generally all practices (including violence) generating boundaries between groups in order to avoid the risk of essentializing the object of analysis. This approach urges scholars and practitioners in the field of peace and conflict studies to recognize the role played by narratives and practices of identification, differentiation, and conflict in the production of social antagonism between groups.

Drawing Boundaries: Narratives and Practices of Communalism

This overview of the critiques moved to the ethnicity paradigm within the field of conflict studies is useful to introduce some of the problematic points related to the concept of communalism and the terms derived from it.

Communalism is regarded here as a narrative produced in the context of identity politics, which is also productive of specific narratives and practices of hostile interfaith relations. Thus, instead of being an aseptic tool for description, it is a meaningful terminology, which contributes to configure its very object of analysis.

In the Indian context this concept has mainly been used to refer to specific identities, politics, groups and organizations having an essentially religious and sectarian basis.[7] Accordingly, the term 'communal conflict' is used to describe unrest, antagonism, violence and competition at the political, social and cultural levels between two or more 'religious communities'.[8]

If unquestioned, this categorization, assuming that religious difference automatically places people into internally homogeneous and reciprocally antagonistic communities, is simplistic[9] but also intrinsically ideological. As noted by Bipan Chandra, 'inherent in communalism is the idea that the social, cultural, economic and political interests of Hindus and Muslims and Christians and Sikhs are dissimilar and divergent because of the fact that they follow different religions' (Chandra 1984).

Hence, the process of essentialization does not apply simply to religious communities but also, and equally important, to an alleged antagonism between them. In this respect, communalism can be regarded as a boundary-drawing narrative, entailing hostile practices of interfaith relations. The implications of this terminology as well as the various circumstances and contexts in which it is employed have to be explored as fundamental elements for the understanding of narratives and practices generating boundaries between groups and communities, as suggested by Barth (1969).[10]

Interestingly, A.P. Cohen argues that a community does not exist out of simple cultural aspects, structures or institutions but as a symbolic construction, through which social boundaries are produced. Thus, communities are 'symbolic forms' (Cohen 1985: 40) adaptable to changing circumstances thanks to the very malleability of symbols, which shape their boundaries in relation to other communities.

The meanings attributed to symbols, rituals and behaviour depend on the interpretations people give to them according to their idiosyncratic experience. In spite of their 'official' form, symbols and rituals have as many meanings as the interpretations attributed to them by individuals. Members are not homogeneously attached to the same cultural aspects, but share a variety of symbols that allow different interpretations to coexist within the boundaries of the community.

The rhetoric of symbols determines the distinctiveness of one community so that 'almost any matter of perceived difference between the community and the outside world can be rendered symbolically as a resource of its own boundaries' (Cohen 1985: 117). Within these boundaries, a variety of interests and motivations finds expression by virtue of the multiple interpretations that symbols allow.

Consequently, it is through the rhetoric of symbols and connected practices that the sense of belonging to a specific community in opposition to a hostile 'other' is configured in relation to contemporary circumstances. Cohen for example underlines the role played by interpretations of the past in reasserting the community's boundaries with respect to other socio-political entities. In this process, leaders provide 'official' interpretations of the past to convey ideological messages.

The movement of the Hindu right in India is an interesting example of the way symbolic discourses and practices construct and continuously negotiate religious communities' boundaries and their internal and external relations.

In *Hindutva: Who is a Hindu*, V.D. Savarkar defines the essential aspects of what he names 'the Hindu civilisation' (Savarkar 1923). In analysing the text, Christophe Jaffrelot (1992) identifies kinship and the moulding of the community's natural historical roots as two fundamental elements on which Savarkar bares the core of the 'Hindu nation':

These are the essentials of Hindutva—a common nation (*rashtra*), a common race (*jati*), and a common civilization (*sanskriti*) (Savarkar 1923).

A Hindu is a member of a *jati*, a kinship group to whom Savarkar attaches racial contents[11] and whose roots are to be found in the so-called 'Vedic golden age'.

A third fundamental aspect of *Hindutva* is territory. According to Savarkar, the uniqueness of Hindu civilization derives from the fact that it originated in the 'sacred geography' of the motherland, in opposition to other 'alien cultures'. The relevance of the sense of belonging to a land emerges in Savarkar's interpretation of the word Hindu (*sindhu*) as: '[...]he who looks upon the land that extends from Sindhu to Sindhu—from the Indus to the Seas—as the land of his forefathers—his Fatherland (Pitribhu), who inherits the blood of that race, whose first discernible source could be traced to the Vedic Saptasindhus [...]' (Savarkar 1923: 115-16).

This speculation represents a fundamental narrative of the Hindu Right's ideology in India, shaping the boundaries of a religious-political community with an exclusive right to rule in India. Therefore, besides establishing symbolic boundaries between the self and the other, this narrative can also be regarded as an ideology of domination.[12]

Moreover, Anand (2005) underlines how a discourse of security informs the kind of identity politics produced and reproduced by the Hindu Right. In this context, 'the Muslim' is portrayed as an object of insecurity, not only for the Hindu self (overpopulating Muslims), but also for the Indian state at large (terrorist Muslim).

By combining the former narrative with the latter, the 'Hindu community' comes into existence through a variety of discourses constructing a myth of a native, glorious civilization, in opposition to 'the Muslim' and his threatening connotations.

Specific practices are related to these boundary-generating discourses. For example, Oza notes that the spatial strategy used by the Hindu Right to affirm their exclusivist claims, especially starting from the 1980s, relegated 'Muslim minorities to the private spaces of their homes and communities; it then placed them at the margins of towns and villages; finally it has sought to erase the landscape of Muslim presence altogether' (Oza 2007: 154). The appropriation of the public space not infrequently occupied by other religious minorities, has played and continues to play a momentous role in conflicts and disputes over religious sites, symbols and rituals as well as debates about minorities' rights.[13]

Boundaries of religious communities and their antagonism with others are therefore the product of specific narratives and practices and not of simple cultural differences. Accordingly, the term 'communalism', with its inherent assumptions regarding sectarianism of and conflict between religious communities, cannot be regarded as a neutral concept but needs to be understood as one of the narratives produced in the context of identity politics and productive of hostile interfaith relations.

Implications of the Ideology of 'Communalism'

The analysis of the circumstances in which usage of the terminology related to communalism originated can help us move to the second point of this analysis regarding the political implications.

In India the term 'communal' has two main, closely interrelated connotations. The one discussed above regards interfaith relations and conflict. The second refers to the intrinsic belligerent and sectarian attitude of particular groupings or movements.

The origins of both meanings can be traced back to the colonial period when the activities of more or less organized struggles started to question the hegemonic power exerted by local traditional elites and the British colonizers.

Aloysius highlights the emergence of political consciousness[14] among the lower strata of society during the colonial times as one of the underlying transformative processes taking place in the Indian socio-political scenario. These movements were different from the upper-caste ideology of the Indian National Congress with which political awakening of nineteenth-century India is usually associated. The various expressions of a rising socio-political consciousness emerged in response to and as a reflection of changing power relations in the social and political systems. Those originating in the lower rings of the power structure found in these changes a possibility to fight against the ideology of ascriptive hierarchy that kept them subjugated, thus exerting a form of power as resistance (Aloysius 1997: 52-5).

Aloysius notes that, despite their extreme variability in terms of geographical location, inspiration and cultural roots, these movements shared a two-fold aspiration. On the one hand, they aimed at removing the existing power system based on an unequal, ascriptive order. On the other, they attempted to play a role in the anti-colonial struggle and the ensuing nation-building process (Aloysius 1997: 19).

The struggle for independence was thus characterized by a double path. The 'nationalists', belonging to the higher ladders of society that aimed at a single, all-India ideology to counter the colonial power, and the movements emerging from below at a more local level, fighting not simply against the British but also for the construction of a new social system within the future independent state.

The more these movements grew the more they were perceived as a challenge to the established structure of power. In the process of legitimization of the Congress movement in national-political terms these grassroots struggles rooted in the vernacular cultures, began to be described as mere expressions of caste/communal consciousness, with respect to the all-India aspiration of mainstream nationalism. In the interaction between different levels of power, the term 'communal' became a political weapon to disqualify claims coming from organized, grassroots movements.

The violence that rocked the subcontinent during Partition marked the final identification of the 'communal' with inter-religious hatred, imbued with an anti-secular, sectarian and therefore anti-national strand.[15]

The term is still used for descriptions of episodes of violence whose explanations focus on the different faith of the people involved. As noted above, this term contains in itself a specific interpretation of the phenomenon, i.e. perpetrators and victims belong to two different religious groups that are, for some reasons, antagonists. Hence, when a communal riot takes place, some sort of competition—economic, political, social or cultural—between two religious communities has to be unveiled to understand the causes of violence.

However, the identification of an episode of violence as communal—the product of Hindu/Muslim antagonism—hinders a more in-depth analysis of such violence and, above all, of the interpretations given to it, both 'official' and 'non-official' as part of the phenomenon itself. The way the event is framed and understood by different actors can shed light on the nature of the phenomenon, and on the impact of different interpretations on the parties involved, in terms of their socio-political positioning.

For example, in the case of the Gujarat pogrom in 2002, the expression 'communal riots' is misleading. To describe the organized, state-assisted massacre of thousands of Muslims as the result of competition between religious groups is at best simplistic (Brass 2002-3: 5-6). In fact, the larger picture of who and what was behind this event, the historical moment in which it took place and how religious symbols and ritual behaviour were used to produce discourses about religious nationalism and the construction of a socio-political order based on discrimination and exclusion runs the risk of being neglected.

The narrative of communalism is inscribable in the dialectics between power as dominance and power as resistance because, besides the essentialization of antagonism between religious communities, it bears a negative value connotation, which has an impact on interfaith relations and the representation of minorities. Hence, the term 'communal' has become a political tool in the hands of different political parties, groups and media, through which they produce discourses and practices about power and social relations.

According to this frame, the association with a specific religion can become a social marker in the sense that a series of rituals and symbols entails a specific kind of positioning with respect to the political and social arenas, according to the community at stake. So, the Hindu Right leaders portray themselves as 'nationalist', while Muslims are said to be 'anti-national', following an 'alien' religion whose fundamental teachings represent a threat to the unity and integrity of India as a nation.[16]

Since 'the communal' is deemed to question the state's pluralistic and secular values, its derogatory connotation applied to groupings and individuals has the effect of delegitimizing their claims, reducing their foundations to sectarianism. According to Ayesha Jalal (1998-9), 'neither the Congress nor the RSS, BJP and VHP combination would plead guilty to the charge of communalism [...] The original sin of being communalist for the most part has been reserved for the subcontinent's Muslims' (p. 2) as if this 'communal consciousness' were inherent to the political and social views of the Muslims (p. 4).

In the light of the above considerations, it is quite telling that, despite the clear politics of identity with its divisive implications, the so-called 'Hindu nationalist' movement is rarely described as communal (Noorani 2000). The processes of labelling are political tools and have an enormous impact on the configuration of social relations and political positioning of groups differently situated in the power structure.

It then becomes quite clear that the use of labels such as 'nationalist' and 'communal' is inscribable in the dialectics between power as dominance and resistance. In India, those movements and organizations named 'communal' in mainstream politics and media rarely occupy dominant positions for, as in the case of the Hindu Right, they would probably opt for a more positively-valued epithet.

In conclusion, the argument challenging the uncritical use of the 'communal paradigm' as a descriptive tool entails an exploration of narratives and practices which configure and transform social spaces and relations, in a constant interaction with power.[17]

Conclusion

In questioning the concepts commonly employed for the study of identity politics and conflict, this paper aims at proposing a reflection on the role the terminology used in academic and non-academic circles plays in contributing to perpetuate the dynamics of dominance and conflict. In fact, as argued above, not only does the concept of communalism present some weak points in terms of its explanatory poignancy, but it also pertains to the paraphernalia of narratives and practices used in the context of religion-based identity politics and conflict.

As suggested by some authors in the field of ethnic conflict studies, the focus on the processes and circumstances in which the opposition between two identified communities becomes paramount in a particular socio-political context reduces the risk of essentializing the object of research and overlooking the relevance of the dynamics of power in shaping, in the present case, interfaith relations.

In addition to this, this paper attempts to show the importance of analysing narratives and practices of religious identity and the way they employ symbols, rituals and actions to configure and reconfigure social boundaries. The uncritical use of concepts such as 'communalism' and 'communal conflict' may, not only hinder an in-depth understanding of such circumstances, discourses and practices, but also reinforce boundary-generating narratives which are part of the object of analysis. This is mainly due to the fact that the very concepts used to describe these social spaces and phenomena belong to the range of tools available for political communication, as evident in the case of the Hindu Right movement. This is the reason why these terms need to be understood as boundary-drawing narratives, entailing specific practices related to the realm of identity politics and as constitutive aspects of the phenomena they are meant to explain.

Notes

1. In order to clarify his perspective, Aloysius incorporates approaches that stress the diversity of forms and domains in which power manifests itself (Lukes 1986; Foucault 1990). According to these views, in the political economy of a society, power emerges in the context of contestation for resources (economic, cultural and intellectual) between groups and collectivities. Second, in the multiplicity of its forms, power is structured around a specific 'nodal point or principle, settling into a harmonious unity in the form of a cultural specificity over a period of time'. This makes power peculiar to each society. Third, power represents aspirations of groups and collectivities having unequal positions and force. Consequently, power can be expressed 'either as dominance or as resistance'. Notwithstanding this conceptual duplicity, there is a degree of ambiguity that blurs boundaries between these two levels (Aloysius 1997: 23-5).
2. According to the author the very absence of a homogeneous and codified anti-hierarchical movement in India is the peculiar characteristic of these forms of resistance which draw part of their power on their very diversity.
3. The case of 'Hindu nationalism' is used here as an example to clarify the argument proposed in the paper. There is, therefore, no attempt to provide a thorough analysis of such phenomenon or to present it as the only form of nationalist and identity politics at work in India.
4. Interestingly, some authors push the critique further by questioning the validity of the very concept of ethnicity. According to Gilley, this concept 'tends to homogenize quite distinct political phenomena' (Gilley 2004: 1155) and even if ethnic markers may be present in political conflict, this does not necessarily mean that such a phenomenon should be labelled 'ethnic conflict' and be regarded as ethnic in its nature. If ethnicity is considered a simple 'focal point for mobilization' then one should question the very existence of a phenomenon called 'ethnic conflict'.

5. The issue of space ownership is momentous in discourses and practices of identity politics. See later for a brief discussion of spatial strategies of legitimization and exclusion of the Hindu Right in India.
6. Barkawi (2004) proposes a similar argument in his study of ethnic hatred between multi-ethnic British imperial forces and Japanese military during Second World War. According to him, war and fighting generated extreme antagonism along ethnic lines, so that conflicting identities, that in retrospect, appear to have motivated the atrocities perpetrated by the two armies, were in fact a product of that very violence.
7. However, in the literature of conflict, communalism is often considered a synonym of ethnicity. See for example, Wilkinson 2004; Varshney 2002; Horowitz 1985.
8. Ayesha Jalal notes that 'such an overarching and loaded term as communalism ends up essentializing the very religiously informed identities, politics and conflicts it purportedly aims at explaining and combating' (Jalal 1998-9: 3).
9. The problem with the use of totalizing categories for social identity has been recognized by various authors and is briefly dealt with in the previous paragraph. For an insightful critique of the Hindu *vs.* Muslim paradigm see Gottschalk 2000.
10. Supra, p. 2.
11. According to Savarkar, *jati* is the social category in which a Hindu is born and that defines, not only the individual's placement into the broader caste to which his/her *jati* belongs, but also some fundamental aspects of the physical appearance and the personality of the members.

    'The word *jati,* derived from the root *jan,* to produce, means a brotherhood, a race identified by a common origin, possessing a common blood. All Hindus claim to have in their veins the blood of the mighty race incorporated with and descended from the Vedic fathers, the Sindhus.' (Savarkar 1923: 84-5)
12. Kapur and Cossman argue that the Hindutva ideology is part of a contest over domination or hegemonic way of understanding the world, and of establishing an understanding that contributes to the legitimation of social power and inequality (Kapur, Cossman 1993: 35).
13. Every year, in the city of Hyderabad, Ganesh Chaturthi, a massive Hindu celebration, takes place. On the tenth and final day of the festival, huge processions starting in different parts of the city reach the various water tanks where the innumerable and colourful Lord

Ganesh idols are immersed. In the district of Sultan Shahi, repeatedly affected by violence, the parade crosses the narrow lanes of the areas mainly inhabited by Muslims. The route of the procession has been changed various times and has become a contested issue, especially after disturbances and violence took place repeatedly on that occasion. In proceeding towards the water tank, the rally converges with other processions in the area of the Charminar, the centre of the Old City commercial activities and the site of the biggest and historic mosque, Mecca Masjid. There the crowd gathers to listen to religious and political leaders addressing the celebration. Because of its connotation as a symbol of cohesion of the Hindu community and of the rituals aimed at appropriating and marking the public space as Hindu, the Ganesh festival is perceived as a 'communally sensitive' event in Hyderabad.

14. Aloysius defines political consciousness as 'the perception of power relations within society and of one's own (individual or group) position in that frame'. It also refers to 'an urgency to take collective action in order to strengthen or alter that position' (Aloysius 1997: 53).
15. It is mainly after Independence that issues of ethnicity and communalism started to question the nature of the Indian democratic and pluralist state. As noted by Aloysius, 'while problems of culture, ethnicity, identity, etc., did form a strong undercurrent during this period, they emerged as a major challenge to state power only in the post-colonial era' (Aloysius 1997: 17).
16. As noted by Ajit Sahi, 'the sort of nationalism that is being projected by the Hindutva lobby is fiercely anti-Muslim. It is premised on a Brahminical worldview. It projects Muslims, but also all non-Hindus and those Hindus who do not agree to its ideology, as "anti-national". The Hindutva groups say they are willing to accept Muslims so long as they don't "look Westward". This is a cunning strategy aimed at forever stoking the flames of divisiveness. For what is a Muslim worth if he doesn't look westward, toward Mecca?' Ajit Sahi, interviewed by Yoginder Sikand for www.countecurrents.org, 10 November 2008.
17. A paradigmatic example is represented by the Ram Janmabhoomi-Babri Masjid case. Van der Veer maintains that the controversy over the religious site in Ayodhya is the result of a planned action by political organizations and movements in relation to a changing political scenario. This action had the scope of homogenizing a 'national Hinduism' in so much as 'the temple-mosque controversy in Ayodhya has thus become a symbolic focus of Hindu and Muslim identities within the Indian nation-state' (van de Veer 1994: 7-10).

References

Aloysius, G. (1997), *Nationalism Without a Nation,* Oxford, New York: Oxford University Press.

Anand, D., 'The Violence of Security: Hindu Nationalism and the Politics of Representing 'the Muslim' as a Danger', *The Round Table* , vol. 94, no. 379, April 2005, pp. 203-15.

Baber, Z. (2000), 'Religious Nationalism, Violence and the Hindutva Movement in India', *Dialectical Anthropology,* vol. 25, no. 1, pp. 61-76.

Barkawi, T. (2004), 'Peoples, Homelands and Wars? Ethnicity, the Military and Battle among British Imperial Forces in the War Against Japan', *Comparative Studies in Society and Ethnicity,* vol. 46, pp. 134-63.

Barth, F. (1969), *Ethnic Groups and Boundaries,* Boston: Little Brown & Co.

Bhikhu, P. (1994), 'Discourses on National Identity', *Political Studies,* vol. 42, no. 3, pp. 492-504.

Brass, P. (1991), *Ethnicity and Nationalism: Theory and Comparison,* New Delhi, Newbury Park (CA): Sage.

Chakrabarty, B. (2003), *Communal Identity in India: Its Construction and Articulation in the Twentieth Century,* Oxford: Oxford University Press.

Chandra, B. (1984), *Communalism in Modern India,* New Delhi: Vikas.

Cohen, A.P. (1985), *The Symbolic Construction of Community,* London, New York: Routledge.

Collier, P., P. Honohan and K.O. Moene, 'Implications of Ethnic Diversity', *Economic Policy,* vol. 16, no. 32, April 2001, pp. 129-66.

De Vos, G.A. (1975), 'Ethnic Pluralism', in L.R.-R. George De Vos, *Ethnic Identity: Cultural Continuities and Change,* Palo Alto (CA): Mayfield Publishing Co.

Fearon, James D. and D.D. Latin (2000), 'Ordinary Language and External Validity: Specifying Concepts in the Study of Ethnicity', retrieved 22 September 2009, from http://web.ceu.hu/cps/bluebird/eve/state building/fearon-laitin.pdf

———, 'Violence and the Social Construction of Ethnic Identity', *International Organization,* vol. 54, no. 4, Autumn 2000, pp. 845-77.

Fenton, S., 'Beyond Ethnicity: The Global Comparative Analysis of Ethnic Conflict', *International Journal of Comparative Sociology,* vol. 45, nos. 3-4, 2004, pp. 179-94.

Foucault, M. (1990), *The History of Sexuality* (vol. 1), London: Penguin Books.

Gagnon, V.P. (2004), *The Myth of Ethnic War: Serbia and Croatia in the 1990s,* New York: Cornell University Press.

Geertz, C. (1994), 'Primordial Loyalties and Standing Entities: Anthropological Reflections on the Politics of Identity', retrieved in April 2008, from www.colbud.hu

Gilley, B. (2004), 'Against the Concept of Ethnic Conflict', *Third World Quarterly*, vol. 25, no. 6, pp. 1155-66.

Gottschalk, P. (2000), *Beyond Hindu and Muslim: Multiple Identity in Narratives from Village People*, New York: Oxford University Press.

Hale, H.E. (2004). 'Explaining Ethnicity', *Comparative Political Studies*, vol. 37, no. 4, pp. 458-85.

Horowitz, D. (2000), *Ethnic Group in Conflict*, 2nd edn., Berkeley, Los Angeles: University of California Press.

Jaffrelot, C. (1992), 'Le syncrétisme stretégique et la construction de l'idéntité nationaliste hindoue', *Revue française de sciences politiques*, vol. 42, no. 4, pp. 594-617.

Jalal, A. (1998-9), 'Exploding Communalism: The Politics of Muslim Identity in South Asia', in B.A. Sugata (ed.), *Nationalism, Democracy and Development: State and Politics in India*, Delhi: Oxford University Press, pp. 1-121.

Kapur, R. and B. Cossman (1993), 'Communalising Gender/Engendering Community: Women, Legal Discourse and Saffron Agenda', *Economic & Political Weekly*, 24 April, pp. 35-44.

Lukes, S. (1986), *Power*, Oxford: Basil Blackwell.

Manor, J. (1996), '"Ethnicity" and Politics in India', *International Affairs* (*Royal Institute of International Affairs*), vol. 72, no. 3, pp. 459-75.

Noorani, A.G. (2000), *The RSS and the BJP: A Division of Labour*, New Delhi: LeftWord Books.

Oza, R. (2007), 'The Geography of Hindu Right-wing Violence in India', in D. Gregory and A. Pred (eds.), *Violent Geographies: Fear, Terror and Political Violence,* New York, Oxon: Routledge.

Savarkar, V.D. (1923), *Hindutva: Who is a Hindu*, New Delhi: Hindi Sahitya Sadan (5th edn., 2005).

Smith, A.D. (1996), 'Culture, Community and Territory: The Politics of Ethnicity and Nationalism', *International Affairs* (*Royal Institute of International Affairs, 1944-*), vol. 72, no. 3, July, pp. 445-58.

Steve, F. (2000), 'Beyond Ethnicity: The Global Comparative Analysis of Ethnicity Conflict', *International Journal of Comparative Sociology*, vol. 45, nos. 3-4, pp. 179-94.

van de Veer, P. (1994), *Religious Nationalism: Hindus and Muslims in India,* Berkeley, Los Angeles: University of California Press.

Varshney, A. (2002), *Ethnic Conflict and Civic Life: Hindus and Muslims in India,* 2nd edn., New Haven, London: Yale University Press.

——— (2003), 'Nationalism, Ethnic Conflict and Rationality', *Perspectives on Politics,* vol. 1, Issue 1, pp. 85-99, Cambridge: Cambridge University Press.

Wilkinson, S. (2004), *Votes and Violence: Electoral Competition and Ethnic Riots in India,* Cambridge: Cambridge University Press.

8

Emerging Class Formation among the Oppressed Castes and its Political Implications

JAVEED ALAM

A number of my Left colleagues and I have often been worried about the fact that the exploited masses have not been getting mobilized across the division of caste and religion. It has been the belief of the communist parties, right from their inception, that the exploited masses have a natural propensity to unite to end exploitation and oppression. It is not that this has not happened. There were glorious peasant struggles in Telangana and Tebhaga and at many other places; there are many works by leftist scholars describing these. Even in normal times there have been long periods of unity of poor and middle peasants and their united political action with the working classes. Modern Indian political history is full of instances of protracted struggles of the working classes. But of late, especially after the Mandal agitation, there has been a decline in the unity among the exploited peasantry and its reluctance to act in an united action with the working classes. In fact, in large areas of northern India there has been a perceptible decline in the political influence and organizational capability of the communist parties, most perceptibly in eastern UP, Bihar and the Punjab—some of the areas where the Left had a sizeable presence once.[1]

In this essay, I want to examine, first, this assumption for optimism about the propensity of the exploited to unite and, then, go on to look at the condition that has led to the decline of the influence of the Left.

I

The beginning of this optimism is with Marx himself. In the *Communist Manifesto,* Marx had quite unambiguously suggested a pronounced trend towards the homogenization of the proletariat, in the sense that it will be more and more the same in England as in France or anywhere else in Europe or America. The basis for saying so was an inexorable trend where 'machinery obliterates all distinctions of labour'. In another similar remark he asserted that with the development of industry the 'ranks of proletariat are more and more equalised'. This takes two forms. On the one hand, cultural and ethnic differences begin to melt away and, on the other, 'narrow mindedness becomes more and more impossible' and so does 'national one-sidedness'. All this is the basis for the simplification of class antagonism and the direct result of the development of capitalism. But with the rise to supremacy of the working class, all these features noted above will 'vanish still faster'.

The ground on which Marx could base his optimism was on the basis of a condition that was uniformly universal all over Western Europe—the rapid dissolution of pre-modern communities; that is to say, the pre-capitalist past was becoming archival. (Archival is not the loss of the past but the loss of something as a presence with us.) In contrast to this, the pre-modern world is a *living presence* in India. In case of Europe if I want to know how people worked, for example, in the guilds, weaved cloth, made the plough or how they spent their leisure time, however, little, with family and friends, I have to go to some or other archive. That is how E.P. Thompson wrote his epic work *The Making of the Working Class in England.* That is why at some point in the first half of the nineteenth century words like kinship or guild quietly disappeared from the political vocabulary, to be replaced by class and industry; this loss and replacement of such key terms can be, in fact, a substantiation of my claim above. Whereas in India, I do not have to travel even 100 miles to get to know that these ways of working and living are not only alive but also vibrant. And this holds true for much else to do with pre-modern attributes like ritual and kinship and status. In other words, the 'past' with us here is not yet a past. It presses for recognition as a presence. We do not live in tenses as a continuum but simultaneously.

The antagonistic atmosphere we live in today is vastly different from any society 'living with modernity'[2] in the West has ever experienced. The rapid dissolution of pre-modern communities of work and status with the rise of capitalism and the emergence of an individuated, autonomous, self-centred, interest maximizing person also constitutes Western modernity. Note in passing the contradictory attributes that go in as a cluster to define a modern person in the capitalist social formation. Both the desirable and the unwanted characteristics in a personality go hand in hand. With us the past is not, to reiterate, yet a past. Our 'past' is always pushing modernity into its opposite. And the working of democracy actually facilitates the working out of this opposition in unpredictable ways.

Ascendant capitalism achieved the dissolution of the pre-modern communities in a simple but very effective manner. It did so by a process of 'dissociation of the labourer from the means of labour', that is, by depriving the peasant and the artisan of the instruments of production, by the dispossession of the labourer. This is what Marx also calls 'primitive accumulation' in the last chapter of his *Capital.* Hundreds of thousands people were thrown out of their land and hearth to move into towns with bare hands to become the working class or make up the ranks of surplus labour. Cut-off from the roots and wandering hither and thither they become bereft of the community and lost all sense of belonging. Hegel, the great teacher of Marx, called this the 'great exodus'. The early making of the working class was preceded by a process of disembedding people from hitherto communities and the slow re-embedding of the people into the working classes. In other words, there was nothing left to mediate between the individual and the state. Everything, every move of the individual, here in our situation, is mediated by the strong presence of primordial communities who also protect the possession of the instruments of labour by individual households. Grounds for optimism of the growing unity of working people, as noted above, therefore cannot be a natural condition with us.

In the background of this profound difference, I want to examine the condition, in the wake of the Mandal phase, that has led to the massive mobilization of the communities of the oppressed, also referred to as the backward classes, Other Backward Castes (OBC) or Most Backward Castes (MBC), and the Dalits and the peculiarly Indian form of communitarian upsurge. The Mandal agitation and the counter-reactionary upper class vandalism backed by sections of the ruling establishment led to the crystallization of long-term tendencies which were underway within the various backward classes and Dalit communities in India. These developments have also given a further impetus to the already assertive movements among the women. But it is important to note and also emphasize, that for a correct assessment of the democratic potential, these movements of the oppressed communities pay no heed to the oppression of women. In fact, they compel women to subscribe to the social and moral codes of the respective communities, all of which are deeply patriarchical and feudal in outlook. Women are made to pay a heavy price if they choose to dissent or defy. With this disqualification in view, let us look at the socio-political forces and the democratic tendencies at work in our society.

II

The trend, which is thoroughly changing the character of the oppressed castes, is based on the internal differentiation and class formation within these caste communities. Two things were happening within these vulnerable communities. First, there was a long period of capitalist development, especially in agriculture, which was followed by land reforms, after Independence. Many of the OBCs became propertied peasants. The long chain of dependence and bondage was snapped. There has been a slow but widespread expansion of education, employment, etc., among the OBCs. New modern classes were slowly emerging. Among the Dalits, reservations as quotas in education and employment and other meekly implemented affirmative action also led to similar results, though on a smaller scale. What thwarted the collective development of Dalits was the nature of land reforms where land often did not go to the direct tiller. Most of the Dalits remained dispossessed of land and were forced to remain agricultural labourers under conditions of coercive wage determination in work and brutality in the social life.[3]

As a consequence of all this, class and income differentiation have been taking place, however uneven, among these castes-communities and therefore a dispersal of earlier forms of power from their traditional leadership. Earlier such castes organized as *jatis* were, and this is important, internally egalitarian because of the same occupation and skill endowment and therefore similar income and consumption levels. The breakdown of the inviolable links between the ritual status and occupation had far-reaching consequences. It encouraged the movement of people, imperceptible though among the oppressed unlike with the *savarnas* earlier, into different occupations and the acquisition of varied and dissimilar skills. With all these developments, *jatis* started becoming internally inegalitarian; the process though has had a different tempo across the distinct castes, and varying in different ways within the same castes in different areas (distinct in Karnataka as against Bihar, for instance) of the country leading to the formation of modern classes within the caste communities. Differentiation and dispersion of inherited bases of property and power, i.e. the individuation of interests as distinct from individuation of persons, if we go by the earlier global pattern of consequences of capitalist development, also sets in process the dissolution of the 'primordial' communities. Nothing of the sort has happened in India, as noted above, nor seems likely to happen in the near future even with the rapid individuation of interests and persons with the spread of capitalism and the deep penetration of market forces.[4] A *thin* stratum of rich peasants, a *bulky* presence of middle peasantry and a *sizeable* number of poor peasants now define the peasantry from among the OBCs.

Within the class formation noted above, a middle class, drawn largely from the rich and also somewhat from the middle stratum of peasants as well has been in the process of formation and consolidation within these caste-based communities. A further result, paradoxical though, of this has been the impetus given to a contrary process, or rather opposite to dissolution, of unification of these communities. Large conglomerates of what were earlier small and varied sub-castes have emerged all over India. How did this happen is a story that need not detain us here. Suffice it to say that it is in the interest of these newly *emergent* middle classes, as distinct from the *established* ones who belonged overwhelmingly to *savarna* castes, to unify these communities as blocs to compete for power and position in democratic contestations, especially the electoral competitiveness. We will refer to these emergent middle classes from among the oppressed as a *neo-middle class* to distinguish it from the *established* one. These two contrary trends, one, the differentiation and undermining of the inherited forms of constitution of castes and, the other, that of the process of internal unification have had a simultaneous run.

The contradiction inherent in the class formation within the communities and the individuation of interests around these did not fructify. In other words, there was rather a negation of the possibilities of the articulation of class tendencies as political positions. Not that this process does not entail class conflict. Rather, the class conflict could not grow into a class struggle because the process described above has acted as a barrier to the coming together of exploited classes from different communities into a bloc, as a unified class. Instead what happened has been a consolidation of the caste groups on scales larger than ever before. Larger movements of the earlier oppressed groups like the anti-Brahmin movement in Tamil Nadu are breaking up into single caste political formations like those of the Thevars or Vanniyars.

Having talked of the neo-middle classes from among the oppressed communities as central to the process described above, let me by way of digression say a few words about the middle class, as a category of description. Middle class in a literal sense is a middling stratum, internally differentiated into a wide variety both by income and lifestyle. Its strongest aspiration is always to move above. But more significantly, it is not a basic class, like, to take instances, the capitalist and the workers or the landlords or the agricultural labourer. Not that it does not have interests of its own, it has. But through aspirations or commitments its interests tend to get aligned to or assimilated into those of the basic classes; those of bourgeoisie and the proletariat or one or the other form of landed property and the toiling masses.

That is how we get both Com. P. Sundaraiah and C. Rajgopalachari as figures of political importance. It is no different with the OBCs or the Dalits. Under the present conjuncture, the middle classes from these communities have generally tended to so define their interest so as be as close to the ruling establishment as possible, as a matter of fact to become one with the ruling establishment.

III

A two-way contest has now come about in Indian society with deep repercussions for the democratic process. First, the neo-middle classes see in white-collar jobs and professional positions the only route to gaining status and prestige in society. Unlike the established middle classes from the *savarnas*, they have no status or prestige or other social assets to fall back on. So to break through into these, monopolized by the established middle classes, is crucial for their self-esteem. Hence there is the clamour for quotas as a necessary aspect of 'social justice'. Secondly, there is a fierce contest on for a share in the power. Self-representation, share in power corresponding to the numerical strength, allotment of ministerial berths, etc., are all a part of what is now called 'empowerment'. These two terms, 'social justice' and 'empowerment', sketch out the self-definition of the politics of the oppressed communities.[5]

As a result, first, it hastened the process of this unification under the neo-middle classes, which also simultaneously is the dominance of the rich peasant, within these communities. This is so because the neo-middle classes who provide the leadership to these communities are from the thin stratum of the rich peasants as a result of differentiation; it is the same whichever caste-community among the oppressed we look at. And if we read this together with the first trend described above, then the Yadavs or the Kurmis or Thevars or the Kunbis or the Dalits are a caste now only in a nominal sense of the term because all the normative markers of what constitutes the *varna* order are being rejected. The oppressed castes no longer consider themselves as lowly because of *karma* or polluted because of the manual work they do or did or any such ordained attribute such as granting a superior status to the *dvija* castes.

They have become a community in every sense of the term. Communities can be identified when they articulate in a socio-political context. A fixed definition of community can be a source of mis-specification. Community boundaries vary as per the context. For example, in the face of the onslaught of the Hindutva forces, Muslims or Christians may consider themselves and act as communities. But in a situation say of strife between the Shias and Sunnis or Catholics and Protestants these then, constitute themselves into different communities in that context, and not as Muslims or Christians. Such examples can be multiplied in different ways; for example, a village gets constituted into communities in a different way during *melas* (common village festivals on auspicious occasions) than when it is in a feud with a neighbouring village or when the distribution of the produce is involved.

If we have a collectivity in a process of formation without the acceptance of any of the attributes which define the relations between *jatis* as set out in the *varna* ideology then the ascription of caste as its mode of social existence is difficult to sustain. This is more so in the realm of politics in India. Democratic politics is, in any case, subversive of ordained hierarchies even if other things were to remain the same; things have in any case not remained the same because of rapid capitalist developments. The available *varna* terms stick as the *varna* ideology provides a common idiom and an over-arching discursive framework. These vocabularies are not so much for internal references or self-images of oppressed castes any more but much more so for mobilization for power to seek *equality* with those who consider themselves superior because they are 'pure'. But it can no longer define the character of the collective as a caste within the caste system as it earlier used to do. It is the upper castes of *dvijas* who still refer to themselves with pride as Brahmins or Thakurs and make all the efforts to enforce caste disabilities to sustain their social domination as a part of the class rule.

These are the communities made up of the oppressed castes, which now are fighting for equality and recognition *vis-à-vis*, on the one hand, the *dvija* castes, and, on the other, against the privileges of the established middle classes. The battle against these two distinct social categories, higher caste status of the upper castes at the ritual level and their social privilege in the secular sphere, is overlapping as well as simultaneous. The battle is fierce and 'ugly'—ugly because everyone among the oppressed is in a hurry to gain all that in the world which will make the claim to equality enforceable. Because of this hurry, everybody is breaking the queue and the 'rules of the game'. Democratic advance is there but in an *untidy* manner. We therefore must be cautious in judging by our sense of parliamentary decorum or social niceties, as much of the media and drawing room conversation does. There is also a sense of hurry to bury the memory of the past relationships with the *savarnas*, a memory made up of a sense of subordination and humiliation.

All this is closely related to what I have called collective unfreedom (i.e. some kind of an absence of freedom which is forced on a collectivity like one or other *jati* and not against the individual *per se*) and the battle for democracy. Even a minimal move towards freedom in conditions of collective unfreedom as prevailed in India, is also simultaneously a call for 'recognition'. Recognition is, as Hegel would tell us, an ideal reciprocal relation between subjects. A call for recognition is therefore also a call for equality, which ought not to negate my being a different person from another. So being recognized and recognizing the other constitutes me as a subject and gives me a sense of self. It therefore follows that the denial of recognition is detrimental to subjecthood. Hegel here is suggesting that the making of an Identity is a *dialogical process* in society. In taking castes as our concern here, I think, it is important to be clear about the distinction between making of Identity and identity politics; one is a necessary condition for being an autonomous actor, an agent, whereas the other leads to *reification* of caste identifications. Yet it is important also to acknowledge that given the earlier nature of unfreedom, the battle for equality will necessarily take a collective form. If Hegel is right, as I presume him to be, then the denial of recognition to the claims for equality of the lower castes in India by the upper castes goes a long way in perverting the values of democracy in India as well as of dignified social existence.

How does this, question of recognition impact on the processes of differentiation and unification of the oppressed communities which we have been discussing so far and whether and how the class formation and class conflict get effected by this question. It is obvious that the movement from class-in-itself to class-for-itself, is substantially impacted, at one level, by the subjective perceptions of the oppressed. At another level, just to mention, we do not have to pursue this dimension any further, as it is determined by the struggles and organizational preparedness of the oppressed through outside fraternal interventions and by the nature of the democratization of the state and other factors related to the process. Lenin therefore is right in saying that the experience and subjective perception of the exploited is not a sufficient condition for a transition from one to the other. Let us therefore look at the question of recognition a little more concretely.

Analytically speaking, recognition works, in contemporary times, i.e. in the period after de-colonization, in two distinct domains, unlike in the theorization in Hegel. One sphere is the state-constitutional site where there is the formal awarding of status,[6] for example, the abolition of untouchability or the acceptance that the backward castes need to be helped through one or another form of affirmative action, as all being equal citizens are entitled to the removal of inherited social disadvantage. The other arena is the society which is the site of social relationships and interactions where, as Hegel maintained, there ought to be the coexistence of unrestricted equality with one's individuality. In a condition like ours, where inequality and implicit non-recognition is a part of the pre-existing social structure, even constitutional conferment of status (or new definitions of citizenship) does not significantly change the social conditions (even market conditions have not been able to do so), yet the constitutional conferment of status is a pre-condition for recognition because it provides for necessary enabling conditions.[7]

What does this contradiction between the two domains, constitutional citizenship and implicit non-recognition at the level of social relations, mean for those subjected to it? How does it work out in practice? At one level, it is a source of ineradicable tension, pain of rejection, and humiliation, and so on. This is important in the making of the subjectivity of the people belonging to these communities. Affirmation at one level of the claim to be a person and citizen and denial at another, at the same time, is both a source of assertion and resistance on the part of the oppressed, and it is also a source of the efforts of the dominant to negate these conditions through subtle modes of exclusion and of retaliation from those who hold power and status in the social order. Individuals and groups may resist denial and exclusion, as they surely do, but many more, are hit at when the retaliation comes. It is the community *per se* which is targeted. It is important to note here in passing that due to the sustained democratic struggles, retaliations are becoming random and ad hoc in the recent period from being systemic as well as systematic as these used to be earlier.

Even so, the retaliations are widespread across the country and often, when directed against the Dalits, brutal and gruesome. In putting the above points together, the nature of making of the subjectivity of the oppressed and the manner of the targeting of the entire communities, we discern an important repercussion of the process of differentiation taking place within these communities. Instead of bringing the exploited and poor strata of the different communities together and forging class unity among them, we see the contrary process of unification, talked of earlier, being reinforced. So here we see the subjective counterpart of the objective process discussed earlier.

Hence we see the oppressed classes remaining within their respective communities and the ascendance of the non-class processes within the domain of ideology of caste and the discursive terms inherited from the *varna* system. The question still remains: Is the form that the politics of the oppressed communities taken, casteism? I will come to this later, in the next section.

I have therefore called the struggle of the oppressed castes, elsewhere in my writings, a struggle for bourgeois equality, no pejorative sense is implied here in the use of the word 'bourgeois'. One can as well call it juristic as against substantive equality, following the use of the terms Marx made in some of his early writings like, for instance, in *The Jewish Question*. Let us look at the very content of the politics of the oppressed for substantiation. There is hardly any worked out economic agenda in their call for 'social justice' as is always the case with the proletarian politics. This politics is not fighting for substantive equality, even Mayawati does not ask for land reforms.

She wants Dalits to have power in the same way as the upper castes always exercised it over others. Whether or not it is a democratic advance is not the central issue. But surely this represents a major shift in the terrain of democracy in India. All this has been a source of new kinds of commitments to the democratic processes, without necessarily a commitment to democratic values or norms, in Indian politics and has given rise to a process of reconsolidation of democracy in India, a uniquely Indian democratic adventure. In passing, to press the point, it would be a rather unique intellectual exercise if someone were to compare this with what Alexis de Tocqueville described for America. The battle for bourgeois equality in India is not being fought, as was the case in the West, between unequal individuals; the serf was individually obligated to the lord and not as part of any primordial group. It is being fought much rather between and by the vulnerable communities which were collectively unfree and found themselves in the realm of juristic freedom and competitive politics all of a sudden, around the time of Independence. They also found their chances thwarted by the established middle class, the *privilegensia*, to coin a neologism, composed of upper castes with English education and Western lifestyles hegemonizing everything from the Indian Administrative Service to clerical jobs.

In passing it is important to realize that there will always be a heavy dose of communitarian angle to all struggles in India because, outside of the working class, all collective assertions will be conditioned by the boundaries, even if somewhat vague and shifting, which earlier defined collective unfreedom. Those from within the communities who snap or seek to even loosen community links will draw a lot of flak from within their communities. Therefore the citizen, while being empowered, taking him as a right bearing person yet embedded in the community, will also feel besieged by community pressures; he is forced not to be different and distinct. This is becoming a source of great tension in India. Ordinary people are becoming individuated persons to different degrees in India—that is, becoming different from the communities within which they are embedded. But the communities do not allow them to assert individualness. Communities demand uncritical affirmation of allegiance from the individual persons, thus thwarting individual democratic aspirations. They are being besieged in this sense.

IV

Let me now terminate one side of my argument. Among the oppressed the appeal to caste is for unification of similar *jatis* into larger collectives and political mobilization for power so as to subvert the very relations of the *varna* order. Caste appeal here therefore is far from being *pure casteism*, as is often alleged.[8] The allegation is based on an over-valuation of surface features and an utter disregard to the inner logic of the deeper processes in Indian politics conditioned by the very specificity of Indian capitalism, retarded in its character.[9] By the way, it is futile for us on the Left to expect a replay of the patterns of development in the wake of capitalist development in the West where communities of primordial bonds were, again as seen earlier, slowly dissolved to be replaced by one supreme primordial bond, the nation, itself polarized into antagonistic classes. In the way that the capitalism in the Third World is incapable of actualizing bourgeois democratic aspiration, it is by a similar logic (of infirmity internal to it) not going to dissolve the pre-modern communities. This infirmity of capitalism has in fact been reinforced both by the policies of colonial regime in fostering and using pre-capitalist social structure and later by the post-Independence ruling establishment making use of feudal vestiges for narrow political gains. The primordial bonds are going to be with us as potent political forces for a very long time to come. Therefore tactical ways appropriate to the situation have to be worked out by the Left forces, for radical advance. One part of the problem is to weaken the *varna* ideological mould which has become the discursive basis of politics while taking forward the democratic aspirations of the oppressed castes which can be part of our charter.

This is not to deny the existence of casteism in Indian politics. I am asking for a more nuanced delineation of what is happening in Indian politics. All I am saying is that the mere assertion and mobilization even when caste vocabulary is used, does not make it into pure casteism; the qualifying term 'pure' is not unimportant.

The question then is: where and how does casteism come into Indian politics. I now want to look at the other side of the coin.

What makes this battle further murky is the second process let loose by the post-Mandal struggles within the realm of social equations. There has been a steady decomposition of the consciousness of the established middle classes into articulated caste interests of Brahmins or Thakurs and so on. The traditionally hegemonic middle class always imagined itself as based on accomplishment, not untrue, but also believed that it had outgrown caste as the basis of its social being. It can now be seen that this belief of being free from caste prejudices was misplaced. What these middle classes, or the ruling establishment that came to power after Independence, missed was the strong presence of national consciousness forged during the freedom struggle. All this together kept the caste solidarity in a muted form. With the passing of time the memories and inheritances of the freedom movement receded. The Mandal agitation shattered the fragile pan-Indian consciousness of the established middle classes. The self-perceived transcendence from caste consciousness, as can now be seen as illusory, has rapidly collapsed in the last decade and more into a heap where they still want to be on the top of the heap. It has taken the form of different spheres of varying upper caste consciousness, separate, but all in close affinity, one to the other. The Brahmin and the Baniya are therefore in a close embrace within the Hindutva fold.

It is easy to understand this process if we remind ourselves that the established middle class was overwhelmingly drawn from its inception in the colonial times from the propertied upper castes. It therefore inherited, in the process of becoming, property, prestige, and power from its prior status. Its hegemony because of the head start in economy, bureaucracy, and other institutions of public life did not make it feel the need to think in terms of caste but could consciously and by habit talk of itself as having transcended the caste barriers. It is this consciousness that has decomposed.

Now as various upper castes, they seek to preserve their privilege by any means but relying mainly on modern discursive jargon. Merit and efficiency is important in any modern society that is why affirmative actions are of such crucial importance for the socially disadvantaged.

But if these same qualities are abstracted from larger considerations of social welfare and equity then this leads to deification and deification can be a disguised mode of defence of vested interest. All this itself is an aspect of the making of caste identity. Note also the reverse direction of changes among the upper caste based established middle classes; from repudiation of caste to being self-referentially caste conscious, note the refrain—there are poor among us the Brahmins. Yes, there are poor among the Brahmins, no doubt. But the well off Brahmin pleading for his poor brethren, does not ask if he is also socially excluded, kicked around if she tries to enter the temple or draw water from the common village well. To say that there are poor among the Brahmin is a factual statement but not to ask if the other conditions, as noted above, prevail for the Brahmin in demanding equality with Dalits or backward castes in affirmative action, the spokesperson for the Brahmin poor is being deeply inauthentic. And, here is the faultline, if one may say so, in the decomposed consciousness of the privilegensia. But what is also important is the way the identities of the vulnerable communities get affected by this adamant behaviour of the upper castes. Here is another reason why the oppressed castes politically band together as castes to defend themselves for their right to be equal. Refusals and denials of the claims of the others by the upper castes and the identification with Hindutva has also brought in the Muslim community on the side of OBCs or Dalits in the battle for equality, depending on the class location of the Muslim community. Muslim masses are similar to the backward castes or the Dalits in terms of occupations and work and leisure, and therefore move towards, in terms of political alignments towards the political formations of backward castes or Dalits.

V

The developments I have described above are deeply conditioned by a historically grounded material force. Let us ask: what was the nature of bondage of the 'direct producer' in the Indian social formation in the pre-colonial times? And, by asking the question about the nature of bondage I am shifting the terms from an earlier debate, whether there was slavery in India. That debate yielded little. After much heat and little light, it quietly died out. But the question of the nature of bondage of the direct producer remains important. This is important because what we today call the Dalit or the OBC or the MBC were the producing classes in India, either in agriculture or in secondary manufacture through household craft production or by working in the guilds. In raising the problem of the direct producer in relation to the oppressed castes I want to point to the fact that these *jatis* were a part of the mode of production in pre-colonial times. Today these *jatis* may no longer be part of the mode of production even if individuals from these *jatis* continue to be so in the remnants of the pre-capitalist mode of production surviving in varied forms in different parts of India. Yet dialectic is involved here. Today the pre-capitalist mode of production does not exist whatever be the nature of the surviving remnants. Yet the disabilities of the social relations entailed within that mode of production survive in various forms including untouchability and physical brutality if one were to resist its enforcement.

All these sections of society, the backward castes and Dalits, were made up of dependent *jatis*—whether as peasants or artisans upon the superior (clean!) castes. What is important to note is the fact that the dependence was of *collectivities* and not just of the *individuals*. This will have long-term implications for the forms of struggles that later emerge. In other words, the direct producers, like elsewhere in feudalism, were unfree. But the nature of 'unfreedom' of the producer in India was of a collective kind unlike the individual unfreedom of the European serf or earlier of the Greek or Roman slave. Not only this but the difference was not just of unequal status but manual work was morally and spiritually downgraded. Further, manual work was morally and hierarchically treated as unclean. The more unclean the work, the greater the degradation of human beings and greater the emasculation of the body because of lower entitlement to food and therefore greater the unfreedom. Unlike slavery which is uniform to the slave, the unfreedom of the direct producer was hierarchically graded, more and less between the producers. India in this is unique, clearly in a deformed way.

Once the scriptural or juristic or structural aspects of this bondage began to crack, as has been happening in India over a long period of time first with the beginning of capitalism and then with the abolition of caste discrimination by the Constitution and in between the various struggles the oppressed have waged, it should therefore follow that the battle for freedom and dignity too has to be of a collective nature. And given that the producer was considered degraded as a human being, the urge for dignity and self-respect tend to gain ascendance over questions of economic relief. But it needs to be noted that dignity is not just a symbolic good. To have dignity one needs education and job and income and other entitlements to be able to present oneself in the public sphere with confidence and self-esteem. And the oppressed castes are fighting for these on a day-to-day basis. Yet the symbolic aspect of dignity remains equally important; we can here see the pride they take in the erection of a large number of Ambedkar statues or the sense of vicarious pleasure in the power, including that of wealth, displayed by Mayawati, former chief minister of Uttar Pradesh.

All this together is, I would like to suggest, the material foundation of the politics of the oppressed 'social classes', to use the language of the Indian Constitution. Both of these—dignity and self-respect—in counterposition to economic emancipation, are, I strongly believe and tried to demonstrate deeply materially grounded. If so, so should be the politics of these oppressed communities. Therefore, to recognise this is to reaffirm Marxism from another new angle.

Acknowledgements

I am deeply indebted to Comrade B.V. Raghavalu, Kumaresh Chakravarty and Aniket Alam for giving me their long critical comments which enriched my arguments. The responsibility for various shortcomings remains mine.

Notes

1. Let us look at a recent instance as evidence. In the 2007 Assembly election in U.P. the communist parties fared as follows:
   CPI contested 21 seats and forfeited deposits in all the 21 seats;
   CPI(M) contested 14 seats and forfeited deposit in 11 seats, won on none of the seats;
   CPI(ML) contested 33 seats and forfeited deposit on all the 33 seats.

2. From the title of my book *India: Living with Modernity*, New Delhi: Oxford University Press, 1999 where many of these things are discussed.
3. Some of this has been discussed in my book, *Who Wants Democracy*? New Delhi: Orient Longman, 2004.
4. As a result of capitalist penetration, the 'subsistence farmer' has disappeared from Indian agriculture. What made them viable was their ability to produce just enough for family needs and keep most of the produce for themselves. Now they cannot do so. They are forced to sell it in the market, often as distress sale. The hedges that protected them from the onslaught of market forces are no longer there. I suspect that most of the suicides are from this stratum.
5. As a digression, let us note in passing: Talking of the strategy and limits of development in India especially within the agrarian sphere a question in passing needs to be raised here. Imagine a situation of land going to the tillers as well, many of whom were agricultural labourers or insecure tenants. As the land reforms were conceived and implemented most of the land got passed on to the occupancy tenants belonging mostly to the intermediate and backward castes. If it had also gone to other tillers including Dalits, what could have been the consequences? It is obvious that the articulation of interests, the constitution of communities and contestations between and within them, and the formation of classes within these castes and communities would all have been so different. The consolidation of the type that took place and the consequent ascendance of caste based communities like Jats, Yadavs, Kurmis, Marathas, Thevars, etc., is inconceivable without the way land reforms got carried out. This question cannot be pursued here. But it is important to raise it as a counterfactual. It provides a link to the relations of production within the agrarian economy and its influence on the question of democracy in India—both its trajectory and inner dynamics. It is just for this reason that I want to add here that what has been said so far and what will be said henceforth about Indian democracy is based on this background of understanding. There is nothing inexorable about the course of development of Indian democracy being analysed here. It has been conditioned, quite deeply, by the peculiarity of the bourgeois condition confronting Indian society. Any pre-existing social formation has many possible ways of developing in terms of the transformational strategies adopted and the nature of development of the popular movements.
6. The constitutional grant of status, for example of equality, is a mere declaration, a *formal* condition. While important and enabling, it may not much alter conditions at the social level. As against this recognition

is an affirmation by each of us to consider the other as equal and therefore deserving of respect and dignity. It is a *reciprocal* stipulation and therefore higher in the normative order.

7. In much of the discussion on recognition (in the previous three paragraphs) where I invoke Hegel so often is drawn from his discussion of '. . . Lordship and Bondage'. See his *Phenomenology of Spirit*, section on 'Self Consciousness', IV.A.
8. See an earlier article, Javeed Alam, 'Is Caste Appeal Casteism? Oppressed Castes in Politics', in *Economic & Political Weekly*, 27 March 1999.
9. I am using the term *retarded* with a specific purpose to characterize Indian capitalism. It is to distinguish it from a uniform condition of under-development as was the case during the colonial period. It is to specify that there may well exist the very highly developed sectors like IT or certain spheres in manufacturing or in the services but these co-exist with the most underdeveloped conditions of production or services like in tribal areas; the posh automobile with the bullock cart on the same roads; best of the scientific research like in CCMB or AIIMS together with the worst of science teaching in a government school; and so on. The idea is to point out that it fails to revolutionize the entire society and leave large parts of populations in conditions of wretched backwardness. It is like a body with a strong torso but weak limbs, they cannot carry the body. India is marked by this feature more than many other societies outside the Western world.

9

Renewed Ethno-Nationalist Insurgency in Balochistan, Pakistan

The Militarized State and Continuing Economic Deprivation

ADEEL KHAN[1]

Since December 2005, Pakistan's army has once again been fighting its own people in the country's most impoverished, marginalized, and violated province, Balochistan. The military government claimed that the operation was launched against militant nationalists who attacked government personnel, buildings, and installations, but its attacks have been indiscriminate and resulted in loss of life and property of innocent people. Militant nationalists maintain that the operation is the Punjabi-dominated army's attempt to strengthen its control over Balochistan's natural resources, which are already being exploited by the central government.

This is the fifth time the Pakistan army has launched an armed operation in Balochistan during the past six decades. One day after the creation of Pakistan on 14 August 1947, the Khan of Kalat (the largest and most prosperous princely state in Balochistan) declared independence, offering Pakistan special relations in the areas of defense, foreign affairs, and communications.[2] Rejecting the offer, Pakistan launched its first military operation in April 1948 to annex Kalat.

In 1958 another operation was launched to quell Balochistan's resentment against the One Unit Scheme.[3] In 1962, the Pakistan army attacked Balochistan to fight against left-wing nationalists. The most fierce and brutal army attack started in 1973 and continued uptil 1977. Some 80,000 Pakistani troops, helped by combat helicopters and the Pakistan Air Force, fought against 55,000 poorly armed Baloch guerrillas.[4] The fifth operation started in December 2005 and is still going on.

This article argues that the violent conflict in Balochistan is unlikely to permanently subside, in the absence of a comprehensive change in the government's approach and policies toward the province. In particular, the militarized Pakistani central state continues to view Balochistan as a source of natural resources, pursuing a largely military solution to lingering socio-economic and political problems. The article begins by providing the socio-economic and political background to the conflict. The next section discusses the evolution of demands for regional autonomy for Balochistan. Section three analyses the emergence of the most recent wave of insurgency, focusing on the Gwadar Port issue and the role of Pakistan's military. The fourth section contextualizes the re-emergence of the Baloch conflict by focusing on its regional and global dimensions. The article then compares and contrasts the new wave of insurgency to previous waves, before discussing possible solutions.

Socio-economic and Political Background

Balochistan is ethnically and linguistically Pakistan's most diverse province. The Baloch are the largest ethnic group in the province but do not constitute a majority. Their number is closely followed by the Pukhtuns (also known as the Pushtuns). The third largest ethnic group is the Brahuis, followed by a substantial number of Sindhis and Punjabis. Interestingly, the majority of Baloch live outside Balochistan, mostly in Sindh and Punjab Provinces.

As the driest province of Pakistan, with severe weather and scarcity of fertile land, Balochistan has little irrigation and farming; therefore the social mode of the people has predominantly been nomadic pastoralism. It was only around some patches of settled areas that tribal life was organized. The livelihood of the people has been dependent on myriad economic activities such as growing crops on small pieces of land, tending pasture land, breeding cattle, sheep, and goats, and trade and work in mines. The social organization of the province continues to be based on tribalism.[5]

Politically, Balochistan has been a fragmented society: the presence of huge deserts, punctuated by settlements, did not facilitate the establishment of a centralized authority. Although the sixth Khan of Kalat, Nasir Khan, in the eighteenth century did succeed in organizing the major Baloch tribes under a military and administrative system, it did not survive his death.[6] Thus, power and control continued to be based on the internal organization of local tribes.

When the British annexed Balochistan in 1884, their only interest in the region was creating a buffer zone between their Indian colony and the Russian empire, and establishing a safe passage from Sindh to Afghanistan through Balochistan. The Khan of Kalat guaranteed that safety but could not control the anti-British tribes attacking the British army. The British termed these attacks a breach of treaty, and when the Khan refused to surrender, he was killed by the British army and his state dismembered. The British divided Balochistan by handing over the western part to Iran and the northern part to Afghanistan. Part of the region became British Balochistan and the rest was divided into the state of Kalat and three puppet principalities.[7]

In British Balochistan, indirect rule was imposed in which the political agent of the governor-general was the head of administration. The tribal chiefs were responsible for managing their own affairs, except on issues of strategic importance, for which they were required to consult the political agent. As the British interest in the region was of strategic military importance only, little changed in the economic and social structure. By the end of the nineteenth century, however, as roads, railway lines, post offices, rest houses, and a cantonment were built for British troops, the neglected economic sector could not remain unaffected. At the same time, when railway lines boosted coal mining, a market economy appeared that led to migrations from peripheral areas to economically developed ones.

The changes that were solely aimed at establishing strategic routes for supplying British troops naturally did not improve the lot of the Baloch people, leading instead to economic deterioration. The astronomical increase in taxation that was collected in kind (wheat) for the British troops led to the landlessness of many peasants.[8] This resulted in the emergence of a large number of tenants and landless labourers. To meet the needs of the British garrison, a new mercantile class was imported from Punjab and Sindh. Thus, these settlers monopolized whatever modern economic relations developed in Balochistan. This triggered nationalist sentiments among the locals. Before the Independence and Partition of India, Baloch nationalists demanded their own state, whereas after the creation of Pakistan, they first refused to be part of the new state. Later, when the Pakistan army forcibly annexed the region, the nationalists started a struggle for regional autonomy.

According to the 1998 census (the most recent one to date), Balochistan has an area of 347,190 sq. km, and its population is 6.5 million, making it the largest province of Pakistan but with the smallest number of people.[9] It has the highest unemployment rate, 33.48 per cent, compared to 19.1 per cent for Punjab and 19.68 per cent for Pakistan overall.[10] Balochistan's literacy rate is 26.6 per cent as against the national average of 47 per cent; only 20 per cent of the people have reliable access to drinking water as compared to 86 per cent of Pakistan; and 47 per cent of the population lives below the poverty line.[11]

Although the government has launched mega-development projects, like the Gwadar Port, there is no 'road map for the social development of a region whose social indicators are the most challenging in South Asia'.[12] There is short or no supply of infrastructure such as roads, communications, and water supply. Balochistan's remote areas continue to present a medieval picture with 'donkey fans' (handheld fans made of cane) used on hot summer nights and long distances covered on camels. Barely 20 per cent of the population has access to electricity. In the absence of sanitation and health care facilities, the incidence rate per 1,00,000 population for tuberculosis is 177 and for malaria 6.56, respectively, which is 30 times the average for the country. The province also has the highest child mortality rate.[13]

Yet, Balochistan, Pakistan's poorest province, is the richest in such natural resources as natural gas, copper, uranium, gold, coal, silver, platinum, as well as potential oil reserves. It provides 36 per cent of Pakistan's total gas production. Gas was discovered at Sui in the Dera Bugti region in 1952. It was piped to Punjab, Sindh, and the North West Frontier Province (NWFP) and became a major revenue earner for the federal government. But gas was made available to Balochistan's own capital, Quetta, only in the 1980s and even today, piped gas is available to a mere four out of 28 districts.[14] Not surprisingly, only 17 per cent of the total gas is consumed by Balochistan and 83 per cent by the rest of the country.

However, the price of gas is much lower than in other provinces. For instance, Balochistan gets $0.29 per thousand cubic feet, whereas Sindh gets $1.65 and Punjab $2.35,[15] but receives a mere 12.4 per cent royalty for supplying gas. The Saindak project for copper exploration has been given to China, which gets 50 per cent of the profit. Of the remainder, 48 per cent goes to the central government and only 2 per cent to Balochistan.[16]

Provincial Autonomy

The major demand of the Baloch nationalists has always been provincial autonomy and local control over their resources. This has been denied to them since the creation of Pakistan. As mentioned above, during British rule Balochistan was a political agency, ruled indirectly by the political agent of the governor-general. After Partition, however, the new state managers centralized the state system.

The founder and first governor-general of Pakistan, Mohammed Ali Jinnah, constituted an advisory council for Balochistan to be run directly by him. In 1955, with the imposition of the One Unit Scheme, any territorial identity Balochistan had was eliminated.[17] In 1958 and the early 1960s when the nationalists were protesting against One Unit and asking for provincial autonomy, the government launched military operations against them. It took Pakistan 23 years to grant Balochistan provincial status in 1970.

The same year, when national and provincial elections were held, the National Awami (People's) Party (NAP) won the largest block of seats in both the NWFP and Balochistan and formed governments there in alliance with a religious party, Jamiat-e-Ulema-e-Islam

(Party of Scholars of Islam). Because the region had been ruled by the central government since Pakistan annexed Kalat in 1948, Punjabis and other non-Baloch dominated the administration. The literacy rate was extremely low, and the central government exploited local resources, which led to overall impoverishment.

Figures collected by the economist Omer Noman for the 1970s are quite staggering: Balochistan's per capita monthly income was $54, only 60 per cent of the Punjab's level. Pakistan's literacy rate was 18 per cent, whereas Balochistan's was 6 per cent. Eighty per cent of Pakistan's gas production was from Balochistan, which saved an estimated $275 million in foreign exchange, but royalties for the local government were only $1.2 million. Out of 830 higher civil service personnel in Pakistan, only 181 were Baloch. In 1972, out of 20 provincial department heads only one was Baloch.[18]

When the NAP government came to power in Balochistan in 1972 it started trying to rectify these imbalances. But the central government of Pakistan's first elected prime minister, Zulfikar Ali Bhutto, was not in favour of such reforms, believing they would go against the interests of the dominant ethnic groups, Punjabis, and other non-Baloch who controlled business and Balochistan's minimal industrial sector. Finally, the clash of interests created so much bitterness between the central and provincial governments that Bhutto, in alliance with the military and civil bureaucracy, which is dominated by Punjabis and Mohajirs (north Indian Muslim immigrants), concocted a case of conspiracy against the NAP government.

In early 1973, in a well-orchestrated operation, Pakistani authorities entered the Iraqi Embassy in Islamabad and discovered a cache of 300 Soviet submachine guns and 48,000 rounds of ammunition. The government alleged that the weapons were destined for Balochistan, some 1,300 km south of the capital, although according to Hussain Haqqani, the 'U.S. diplomats and Pakistani intelligence officials knew that the Iraqi arms were meant for Baloch rebels in the *Iranian* part of Balochistan—Iraq's response to Iran's support for Kurdish rebels in Iraq'[19] (emphasis mine).

The elected NAP government was dismissed, and governor's rule was imposed. Hence, the Balochs were not even allowed a year to run their own affairs.

The Baloch response to the action was to launch an armed struggle that soon turned into a bloody war with the powerful Pakistan military. The Bhutto government called out some 80,000 troops, with air cover from the Pakistan Air Force. Iran's government provided 30 Cobra helicopters with their own pilots to fight 55,000 Baloch guerrillas.[20] The conflict cost the lives of an estimated 3,300 army troops, 5,300 guerrillas, and thousands of civilians.[21]

The Bhutto government was toppled by the military in July 1977. The chief of army staff and leader of the coup, General Zia ul-Haq, declared a ceasefire, called back the troops, and as a gesture of goodwill released NAP leaders and workers from prison. Nonetheless, most of the major Baloch leaders, with their secular politics and contempt for military rule, saw Zia as a religious-minded military dictator and could not accept his rule. They therefore went into exile and returned to Pakistan only after Zia's death in 1988.

For more than two decades, Balochistan was relatively calm; the nationalists realized they could not win a war against Pakistan's powerful army. But the bitter memories of the 1970 war lingered in their minds, for the army had indiscriminately bombarded civilians, and thousands of families lost almost everything they had.[22] During Zia's rule, nationalists were less restive because the government had launched some development schemes—construction of roads and small dams and the expansion of power transmission and grid stations, which boosted agriculture. Quetta received piped gas from Sui for the first time since the discovery of it four decades earlier. Also, starting with Zia's party less elections in 1985 and continuing with several elections from 1988-99, there was renewed political activity in which Baloch nationalists participated fully. Indeed, Attaullah Mengal, the NAP chief minister whose government had been dismissed by Bhutto in the 1970s, was indirectly involved in this political process, and Mengal's son, Akhtar Mengal, became chief minister of Balochistan in 1997.

The New Insurgency

In 1999 that political process came to an end when a coup led by General Pervez Musharraf toppled the elected government of Prime Minister Nawaz Sharif. The Baloch always feel more alienated when there is army rule because in the Punjabi-dominated army they have almost no representation. On the other hand, Musharraf further infuriated the nationalists by announcing mega-development projects in Balochistan, including exploration of natural resources and the construction of the Gwadar Port and two army cantonments, with hardly any representation of or benefits for the Baloch.

The Gwadar Port Issue

The main trigger for the new wave of nationalist militancy was the Pakistan central government's announcement in 2001 that it would build a port—with Chinese participation—at Gwadar on the south-west coast of Balochistan. The port is one of the mega-projects with no local participation. When President Musharraf signed the project agreement with Chinese Vice-Premier Wu Bangguo on 24 March 2002, no representative of the provincial government was present.[23]

Work on the project, solely run by the federal government, started that month, with China paying $198 million of the total construction cost of $248 million and providing 450 engineers and workers.[24] The Gwadar Port is designed as a 'regional hub for transit and transhipment of goods for Afghanistan, Central Asia, and the Middle East', and its city is designed to replicate Dubai.[25] This is huge transformation for a poor and isolated fishing town. Although the locals and Baloch nationalists welcomed the initial decision by the elected Nawaz government in 1992, there is now increasing suspicion about the real intentions of the central government and Pakistan army. Without local participation, residents have started viewing the project as the central government's plan to colonize them. And there are good reasons for that perception:

> Some observers share the view that the Gwadar project is one of the biggest land boondoggles in Pakistan's history. . . . [T]he local people owned the land through generations but lacked documents of ownership. The elite

have bribed revenue clerks to register Gwadar land in their names; the land was then resold at rock-bottom prices to developers from Karachi, Lahore, and other major cities . . . illegally allotted to civilian and military bureaucrats living elsewhere. . . . [T]he poor and uneducated Baluch [i.e. Baloch] population had been shut out. . . . Gwadar became a lightning rod for Baluch hatred of Punjabi-ruled Pakistan.[26]

Though Pakistan's army has been notorious for land grabbing in other parts of the country, especially Sindh, in Gwadar's case the army's tactics of treating the land as a no-man's land seem to have broken its own record. Baloch nationalists believe:

The Pakistani army is the biggest land grabber. . . . It is giving away the coast of Baluchistan [Balochistan] for peanuts, to the Punjabis. . . . In Gwadar, the army is operating as a mafia, falsifying land records. They say we don't have papers to prove our ownership of the land, though we've been there for centuries.[27]

The livelihood of the people of Gwadar for years has depended on the fishing industry. But a key part of the city was allocated for construction of the port. Since this started in 2002, there has been no improvement in the living standard of the local people. Indeed, a parallel town is being built close to the port to distinguish new settlements from the old town.[28] A five-star hotel has been built on top of the hill, overlooking the port and slum city of Gwadar, which provides food and accommodation to foreign workers and well-to-do tourists from Karachi. The port, hotel, and surrounding area allocated for a naval base, an elite housing enclave, and a high-class coastal resort are protected by paramilitary checkpoints. There is no access for ordinary local people.

As far as the old Gwadar city is concerned, it still lacks basic amenities in sectors such as health, education, and sanitation. There is a hospital, but it has no modern facilities. There is one intermediate college, which has two shifts, morning and evening, one for boys, one for girls. There is no institution for technical education. Garbage dumps are spread all over the town. Since the construction of the port, there has been a rapid increase in the population as people from surrounding areas moved in seeking jobs and better living standards;

but there has been no increase in resources allocated for them.[29] As a high city official said in an interview with the author:

Gwadar used to be a poor but peaceful town with no class differences. With the development of the port and new township, however, that is changing. The gap between the locals and non-locals is in fact the gap between the poor and the rich. It's a gap between development and the locals. The development should have been for us and then others could come and have a share. But unfortunately that is not the case. With the building of Gwadar Port, the locals, naturally, hoped that it would bring prosperity to them. But what we see today is quite disappointing. Gwadar land has been allocated to the personnel of military and civil bureaucracy. As if that was not enough, now people of the old Gwadar town are threatened [with having] to leave their ancestral land and move elsewhere.[30]

In a separate interview with the author, Hussain Ashraf, a two-time minister in the Balochistan cabinet, said:

The central government claims that Baloch *sardars* (tribal chiefs) are anti-development. It's laughable for Gwadar because we do not have any *sardars*. We are not tribal people. We are fishermen. The question is: what do they mean by development? Building cantonments and naval bases? That's not development. That's colonization. For the last 55 years we were not allowed to benefit from our resources. Sui gas goes to the rest of Pakistan but we do not have it. Frankly, they want to eliminate us. We did not see a better future yesterday. We do not see a better future today. The only future that we can see is that Gwadar town will become (the) Lyari of the new Gwadar town.[31] We are the Kurds of Pakistan.[32]

It is estimated that the development schemes and projects in Gwadar announced so far will require at least 1 million workers. Gwadar's population is only 60,000, with little education and skills. That means outsiders will be invited to come and work on the projects. Already 'almost all the construction contracts (have been) awarded to non-Baloch, mainly Punjabi, firms. . . . Of the 600 personnel that worked on the first phase of construction, only 100 were Baloch, and they were mainly day-laborers.'[33] This is a nightmare scenario for Baloch nationalists who believe the influx of outsiders will eventually outnumber the Baloch population.

Role of the Military

A report by the ICG in 2006 placed the responsibility for the worsening conflict in Balochistan squarely on the Musharraf government and the military command. The report noted that 'tensions between the government and its Baloch opposition have grown because of Islamabad's heavy-handed armed response to Baloch militancy and its refusal to negotiate demands for political and economic autonomy'.[34] The Baloch nationalists as well as liberal and independent circles in Pakistan tend to agree with this line of argument.

The Pakistan military, however, does not seem to agree. As pointed out earlier, the Pakistan army has always been more inclined to find military solutions to political and administrative issues. The attitude of the Musharraf regime toward the Balochistan problem may well have been the worst in Pakistan's history. Soon after coming to power, Musharraf started talking about the construction of the Gwadar Port and two cantonments. When Baloch nationalists expressed their resentment, the president's argument was not different from that of his predecessors, including President Ayub Khan and Prime Minister Bhutto, but his tone was widely perceived as stubborn and aggressive. Musharraf's point was that tribal chiefs were anti-development because they feared losing control over their people. Later amending his stance, he insisted that only three out of 78 tribal chiefs, namely, Nawab Akbar Bugti, Nawab Khair Bux Marri, and Sardar Ataullah Mengal, were 'troublemakers'.[35] Musharraf, on local private television channels, warned Baloch militants that it was not the 1970s and that if they did not get in line, 'they will be struck with weapons—they will not know what happened to them'.[36]

The Baloch nationalists largely laughed off this attitude, apparently agreeing that it was not the 1970s, when they were neither properly organized nor adequately armed. How a simmering insurgency of over two decades with no open armed conflict was turned into a bloody armed conflict by the Musharraf regime becomes clear with a look at the HRCP report. This chronicled the major events after Musharraf took over power on 12 October 1999.

In January 2000, unknown assailants assassinated a judge of the Balochistan High Court. The central government responded by arresting an octogenarian nationalist leader, Nawab Khair Bux Marri, and keeping him in solitary confinement for 18 months. Soon after the arrest, the Baloch Liberation Army (BLA) emerged. Although it has largely cloaked its identity, the organization claimed responsibility for a number of bomb blasts, acts of sabotage, and rocket attacks on government installations.

In June 2002, army troops were deployed in the gas-rich region of Dera Bugti to besiege and blockade the town. Nawab Akbar Bugti, chief of the Bugti tribe, and his tribesmen were given a deadline to surrender. Bugti and others were accused of providing protection to criminals and terrorists responsible for rocket attacks on gas installations in Sui. Incidents of violence increased steadily with the pace of construction in Gwadar, the expansion of cantonments, and the acquisition of land for cantonments and other military enterprises.

In January 2005, the rape of a female doctor, Shazia Khalid, working at the Sui Hospital complex in Dera Bugti was reported in the press. Bugti accused an army officer; the government tried to cover up the incident. The officer was allowed to give a lengthy statement on state-owned Pakistan Television, presenting his side of the story; the president publicly vouched for the officer's innocence.

In February 2005, paramilitary forces raided locations at New-Kahan, a Marri tribe area in Kohlu district. Local people, including women and children, were allegedly roughed up, and a Pakistani flag was hoisted on the guesthouse of the *sardar*, a gesture that it had been conquered. In March 2005, tensions were high when patrols of the Frontier Constabulary (FC) and armed Bugti tribesmen came face to face, leading to harsh words. An exchange of fire with rocket launchers followed. According to credible reports, eight paramilitary personnel died while 62 local people were killed in the attacks by security forces. On 14 December eight rockets were fired at a paramilitary base on the outskirts of Kohlu city as President Musharraf visited it. On 15 December, rockets were fired at a helicopter carrying the inspector-general and deputy inspector-general of FC in Kohlu, injuring both.[37]

The HRCP report also included reports of arbitrary detentions, torture, disappearances, and abuse by security forces. The report covered events through December 2005 and was published in January 2006. Since then, violence in Balochistan has increased exponentially as the military has launched operations against the militants. The mini-war has resulted in the displacement of thousands of people, mostly women and children. The conflicts in Dera Bugti and Kohlu alone have forced 84,000 people to leave their homes.[38] The situation further deteriorated with the killing of Akbar Bugti, one of the three nationalist leaders that Musharraf described as 'troublemakers', in August 2006. Bugti, along with 37 of his tribesmen, was killed when helicopter gunships dropped bombs at his hideout as part of the military operation. Twenty-one security personnel also died in the attack.[39] To condemn the killing of Bugti, Baloch nationalists held a grand *jirga* (tribal elders' meeting) attended by more than 380 leaders, including 85 tribal chiefs, belying Musharraf's claim that he enjoyed the support of all but three tribal chiefs.[40] The killing sparked widespread protest rallies in Balochistan and some parts of Sindh.

As violence increased in Balochistan, so did the number of missing persons. With the military regime's change of tactics from a low intensity approach to one of full frontal attacks a large number of Baloch citizens started disappearing. According to one Baloch nationalist, some 8,000 to 12,000 Balochs have disappeared. He said that a couple of years ago the interior minister acknowledged that around 5,000 Balochs had been arrested but added that the figure has gone up.[41] It is a measure of the seriousness of the matter that in August 2007, provincial opposition leaders moved three identical motions in the Balochistan parliament asking the government to 'take notice of the violation of the constitution by intelligence agencies and arrest of political activists without fulfilling legal requirements'.[42]

The military also employed an ideological push to counter secular nationalism with religious fanaticism. The Balochs are deeply religious people in their social lives, but their politics has always been secular. The reason is simple: they have fears about the loss of their ethnic identity but have never felt a threat to their religious beliefs. Baloch nationalists are strongly opposed to mixing religion with politics and therefore have no sympathy for the Taliban. Despite a ban on *madrasas* (seminaries) as part of Pakistan's contribution to the US 'War on Terror', the Pakistani federal government, through the Ministry of Religious Affairs (MRA), continued to support their establishment. In a region where the lack of secular education is more striking than any other province, and where 50 per cent of children are compelled to attend these religious schools, it is not surprising that the national budget for the MRA is $15.4 million while the allocation for the secular education ministry is only $2.56 million.[43] Baloch nationalists see the government's support for fundamentalist parties as the 'Talibanization' of Balochistan.[44]

In the Musharraf regime's national and provincial elections in 2002, the government and its intelligence agencies actively supported the conserva-tive religious alliance Mutahida Majlis-e-Amal (United Action Forum, MMA) against secular nationalists. Subsequently, the ruling party in alliance with the MMA formed the government in Balochistan in 2003. The MMA was dominated by a Sunni (the majority sect in Pakistan) party, Jamiat-e-Ulema-e-Islam, Fazl-ul-Rehman group (JUI-F). JUI-F is widely believed to be a staunch supporter of the Taliban. It has a wide network of *madrasas* throughout Pakistan, but the majority of them are in the NWFP and Balochistan. While in power, the JUI-F poured 'resources into their *madrasa* network to consolidate and expand their political hold over the province'.[45] The Sunni JUI-F's ascendance to power sparked sectarian violence in the province, leading to terrorist attacks on five major Shia processions and mosques since 2002. The deadliest came on Ashura, the holiest day for the Shia sect, in 2004, with the anti-Taliban Shia Hazara community as the main target. It left 45 people dead in Quetta.[46]

Regional and Global Interests

Strategically located, Balochistan shares its western border with Iran and its northern border with Afghanistan. With the construction of the Gwadar Port, Balochistan has also attracted the interest of China, Central Asian states, and the United States. In the 1970s, it was quite obvious that India and Afghanistan were supporting Baloch nationalists: the two states had long-standing territorial disputes with Pakistan. But that situation has now changed. Afghanistan is occupied by the allied forces and increasingly threatened by the resurgence of the Taliban.

As far as India is concerned, as a growing economic power, its interests have shifted from strategic to economic. If in the 1970s instability in Pakistan was in the interest of India, today it is political stability in Pakistan that India finds favourable to its economic ambitions. Energy-starved India is keen on the proposed 2,600-km Iran-Pakistan-India gas pipeline, of which some 750 km will pass through Balochistan. Thus, instability in Balochistan goes against Indian interests. India has openly and repeatedly criticized Pakistan army operation in Balochistan, but here too its aim is to gain the sympathy of Baloch nationalists for future economic gains, rather than to destabilize Pakistan. India is also interested in Afghanistan and Central Asian states for economic reasons, for which stability in Balochistan is imperative. The rhetoric that the previous Musharraf regime used about Indian support for Baloch nationalists, without providing any evidence of such involvement, has reached new heights with the claim by Rehman Malik, the new civilian government's advisor to the prime minister on interior affairs, that 'Russia and India were supporting the Balochistan Liberation Army (BLA) in its secession bid'.[47]

Iran, because of its own considerable Baloch population (1.2 million) near the Iran-Pakistan border, has always been wary of any nationalist uprising in Balochistan. Indeed in the 1970s conflict, the Shah of Iran provided Pakistan with $200 million and US-supplied combat helicopters, some of them manned by Iranian pilots, to crush the Baloch armed struggle.[48] Economically, too, stability in Balochistan helps Iran, as one of the world's largest oil and gas producers, to supply gas to India and Pakistan.

In the 1970s, the US interest in Balochistan was restricted to its concerns about the Soviet Union's influence in the region. After the 2001 terrorist attacks in the US, however, the situation has seen a sea change. US forces are engaged in a protracted war against the Taliban in Afghanistan. The porous border between that country and Balochistan makes the Pukhtun-dominated (the majority of Taliban are ethnic Pukhtun) northern region of the latter a safe haven for the Taliban.

The US also does not want anything to divert the Pakistan army from its assigned job of active contribution to the so-called 'War on Terror'. As far as secular Baloch nationalism is concerned, in the absence of a communist threat the US could not worry less. However, despite the fact that there is no love lost between Baloch nationalists and the Taliban, political instability and the serious law and order situation in Balochistan have made easier the Islamic militants' efforts to recruit and train. This is as distressing to the US as it is to Baloch nationalists.

Another worry for the US construction of the Gwadar Port with the help of China, which will naturally facilitate a strategic superiority in the Indian Ocean for the emerging economic giant, i.e. China. Washington is also opposed to the proposed Iran-Pakistan-India pipeline, believing that it will boost the Iranian economy and 'reduce the West's economic leverage over Tehran—economic leverage that is necessary to persuade Iran to abandon its nuclear ambitions'.[49]

Nationalist Militancy: Past and Present

There are stark differences between the nationalist insurgencies of the past and the current one. There are three major factors distinguishing the new militancy from the previous ones: emergence of a middle-class leadership and cadre, easy availability of sophisticated weapons, and unity among various tribes and classes. In the past, nationalist parties led by tribal chiefs organized armed resistance to the government against its intervention and intrusion. They fought against the military as a poorly armed guerrilla force from hideouts in the mountains.

Today, however, the situation is different in many ways. There is no nationalist political party thus far that has claimed responsibility for the violence. The nationalist movement is no longer restricted to guerrillas in mountains. There is sporadic violence all over Balochistan, in cities as well as in remote areas. Although the targets are usually government installations and personnel, civilians also suffer loss of life and property. The central government claims that the BLA, supported by nationalist tribal chiefs, namely Attaullah Mengal, Khair Bux Marri, and the late Akbar Bugti, is behind the violence. But it has not been able to provide any evidence for that.

The BLA keeps claiming responsibility for attacks, but it is still not clear who is its leader, how it recruits its activists, and from where. It is speculated that there is not one but three groups, the others being the Balochistan People's Liberation Front (BPLF) and the Balochistan Liberation Front (BLF).[50] An opposition member of the Balochistan assembly during the Musharraf regime, Kachkool Ali Khan, agreed that there was more than one militant group 'with different tactics but an identical goal—to protect the Baloch people from an oppressive and exploitative center'.[51]

Despite the government's allegations, it is quite obvious that this time the movement is not led and controlled by tribal chiefs. During the past three decades, a new generation of leadership and cadres has emerged belonging to the urban middle classes. There are two organizations with substantive support among this class, the Baloch Students Organization (BSO) and the National Party (NP). The BSO is an old organization formed in 1967. It 'represents educated Baloch middle class and students' as an independent political force with demands for 'jobs for Baloch youth and recognition for Balochi [the language] as a medium of instruction in the province'.[52] The BSO is a leftist organization opposed to the tribal system; it advocates a modern democratic system for Balochistan. Its cadres were fond of the leftist former NAP governor, the late Mir Ghous Bux Bizenjo, who, though chief of the Bizenjo tribe, lived and behaved like a middle class intellectual.[53]

The NP, led by Abdul Hayee Baloch, is a post-1970s conflict phenomenon. The NP's support base is the Makran Division in the south and the coastal areas that are not in the grip of the tribal system. With its educated middle class cadre, the NP on the one hand is opposed to the tribal system, but on the other it rejected the Musharraf government's claim that tribal chiefs were responsible for Balochistan's problems. Instead, the party placed the blame for the crisis 'squarely on the military's shoulders'.[54]

The second factor that distinguishes the new insurgency from the previous ones is the easy availability of sophisticated arms and ammunition. The long war (1979-92) by Afghan *mujahideen* (holy warriors of Islam) against the Soviet invasion of Afghanistan and the communist regime in Kabul was covertly but heavily supported by the West and Middle Eastern states via the Pakistani army. A large amount of foreign arms and ammunition made their way to the local markets in Pakistan, particularly to the western and northern border areas. Balochistan, after the NWFP, was the major pipeline for the flow of arms to the Afghan Islamist groups. Sophisticated arms flooded the province as army officers sold them to local buyers.[55] Baloch leaders claim that financial contributions to the nationalist cause by rich Baloch compatriots and sympathizers have made it easy for militant nationalists to buy weapons 'in the flourishing black market along the Afghan frontier'.[56]

The third factor is the unity among the various tribes and classes for the cause of provincial autonomy and local control over resources. The central government used to play one tribe against another to weaken the nationalist movements in the past. This time, however, the military is confronted with a united nationalist movement comprising a majority of the tribes.

The unity among the tribes has more to do with demographic changes in the province and a change in the nature of nationalist leadership and its tactics than with a change of heart on the part of tribal leaders. In previous conflicts, certain tribes, namely, the Marri, Mengal, and Bugti, would confront the central government demanding provincial autonomy and control over local resources. But most of the other tribes would either stay out of the conflict or side with the government.

In the new insurgency, the three radical tribes are not directly involved, or at least have not claimed to be involved. According to available information, the new movement is led and supported by a young, educated middle-class leadership and cadre.[57] The attacks of the insurgents are not restricted to certain regions and localities but are carried out throughout the province. Under the circumstances, the tribal leaders who would be inclined to side with the government feel threatened by the insurgents, whereas the nationalist tribal leaders seem to be quite happy with the militant nationalists' activities. Thus, uniting with other tribes and not appearing to look like government sympathizers seem to be tactical moves.

The fourth factor is that Pakistan's law and order and security situation has deteriorated so badly that the military is in no position to concentrate on Balochistan. Pakistan's military is deeply engaged in the NWFP-Afghanistan border areas as part of the 'United States' 'War on Terror' and also faces its own conflict in Kashmir. In the 1970s conflict, when the military concentrated on Balochistan with no other distractions, it still lost over 3,000 of its personnel.

Toward a Possible Solution

The seriousness of the crisis in Balochistan forced the ruling party-dominated Senate (Upper House) under the military regime to set up a committee in 2004 to explore the reasons behind the crisis and come up with recommendations. It is obvious from the Report's 2005 recommendations that none of the Baloch grievances are unfounded. The recommendations included:

> Maximum representation for the province on the boards of Pakistan petroleum, oil, and gas development corporations; allocation of 5% of the total expenditure of a successful exploration company awarded concession in an area, for social welfare projects; strict implementation of the 5.4% employment quota for the Baloch in federal ministries, divisions, corporations, and departments, and compensation for the lack of Baloch recruitment in armed forces and civil security forces; immediate shifting of Gwadar Port Authority head office from Karachi to Gwadar; more than 50% representation for Balochistan on the board of directors of this authority; allocation of 7% of gross revenue collected by Gwadar Port Authority to the development of Balochistan; preference to the locals in employment at Gwadar Port followed by the people of Makran [District] and the rest of Balochistan; and establishment of a fisheries training institute, a vocational technical training institute, a research institute, and degree colleges for the local youth of Makran and Balochistan; removal of the unnecessary presence of FC, Coast Guards, and check posts from interior of the province; review of cases of political workers arrested in Balochistan, release of persons implicated in minor offenses; postponement of building cantonments at Gwadar, Dera Bugti, and Kohlu till major issues are resolved.[58]

Because the report recommended a fair representation for the Baloch, it had the potential to have a positive impact on the situation in the province, but the recommendations were put into cold storage and never implemented. The government-appointed author of the report blamed hawks in the military for non-implementation, not the Pakistan army and the Musharraf regime. Not surprisingly, in the report itself, the army's misdemeanours in Balochistan were not taken into account, except one: acquisition of vast lands for housing and commercial purposes by the armed forces. Another important point is that the report tended to address legalistic and constitutional matters rather than political and administrative ones.

As military intervention in Balochistan has become the major cause of violence in the region, its withdrawal needs to be addressed on a priority basis. That is why both the ICG and the HRCP have recommended that reliance on a military solution should be ended by immediately stopping army action, sending troops back to their barracks, and restricting their role to guarding the province's land and nautical borders. The ICG recommended that to de-escalate the situation, the government should withdraw the FC, replacing it with provincial security forces that are firmly under provincial control; dismantle all check posts manned by paramilitary and other federal security agencies; halt construction of cantonments and end plans to construct additional military or paramilitary facilities.

Taking note of the widespread disappearances, the report demanded immediate production of all detainees before the courts and release of political prisoners, an end to the political role of intelligence agencies, military and civil, barring them from detaining prisoners, withdrawal of travel restrictions, internal and external, on Baloch opposition leaders and activists, ending of intimidation, torture, arbitrary arrests, disappearances, and extrajudicial killings, allowing all political parties to function freely, respecting the constitutionally guaranteed rights of speech and expression, assembly, association and movement, and respect for the constitutional obligation to preserve and promote distinct language and culture.[59]

The Baloch demands are not very different from the recommendations of the ICG and HRCP. They demand the following: an end to the construction of military and paramilitary cantonments, and redirection of funds toward the socio-economic development of the province's conflict-stricken districts, immediate assessment of damage caused to the displaced populations of Dera Bugti and Kohlu districts and arranging the repatriation of displaced people and compensation to them, cancellation of all allotments of civil/military lands made in 1999-2008 in Gwadar and Lasbela districts, a policy of paying equal wellhead prices for gas and a 30 per cent royalty to Balochistan, and an end to the intelligence agencies' role in Balochistan's political, social, and tribal affairs (the agencies are regarded by the majority in the province as a source of instability, which provokes conflict among the tribes and the political parties).[60]

After the forced resignation of Musharraf in August 2008, although the situation in Balochistan remains the same, the rhetoric of the civilian government in Islamabad is different. The elected government has offered an apology to the Baloch people for the excesses perpetrated on them. It has decided to abolish 35 of the 54 security check posts and remove the names of Baloch leaders from the Exit Control List, which forbids citizens from leaving the country. These are positive steps, with a potential to assuage Baloch grievances. The civilian government, however, has not said anything about the issue that sparked the current wave of violence in Balochistan, the presence of troops. Obviously officials are in no position to confront the powerful military command. It is believed that at one stage during the 1970s crisis, Zulfikar Ali Bhutto was willing to negotiate with the NAP leaders and pull out the troops he had sent to crush them. But the military command refused to comply, arguing that 'after a considerable loss they had better clean up'.[61]

There are no indications that the military mindset has since changed. Indeed after long years of repressive military regimes under Zia ul-Haq (1977-88) and Musharraf (1999-2008), the Pakistan army seems more confident about its crisis tactics. The shaky nature of the civilian government, and the military command's behind-the-scene control over issues of national and international significance, will render meaningless any meaningful effort to find a political solution to the Baloch crisis. The Baloch militants are not unaware of this. Despite the civilian government's goodwill gestures and its decision to remove most of the security check posts, violence in Balochistan continues unabated.

Conclusion

What lies at the heart of the Balochistan crisis is the insensitivity and shortsightedness of successive governments, starting from the inception of the Pakistani state. The real issue in Balochistan was, and continues to be, political and administrative. A political solution to the problem has not been sought because Pakistan's civil and military establishment has always been unwilling to accommodate elective politics and representative rule. The history of Pakistan is one of bureaucratic and military subversion of democracy. So much so that even the first democratically elected government of Zulfikar Ali Bhutto tended to depend on that establishment, eventually causing its own downfall and disruption of elected rule.

Repeated interventions of the military in politics and its subversion of representative rule have left Pakistan at the mercy of its armed forces. Pakistan's military is so entrenched in the power structure of the state that it is difficult to imagine it will ever come under the control of an elected civilian administration. A Baloch nationalist, Kachkool Ali Khan, has aptly said: 'The people of Pakistan did not get a nation—the Pakistan army got a state.'[62]

The state that the army got has been systematically turned into a military empire. Civil and democratic institutions have progressively been weakened and brought under the empire's control. No matter whether the country has civilian rule or military, real power remains in the hands of the military command. That command treats Pakistan as its fiefdom and the people as its subjects. It has earned the dubious distinction of being an army that keeps trying to conquer its own people whenever they refuse to follow its diktat. In 1971 the military massacred Bengalis in the east wing of the country. During 1973-7, it massacred the Baloch. In 1983 it humiliated, jailed, and killed Sindhis. Today, it is once again involved in the killing of the Baloch. It also has the notoriety of an army that has repeatedly intrigued against civilian governments and was instrumental in their dismissals.

This article has argued that the conflict in Balochistan is unlikely to be resolved, in the absence of a comprehensive change in the Pakistani state's attitudes and policies toward its peripheral regions. Under the circumstances, it is unrealistic to think that the military will voluntarily relinquish political power to elected representatives in the near future. While talking to a senior civil servant who worked in key positions in various troubled areas of Pakistan, the author asked what he thought was the solution to the problem of militancy. The civil servant's answer: 'Disarm the army and bring it under civilian control'.[63] Politically and logically an appropriate idea indeed, but practically, near impossible at the moment.

Notes

1. Adeel Khan would like to thank Siddiq Baloch, a senior journalist and Baloch nationalist, for providing him with contacts in Gwadar and for insights on the Balochistan crisis. He also thanks UNE Asia-Pacific Research Theme Group for seed funding for fieldwork in Pakistan.
2. For details, see Adeel Khan, 'Baloch Ethnic Nationalism: From Guerrilla War to No-where?', in idem, *Politics of Identity: Ethnic Nationalism and the State in Pakistan*, New Delhi: Sage, 2005, pp. 109-26.
3. Under the scheme, the four regional entities of the west wing of Pakistan were amalgamated into one unit to establish some parity with the country's east wing, Bengal (now the nation of Bangladesh), because of the latter's overwhelming majority in population. See ibid.
4. Selig S. Harrison, *In Afghanistan's Shadow: Baluch Nationalism and Soviet Temptations*, New York: Carnegie Endowment, 1981, p. 3.
5. Nadeem Qasir, *Pakistan Studies: An Investigation into the Political Economy, 1948 -1988,* Karachi: Oxford University Press, 1991, p. 26.
6. Selig Harrison, *In Afghanistan's Shadow*, op. cit., p. 16.
7. Ibid., p. 19.
8. During 1879-80 and 1902-3, there was an 82 per cent tax increase in Sibi, and between 1882 and 1895, a 350 per cent increase in the Quetta region. Yu V. Gankovsky, *The Peoples of Pakistan: An Ethnic History,* Moscow: Nauka Publishing House, 1971, pp. 203-5.
9. Population Census Organization, Pakistan, <http://www.census.gov.pk/Demographic Indicator.htm>.
10. Ibid.

11. Senate of Pakistan, *Report of the Parliamentary Committee on Balochistan,* no. 7 (November 2005).
12. Syed Fazl-e-Haider, 'Social Development in Balochistan', *Dawn* (Karachi), 23 January 2006.
13. Ibid.
14. International Crisis Group (ICG), 'Pakistan: The Worsening Conflict in Balochistan', *South Asia Report,* no. 119 (14 September 2006), p. 16, <http://www.crisisgroup.org/home/ index.cfm?id=4373&=1>.
15. Syed Fazl-e-Haider, 'Gas Subsidized at Balochistan's Expense', *Dawn*, 21 August 2006.
16. Shamim-ur-Rehman, 'Nothing but Provincial Autonomy', an interview with nationalist leader Mir Hasil Bizenjo, ibid., 12 February 2006.
17. Adeel Khan, *Politics of Identity*, pp. 115-16.
18. Omer Noman (ed.), *Pakistan: A Political and Economic History since 1947* (revised and updated) London: Kegan Paul, 1990, pp. 64-5.
19. Hussain Haqqani, *Pakistan: Between Mosque and Military*, Lahore: Vanguard, 2005, p. 102.
20. The Iranian regime of Shah Mohammad Reza Pahlavi feared that the insurgency would spread across the border to 1.2 million Baloch of eastern Iran. Selig S. Harrison, 'Pakistan's Baloch Insurgency', *Le Monde Diplomatique* [Diplomatic World] (October 2006), <http://mondediplo.com/2006/10/05baluchistan>.
21. Ray Fulcher, 'Balochistan's History of Insurgency', *Green Left* (Australia), 30 November 2006, <http://www.greenleft.org.au/2006/693/35987>.
22. Siddiq Baloch, Baloch nationalist and senior journalist, telephone conversation with author, September 2008.
23. Frederic Grare, 'Pakistan: The Resurgence of Baluch Nationalism', *Carnegie Endowment's South Asia Report*, Washington, D.C., no. 65, January 2006.
24. ICG, 'Pakistan: The Worsening Conflict in Balochistan', pp. 14-24.
25. Ibid., pp. 14-15.
26. 'The Great Land Robbery', *Herald* (Karachi), June 2008, quoted in Robert D. Kaplan, 'Pakistan's Fatal Shore', *Atlantic* (May 2009), <http://www.theatlantic.com/doc/print/200905/ kaplan-pakistan>.
27. Quoted in ibid.
28. The author visited Gwadar in January 2008.
29. Abdul Ghaffar Hoth, deputy mayor of Gwadar City, interview with author in Gwadar, January 2008.
30. Ibid.

31. Lyari is one of the poorest suburbs of Karachi, inhabited by mostly Baloch people.
32. Hussain Ashraf, interview with the author in Gwadar, January 2008.
33. Ray Fulcher, 'Balochistan's History of Insurgency', op. cit.
34. ICG, 'Pakistan: The Worsening Conflict in Balochistan', p. i.
35. Report of the Human Rights Commission of Pakistan's (HRCP) Fact-Finding Missions, 'Conflict in Balochistan' (December 2005-January 2006), p. 37.
36. Ibid
37. Ibid., pp. 45-6.
38. ICG, 'Pakistan: The Forgotten Conflict in Balochistan', *Asia Briefing*, no. 69 (October 2007), p. 5.
39. Saleem Shahid, 'Bugti Killed in Operation: Six Officers among 21 Security Personnel Dead', *Dawn*, 27 August 2006.
40. ICG, 'Pakistan: The Forgotten Conflict in Balochistan', p. 12.
41. Ibid., p. 5.
42. Amanullah Kasi, 'Motions on Missing Persons Disposed Of: Matter Sub Judice, Says Balochistan Minister', *Dawn*, 10 August 2007.
43. Ray Fulcher, 'Balochistan's History of Insurgency', op. cit.
44. Ibid.
45. ICG, 'The State of Sectarianism in Pakistan', *Asia Report*, no. 95 (18 April 2005), p. 20.
46. Ibid.
47. Mumtaz Alvi, 'Russia, India Supporting BLA, Malik Tells Senate', *The News* (Karachi), 23 April 2009.
48. For details, see Adeel Khan, *Politics of Identity*, op. cit.
49. Subhash Vohra, 'U.S. Concerns over India-Iran Gas Pipeline', *Voice of America*, Washington, D.C., 18 June 2008.
50. ICG, 'Pakistan: The Worsening Conflict in Balochistan', p. 12.
51. Ibid.
52. Ibid., p. 11.
53. This author observed this while attending a BSO convention in Quetta in late 1980. He had also interviewed Bizenjo several times in Karachi for *Dawn*.
54. ICG, 'Pakistan: The Worsening Conflict in Balochistan', p. 10.
55. Baloch telephone conversation.
56. Selig S. Harrison, 'Pakistan's Baloch Insurgency', op. cit.
57. Baloch telephone conversation.
58. Senate of Pakistan, *Report of the Parliamentary Committee on Balochistan*, pp. 95-100.

59. ICG, 'Pakistan: The Worsening Conflict in Balochistan', op. cit., p. 3.
60. Sanaullah Baloch, 'Undoing the Damage', *Dawn*, 31 March 2008.
61. Abdul Hayee Baloch, cited in Adeel Khan, *Politics of Identity*, op. cit., p. 123.
62. ICG, 'Pakistan: The Worsening Conflict in Balochistan', p. ii.
63. The interviewee wanted to remain anonymous.

10

China's Policies and Practices towards Ethnic Uighurs in Xinjiang and the Impact of Modernization/ Globalization on Ethnic Identity

K.R. SHARMA

This paper has three major thematic components. One, it discusses the People's Republic of China's policies and practices towards her ethnic/religious minorities in general and Uighurs in Xinjiang in particular. Of China's 55 odd ethnic nationalities, three consider themselves as nations and therefore their ethnos, ethnonyms and ethnogeneses are quite strong, both in its primordial as well as its contextual/circumstantial sense. Chinese state and the Chinese Communist Party have failed to denationalize (or nationalize) and 'Hanize' them. These three nationalities are Tibetans, Uighurs and Mongols. Tibetans and Mongols follow Buddhism while the Uighurs of Xinjiang are believers in Islam. This statement of mine needs a small caveat. In the last three decades or so, the Mongols and the Hans have achieved considerable levels of mutual reconciliation and Mongols may well be the next candidate for assimilation. The second focus of this paper is on the ethnos and ethnogeneses of Uighurs living in Xinjiang. China's policies in Xinjiang and Tibet can be frankly described based on ethnocide. As a reaction to and in response to the ethnocide, the Tibetans in Tibet and Uighurs in Xinjiang are engaged in preserving, inventing and reinventing their respective ethnogeneses. In the last several decades this titanic struggle between ethnocide and ethnogeneses has assumed serious and explosive dimensions. My focus here is primarily on Xinjiang. Any reference to Tibet if any, is in the nature of supporting and substantiating my arguments pertaining to the ethnic tangle in Xinjiang. The third and the last section of this paper is somewhat autonomous and still profoundly related to the protean theme of ethnicity. As the world is modernizing and globalizing fast what could be the possible consequences—intended as well as unintended—of this on the germane question of ethnicity. Instead of marshalling abstract, empty and bookish arguments on this problematic, being a student of Chinese society and polity, I have situated and contextualized my thoughts and comments almost exclusively on China theme.

Xinjiang (earlier called Sinkiang) is gifted with an extremely important geographical location. Much of Xinjiang's strategic significance whether it is a 'pivot' or a 'pawn' is due to this dominant factor. It is a very resource-rich province of China containing significant reserves of oil, gas, coal, timber and several critical metals needed for China's economic growth. It is also China's western gateway to reach her several important neighbours. Some of these immediate neighbours are China's good friends and even allies while few others are her competetors and even potential rivals. Xinjiang is also China's entry point to Europe and West Asia and therefore has unprecedented potential in terms of trade, travel and communication. It is fast becoming a modern replay of the old historical Silk Route. Speaking in the idiom of strategy syndrome, Xinjiang occupies the position of a nerve-centre of central Asia. The above-mentioned attributes of Xinjiang are not the focus of this paper.

Instead, I propose to look at the province as a rich laboratory and a problem area for China's policies and practices towards her ethnic and religious minorities. Xinjiang is also China's Moslem face to her Central Asia neighbours in particular and to the Islamic world in general. The main burden of my thesis is that the Uighur people there are facing a tough fight for preserving their religious and cultural identity. It is a titanic fight for survival. The Chinese Communist Party and the Chinese state are systematically focused on 'Hanizing' and forcefully 'assimilating' the Uighurs there.

China is a relatively homogeneous state. Approximately only 10 per cent of its 1.4 billion people belong to non-Han stock while the remaining 90 per cent are Hans. Since 90 per cent of China's population are Hans, one should resist the temptation of concluding that China as a nation is a unified and united entity. The reality is far from this. I shall return to this theme of China's homogeneity and national unity later in my paper. Minority people in China number around 130-40 million. Of the 55 recognized minorities of China, the most prominent are Chuang (Koreans), Mongols, Tibetans, Uighurs, Kazaks, Kirghis, Moslems (Huis), Uzbeks, Dais, Bais, Kawas, Yie and several others. Out of China's 31 odd provinces, minority nationalities are scattered over 15 or so. Several provinces like Tibet, Inner Mongolia, Xinjiang, Yunnan, Gansu, Guangxi are heavily peopled by minority people. It is significant to remember that Chinese state registers and recognizes her citizens as a member of the ethnic groups and this ethnic identity of people is stamped on their residence registration papers (*hou-kou*) and passport. Technically speaking, ethnicity is a part of one's identity in China. Religious belief is never mentioned in the census or on the *hou-kou* documents.

A careful look at the ethnographic map of China would make it clear that these 10 per cent people of China, numbering between 130 and 140 million and belonging to 55 odd ethnic minorities occupy 50 per cent plus space of China's land mass. Huge chunks of these areas are deserts, mountains, and rivers which makes them hard and inhospitable. Added to this, these areas are the frontiers and borders of China which are sensitive and therefore vital to China's foreign policy formulators and even important from defence and strategic points. The implications are crystal clear. The loyalties of these 'frontier' people to Beijing's regime becomes one of the categorical imperatives for China. Most of these people occupy the space loosely referred as 'outer China' differentiating them from 'Inner China'. To restate this fact in terms of ancient, medieval and even modern history, these areas were added and readded to the Chinese empire by Mongol (Yuan dynasty) and Mauchu (Ching) rulers of China. It stands to reason to argue that Beijing ought to keep these minorities satisfied and in good humour. Antagonizing these people resulting in their estrangement and alienation is no longer an option available to China since she harbours the ambition of becoming a global player.

Ethnic minorities can be defined as groups holding together by ties of common descent, language, religious faith and cultural distinctiveness feeling themselves to be different and distinctive from the majority of a given political entity. It is this emotive (self-ascriptive) sense of 'togetherness' and 'ancestry' which gives them a personality and identity of their own. Also, it is this sense of 'belonging' which makes them feel 'us' and 'them' 'a category of distinctiveness and differentiation'. It is pertinent to note here that while the differentiation of class and profession is easily mutable, the identity marks of ethnicity are not. Ethnicity has two major dimensions of identity. The major part of this identity is primordial while residual is situational or/and contextual. In the subsequent pages of this paper, I shall have more occasions to comment on these two major components of ethnic identity.

Commenting on the dynamics of relationship between the dominant ethnic groups (nation) and the ethnic minority or minorities (nationalities), social scientists worldover have a near consensus about the theoretical matrix. These two competing and therefore alternative frameworks are that of integration and assimilation. Integration is the process whereby ethnic minorities while retaining their indigenous and primordial characteristics, start shifting their political activities, expectations and even loyalties to a new centre, that is, towards the nation. Conversely, an assimilated nationality would actually merge and comb with the dominant/ruling nationality. Once assimilated, it would cease to exist as a separate group. If, only integrated, it would not cease to exist. The ethos of integration expect the ethnic minorities only to re-cast and re-orient their feelings of sub-nationalism to a political corporate centre. An assimilationist approach is totally opposed to the very idea of sub-nationalism. Normally, coercion of one kind or another is always associated with the policy of assimilation while the major burden and thrust of integration is partly through persuasion and partly through social and economic incentives. These incentives, more than personal, are based on economic entitlements and development. Anthropologists rightly associate assimilation with racist psyche and even with racism. The old concept of 'melting pot' symbolized the pathos and pathology of assimilation. In a democratic and forward looking polity the concept of 'melting pot' is being replaced by what the historian Carl Degler called the 'salad bowl' approach. The ethos of 'salad bowl' syndrome respect cultural, ethnic and religious pluralities with their diversified variables.

In the last six decades or so the policies and practices of the Chinese communists towards her minority nationalities have undergone several twists and turns. A small comment on the pre-1949 policy matrix. During the Jiangxi Soviet, a young idealist Mao—literally in the theoretical footsteps of Marx, Lenin and Sunyat-Sen—declared that all the minority nationalities (after the liberation) shall be granted the 'right of self-determination' including the right to secede. Even this did not motivate and entice the minority people to join Mao's plank of revolution. The overwhelming number of China's minorities kept aloof from the Chinese communist revolution and no wonder, then, the Chinese communist revolution was almost a Han affair and the Revolution's geographical spread remained confined to what is loosely referred to as 'Inner China'. After coming to power in October 1949 the Chinese Communist Party realized that 'self-determination' for ethnic minorities was neither viable nor desirable. Accordingly, the 'self-determination' policy paradigm was immediately replaced by 'autonomy' syndrome.

Beginning 1949 (October 1949 when China became the Peoples Republic of China), four distinct phases can be discerned about China's policy towards her ethnic minorities. From 1949 to 1956-7 the Chinese communists adopted the policy of integration towards her minorities. Flexibility, caution and pragmatism were the watchwords. The minority areas were granted autonomy in substantive degrees. Special Autonomous Areas were carved out. Cultural, linguistic and religious differentiations were tolerated and even encouraged. Tibet was treated as a special case, to be handled softly. In 1957-8 this policy was suddenly reversed. With the onset of the People's Commune, Great Leap Forward and General Line (the so-called, Three Red-Banners of Mao) which constituted the first major phase of Mao's radicalism, the party and the state adopted a tough posture towards ethnic minorities. In 1957 Mao, under the impact of his Permanent Revolution theory, announced that the 'Nationality question is basically a class question'. The policy implications were obvious. Between the Chinese state and the ethnic minorities, the dynamics of class struggle would apply. This phase was frankly based on assimilationist parameters. Han 'Chauvinism' was no longer the evil. Instead, sub-nationalism or 'local nationalism' was identified as the problematic. Local nationalism was equated not with centrifugalism but with 'separatism'. The religious and cultural distinctiveness of the minorities were frowned upon. A state policy of heavy Han migration to select minority areas, specially into Inner Mongolia, Yunnan and Xinjiang was unfolded. The idea behind this policy was to outnumber the minority people in their own locale. Large number of Han cadres, technicians, specialists, semi-specialists, skilled and non-skilled workers and retired army (PLA) people were transferred and settled in minority areas. The study of Chinese language (Mandarin) was made obligatory in most minority areas.

The third and the most tragic phase began with the Cultural Revolution in 1966 and continued till the death of Mao in 1976. This phase was frankly based on forcible and violent assimilation of minority nationalities. Suppression, control, domination and ruthless absorption became the salient characteristics of this phase. Mao's so-called Great Proletarian Cultural Revolution (GPCR) was a catastrophe for the entire Chinese nation and for the minority nationalities, it was a tragedy of unprecedented magnitude. Minority people were treated as if they were the class enemies of the Communist Party and the Chinese state. China's post-Mao leaders in their well-known assessment of this period (Resolutions on Certain Questioning of History) in 1981 characterized this period as the phase of 'feudal and fascist dictatorship'.

To be very concise and concrete, the five policy measures proved to be disastrous and deadly for the ethnic minorities during this period (1966-76).

(a) Most of the top and even middle level leaders in minority areas were purged and replaced. At the beginning of the Cultural Revolution Wang Enmao was in power in Xinjiang, Zhanggu hua in Tibet, Ulanfu in Inner Mongolia, Yan Hungyan in Yunnan and Wangfeng in Gausu. Wang Enmao was holding the highest party and the military office in Xinjiang. Ulaufu was the chairman of the Inner Mongolian Autonomous Republic as well as the chairman of the State Council's Nationalities Affairs Commission. By the end of the first year of the Cultural Revolution all except Wang Enmao were removed and replaced by hard-liners. Eventually, Wang Enmao too was forced to go. The purges of the minority cadres at the middle levels was a heavy one. In certain areas (Mongolia, Yunnan) 70-80 per cent of the local minority cadres were replaced. The purged cadres were replaced either by Han cadres or by hard-liners of the minority people.

(b) The territorial sanctity of the minority areas was violated and tempered. The Inner Mongolian Autonomous Republic was dismembered and several parts of the province were amalgamated with Jehol, Gansu and Suiyan. A large number of Tibetans were forced to settle down outside Tibet.

(c) A deliberate and systematic policy of settling Han people into the minority areas was planned and executed by the state. Mongols were reduced to a hopeless minority in Inner Mongolia. For four million Mongols there were 10 million plus non-Mongols (mainly Han people) in Inner Mongolia. In Yunnan, the several minority people were greatly outnumbered by Hans. The Xinjiang Autonomous region with its majority of Uighurs, Kazaks, Kirghis and Uzbeks (all Moslems of Turkic origin) were heavily targetted by Han migrants for settlement. China's largest minority people—the Chuangs (Koreans) were outnumbered almost three to one in Guangxi province. Tibet was the only minority area which was spared from this flux.

(d) The religious practices, the social and cultural customs, the food, the folklore, the local language and the literature of the minority people were ridiculed and attacked. The Red Guards (school and college children in their early 20s who could not even correctly write Marxism-Leninism in Mandarin language) entered the minority areas to 'exchange revolutionary experience' made Buddhist temples, pagodas and Islamic mosques—all centres of

> worship and reverence—as the main focus of their anger. Several internationally famous, religious monasteries and pagodas in Tibet and Mongolia were completely or substantially destroyed. Out of the 2,300 plus Buddhist temples and pagodas in Tibet, nearly 2,000 were destroyed. The destruction of the famous Ganden monastery in Tibet at the hands of the Red Guards is a well-known episode. The Red Guards in Tibet had dug out the dead remains of the 5th through 9th Panchen Lamas, dismembered them, threw the remains on the streets of Xigaze and Lhasa. Panchen Lama's last public ceremony was to formally reopen the (destroyed) Great Stupa and perform the burial ceremony of (5th through 9th) the Panchen Lamas at Xigaze. In Xinjiang several mosques were burnt and destroyed. Pig's meat was tied around the necks of Moslem clergymen (*imams*) and they were paraded on the streets in Urumchi, Kashgar and several other cities of Xinjiang. The religious symbols of minority people were characterized as the 'tail of feudalism'.

The ethnic-specific features of the minorities were refuted and ridiculed. Jiang Qing, Mao's wife and her radical associates (the Gang of Four) had ordained that minority nationalities are 'no better than foreign invaders and aliens'. She also opined that their 'culture had an outlandish flavour'. The radicals reasoned that since China has already achieved socialist transformations, then, why the special characteristics of the minorities to be recognized and preserved? In a word, during the chaotic ten years of Cultural Revolution, the whole country went through a traumatic time but for the minority peoples of China—particularly Inner Mongolia, Tibet and Xinjiang—this trauma and humiliation was doubly cruel.

This paper is not about the so-called 'Great Proletarian Cultural Revolution' and its pernicious and tragic affects in China. Since the 1990s any comment and critical discussion on Maoism and his cultural revolution is a forbidden area of research and public discourse in China. Mao's acts of omissions and commissions once fully exposed and documented would put to shame even Stalin and Pol Pot.

The Third Plenum of the 11th Central Committee of the CCP formally bade goodbye to Mao's radical policies. With the process of de-Maoization and Deng's market-based reforms, a whole series of new policy initiatives on various domestic and international policies were unfolded. Pertaining to ethnic minorities, Huyao-bang's visit to Tibet in 1980 was the turning point. The 'left' and 'radical' policies on minorities were replaced by liberal and flexible measures. The new leadership candidly accepted the mistakes (rather blunders) of the Cultural Revolution period and a new beginning was sought to be made to assuage the injured feelings of the ethnic minorities. The individual wrongs done to the minority nationality leaders were sought to be undone. A large number of dismissed cadres—both dead and alive—were 'rehabilitated' politically. The 1982 Constitution incorporated several new formulations and clauses assuring minority people that the state would respect their autonomy. If Mao and his radical cohorts quoted Marx in support of the Cultural Revolution, this time, Deng and his supporters also quoted Marx to justify their new initiative. The science of quoting Marx against Marx has been fully mastered by a section of academia oriented ideologues of the CPC. The Chinese Academy of Social Sciences with its academic contingent of tens of thousands plus salaried experts excel in this. These social scientists work on government/party assigned 'policy priority' subjects. They do not and cannot function as independent and objective think-tanks. For this role, they shall have to wait the arrival of democracy and liberal ethos.

The oftquoted phrase of Karl Marx (reference to his letter dated 5 March 1852 to J. Weydemeyer) that the 'existence of classes is of much shorter duration than of nationalities and after withering away of the former the latter will remain in existence for a long time' is being printed and reprinted by the Chinese media. Lenin has also been quoted in support of this flexible policy initiative towards minorities. Lenin's comment in his ('Left Wing Communism: an Infantile Disorder') (1920) that 'national distinctions will continue to exist for a long time to come even after the dictatorship of the 'proletariat has been established on a world wide scale' is being quoted frequently. Once, I asked a senior professor at Chinese Academy of Social Sciences in Beijing whether they were not aware of these famous quotes of Marx and Lenin and why they did not underline these quotes earlier? Of course, he was conspicuously silent.

This liberal and relaxed policy paradigm—openly based on the dynamics of integration—is being observed in China except in two provinces—Tibet and Xinjiang. Inner Mongolia has been a huge beneficiary. In Tibet and Xinjiang the ethnic minority scenario has much worsened in the last two to three decades. The Chinese state and the CCP have adopted much harsher and oppressive ways to tackle the problematic there. In the following few paragraphs, I shall be attempting to state the fact-sheet in Xinjiang.

For the last three decades or so, the ethnic conflict between the Uighurs and Han Chinese state in Xinjiang is visible, demonstrative and self-evident. The data-wise details with fatal casualities have been listed in several publications and hence I need not repeat them here. A careful counting of these figures lead me to believe that this ethnic conflict has claimed the lines of several thousand people with hundreds executed by the state. There have been umpteen number of clashes between Uighur protestors and the para-military forces of the state. There have also been communal clashes between Uighurs and the Hans there. Acts of terror and bomb blasts have also added to this figure. Of those executed, some of them publically in the presence of thousands of onlookers, almost all of them (except a handful), were Uighurs.

Also, in the last three decades or so, an academically rich corpus of well-documented and richly researched scholarly works on Xinjiang and its problematics have emerged. Publications based on research/fieldwork undertaken in Xinjiang and researcher's proficiency in Uighur language and Mandarin have enriched both the information and knowledge on and about Xinjiang. As a result of this, Xinjiang is no longer an under-researched and 'little known' area. Academic as well as journalistic interest on Xinjiang continues to be on the upswing.

There is a near-consensus among the scholars that a volcano-like situation is developing there. If the fault-lines are not corrected promptly there, the volcano may erupt anytime. Uighurs are a mistreated, humiliated and an alienated minority there. On the contrary, if one believes the Chinese state/party narratives on

Xinjiang, then, except the fact that a handful of Uighur terrorists taking inspiration from outside indulging in acts of sabotage and violence occasionally, there is no other important problem in Xinjiang. These official narratives are based on propaganda and make-belief. Occasionally, all governments world over indulge in telling lies. In a democracy since there are multiple checks and counter-checks, the lies and untruths spoken by the governments get exposed in the public domain. The Chinese—both the party and the government—have converted this task of telling lies into a fine art. For 40 years or so, I have been telling my Chinese politics students that for getting at the bottom of things and to have a realistic and correct picture of China, it is not enough to read between the lines but one should learn to read 'against' the lines. China's official discourse on her ethnic tangle in Xinjiang and Tibet is a good example of this.

Xinjiang continues to be in a flux because the state has escalated its levels of dominance and suppression over Uighurs, who in turn continue to be resentful and restless. Occasionally, a microscopic minority of separatists and practitioners of terror among Uighurs resort to violence. New facts and new grounds of disaffection and discrimination are being created almost everyday. What could be the likely consequences is difficult to foresee. One thing is clear, the situation is far from 'tranquil'. Uighurs have a long list of grievances and it appears that a lot of these grievances are genuine. These grievances can be grouped in four major categories. They are produced and reproduced when China acts: (a) as an empire; (b) when China attempts to assimilate the Islamic minorities there civilizationally; (c) when China's narratives and policy instruments forcefully herd the Uighurs towards the Grand project of nation-building, and finally; (d) when Hans through the method of migration/influx continue to change the demography and population mix of Xinjiang. All these four phenomenons which constitute the basic elements of the ethnic tangle in Xinjiang needs some observations and some qualifications.

The historically traditional relationship between the frontier people of Xinjiang, Manchuria, Mongolia, Tibet and to a great extent Yunnan with China has been that of an empire and its tributaries. In times when the Chinese empire was weak and in decline, these frontier people asserted and repeatedly reasserted their independence. Even during the Chinese centre's strong position, these frontier people were never 'governed' by China. It was an indirect rule through proxy. This is the historical meaning of expressions like 'Inner China' and 'Outer China'. A careful look at the demographic map of China of the seventeenth century would persuade one to the fact that China's territory, then, was just 50 per cent of its present one. This is also true that these frontier areas were added earlier by Hans and later crucially to the Chinese empire by the non-Han dynasties. This conquest or reconquest of these frontier non-Han people were achieved by Yuan (Mongol) and Ching (Manchu) dynasties. That was one important reason why Chiang Kai-Sheik and Mao Ze-dong in their youthful revolutionary times had promised them the right of self-determination including right to secede. It is an entirely different issue that both of them, otherwise antagonistic in many ways, went back on their respective promises.

The communist government of China denies vehemently that China is behaving like an empire towards these frontier people. Notwithstanding this denial, patterns of China's behaviour and superpower intents and ambitions make it explicit enough. What is implicit is much more than enough. I have no hesitation in saying that for these frontier people of Xinjiang—I surmise the case of Tibet and Mongolia is not much different—China is still behaving in the mould of an imperial and majestic power. China is treating Xinjiang as its most prized colony. It reminds one of the British description of India as the 'jewel in her crown'. Xinjiang is more than a jewel in China's crown. Its importance goes much beyond its geo-strategic position in Central Asia when Owen Lattimore had termed it as a 'pivot' of Asia. A secured and fully assimilated Xinjiang could be a 'pivot' of China's energy security. It is becoming the main source and the main transport conduit for the energy needs of China. In turn, China's candidacy for major global power depends on the fulfilment of China's energy requirement. China has to take cognizance of the fact that Xinjiang is the Islamic face of China and China's energy security heavily depends upon the Islamic world. It is in China's own interest to treat the people of Xinjiang with little compassion and benevolence.

Hypothetically, granting the fact that after China's conquest or reconquest of Xinjiang, now it is a part of Chinese empire, even then, a careful perusal of China's governance—more of a misgovernance—of Xinjiang is a classic example of internal colonialism.

China is a civilization and the learned and the knowledgeable Chinese look at their country civilizationally. She has a rich and proud legacy. This is perfectly correct. This is their civilizational belief that Confucian China does not need Western style democracy. May be, but this is a half truth or may be, not true at all. There is a healthy debate going on this issue within and outside China. Supporters of authoritarianism are invoking Confucianism and opining that China is better without democracy. The votaries of democracy including the Chinese protagonists inside China, are producing counter-arguments stating that democracy is a universal value and no longer a culture-bound habit. One Chinese intellectual who is an engaged supporter of democracy told me that contemporary China has gone much beyond Confucianism in many other critical aspects of socio-economic life. Even culturally, China is qualitatively different and even contrastive to many core values of Confucianism.

The Han's civilizational pride prompts China's policy makers and implementers to Sinicize and Hanize the Uighurs in Xinjiang. It is a strong belief of many Chinese that whosoever came to China and settled there, whether he was a foreigner or a 'barbarian', was eventually sinicized. This statement has a considerable element of truth in it. The Mongols and subsequently the Manchus—both foreigners and 'barbarians'—came to China as conquerors, settled down and finally were sinicized and even Hanized. Contrary to this argument and to the Han's delight, the Uighurs of Xinjiang also view themselves civilizationally. The Uighurs of Xinjiang—even the non-Uighur Moslems there—have a strong sense of ancestry. It is true that the expression 'Uighur' went out of circulation for about five centuries until it was revived in the 1930s. The Islamic identity of Uighurs is reasonably strong. Discounting the religion factor proportionately, the other markers of their ethnic identity are extremely robust and solid. During the period when the word 'Uighur' was out of vogue, the ethnogeneses of Uighur generated and regenerated in resistance to their political opponents and cultural ethnociders—struggle produced by praxis—assumed somewhat primordial character. Between 1950s and 2009, Uighurs in praxis with Hans and Chinese state have produced tons of ethnogeneses. Without taking Huntington very seriously at the global level, what one is witnessing in Xinjiang (more so in Tibet) is a clash of 'civilizations'. Without extrapolating this argument further, it is enough to say that the Uighurs too have a strong civilizational 'hang over'. In terms of 'imagining' national identities, the Moslem population of Xingiang, particularly Uighurs, view themselves as a part of the ancestry of the Ottoman civilization. Present Turkey which is divided, sick and a part of Europe is not a model of course. That is the reason why Uighur nationalism is inward and not outward looking.

The Uighurs strongly feel that the Han's attempts to suppress their language and literature and to impose Chinese language on them is a civilizational project. One Uighur academic argued with me, with a sense of conviction, that a slow but sure way to 'kill' any ethnic group is to 'kill' its mother tongue. The literature, folk tales and myths based on and propagated through their language would automatically wither away. In reaction, most of the 20,000 mosques in Xinjiang, have developed the facilities to teach Uighur, Arabic, Persian and even select Urdu to the Uighur boys and girls. Uighurs are taking this as a civilizational challenge. One Uighur intellectual argued with me that 'If I must learn Chinese for career advancement' then why should I not master English, the language of globalization which the several hundred million Mandarin speaking Hans are also learning?' Also, more and more Uighurs are going to Haj and coming back with a strong Islamic identity. It seems that radicalized and political Islam is making a slow but sure entry into Xinjiang.

From the 1880s onwards, China's march towards nation-building began. There is no escape from this fact. As a nation China is young. In fact, she is a nation-in-making like India. In this article, I have argued that Mao (1949-76) had replaced culture with ideology. His attempts to substitute culture with ideology (in this case Marxism-Maoism) failed. Present-day reformist leadership has replaced ideology with nationalism. Nationalism is the ideology of nation state and nation-building. The anti-imperialist edge of Chinese nationalism is practically over. She is no longer an aggrieved and dissatisfied power. The internal rough edges of nation-building enterprise have sharpened. This is clearly reflected in China's handling ofher minorities, cultural, religious, ethnic and political. Instead of respecting and celebrating their diversities, China feels that they are at odds with her nationalism. Then, no wonder, China does not make meaningful distinctions between 'autonomy', 'separatism' and 'splitism'. Demand for autonomy is not a demand for separatism and secession. In the name of 'historical materialism' from 1949 till the 1980s disciplines like sociology, psychology, political science and management disappeared from the Chinese academic syllabus and public domain. Chinese scholars lost almost half-a-century of scholarship in these branches of social sciences which alone can help China to tackle her ethnic tangle.

Finally, the phenomenon of mass Han migration—in fact an influx—into Xinjiang has already produced a Han majority there. Turkic Islamic minority people, fear that they have 'lost their homeland' already. It is a feeling of having been swamped and submerged. There is a heavy smell of internal colonialism in this. No amount of sophistry on the part of the Chinese state can justify this.

The fact sheet on Xinjiang, based on the above-mentioned four policy dynamics, Xinjiang is a split province whose population has became highly polarized. To put this in simple social science language, the Uighurs of Xinjiang are economically poor and are the have-nots. Politically, they are powerless. The real political power in China belongs to the Communist Party and the representation of minorities—in this case Uighurs—is negligible. Culturally, they feel subjugated. They are among the 'wretched of the earth' described by Franz Fanon. One Uighur intellectual—half Uighur and half Marxist—told me in Beijing that the power holders in Beijing and Xinjiang should read Karl Marx's *Economic and Philosophical Manuscript* where the author diagnoses the phenomenon of 'human alienation' under capitalism. I tried to correct him that the author of *Manuscript* had till then not become the Marxist of *Das Kapital*. The Uighur intellectual wouldn't listen to me. He concluded that 'in his mind there is still a bit of Marx (not Marxism of Mao) but in his heart there is Uighur ethnicity.

Ethnocide and Ethnogenesis of Uighurs in Xinjiang

Speaking in simple vernacular, ethnocide means extermination of a culture. It is a planned systematic and symmetrical (as opposed to asymmetrical) destruction of the cultural identities of an ethnic group. The cultural identity of an ethnic group involves its native language and literature, religious rituals, belief systems, ceremonial symbols, myths, customs, etc. An extreme example of ethnocide may even involve relocation/displacement of an ethnic group from its homeland to reservation. Even without resorting to relocation, and pushing ethnic groups to an isolated corner on the periphery, the same goal can be achieved by a massive migration of dominant groups to select and strategic areas. The Chinese state in Xinjiang has adopted the latter strategy to achieve its goal. The story of Han migration into Xinjiang has been discussed in parts of this paper. Few observations on the theme of ethnocide and ethnogenesis are called for.

Ethnocide cannot be achieved in one stroke. It has to be a process and quite often a long drawn one. It is a truism that the most enduring and ubiquitous trait of any strong ethnic group is its language, culture, rituals and religious beliefs. In fact, the strength and the distinctiveness of any ethnic group with strong ethnos (ascriptive psychology of differentiating between 'us' and 'others') depend on this identity marker. These markers may be described as germane and primordial. Therefore, the policy goals of ethnocide are precisely to considerably weaken them. If these marks of identity refuse to weaken and are waning fast, then they have to be erased and demolished. The philosophy of ethnocide is based on a racial psyche of the dominant ruling nationality group. This tendency to ethnocide also emanates from a feeling of strong ethnocentrism. I shall return to the theme of Chinese ethnocentrism later.

Ethnogenesis is normally a reaction against ethnocide. If the ethnos of an ethnic group are very strong and enduring and the levels of self-esteem are high and it is in a position to mobilize the collective resources of its group or succeeds in mobilizing international opinion in its favour, then a clash between ethnocide and ethnogenesis become almost unavoidable. In those cases, where the identity marks of any ethnic group are weak, somewhat artificially acquired (not innate and organic) and therefore malleable, such a community offers itself for assimilation. Out of 55 odd ethnic minorities of China numbering 130-40 million people, many have been integrated/assimilated in Han collectivity. The largest minority people of China—the Chuang of Korean origin—numbering about 20 million have been substantially, if not fully assimilated. The Manchus, Dais, Yis and many smaller groups have also been accultured in the Han national mainstream.

Three nationalities of China consider themselves as separate nations and are offering strong resistance to Chinese attempts to eliminate them. These are the Tibetans (Buddhist faith), the Mongols of Inner Mongolia (also of Buddhist faith) and the Uighurs, the Turkic Moslems of Xinjiang (Islamic faith). Tibetans and the Moslems of Xinjiang, in particular Uighurs, are offering a tough resistance to the Chinese policy of ethnocide. In Tibet it is a life and death struggle between survival and extinction. Dalai Lama's singular contribution apart from spreading the message of non-violence universally has been that he has immensely succeeded in empanelling the demand for Tibetan autonomy on international agenda. Since the focus of this paper is neither on Tibet nor on Mongolia, I propose to confine myself exclusively to Xinjiang.

As stated earlier an ethnic minority whose ethnos is weak and is only a prototype of its social mannerism, starts 'melting in the pot'. When subjected to the policies of ethnocide. It may not only offer itself for integration but it gets even ready for assimilation. Quite often it becomes more Christian than even the Pope, as the saying goes. This is what has precisely happened with the Manchus. This is also happening, slowly but surely to China's minority nationalities in Yunnan. Shih Shirpann offers an excellent laboratory for this case study. As stated above, the total population of Moslems (called Huis) in China is around 22 million. Of this, 12 million are Huis. These 12 million Huis speak Chinese. All of them read and write Mandarin. What is equally important, is that all of these 12 million Huis profess faith in Islam. Several components of their ethnos have either become weakened considerably or have waned or/and are still in the process of withering away. Of course, eating pork is taboo for them. They are spread over nearly 14 provinces of China. In a way they are 'scattered'. A good number of them do not have access to mosques because of around a total 23,000 mosques in China, 20,000 alone are located in Xinjiang. Many Huis do not observe the month of Ramadan. It is believed that a good number of them offer *namaz* at home at least twice a day, once in the morning and again in the evening. These 12 million Huis (of non-Turki origin) whose mother tongue is now Mandarin have been substantially integrated into the Han mainstream. Still occasionally some incidents of friction and even conflict do arise. For example, about 1,000 Huis in the late 1980s and early 1990s were killed in ethnic clashes in the province of Yunnan.

The ethnos of 10 million Moslems (of Turkic origin) in Xinjiang are qualitatively different from the remaining 12 million Huis of China. Uighur, originally it is believed, was the name of one of the tribes who came to Central Asia some 2,000 years back. It is believed by many anthropologists and historians that the Chinese word Hue or Hui was originally the transliteration of the word Uighur. Also, the language that the Uighurs spoke belonging to one of the main Turkic family language group—was also called Uighur. What are the implications of these two important facts? The ethnos of the Uighurs had a linguistic and a primordial (albeit tribal) foundation. Once settled in Turkestan (the name Xinjiang, in Chinese language means new territories was coined only in the eighteenth century) the geographical locale became another important identity mark. The Uighurs started describing themselves as 'oasis people' for the simple reason that they settled around and near the several hundred oases carved out by the flowing waters of the glacial mountains of basins. Almost 2 millennia back, abandoning a nomadic life, the Uighurs settled for agriculture around those oases and started calling themselves oasis people. Religion as one of the markers of their ethnic identity was added somewhat later. To begin with, the Uighurs were strong believers in Shamanism which was replaced partially by Machenianism of a Persian variety. When Buddhism was actively travelling on the Silk Route they become Buddhists along with Mongolia and Tibet. The 1,000 magnificent temples in Xinjiang are still a living testimony of Buddhism in this region.

Beginning from the tenth century onwards, a good number of them were converted to Islam. This process of conversion to Islam was slow but spontaneous. It took more than 300-400 years for Islam to acquire a near total sway over the entire region. Oasis identity and Islamic identity were not at odds with each other. Of this 10 million Moslem population of Xinjiang around 8 million are Uighurs and the remaining 2 million are Uzbeks, Tajiks, Kirghis and Tatars who also speak their own native languages like Uzbek and Tajik belonging to the Turkic language family. It needs to be mentioned here that these 2 million non-Uighurs do not have a very cordial and intimate relation with the Uighurs. This is not to say that they are in a warring relationship. However, these 2 million non-Uighur Moslems and the 8 million Uighurs have failed to offer a joint resistance to the Chinese efforts to ethnocide Xinjiang. Beijing's policy of divide and rule is also paying rich dividends. Moreover, the non-Uighur Moslems are also displaying anxieties and concerns against the Uighur's hegemonistic tendencies. Notwithstanding this silent but real schism, the non-Uighur Moslems are also devout believers and practitioners of Islam.

The Islamic identity of Uighurs is getting stronger by the day for the last 50 years or so. Partly it is a commensurate reaction against the Han policy of ethnocide. Uighurs are busy inventing and reinventing their ethnogeneses. This whole process of reinventing their ethnic identities is not only extremely challenging but it demands creativity as well. In case of the Tibetan people, efforts at preserving and reinventing their Tibetan identity has been a success. The local resistance of the Tibetan people (based on non-violence and passive resistance) and Dalai Lama's 'charismatic' leadership have proved immensely productive. Of these two basic factors Dalai Lama's leadership has received a lot of public attention and scholarly scrutiny. Unfortunately, the passive and non-violent resistances of the Tibetan people living in Tibet and outside Tibet (more Tibetan people are living outside Tibet in China than in Tibet) have not received the attention of academia interested in Tibetan affairs.

A few comments on the ethnogeneses of Uighurs of Xinjiang. Since Xinjiang was made a Chinese province under the Manchus there always has been serious and in fact intractable problems between the Hans and the Uighurs. Mao promised them the 'right of self-determination' Jiangxi (Kiangsi) Soviet (1934-9). Once the Chinese Communist Party came to power in October 1949, the promise of 'right of self-determination' was changed to 'autonomy'. The period from October 1949 till 1957 was the golden period of China's ethnic minorities. Trouble started brewing during the period of the 'Hundred Flowers' (1957) when Mao offered the Chinese people the right to comment, criticize and even articulate their grievances against the government and the party openly. The mainstream leadership of Uighurs openly articulated its demand for a separate space for Uighurs. Even a section of Uighur elites went to the extent of reminding Mao about his solemn promise of 'self-determination' to Xinjiang. Chinese people openly demanded freedom and democracy. What was the result? Mao's 'Hundred Flowers' started wilting within a hundred days and the Chinese Communist Party had to launch a 'rectification' and 'anti-rightist' campaign.

In his quest for 'revolutionary immortality' under the rubric of 'permanent revolution' and as a consequence of Sino-Soviet schism which led Mao to believe that the Soviet Union under Nikita Khruschev had 'betrayed' revolution Mao launched his policy of Three Red-Banners. It was a race towards hastened transition to socialism and even communism. This style of communism proved a disaster for China. The 1958-61 famines claimed a whopping human toll of nearly 30 million people. This unprecedented famine proved more catastrophic for minority areas which had a weak economy and underdeveloped agriculture.

As a consequence of famine and Sino-Soviet schism, about 70,000 Uighurs, Kazakhs and Kirghis crossed over to the neighbouring Soviet Union. To avoid collectivization of livestocks, millions of animals were slaughtered and consumed by Xinjiang farmers in their oasis locales. Economically things got stabilized and became normal by 1962-3. China regained the 1957 levels of production. Mao's radical 'impetuosity' instead of waning started ascending greatly. This was articulated in the form of the 'Great Proletarian Cultural Revolution' (technically 1966-9 but ideologically 1966 till Mao's death in 1976).

Mao's so-called 'Cultural Revolution' degenerated into a prototype of civil war within the Chinese Communist Party and within China.

The Chinese Communist Party under Deng's leadership in 1981 termed the Cultural Revolution as Mao's 'feudal fascist rule darkest in Chinese history'. Let me not waste time on the narratives of the Cultural Revolution and exclusively focus my comments on the disastrous impact of the Cultural Revolution on minority areas of China and Xinjiang in particular.

In 1962 in an important interaction with a delegation of American blacks visiting China, Mao made an extremely consequential statement on the problematic of ethnic nationalities. He said, 'The ethnic minority question in the ultimate analysis is a question of class struggle'. The implications were clear and categorical. If the dynamics of class struggle are to apply between the Han's and ethnic minorities of China, then it can be resolved and won only through force and ethnocide. This policy of ethnocide was fully put to test at least in three ethnic minority areas, viz., Inner Mongolia, Tibet and Xinjiang. All the moderate leadership (in Communist Party as well in the government) was replaced by hard-liners. Millions of young school (senior secondary) and college students were sent (to use sinologist's vocabulary 'rusticated') to minority areas to 'exchange revolutionary' experiences with the masses. Mao's wife Madam Jhiang Qing, in her famous statement proclaimed 'When China has already socialism (she said very soon China shall attain communism), then why these ethnic and minority distinctions'. Mongolia and Xinjiang were the hardest hit during the Cultural Revolution. China's policy towards these three ethnic minorities—Mongols, Tibetans and Moslems in Xinjiang was clearly based on ethnocide. In certain critical situations when minorities in these three provinces resisted, the policy started assuming certain features of genocide.

Mao and Maoism ruled China till 1976, a period of approximately 27 years. From 1976 (both Zhou En-lai and Mao died in 1976) till 1978-9 China was in a flux and this period was a sort of interregnum. 1979 onwards, Deng Xiao-ping and his reformist associates inaugurated a new epoch (in fact, a new age) in China. China under Mao's revolution and China under Deng's reform are in fact two Chinas based on different reasonings and premises. Beginning from December 1978 till date China has undergone several kinds of transformations—economic, social, cultural, and ideological and foreign policy shifts. What a contrast between the so-called revolution and structural reforms? Even on the question of policy shift towards ethnic minorities, this paradigm shift is visible. It is more accommodative towards those minorities who are willing to integrate/assimilate in what China calls the 'national mainstream' which frankly amounts to 'Hanization'. This accommodative and flexible option is not available to the Uighurs of Xinjiang and the Tibetans of Tibet. It is also true that the Chinese state has made unprecedented heavy investments in Tibet and Xinjiang which has resulted in higher economic growth and a higher per capita GDP. However, the policy matrix on the ethnic problematic pertaining to Tibet and Xinjiang continues to be based on ethnocide.

In my analysis above, I was referring to the China-centric mindset of the Chinese elites. Right from the ancient time when the Han dynasty and Confucianism had acquired political and cultural roots in China, the concept of a China-centric mentality started shaping. The very concept of a 'middle kingdom' emanates from China's collective consciousness that China is the reference point of civilization. Those who are 'outsiders' are either 'barbarians' or fit candidates to be 'civilized'. The concept of *Han Ren* (Han man) is as old as the Han dynasty but the concept of *Han-minzu* (Han nationality) is a late nineteenth-century phenomenon. This shift from Han Ren to Han-minzu started evolving when China started developing the consciousness of a nation. The shift from civilization to empire and finally to nation is merging into a hybrid form of superpower ambition which China's present leaders believe is well within its striking distance. Let me offer a new name to this national aspiration of China and in the absence of a better expression (at my command) I call it 'Han ethno-centrism'. China's ethno-centrism is so strong that the space vacated by the decline (some say withering away) of ideology (Marxism-Maosim) is being filled up by this ethno-centrism. If the one ideology which has not declined and weakened in China in the last hundred years or so, it is Chinese nationalism. In fact, after the disintegration of the USSR and the rest of the socialist/Marxist world, this psyché of China-centric nationalism is getting stronger. On occasions, this syndrome does not hesitate to acquire chauvinistic, aggressive and even expansionist overtones.

It is this format of militant nationalism which prevents her from distinguishing between autonomy, separatism and independence. In my considered opinion Tibetans and Uighurs are demanding, as of today, only a meaningful autonomy so as to preserve their cultural identity and self-esteem. May be only a handful of elements among the Uighurs do dream for national independence but their number can be counted on one's fingers. For China any demand for autonomy and dignity by these two nationalities, Uighurs and Tibetans, is perceived as a call for separatism.

A few more comments on China's ethno-centrism. In contemporary parlance, the term 'ethno-centrism' remains in use as a reference to culturally-biased judgement. *The Dictionary of Anthropology* (Barfield 1997, p. 55) defines ethno-centrism as 'the belief that one's own culture is superior to others'. The diversities of language, culture, rituals, festivals, and symbols of non-Han ethnic groups are viewed as irritants, funny and even as new fangled ideas to an ethnocentrist. Tolerance towards 'other's' diversities and their identity marks are objects of ridicule and scorn rather than of celebration. Ethno-centrism and democracy do not make good partners. Chinese elites view them as 'thesis' and 'anti-thesis'. Synthesis to the Chinese is a complete victory of anti-thesis over thesis. Hanization of these 'diversities' is the ideal solution. Unless this 'Hanization' or 'nationalization' of these 'backward' and 'uncivilized' nationalities is achieved, China's ethno-centrism is incomplete. So runs the argument in Beijing, at times stated covertly and at times overtly.

As stated above, the strong feeling of this Middle Kingdom syndrome, referred to here as ethno-centric psyché, has been a protean theme of China's ascriptive narratives of herself. This thought permeates all the three essential ideological constructs, viz., China as a civilization, China as an empire and China as a nation. I am strongly of the opinion that these are the only three meaningful and real approaches to understand and evaluate China. China as a civilization, China as an empire and China as a nation (in fact, a nation in the making) are the only useful and viable categories for the sinologist studying China. An ideological approach alone; albeit Marxism, Leninism never made any sense to understand China. That is one main reason why Marxist and Leftist analyses of

China (from 1949-76) proved completely off the point. In the entire recorded history of China, very glorious and rich otherwise, of the last 5,000 years, there have been only four historic occasions when this China-centric pride of the Hans was challenged. The first time was when Buddhism from India intellectually and philosophically 'invaded' China. In its long glorious history, China for the first time was contrasted with a thought that some other country (other than China) can be equally civilized. Buddhism found an easy and wide acceptance in China. The second occasion when China's national pride was humbled was in sixteenth century when Mongols, successfully breaking through the Great Wall defeated China and established the first non-Han dynasty and ruled for years. The third occasion when China felt slighted was when Manchus came from Manchuria, again crossing and breaking through the 'Great Wall' conquered China and established the Ching (in Chinese it means pure) dynasty which was overthrown by the 1911 Revolution of China. This shocked China both as a civilization and as a empire. The last occasion when China felt 'humiliated' was when the Western capitalist/colonial powers (beginning with the First Opium War) converted China into a 'semi-colony'. When Buddhism permeated China, it was a civilizational shock. However, the Mongol and then Manchu conquest of China was a shock to the Chinese Empire. Civilizationally, both the Mongols and the Manchus were much inferior to the Chinese civilization. It was because of their sense of civilizational inferiority that Manchus subsequently offered themselves for assimilation and became a part of China's civilizational mainstream. The present leadership of China is determined that China shall not face such shame anymore. This concern of China is absolutely justified.

One more small but pertinent comment on ethnocide and ethno-genesis. As stated above, ethno-genesis is substantially—if not invariably a reaction against ethnocide. This contest and the confrontation between the two is a fight for survival and extinction. The stakes are very high. This conflict produces winners and losers. The winner walks away with everything and in return the loser relinquishes almost everything including his identity and self-esteem. If the contest is based on the matrix of 'Integration' then both the contestants are winners but since ethnocide is based on the matrix of total assimilation and absorption, the ethnic minority is a sure loser. For the dominant group, it is a quest for glory and pride, but for an ethnic minority, it is a titanic struggle for survival. If the ethnos of the ethnic group are innate, organic and authentic and therefore not a part of their acquired mannerism and if several other factors are favourable, then the ethnic group has a chance to remain floated.

As of today, it would be professionally hazardous to comment whether the Uighur and several other Turkic Islamic ethnic minorities will swim or get drowned in the coming 4-5 decades. Dru. C. Gladney and several other distinguished scholars have done ground-breaking academic research on the Xinjiang problematic. Many of these scholars, in particular Gladney, opine that the chances of surviving the ethnogenesis by the Uighurs are reasonably strong. In a significant research work based on intensive and extensive fieldwork on Uighurs, Gladney has produced a very convincing proof of enduring ethnic identity of Uighurs.

Ethnogenesis is a continuous act of regeneration and reinvention. It demands creativity and imagination. It cannot be achieved by dogmatic and a sectarian element of leadership in any ethnic nationality. If an ethnic group successfully modernizes the core trad-itional value markers and rituals which deserve to be modernized, then it is strengthening the roots of its ethnogenesis. In this sense ethnogenesis of Uighurs in the last half a century have incorporated new and living tissues in their cultural tapestry. Ethnogenesis is much more than updating the traditions. In fact, all the traditions of an ethnic minority which claims to be living and dynamic need not be modernized. Periodically, with an intervention of decades and centuries, an honest assessment should be made about the traditions and legacy of the group's identity. The retrogressive, the backward looking and undemocratic (more so anti-democracy) corpus of legacy should not be and in fact cannot be updated. Only the robust, forward looking and egalitarian component of the group's legacy qualifies to be taken up for ethnogenesis. Every great universal *dharma* contains a hugely rich tradition of compassion and equity oriented values. These values and traditions qualify to be reinvented. The fact of the matter is that this intellectual enterprise called ethnogenesis can be achieved only by saints, sufis and social reformers.

Any great civilization or a religious system which periodically fails to produce such great minds is surely heading towards its decline. This innovating mission of updating and renovating the ethnic culture relevant and acceptable to the believing groups cannot be performed by NGOs and other well-meaning collectivities. An innovator and an inventor is much more than an angry agitator. A mind (and soul) full of quest and genius alone can be an innovator. Innovating and reinventing culture and tradition requires extraordinary skill and qualities of investigation and synthesis. A Martin Luther King, a Vivekananda, a Gandhi and a Dalai Lama alone can achieve this stupendous task. The concept of non-violence is as old as the hills. However, the way Gandhi and later, Martin Luther King and Dalai Lama revived and in fact reinvented non-violence and compassion speaks volumes of the science and art of creativity and regeneration.

Let me illustrate my argument by giving a concrete example of one such rich reinvention of tradition by the Uighurs in the last couple of decades. Uighurs in particular and several other ethnic groups of Islamic faith in Xinjiang used to have the tradition of *Mashraf*. This ritual, in the good old days had multiple objectives. It was an occasion for celebration when a young Uighur male graduated to adulthood. The entire tradition fell in disuse and even when used was reduced to a prosaic and dull family ritual. Its social, moral and religious content got divested. This traditional form of Mashraf had almost disappeared in Kazakhstan during Stalin's purges in the late 1930s. However, in the valley of Xinjiang this tradition escaped total decimation but suffered a considerable decline even there. During the Great Leap Forward (1958-62) and the Great Proletarian Cultural Revolution (1966-76) it had practically disappeared in Xinjiang also.

In the face of Han ethnocide, the Uighur religious elites and community leaders decided not only to revive Mashraf but also to update and reinvent it. Now, there is a rich, varied, socially relevant and authentic scholarly literature available on the theme of Mashraf. A reinvented and revived Mashraf is no longer an old family affair to begin and end with a family feast. Every *mahalla* (segregated locality) in Lee Valley and other parts of Xinjiang richly peopled by Uighurs have created a network of Mashrafs. An average Mashraf is organized in a group of 30 (or even more) male Uighurs. This group of Uighur youth is called *Ottuz* or *Oghul*. In folk parlance it is referred to as 'thirty sons' (normally it has more than 30 youths). A Mashraf gathering normally on a weekend starts around 6 p.m. and lasts till 10 p.m. The old tradition of teaching to the new adults about their duties and obligations to the family and the community is conducted. There is also dancing and singing. The dimension of music and romance has been added (love themes based on *ashiq* and *mashooq* from Indian movies pirated through Pakistani traders). Also a one-hour religious discourse on Islam and its egalitarian traditions is delivered by learned scholars. Finally an event of Mashraf ends with a rich and ethnic Uighur feast. These Mashraf events are taking the form of community participation which promotes a communitarian and an altruist face of Islam thus solidifying and cementing the Uighur ethnos. When it was revived in Lee Valley in the 1980s in the wake of Deng's reforms to liberalize religious practices, one of the foci of those Mashrafs was to wean away the Uighur youths from drug and alcohol which was spreading like a virus in Xinjiang. (Xinjiang has the largest percentage of HIV positive patients in entire China.) Soon, it developed into an occasion of social and religious reform and an instrument of acculturization of Uighur youth to Islam. A young Uighur who does not participate in Mashraf is considered uncultured and even uncouth. The Chinese state and the Xinjiang Communist Party leaders were not happy about the revival of Mashraf, notwithstanding the stronger revival of religion and even religiosity throughout China.

The revival and reinvention of Mashraf which eminently qualifies to be a good illustration of ethnogeneses could not have gone unnoticed by Chinese authorities. In 1994 at Kuldja the largest city in the Lee Valley, a group of intellectuals, students, traders and community leaders assembled to debate the 'fate of their people and the nation'. The meeting decided to have a big gathering of several thousand at a Mashraf. Such gatherings were gaining currency and sports activity—soccer in particular—was getting acceptability in Lee Valley. In fact, these Mashraf gatherings had started assuming the form of a sort of grassroot movement of cultural solidarity with subdued political undertones. At the same time the movement was 'creating a sense of national unity among young Uighur men who were finding in Islam an empowering world view and alternative'. Mashraf was emerging as a small challenge and thus an alternative both to Confucianism and Marxism.

In mid-August 1995 Xinjiang's annual football match of Mashraf was decided to be organized. When the organizers approached the authorities for permission, they were told to deposit 50,000 Yuan as fee. The organizers collected this amount and approached the local authorities, who now raised the fee to 100,000 Yuan. The organizers even then agreed for this raise and decided to collect this amount partly through donation and partly through the sale of tickets. The authorities now flatly refused the permission to hold the football match. What was more astonishing was that the authorities on 14 August 1995 with the help of the local police removed all soccer goals from football fields of all the school's in the city. When the Uighur youths protested against this policy of highhandedness of the police and authorities, the police used force against demonstrators, arresting many and injuring hundreds. The authorities dubbed the proposed football Mashraf as an expression of Uighur nationalism and 'separatist' aspirations. It was this pent-up resentment of Uighur youths which exploded in February 1997 when several thousand Uighur youths carrying banners (with verses from the Koran written on it) organized a protest march. The authorities suppressed it with even greater force. May protesters were shot dead by the police. Hundreds died, thousands were injured and several hundreds were sent to jail. Within a month the 'judiciary' of Xinjiang awarded 'execution' to about a dozen youth by dubbing them splitters'.

This paper focuses on the ethnocide policy of the Hans and the Uighur's attempts of resistance by consolidating and even reinventing its ethnogenesis. In the last two decades two epoch-making events have occurred in world politics which have hugely impacted the processes and content of ethnocide and ethnogenesis in Xinjiang. Paradoxically, neither the Hans Chinese nor the Uighurs of Xinjiang are the author of these two events but both are facing its brunt. In the 1990s, the USSR and several other communist countries met with disintegration and dissolution. Here I am not concerned with the causes of this collapse. The collapse of the Soviet Union and many communist countries was the most ideologically and politically consequential event of the later half of the twentieth century. This collapse was an internal and authentic one. Obviously, it was a multi-causal phenomenon. There were several serious fault lines in the system which instead of being repaired in time and re-fixed continued to get complicated. From the point of view of a serious debate on the ethnicity problematic, two major fault lines should be mentioned. These two fault lines had and continue to have an intimate and decisive impact on ethnicity. One, the democracy deficit relationship between the dominant ethnic majority and the minority ethnicity. Second, the Soviet Union had serious historical, linguistic, religious and ethnic distortions produced by the ethnocide policies of Stalin. In other words, the Marxist discourse and action programme to resolve the ethnic problematic was basically flawed. One USSR has resulted in the birth of fifteen independent countries called CIS (Commonwealth of Independent States). Yugoslavia, Albania, Czechoslovakia, Romania, Bulgaria and several other communist countries also went the Soviet way. There were many fault lines in these communist states. I do not propose to comment on those fault lines. One common fault line in the USSR and several multi-ethnic communist countries was the systematic wrong handling of nationalities problematic. Stalin's brutal policy based on force and ethnocide was responsible for disintegration on ethnic/ nationalities lines. It is not a coincidence that Soviet Union which appeared to be an impregnable monolith till it started crumbling has disintegrated along its historical, religious, linguistic and ethnical fault lines. The fifteen CIS states are the consequences of those fault lines. Several other so-called communist countries in eastern and central Europe—Yugoslavia, Albania, Czechoslovakia, Romania, Bulgaria also split along the racial, linguistic, religious and ethnic fault lines on the Soviet pattern. The CIS, three Central Asian Republics—Kazakhstan, Kyrghistan and Tajikistan—share common borders with Xinjiang (the other states which have a common border with Xinjiang are Russia, Mongolia, Afghanistan, Pakistan and India). This disintegration of the Soviet Union and several other Soviet bloc countries along the historical, religious, cultural, linguistic and ethnic fault lines has taught several important lessons to the Uighurs and other Moslem nationalities of Xinjiang. It would be an academic folly to argue that China shall go the Soviet way. China has successfully graduated out of the unpleasant and disastrous legacy of Marxism and Maoism. While in Soviet Union, the non-Russians constituted almost 50 per cent of the total population and hence had a numerical weightage on the ethnic tangle. Notwithstanding the fact that China—both as a civilization and as a nation—is much more homogeneous, the emergence of these states on the common borders of Xinjiang has rekindled a hope among the Uighurs that in an event of China's disintegration they would redeem their dreams of having an independent Uighurstan. To put it bluntly, the fact of Soviet Union's disintegration and the emergence of the three Islamic states of CIS on the borders of Xinjiang, have emboldened the Uighurs of Xinjiang to dream of a similar destiny. I repeat, it would be an act of foolishness and supreme ignorance (about China) to argue that China will go the Soviet way. Conversely, to argue that China is an absolutely impregnable monolith of unity and strength and therefore totally immune from such an eventuality is to believe the surface and ignore the sub-terranian reality. China has several serious fault lines. As a student of Chinese politics I can enumerate these fault lines of China clearly visible to the sinologists. The emerging middle class of China numbering 300 million people plus are demanding more transparency and freedom. They are repeatedly articulating their demand that the government be accountable to the people for their acts of commission and omission. The increasing gap between the haves and have nots has already crossed tolerable thresholds. The regional imbalance between the developed parts of China and backward regions has emerged as a major point of discord. The all-pervading corruption and nepotism in the Chinese government and the Chinese Communist Party has acquired Olympian heights. The credibility and legitimacy of both the party and the government have touched the lowest depths. In a word, Mr. Democracy is giving a knock at the gates of the Middle Kingdom.

The second major event which again has neither been authored by the Hans nor by the Uighurs but has a huge bearing on the ethnic tangle in Xinjiang is the epochal event of 9/11 in the United States. The Islamic terrorist attack on America has generated a near universal alert against terrorism. Radical/political Islam is the butt of this disapproval and alert. A strong and effective world opinion has emerged and continues to emerge that in several countries, the Muslim populace radicalized by political Islam is becoming problematic. In a reductionist way, a deductive logic from this belief is spreading the message that Moslems in those societies where they constitute a meaningful minority are trouble-makers. China has successfully exploited this argument within China and even outside it. The Chinese authorities are busy propagating through policy speeches and public discourses on ethnicity that Muslim Uighurs of Xinjiang are the wrongdoers and not the victims. On this count, Chinese state propaganda is both intensive as well as effective. Several Uighur organizations operating outside China have been declared unlawful bodies both by the US and the UN. This has been a serious setback to Uighur's legitimate demands for autonomy and justice. Fortunately for China, since there is not much of political/radical Islam in Xinjiang, there are not many ethnic soldiers there. Since there is no democracy there, there are not many political entrepreneurs among the Uighurs who can think of practising identity politics and mobilize their brothers for a political change. The option is not available to the Uighurs of Xinjiang. This option is not available to the Hans either.

To conclude, both the contestants, the Chinese Communist Party and the Chinese state on the one hand and the Uighurs of Xinjiang on the other, suffer from democracy deficiency. Inherently, there should be no major incompatibility between the Islamic commitment of Uighurs and democracy (on account of the fact that there is no radical/political Islam among Uighurs) in Xinjiang. For China, opting or not opting for democracy is a civilizational choice. China's capacity to conceive and conceptualize out-of-box thinking is impressively amazing. The way China, under Deng's leadership, cast away the straightjacket of Marxism and Maoism speaks volumes of her capacity to rediscover and reinvent herself. This paradigm shift which occurred in the 1980s and continues to consolidate and expand its reach has no parallels in history. China has learned and continues to learn a lot of new lessons from her competitor and also her role model, viz., the United States. Instead of treating her minorities as subjects she has to learn how to treat them as citizens.

This can happen only with the aid and advice of Mr. Democracy. In the end, the Uighur population of Xinjiang can be divided into three broad opinion groups. One extreme end is a miniscule minority of radicalized/politicized Islam who are Pleading for Uighur's right of self-determination in the proposed form of Uighurstan. This group is pleading for a confrontation and clash with the Hans and the Chinese state. The second opinion group consists of those Uighurs who have been substantially converted to the idea of integration in the Han mainstream. This group finds opportunities as well advancement through the modicum of reconciliation. This group is also in a hopeless minority. The huge middle consists of those people who will be satisfied if the Chinese state confers upon them genuine autonomy in the field of language, culture and religion. By and large this huge middle belong to the secular persuasion. If the ground situation in Xinjiang continues to worsen. I am afraid the Islamic fundamentalism may start gaining an upper hand at the cost of the secular middle.

11

Nepal

Rise of Ethnicity and the Agenda of Inclusive Democracy

KRISHNA HACHHETHU

Nepal has embarked upon the twenty-first century with an agenda of restructuring the states in the form of inclusive democracy. A number of epochal events placed Nepal on the road of a new destination. These were the unprecedented mass uprising of April 2006 (known as the *Jana Andolan* II) in which 3 to 4 million people in a country of 23 million participated directly; a decade long civil war (1996-2005) between the security forces of the state and the guerrillas of the Communist Party of Nepal, Maoists or CPN-Maoists, culminating in the mainstreaming of the former insurgents into a system of peaceful multiparty competition. The April 2008 elections to the Constituent Assembly (CA) were followed by negotiations among the competing ideologies and interests with a task of framing a new constitution in the spirit of the goals of *Jana Andolan* II; and demise of monarchy—an institution that had long been considered as a 'symbol and substance of national unity and nationalism of Nepal' —in May 2008. Above all, there has been the rise of ethnicity—visible in the emergence of ethnic and regional movements in the post-1990 democratic space backed by international conventions and communities and geared up by ethnicization of politics and politicization of ethnicity. This has brought in a paradigm shift in Nepal's nation-building project from that of assimilation into the fold of dominant hill caste's culture, to accommodation of social diversity, along with the declaration of Nepal as a republic, secular and pluralistic state. Nepal has adopted a new electoral system—a system combining 'first-past-the-post' (FPTP) and proportional representation (PR)—ensuring representation of different social segments in political power structure in proportion to the size of their population. Along with hill Hindu high castes, excluded ethnic groups like the *madheshi* community (people of plains land origin), Dalits and women are legally recognized as political constituencies. Moreover, the federal project under consideration is hoped to become a big step forward for promoting inclusive polity. Emergence of regional parties as balances of a hung parliament (CA) in the present bipolar mainstream politics—Maoist as one pole and traditional parliamentary parties in another pole—also suggests the emergence of a new trend, i.e. the transformation of identity movements into political power. The new constitution in the making by the CA has to give a legal/constitutional stamp to Nepal as an inclusive state.

Past Experience of Nation Building

Nepal is home to 101 caste/ethnic, 91 linguistic and 9 religious groups. Based on caste, ethnic, regional, cultural and linguistic cleavages, Nepali population can be broadly classified into three major groups: *pahadi* (hill people) and *madheshi* (plain people); *jat* (caste groups) and *janajati* (ethnic/tribal groups); and high caste and low caste Hindus (within *jat*). As a consequence of the historical process of national integration high caste culture—monarchy, Hinduism and Nepali language were effectively enforced as the three key pillars of Nepali nationalism—thus diversity has been translated into inequality among the different social groups.

Monarchy has played a central role in the evolution and unification of Nepali state. Prithvi Narayan Shah, the king of Gorkha principality, established modern unified Nepal by conquest. He, thus, introduced the Shah regime based on the right of sword. The utility of sword for territorial expansion was, however, effectively blocked following the end of war with British India in 1816 and demarcation of the political territory of the kingdom. Hence, the legitimacy of sword was confined to and symbolized with the royal army, which was, however, significant in retaining control in conquered areas. But the symbol of the sword was not sufficient to establish legitimacy among the people of the vanquished lands. Absolute control of political authority, monopolization of economic resources, and penetration and expansion of social value systems of the victorious groups in vanquished areas were some of the mechanisms that the Shah rulers and the subsequent Rana rulers used to consolidate their respective regimes. It was, as one critic observed, an 'empire model' of national integration (Pfaff-Czarnecka 1997: 421).

Prithvi Narayan Shah adopted both strategies together, i.e. respect for the pluralistic characteristics of Nepali state and assimilation into Hinduism, as his motto was to make Nepal an *asli hindustan* (pure Hindu state). For the successors of P.N. Shah, Nepal as *asli hindustan* had become the *mul mantra* in the state-designed project of national integration. It also manifested the source of legitimacy of the Hindu king, derived from divine right. The Shah/monarch, as a hereditary institution, was enforced by the traditional Hindu view of the nobility of birth, as it was an accepted tradition all through the ancient and the medieval times. The Hindu polity places the king as a sovereign lord, a protector of territory and of subjects, a guardian of moral order, an upholder of traditions, and the source of all spiritual and temporal power (Sharma 1997: 475). As the ideology of Hindu religion and polity provided legitimacy to the Shah regime, the rulers tried their best to spread Hinduism all over the country. In the post-unification period, 'the process of Hinduization was intensified' (Baral 1991: 56). So kingship along with the Hindu religion played a key role in the construction of the Nepali state and identity.

The Hindu polity—in which monarchy and religion have decisive roles—was further enacted more rigidly during the Rana period (1846-1951). The Rana prime ministers were also monarchs by title (*Shree Tin Maharaj,* king of Kaski and Lamjung) and by the authority they enjoyed. Jung Bahadur Rana, founder of the Rana regime, promulgated a Civil Code in 1854 providing a legal framework to Vedic prescription of social order in hierarchical caste society. The Civil Code 1854 classified the people into three broader categories in ascending order: (a) *Tagadhari* (sacred-thread wearing castes) at the top, (b) *matwali* (alcohol-drinking castes and ethnic groups) in the middle, and (c) 1. *Sudra* (impure but touchable) and 2. *Acchut* (impure and untouchable castes) at the lowest position. The Code violated the very notion of national integration, i.e. equality among the people of a given territory/state. The Code discriminated the people of different caste hierarchy in the judicial system and in distribution of the state resources. By putting ethnic groups into the fold of Hindu-based hierarchical caste system, the Code translated diversity into inequality.

The partyless panchayat system under absolute monarchy (1960-90) upheld the old symbols and practices, though the new Civil Code of 1963 is a radical departure from the past as it recognizes the universal principal of equality of people. The legal abolition of caste discrimination was/is, however, hardly translated into practice because of self-contradiction of the value system that the state ushered. The Hindu religion and caste system is complementary and the ruler's adherence to Hindu religion was well reflected in late king Birendra's perception of the source of legitimacy of monarchy. He said, 'In Nepal, the monarch and his subjects have been governed by Dharma, a system drawn from the Hindu religion. The King cannot change this value system' (quoted in Shaha 1975: 7). His predecessor king Mahendra, the founder of the panchayat regime, legally identified Nepal as a Hindu state as it was explicitly mentioned in the Constitution of Nepal 1962 for the first time, unlike the previous constitutions. So the king and Hindu religion were retained as the core components of Nepali nationalism.

The panchayat system spread the Nepali language, which has already received a status of official language since 1930. Even before the introduction of the panchayat system, the state took a policy of promotion of Nepali language at the cost of other languages. Here, recommendations made by Nepal National Education Planning Commission (1955) are worthwhile to mention.

> Nepali should be the medium of education, exclusively from the third grade on, and as much as possible in the first two grades. No other languages should be taught even optionally, in the primary school because few children will have need for them, they would hinder the reaching of Nepali . . . other language will gradually disappear and greater national strength and unity will result. (quoted in Bhattachan 2003: 26-7; Whelpton 1997: 49)

With state protection and promotion, Nepali language—being the official language and medium of education as well—has increasingly received prominence with the development of infrastructure, particularly in education, media, transportation and communication. Internal migration also contributed to developing Nepali as *lingua franca* of the country, and so, as a powerful means of national integration. The dominant trend of migration in the pre-1950 period was from the west hills (original homeland of Khas/Nepali-speaking people) to the east hills (*janjati* dominated area) and later from north (hill) to south (plain *tarai*). The migration of hill people to *tarai*—a traditional homeland of tribal people and the people of Indian origin—led to change in its demography. At present, nearly one-third of the total *tarai* population is those of hill migrants, mostly Nepali-speaking people.

Centralization of politics and administration was another instrument of the state's project of national integration. Though decentralization, balanced regional development, and people's participation were some of the buzz words the panchayat regime propagated, the system itself was highly centralized. So the objective set in the decentralization project was largely confined to paperwork, which obviously had adverse impact on national integration in the real sense and also to the survival of the regime itself. The model of national integration what the panchayat system prescribed was homogenization and assimilation of diverse groups into the fold of *parbatiya* Hindu culture. Disregard to pluralism was expressed in slogans, like 'our king, our country' and 'one language, one dress, and one culture'. In sum, the panchayat system upheld and espoused traditional components, i.e. kingship, Hindu religion and Nepali language, and added new contents like decentralization, development and coexistence in the state-designed scheme of national integration.

The 1990 mass movement ended the panchayat regime and restored democracy. The new constitution brought out fundamental changes in the political system of the country—from partyless to multiparty system, reduction of king's position from absolute to constitutional monarchy, and promotion of people's status from subject to citizen. The newly-established democratic regime was associated with the principles of popular sovereignty, fundamental and human rights of the citizen, representative government, and an independent judiciary. Were such changes significant to reset the state's ideology *vis-à-vis* ethnicity? The 1990 constitution stood in between. On the one hand, it recognizes the pluralistic character of Nepali society consisting of diverse cultural and linguistic groups, which was widely appreciated as a major departure from the historical model of national integration (Sharma 1992: 7; Fisher 1993: 14; Gurung 1997: 502; Pffa-Czarnecka 1997: 419). But the government ignored the constitutional commitments, i.e. to 'maintain cultural diversity', right 'to promote literature, scripts, arts and culture of different groups', freedom 'to protect religious places and trust' and recognition of other than Nepali (language of the nation) as 'languages of nationalities'—at the implementation level. On the other hand, the 1990 constitution upheld a number of features of Nepali nationalism adopted since 1951 and before. Particularly from the end of the Rana regime in 1951, the components like kingship, Hindu religion, and Nepali language, and the concepts of citizen, equality, and unity and harmony of different social groups have been adopted as ingredients of the nation state of Nepal. As the 1990 constitution recognized Nepal as a unitary, Hindu, and monarchical state, and Nepali as the official language as before, many things remained unchanged in the basic characteristics of the Nepali state.

Since the time of unification of Nepal, the rulers—Shahs, Ranas, Panchas and party leaders—had tried to develop Nepal as a homogeneous, monolithic and unitary state providing protection to one language (Nepali), one caste group (hill Bahun-Chhetri), and one religion (Hindu), ignoring the reality of diversified and pluralistic character of the Nepali society. Besides, the state-designed 'Nepalization' process—through Hinduization, spread of the *parbatiya*'s culture, institutionalization of caste system converting separate identity of ethnic groups into caste structures, and centralization of politics and administration—had led to increase in disparity among different social groups. The hill high caste Brahmin-Chhetri and Newar have long been in a privileged position. Other groups, i.e. *janajati*, *madheshya* and dalit are generally marginalized. The legacy of history is well reflected in unequal distribution of socio-economic resources of the country and in representation of political power structure of the country.

The old model of national integration resulted in placing the ethnic groups in a disadvantaged position. So, the rise of ethnicity in Nepal is intended towards curtailing power of the dominant group (hill Hindu high castes Brahmin and Chhetri) and also is motivated for assertion of identity, sharing of economic resources and greater representation in political power structure of the country.

Democratic Space and Ethnic Movement

Ethnic and regional activism for inclusive democracy was first noticed at the dawn of democracy in Nepal in 1951 and revived after the restoration of democracy in 1990. The 1959 general elections were prelude to assimilate the hill ethnic groups and *madheshi* community into the body politic from complete exclusion in the past under the Shah and Rana regimes. Hence, their representations in the elected bodies have continued albeit in a much lower proportion in comparison to the strength of their population. Particularly after the replacement of a partyless panchayat regime by a multiparty system in 1990, ethnic movements are accelerating. The restoration of democracy with the principles of popular sovereignty, equality, freedom and cultural rights has provided a platform for ethnic activism. The advent of democracy has, therefore, been followed with the rise of ethnic consciousness and awareness. Over time, the political parties have gradually become more receptive to the cause of excluded groups, accommodating them, although only a token accommodation, in the party apparatus and amplifying party policy platforms related to ethnic issues with each successive parliamentary election in the 1990s (Hachhethu 2003). Although the parliamentary parties' offer to include previously excluded groups were not clear, nor were they specific about the modality of inclusion, their realization of the need for inclusive democracy, even in rhetoric, had its impact, making the post-1990 democratic state somehow responsive to the question of identity. The inclusion of caste/ethnic content in the national census (via a separate section for

Table 11.1(a): Human Development by Caste and Ethnicity, 2006

	Dominant Groups			Marginal Groups			
	Bahun	Chhetri	Newar	Madhesi	Janajati	Dalit	Nepal
Life Expectancy	68.1	60.6	68.0	61.6	62.9	61.0	63.7
Adult Literacy Rate (%)	69.9	58.4	68.2	42.3	51.7	38.0	52.4
Means Years of Schooling	5.4	3.7	4.7	2.4	3.0	1.7	3.2
Per Capita PPP Income US$	2,395	1,736	3,097	1,094	1,405	977	1,597
Life Expectancy Index	0.718	0.594	0.717	0.610	0.632	0.601	0.645
Educational Attainment Index	0.586	0.471	0.558	0.335	0.410	0.292	0.421
Income Index	0.5301	0.4763	0.5730	0.3993	0.4410	0.3804	0.4624
Human Development Index	0.612	0.514	0.616	0.448	0.494	0.424	0.509
Ration to HDI Nepal = 100	120.1	100.8	120.9	88.0	97.1	88.3	100.0

Source: UNDP/Nepal, 2009, *Human Development Report 2009*, Kathmandu: UNDP/Nepal.

Table 11.1(b): Integrated National Index of Governance, 1999

	Dominant Groups		Marginalized Groups				
	Bahun/ Chhetri	Newar	Madhesi	Janajati	Dalit	Other	Total
Court	77.0	13.6	7.6	1.7	0	0	235
Constitutional Bodies	56.0	24.0	12.0	2.8	0	0	25
Cabinet	62.5	9.4	15.6	12.5	0	0	32
Parliament	60.0	7.6	17.4	13.6	1.5	0	265
Public Administration	77.6	17.6	3.7	1.2	0	0	245
Party Leadership	58.8	10.9	15.8	15.2	0	0	165
Leadership: Local Elected Bodies	55.5	15.7	16.2	12.0	0	0	191
Leadership: Commerce and Industry	16.7	47.6	35.7	0	0	0	42
Leadership: Educational Arena	77.3	11.3	7.2	2.1	1	1	97
Leadership: Cultural Arena	69.1	17.9	0	4.9	0	0	123
Science/Technology	58.1	29.0	9.7	3.2	0	0	62
Civil Society Leadership	75.9	14.8	7.4	1.9	0	0	54
Total	66.5	15.2	11.2	7.1	0.3	1	
Population (%)	31.6	5.6	30.9	22.2	8.7	1	
Difference With Population (%)	+34.9	+9.6	-19.7	- 15.1	- 8.4	-1	

Source: Govinda Neupane (2000), *Nepalko Jatiya Prasana* [Question of Caste/Ethnicity in Nepal], Kathmandu: Centre for Development Studies.

both *janajatis* and dalits) and in plan documents, news broadcast in mother tongues by the government-run radio and television, and the setting up of commissions and committees to address the problems of *janajatis*, dalits and *madheshis* can be considered as positive response by the state to ethnic assertions of identity. The state's response was, however, conservative in that it did not match the radicalization of ethnic movements, particularly in the aftermath of the post-*Jana Andolan* II period.

The post-1990 party system, because of it's over articulation of the principle of individual rights of citizen, ignored the significance of collective rights and so the constitutional designation of Nepal as a 'multi-ethnic and multi-lingual state' lacked any substantial policy and programme to address the problems of the excluded groups. Moreover, competitive politics in line with caste, ethnicity, language, and region was prohibited constitutionally. This provision was, however, implemented loosely and flexibly. As a consequence that the post-1990 party system discouraged the principle of collective rights, the ethnic and regional aspirations were largely ventilated from other platforms.

Ethnic Platform

The disadvantaged in Nepal fall into three large groups: *Janajatis, Madheshis* and Dalits. Each of these groups has their own organization(s) to speak on behalf of the group as a whole. The Nepal Federation of Indigenous Nationalities (NEFIN) and its 48-member organizations have focused more on the problems of *janajatis*. Dalit activism has been promoted largely by the NGO movement having links with INGOs and backed by several donors. The Dalit NGO Federation is an umbrella organization of 102 NGOs. The number of actors championing the cause of *madheshis* has increased with the rise of the *madheshi* parties (Madheshi Janaadhikar Forum or MJF, Tarai Madhesh Loktantrik Party or TMLP) and the two splinter groups of the CPN (Maoist)—Janatantrik Tarai Morcha (JTM) led by Goyait and another by Jwala Singh—in addition to the Nepal Sadbhabana Party (NSP).

International Environment

The ethnic activism in Nepal has already been internationalized. The international environment, particularly the UN Declaration of 1995 to 2004 as the International Decade of Indigenous People, has provided additional impetus to highlight the problems of ethnic groups within the country and also to link local initiatives as part of the global movement. Ethnic exclusion is one of the key concerns of donor countries in their much-weighted scheme of 'conflict management', 'peace building' and 'constitution making'.

CPN-Maoist

Among the competing forces rushing to cash in on the post-1990 ethnic rise, the CPN-Maoist seems more successful than others both in mobilizing the ethnic capital and in giving a political framework to ethnic demands, i.e. autonomy and federalism. Its concerted efforts to blend ethnic rights with the class ideology are evident in the formation of 11 ethnic and region-based frontier organizations. Furthermore, based on ethnicity and regionalism, the CPN-Maoist proposes a federal structure. So the ethnic issue has gained new importance and strength as the Maoists have gained influence and power (Hachhethu 2008-9).

The accumulative effect of politicization of ethnicity from different platforms is quite visible both in bottom-up movement and top-down policy. Census data reveals disassociation with Hindu religion and Nepali language as the population of people professing them decreased from 87 per cent in 1991 to 80 per cent in 2001 and from 52 per cent in 1991 to 48 per cent in 2001 respectively. Such a trend of differentiation with Hindu religion and Nepali language is likely to increase in the near future. To be a non-Hindu by origin is one of the qualifications of being a *janajati*, according to the NEFIN definition. Survey findings (2004 and 2007) show that people's preference to ethnic/regional identity is on the rise and identification with national identity is down (from 58 to 43 per cent). This is indeed distinct to the case of people living in plains, known as *madheshi*. The rise of *madheshi* nationalism over time is distinct to that of the proportion of people of *madheshi* origin (across caste, ethnicity and religion) who preferred to identify themselves with ethnic/regional identity, rather than with national identity, increased from 19 per cent in 2004 to 46 per cent in 2007. The *madheshi's* preference to identify themselves with national (Nepali) identity decreased from 40 to 18 per cent over the last three years (Hachhethu 2004; Hachhethu et al. 2008). On emergence of ethnicity and regionalism as a dominant part of the Nepali polity, a foreign expert on Nepali society and politics observed 'If the period 1960 to 1990 was one of nation-building, the 17 years since then has been a time of ethnicity-building' (Gellner 2007: 1823).

Politicization of Ethnicity and Ethnicization of Politics

Ethnicization of politics, one of the dominant phenomenons of contemporary Nepal, is formalized by the Interim Constitution 2007 (IC) with its several provisions. The most important provision is constitutional guarantee for the representation in the CA on the basis of caste, ethnicity and region. The CA election result shows a decline of national political parties and those contested with ethno-regional identity and one which blended class and ethnicity gained more than their own expectation. Ethnic and regional based politics, which was constitutionally prohibited till the recent past, is likely to be an important characteristic of Nepali politics at present and the future.

Inclusive democracy is one of the three key agendas (two other agendas are republic and conflict transformation) of restructuring the Nepali state, an ambitious nation building project carrying out since the April 2006 mass uprising, known as *Jana Andolan* II. Inclusive democracy is, at the moment, primarily understood as the representation of social segments into the state structure in proportion to the size of the population of each group.

In the aftermath of the April 2006 *Jana Andolan* II, the ethnic movement geared up from a quest for identity to pressure for power sharing. Nepali state and government, dominated by the eight parties including the CPN-Maoist, appeared liberal on issues related to the identity question converting Nepal from a Hindu to a secular state and recognizing a need of bi/multi-language policy for the future. But it failed to preempt, in the early phase of transition, to ethnic and regional aspiration of power sharing. So, the promulgation of the IC 2007 added a new dimension to transitional politics. It sparked a battle for inclusive democracy by various social forces who felt that their interests had not been represented in the IC. Previously, transitional politics were dominated by a series of negotiations between the SPA and the CPN-Maoist, and social groups such as dalits, women, *janajatis* and *madheshis* played the role of pressure politics and lobbied for the recognition of their concerns in the process of constitution making. They were frustrated by the absence of any specific content on inclusive democracy in the IC. Reacting to this deficiency in the IC, they went to the streets launching a very aggressive movement.

The *madhesh* uprising of January-February 2007 was powerful in terms of popular participation and its impact. During this 21-day long violent movement participated in by large masses of people of plains origin, 27 people lost their lives, compared to 21 in the April 2006 uprising. Connected to the *madhesh* uprising was the tragic massacre of 27 Maoists in Rautahat, a tarai district. The *madhesh* uprising brought the transitional authority in favour of federalism. At times *madhesh* movement was taking momentum other social forces like *janajati*, women and dalits were also busy in launching their own movements which were more assertive, aggressive and effective. As these social forces gained strength from the movements they launched, their role changed from that of lobby group before the promulgation of the IC to key actors directly negotiating with the government.

If republic, peace building and the restoration of the multiparty system are the key issues contained in all the agreements made between the SPA and the CPN-Maoists, inclusive democracy is the pivotal issue in the agreements made between the government and the various social groups. Among several social groups engaged in the post-April 2006 transitional politics for inclusive democracy, the *janajatis* and *madheshis* are two major powerful groups with whom the government made separate agreements several times before the April 2008 CA elections. Obviously, all of these agreements were centred on advancing Nepal into an inclusive democracy. Consequently, the IC 2007 was amended twice in a short span of time to incorporate some of the key issues of the ethnic/regional movements, i.e. federalism, PR with inclusive representative system, and an increased number of seats for the *tarai* in the CA (from 43 to 49 per cent). These are some of the most important and substantial elements of inclusive democracy. Some concrete achievements made during the two-year transition period (from the time of the April 2006 popular uprising to the April 2008 CA election) for translation of a broad principle of inclusive democracy into specific contents are listed below:

- Nepal is a secular state.
- All the languages spoken as mother tongue in Nepal are the national languages of Nepal. The use of one's mother tongue in a local body or office shall not be barred.
- In pursuance to inclusive democracy, a bill of Civil Service is amended adopting a new provision of 45 per cent reservation in bureaucracy for excluded groups, women, Dalit, *janajati*, handicapped and backward communities.
- At least one-third party committee members should be female and there should also be due representation from the Dalits. Besides, selection of candidates to the elections by political parties should be in conformity to inclusive democracy ensuring due representation from the ethnic groups, Dalits, peasants, labourers, people residing in different ecological/geographical areas, and of course one-third from women.
- By its first amendment on 9 March 2007, the IC ensures the establishment of a federal system by a new constitution to be made by the CA.
- It provides a provision of 601 members of the CA: 240 to be elected under the FPTP, 335 to be elected by the PR and 26 nominees by the Cabinet. There is provision for inclusive representation in each of the three categories of CA members.

    1. For the candidacy under the FPTP, the interim constitution directs political parties to follow the norms of inclusive representation. Since this is not binding provision, political

parties, except the CPN-Maoist, were least inclined to offer inclusive candidacy, particularly women and Dalit for the FPTP constituencies. However, extension of seats from 43 per cent (83 out of 205) in the past into 48 per cent (116 out of 240 from FPTP) for 20 *tarai* districts contributed to the higher representation from *madhesh* or of *madheshi* people.

2. Distribution of CA members is weighted in favour of the PR, 56 per cent or 335 out of the total 601 seats. Here, parties are bound to follow social-based representation in proportion to size of their own population, like 31.2 per cent for *madheshis*, 13 per cent for Dalits, 37.9 per cent for ethnic groups, 4 per cent for backward region, and 30.2 per cent for others (hill Brahmin, Chhetri, Thakuri, etc). Out of these 50 per cent from all groups should be women.
3. For the remaining 26 seats to be nominated by the cabinet among the distinguished persons, a condition is inserted after agreement between the government and NEFIN in July 2007 that the chances would be given to persons belonging to 59 listed *janajati* who failed to be represented as a result of election under the FPTP and PR.
4. There is another provision favouring minority/ethnic-based parties that those contested in less than 30 per cent seats are exempted from the provision of inclusive candidacy under the PR system.

The CA election is, therefore, credited for power shift in regard to the social make-up of the political power structure. The CA elections along with the constitutional provision of caste/ethnic-based representation for 56 per cent seats (allocated under PR system) of total 601 members of the CA, provided an outlet for translating identity movement into political power. The April 2008 CA election is remarkable in producing inclusive representation of different social groups in the CA in proportion close to the size of their own respective population. Out of 101 caste/ethnic groups reported in the population census more than 60 groups have found place in CA.

Table 11.2: Societal Representation in Parliament in the Past and the CA at Present

Caste/ethnicity	Population (%)	House of Representatives (%) of 205 seats			CA	
		1991	1994	1999	No	%
Hill high castes	30.8	56	63	60	196	34
Hill ethnic	28.5	24	18	20	147	26
Madheshi caste	14.8	9	11	14	124	22
Madheshi ethnic	8.7	9	7	5	45	8
Muslim	4.3	2	1	1	16	3
Dalit	12.9	0.5	–	–	47	8
Total					575	100
Women	50	3	3	6	190	33

Looking through the caste/ethnic composition, the CA can be said a departure from the past as the faces of the hill Hindu high castes, Brahmin and Chhetri, reduced substantially from 56-63 per cent in the HOR of the 1990s into 34 per cent in the CA, only 3 per cent higher than their strength of population (31 per cent). For the first time in the history of Nepal, the *madheshis* (including caste, ethnic, dalit and Muslim) gain a higher representation (34 per cent) than its population size (31 per cent) against the past record of their representation as only around 20 per cent. The *janajatis* (of both hill and *tarai*) have also a strength of 34 per cent—though it is 3 per cent lower than their population size (37 per cent)—which is significant as its representation in the past was around 25 per cent. Representation of dalits also increased from less than 1 into 8 per cent. Having one-third women in the CA is also a new phenomenon.

References

Baral, Lok Raj (1991), 'Minority Groups in the Kingdom of Nepal: Status, Dynamic and International Implications', *Ethnic Studies Report*, 9: 1, pp. 56-64.

Bhattachan, Krishna Bahadur (2003), 'Minority Rights: Country Report-Nepal' (a report under publication).

CBS (2002), *Population Census 2001: National Report*, Kathmandu: Central Bureau of Statistics.

Constitution of the Kingdom of Nepal 1990.

Election Commission (2008), *Result of the 2008 Constituent Assembly Election*, Kathmandu: Election Commission.

Fisher, William F. (1993), 'Nationalism and the Janajati', *Himal*, 6: 2, pp. 11-14.

Gellner, David N. (2008), 'Caste, Ethnicity and Inequality in Nepal', *Economic and Political Weekly*, XLLII: 20.

Gurung, Harka (1997), 'State and Society in Nepal', in David N. Gellner, Joanna Pfaff-Czarnecka and John Whelpton (eds.), *Nationalism and Ethnicity in a Hindu Kingdom: The Politics of Culture in Contemporary Nepal*, Amsterdam: Harwood Academic Publishers, pp. 495-532.

Hachhethu, Krishna (2003), 'Nepal: Party Manifesto and Election', *Nepali Journal of Contemporary Studies*, 3: 1.

——— (2004), *State of Democracy in Nepal: Survey Report*, Kathmandu: SDSA/N and International IDEA.

——— (2008-9), 'The Communist Party of Nepal (Maoist): Transformation from an Insurgency Group to a Competitive Party', *European Bulletin of Himalayan Research*, 33-4, Autumn 2008 and Spring 2009.

Hachhethu, Krishna, Sanjay Kumar and Jiwan Subedi (2008), *Nepal in Transition: A Study on the State of Democracy*, Stockholm: International IDEA.

Interim Constitution of Nepal 2007.

Neupane, Govinda (2000), *Nepalko Jatiya Prasana* (Question of Caste/ Ethnicity in Nepal), Kathmandu: Centre for Development Studies.

Pfaff-Czarnecka, Joanna (1997), 'Vestiges and Visions: Cultural Change in the Process of Nation-Building in Nepal', in David N. Gellner Joanna Pfaff-Czarnecka and John Whelpton (eds), *Nationalism and Ethnicity in a Hindu Kingdom*, pp. 419-70.

Shaha, Rishikesh (1975), *Nepali Politics: Retrospect and Prospect*, Delhi: Oxford University Press.

Sharma, Priyag Raj (1992), 'How to Tend this Garden', *Himal*, 5: 3, pp. 7-9.

——— (1997), 'Nation Building, Multi-Ethnicity, and the Hindu State', in David N. Gellner, Joanna Pfaff-Czarnecka and John Whelpton (eds), 1997, *Nationalism and Ethnicity in a Hindu Kingdom*, pp. 471-94.

UNDP (2009), *Nepal: Human Development Report 2008*, Kathmandu: United Nations Development Programme.

Whelpton, John, 'Political Identity in Nepal: State, Nation and Community', in David N. Gellner, Joanna Pfaff-Czarnecka, and John Whelpton (eds), *Nationalism and Ethnicity in a Hindu Kingdom*, pp. 39-78.

12

From Winning the Secessionist War to Addressing Ethno-Political Challenges in Sri Lanka

R.A. ARIYARATNE

The decisive military victory scored by Sri Lankan security forces over the LTTE has lain to rest what the *SIPRI Year Book* 2009 termed as 'The World's Deadly Armed Conflict'. For the rest of the world plagued by ethno-political insurgencies, the writing on the wall is clear, as pointedly proclaimed by *Wall Street Journal*: 'For all those who argue that there is no military solution for terrorism, we have two words: Sri Lanka'. For the Sri Lankan government and its citizens the post-war scenario poses a daunting array of challenges in order to convert the military victory into lasting peace for the entire country. Rehabilitation and resettlement of nearly 300,000 war-displaced Tamils, including 20,000 or so ex-LTTE combatants, is the immediate concern of the government agencies. This requires, in addition to adopting requisite resettlement logistics, a visible shift of attitudes from sympathy for the IDPs to an affirmation of their rights and dignity as Sri Lankans. Then comes the more formidable task of addressing the legitimate aspirations of the disaffected Tamil community and politically disadvantaged other communities, such as Muslims and Tamils of recent Indian origin, through a comprehensive package of political reforms. Several piecemeal solutions experimented in the past have failed to link the marginalized ethnic communities with the central governing process.

Sri Lanka is now at the cusp of a golden opportunity to design a new constitutional framework based on effective power sharing between the provincial legislatures and the central parliament. Since the majority of Tamil, Muslim and Sinhalese disadvantaged communities live mostly in outlying areas of the island, power sharing will offer them the ideal opportunity to become an organic link to associate themselves with the central decision-making processes while keeping their ethnic and cultural identities intact at the respective territorial bases. If such an arrangement of power sharing could be adopted successfully, it will usher in an era of peace-politics in Sri Lanka, minimizing regional imbalance in elective representation causing disaffection among marginal communities, and redirecting strong beliefs that foster behaviours contrary to the law of the land or by changing the law of the land to reconcile with the principles of those beliefs. Unless this transformation can be effected within the bounds of the legislative process, the existing maladjustment of the governing structures contra aspirations of the marginalized communities, is bound to haunt Sri Lankan politics for the years and decades to come.

Deriving from the Greek word *ethnos*, meaning people or tribe, in contrast with *genos*, Greeks in city states, and used in a derisive sense to denote 'pagan/heathen' groups during the middle ages, the term 'ethnic' has undergone many an interpretation since it entered the modern demographic vocabulary in the late nineteenth century. Without going into long-drawn intellectual debates between 'primordialism and instrumentalism', 'constructivism and essentialism' and 'survivalism and evolutionism', suffice it to say that both primordial bonds between a given group of people and values acquired in the process of power struggles have, in varying degrees and at various levels, contributed to the modern day perceptions of ethnicity. In a general way, any hereditary group having its roots in ancient or relatively recent times, with shared values, styles of life, cultural identities and consciousness of common destination, can be considered an ethnic group.

Yet, no definite interpretation of the term 'ethnicity' has so far been crystallized, and it continues to mean different things to different people at different places. In modern times, the practice has been to use the term 'ethnic group' to refer to minority and marginal subgroups but of late, in demographic surveys in particular, the tendency has been to subsume even the major elements in societies under this term. However, arising from diverse conceptions of what constitutes an ethnic group, classification of population segments do not follow a common pattern. In Britain, 'ethnic' popularly connotes 'race', but interactions between the domestic population and 'races' and those within naturalized immigrant communities, are referred to as 'ethnic relations'. In the USA, Black Americans are considered a 'race', and ethnics are descendants of recent immigrants from non-English-speaking countries like Mexico, Puerto Rico, Cuba, China and Japan and other parts of Asia, and native Indians. As Asian populations are hard to define in terms of ethnicities, the population surveys are in the habit of grouping them under broad categories: India—Aryan 72 per cent, Dravidian 25 per cent; Pakistan—Punjabi 44 per cent, Pasthun 15 per cent, Sindhis 14 per cent; Nepal—Chetri 16 per cent, Bahun 12 per cent; Bhutan—Northern Butanese 60 per cent, Ethnic Nepalese 25 per cent; Maldives—Dhivehi 98 per cent; Bangladesh—Bengali 98 per cent; Sri Lanka—Sinhalese 74 per cent, Sri Lankan Tamils 12.6 per cent, Indian Tamils 5.1 per cent, Moors 7.2 per cent.

Taken as a whole, none of these so-called ethnic blocs provide a sound basis for understanding the pathways generating tensions among them or between them and state structures in their respective countries. Nor are these entities monolithic in composition or remain static over the passage of time. As Ted Gurr pointed out:

> The salience of communal identifications varies over time. The psychological bases of group identification are reinforced by cultural, economic and political differentials between the group and others: treat a group differently, by denial or privilege, and its members become more self-conscious about their common bonds and interests. Minimize differences, and communal identification becomes less significant as a unifying principle . . . all collective identities, whether centered on a communal group or a national state, are to a degree situational and transitory.[1]

What is useful in the search for clues to understand the process in which legitimate ethnic aspirations enter into a collision course with those of neighbouring groups or with the state is to explore the underlying causes of this transformation. Among them are facets of modernization bringing the disparate ethnic communities into a whirlpool of shared activities leading to greater socio-economic integration. When the political order is unable to adjust itself to absorb the pressures engendered by ensuing changes, sections of the constituent population, especially those who are numerically weaker, begin to entertain fear of the future of their individual communities. When this apprehension enters the stream of consciousness, ethnic identities which may have remained quiescent for years are called forth and reinforced by memories and myths. In these circumstances, as David A. Lake comments, ethnic security dilemma becomes an 'insecurity dilemma'. 'Given a fear of future exploitation, the party that is likely to become weaker may choose to fight now rather than later'.[2] This aptly and succinctly sums up the motivational process behind the Sri Lankan Tamils' convergence toward a militant struggle to defy the writ of the state and to form an autonomous region for themselves. The military wing of the Tamil militancy now stands defeated, but the direction in which the Tamils' ethnic aspirations would move in the overall Sri Lankan polity remains uncertain.

Emergence of Sri Lanka's Ethno-political Conflict and State Response

In Sri Lanka, the passage from the British colonial rule to statutory independence in February 1948 did not accompany a vibrant freedom struggle or mass involvement in it in any appreciable degree. The landmark constitutional provisions of universal franchise (1932) and independence status (1948) were handed out to the Sri Lankan political elite on a platter. The departing British could no longer delay granting self-governing powers to the 'loyal' Sri Lankan subjects when Whitehall had decided in favour of granting independence to 'seditious' Burma and virulently anti-British India. The paradigms of ethnic identity formations did not in any appreciable level influence the imperatives of the transfer of power. As elsewhere in the newly-independent former colonial territories, in South Asia,

The acquiescence of the ethnic groups in the acceptance of the post-independence state system was largely taken for granted. The voices of resistance and protest at the imposition of the new order were too mild and/or were overshadowed by then existing more crucial problems. Once the democratic process, despite its severe limitations, percolated the peripheral segments, hitherto excluded from the main currents of nationalism, nation building and state building, the myriad ethnic groups vied for participation and inclusion in the political process.[3]

Successive waves of immigrants, warlords and their auxiliary forces entered the island and made it their permanent home from the pre-Christian era.

Sri Lanka has been from time immemorial the home of various ethnic groups. There have been political and social conflict among them, but the kind of ethnic consciousness and disruptive prejudices that have surfaced in the nineteenth century and continue to plague the island were not part of Sri Lanka's pre-colonial history, writes reputed Sri Lankan Tamil historian, I.K. Indrapala.[4]

What is germane to our discussion here is how the overall population, with ethnic disaggregation, had been composed at the time of attaining independence. Of them, descendants of south Indian Dravidian stock came to occupy the northern and eastern parts while the south became the predominantly Sinhalese region of the island. At the census of 1911, over 85 per cent of (Ceylon) Tamils lived in the northern and eastern provinces as against the Sinhalese residing in these two provinces constituting less than 2 per cent of their entire population.[5] Interethnic interaction, by and large, was confined to the realm of nascent middle class—professional and business circles. Even within such superficial groupings, they saw one another *not* face-to-face but always in relation to a third party—the British rulers. Thus even as late as the beginning of the twentieth century, they were strangers to the notion of common destiny. Lanka was not 'it' as England was to Shakespeare, but at best 'she' in the broad sense of being a mother to all her children, but could not say 'we' until after the turn of the century.

When the Sinhala-Tamil and Muslim elite came round to form the Ceylon National Congress (CNC) in 1919, political calculations based on ethnic apportionment had already permeated their mindsets. The CNC platform collapsed barely three years after its formation. The Tamil leadership drifted further apart when territorially-based elections were introduced to select legislative council members and communal representation was abolished alongside the introduction of universal adult franchise in 1932. The independence status granted to Sri Lanka in 1948 deemed the landscape to be one in which the majority Tamil areas are amalgamated with the rest of the island as a single state. The mandate was to form a 'state nation': an independent 'state' was to be formed first, facilitating conditions to form a 'nation' within it subsequently.

The post-independence political development in Sri Lanka is a tale of the failure to instill a sense of broad national consciousness across the width and breadth of the country. Given the nature of the unitary constitution adopted in 1948 and the yawning disparity between the majority-minority segments among the constituent population, the possibility of a common political outlook emerging in the new dispensation seemed remote. Among the several causes contributing to this ethnic 'mismatch' are two vital changes in the demographic composition. The first was the dilution of the 'low-country' and 'Kandyan' (hill country) identities among the Sinhalese as a result of the inexorable onslaught of market forces and improved road network. On the eve of independence, the Kandyans accounted for 25.81 per cent as against 43.60 per cent of low-country Sinhalese in the total population. As their distinctive cultural peculiarities gave way to forge a common Sinhalese community in the post-independence period, together they came to form the electoral majority of the island. As simple logic dictates, fortunes of the numerically smaller communities decline as the stakes of the majority get strengthened.

Yet another change in the demographic front has given a new twist to Tamil political fortunes. The indigenous Tamils had all along been living as a group apart from the island's Indian Tamils—descendants of estate labourers brought to work in the tea and rubber plantations. The first census surveys took count of the two groups separately showed an excess of 'Indian Tamils' over the local Tamils, as the following figures show:

	1911	1921	1946
'Ceylon' Tamils	12.86	11.50	11.02
'Indian' Tamils	12.93	13.39	11.72

However, after independence the 'Indian' segment of the Tamil population suffered two major setbacks. First, the majority of them were disenfranchized by two parliamentary Acts redefining citizenship and the right to vote. Then a large number of them opted to return to India under the Sirimavo-Shastri agreement concluded in 1962 and J.R.-Rajiv agreement signed in 1988. The result is that their numerical strength *vis-à-vis* local Tamil population weakened significantly, leaving the field open to the latter to represent and orchestrate most issues which has a bearing on Tamil interests. By then the caste, religious and geographical diversity among the Sinhalese had been reduced significantly for them to present themselves as a community with common political identity and destiny. The Sri Lankan Tamils were on the way to become the largest minority group, but their numerical strength within the total population (12.5 per cent) was too weak to challenge the supremacy of the Sinhalese (74 per cent).

Notwithstanding this numerical disadvantage, the local Tamil community had come to regard itself as one of the two majority communities inhabiting the island *vis-à-vis* the much smaller Muslim, Indian Tamil, Malay and Eurasian communities. Three factors reinforced this belief. One is the existence of a presumably fraternal Dravidian population in south India together with whom they constitute an overwhelmingly bigger majority over the Sinhalese. Second, their leaders cherished the memories of the parity of status that they enjoyed with the Sinhalese in the legislative council representation until 1922—a position they did not wish to forsake even after independence. The Tamil leaders always maintained that this parity status as confirmation of their permanent right to be represented on an equal footing with the Sinhalese. Third, the community had a disproportionately high share in the upper echelons of government service, due partly to the lead that they had in English literacy over the Sinhalese, and partly to the 'most favoured community' position held by them in the eyes of the colonial rulers. In public affairs, therefore, Tamil leadership exuded an unmistakable air of superiority over its Sinhalese counterpart. At the approach of independence, the cumulative effect of these perceptions on Tamil mindset operated to run counter to accepting an inferior position in politics, while the Sinhalese were confident that they would have the edge in any political contest with the Tamils by virtue of their superiority in numbers. It was a matter of time before these irreconcilable stances entered into a collision course on the political front.

Government Response 1948-1990: From Reconciliation to Confrontation

In 1948 Sri Lanka attained independence with all the trappings of the international state system. Even centuries after the Treaty of Westphalia in 1648, independent status of a country deemed to equate national security with state sovereignty encompassing a fixed territory and its citizenry as a whole. But from the outset, Sri Lanka was faced with the inbuilt conundrum of harnessing the ethnically-oriented loyalties of its constituent people to sustain a common nationhood. As Urmila Phadnis observed, 'Broadly speaking, the Sri Lankan political system, as it has evolved, has not been that of the "ethnically dispersed" (as in India), but is an "ethnically central" system'.[6]

This pattern is inextricably intertwined with the partly primordial and partly constructed phenomenon of the peoples' political loyalties overlapping the ethnic bonds. 'Us and Them' syndrome had set in the political culture even in pre-independence political bargaining, as exemplified by the demand for 50:50—equal number of seats in the legislature for minority communities and the Sinhalese majority. On the threshold of attaining independence a section of the politically articulate Tamils formed the 'Federal Party', with establishing an autonomous state for Tamils as its avowed aim. At the other end of the pole, the Sinhalese political parties came increasingly under the spell of winning popular rural vote in the south of the country in order to enhance their position *vis-à-vis* their local and ethnic rivals.

At the general elections of 1956, the Sinhalese majority rule was firmly enthroned in governance, never to be challenged in future, either democratically or constitutionally.

From then on, the provisions dovetailed in the 'old order' conferring differentially advantageous situations for the minorities, especially Tamils, were removed one by one and new provisions favouring Sinhalese-Buddhists were introduced into the governing process, e.g. the 'Sinhala Only' Official Language Act (1956), followed by legislation enforcing media-wise standardization and district quota system in the selection of students to the universities (1971), dispensing with the secular independence constitution together with minority safeguard provisions embodied in it (1972), and finally, promulgation of the second Republican Constitution coupled with 'dictatorial' Executive Presidency.

Meanwhile the Tamils' disaffection entered into a phase of militancy, eventually giving rise to a full-fledged guerrilla movement under LTTE. In between there has been two major bouts of anti-Tamil rioting (1958 and 1983), military intervention by India, followed by its imposition of a peace accord, seven rounds of peace negotiations, and four phases of 'Eelam War'. The IPKF induction created a curious twist in the ensuing conflict: the LTTE turned their guns against the Indian *jawans* who had entered the scene ostensibly to save the Sri Lankan Tamils from the alleged clutches of Sinhalese domination. Those in LTTE's support base in Tamil Nadu did precious little to save their fraternal 'freedom fighters' across the Palk Straits from the armed onslaught carried out by the Indian military forces. This episode provides convincing affirmation of the theory that all ethnic identities are subject to ebb and flow depending on the ground situation and contextual realities.

One other significant factor contributing to the alternating hyped up activism and indifference on issues affecting Sri Lankan Tamils is the extremely maudlin political culture in Tamil Nadu, with all political groups contending for power both in the state as well as national assembly tending to make political capital out of the predicament of Sri Lankan Tamils. Tamil Nadu's penchant for intimidating Colombo received a temporary setback when Prime Minister Rajiv Gandhi was assassinated at the hands of an LTTE suicide activist, but once again reverted to the familiar threatening posturing when the LTTE's last-ditch fighting coincided with the Indian Lok Sabha elections. Several TN leaders publicly proclaimed their readiness to 'liberate' Sri Lanka's Tamil inhabited areas by show of force, but no sooner the Congress mustered enough electoral support to retain power at the centre and LTTE suffered humiliating defeat in May 2009 than did coteries of Tamil Nadu protest enter yet another period of hibernation.

'Guernica' Period of Sri Lanka's Conflict: 1990-2009

The highly turbulent sequence of events that engulfed Sri Lanka during these two decades is analogous, if not more gruesome, to the turmoil prevailed after the Spanish city of Guernica fell under fascist spell in 1937. The specter of physical destruction, emotional trauma and anguish felt by the ordinary masses so artistically depicted in Picasso's monumental painting *Guernica* were present in their gory detail in this intensified fighting phase of the Sri Lankan conflict.

Following the anti-Tamil pogrom of 1983 and punishing the mighty IPKF from 1987-9, LTTE graduated from being one of the dozen or so, the then existing Tamil protest groups, into a deadly terrorist outfit in the 1990s. They constantly engaged the state military, successfully carried out bombing forays into vital government institutions including oil refineries, Central Bank and international airport, assassinated prominent politicians both Sinhalese and Tamil, and deployed with devastating effect their newly invented weapon, suicide bombing, against civilian targets. Sri Lankan armed forces, long accustomed to rely on extrajudicial means to deal with potential 'trouble makers' swiftly swung into action with equally ferocious attacks on suspected Tamil insurgent groups.

The state agencies had neither the capacity nor disposition to bring to book the perpetrators of these killings. 'Any thing is fair in war and love for enjoying power' seemed to have been the government rationale. A regime in the South at one stage was dabbling in an uncouth game of pitting the LTTE against the IPKF in spite of the fact that the latter had been invited to the northern battlefield by the then executive president of the island. It is now common knowledge that the regime in question gave the Tigers truckloads of weapons and bag loads of money to facilitate the anti-Indian drive. Ironically, when IPKF withdrew, LTTE turned its guns—literally some of which had been given to it by the government—against the government security forces, and finally the president then in power.

As an organization built around the unquestionable loyalty to and authority of a single leader, LTTE was not under any compulsion to account for the punishments meted out to its cadres. Quite simply, the Tigers preferred to openly execute the opponents and would-be defectors, and even showed no conscientious scruples when ordering the summary killing of nearly 600 policemen who had surrendered themselves to them on the orders of the government in the south. In general, only a handful of killings entailing insurgency and counter-insurgency operations conducted within this span of time reached the stage of investigation, and much less prosecution and punishment.

Aside from uninvestigated murders, the other most disconcerting phenomenon characterizing the local Guernica scene has been the recurrent incidents of unexplained disappearance of individuals, families and sometimes small communities. Some of these might have occurred when individuals left the country or family group on their own volition and without any involvement by either of the parties to the conflict. However, what is relevant to our discussion here is the issue of enforced disappearances. Under international law, 'an enforced disappearance occurs when state authorities detain a person and then refuse to acknowledge the deprivation of liberty or the person's whereabouts, placing the person outside the protection of the law'.[7] During the period under review, thousands of 'disappearances' occurred in all parts of the country, the majority of which up to date remain uninvestigated and therefore unsolved. The victims are primarily young ethnic Tamils who have disappeared without trace after being picked up by the government forces or pro-government Tamil armed groups acting either independently or in conjunction with the security forces. Allegations on this count have been levelled also at the militia under the LTTE breakaway faction led by Karuna, and Eelam Peoples' Liberation Front (EPDP). The alleged abductions appear to have been conducted either to settle scores with the LTTE or to extort ransom—with security forces turning a blind eye.

All along successive governments in the south have continued to downplay the scope of the problem. The government response has been in the direction of leveling counter-allegations that these 'disappearances' could have been the result of 'personal grudges' or part of a sinister campaign aimed at the state's image. Its standard practice has been to appoint commissions to 'sit, deliberate and dispose' the referred cases, but as yet none of them have yielded concrete results. The fate of thousands of 'disappeared' persons still remains shrouded in mystery. In the words of the Human Rights Watch, 'The cost of this failure is high. It is not measured in lives brutalized and lost, but in the anguish suffered by the family survivors'.[8]

Even at this late hour, the accretion of public opprobrium on this count could be staved off in part at least if immediate measures are taken to:

(a) publicly acknowledge the scope of past and recently occurred disappearances.
(b) reform the detention procedure in keeping with internally accepted norms and practices, such as allowing the detained person to contact family members and unimpeded access to legal counsel.
(c) vigorously investigate and prosecute those responsible for abductions and 'disappearances'. The scope of this issue has now transcended the north-eastern battle scene and entered the southern borders.

It seems unlikely that the culture of impunity that helps spawn acts of abduction, disappearance and extrajudicial killing will disappear in the foreseeable future. The emergency legislation under which these incidents occur has been in existence for the last thirty years. The European Union Experts' interim report on Sri Lankan human rights situation comments: 'Criminal offences are vaguely defined and the regulations contain provisions that excessively limit or eliminate the accountability of state agents. Basic fair trials are undermined in the emergency regulations'.[9]

Undoubtedly such criticism is indeed valid with regard to the pre-2009 situation as it is now, considering the fact that there are at least 71 Regulations, Proclamations and Gazette Notifications currently existing under emergency law.[10] But the problem is that terrorism and imposition of emergency regime have entered into a vicious circle in which one feeds the other, and governments all over the world invariably resort to extraordinary legislation to deal with acts of terrorism. As the simple deductive logic has it, if terrorism can be reduced to a minimal level, law and order will return, thereby obviating the need to maintain draconian legislation and harsh methods of law enforcement.

Addressing Ethnic Challenges after Winning the War

There has been several attempts to resolve the deadlocked political situation since the Indo-Sri Lanka Peace Accord (1987) failed to produce the desired results. The ceasefire agreement initiated by the Chandrika Bandaranaike government ended unceremoniously when the LTTE destroyed several ships carrying provisions to the north. Thereafter fighting re-ignited with a vengeance until a fresh CFA was signed in February 2002, followed by six rounds of peace talks conducted in various parts of the world. All of them came to naught as the LTTE decided to withdraw from talks and re-engage the government forces. When the Mahinda Rajapaksha government was voted into power in late 2005, one of its priorities had been to restart peace talks with LTTE, but yet again the effort had to be abandoned as the latter resumed attacks on government security forces.

Finally, all options narrowed down to Armageddon. The ensuing military confrontation came to a decisive end with the comprehensive defeat of LTTE forces in May 2009, leaving behind a bewildering array of issues, both new and old, to contend with. What has confounded the end-of-the-war chaotic situation is not just the sheer multitude of persons affected by the raging war, but also the fact that thousands of them had to be accommodated within a time span of two or three weeks—a point underscored by President of Tamil United Liberation Front, V. Anandasangaree when he revealed that '. . . in one night alone over 85,000 IDPs broke the LTTE cordon and crossed over to the government controlled area. Several thousands followed them later'.[11]

Broadly, the persons displaced by conflict at different stages of its evolution can be classified under four different categories: (a) Tamil, Sinhalese and Muslim IDPs displaced during the first waves of the conflict, 1990-2006; (b) the externally displaced living in India; (c) Tamil diaspora in the Western world; (d) war-displaced after 2006.

(a) *The IDPs*

Currently, the congested conditions prevailing in Vanni camps have attracted adverse criticism both locally and internationally. But, conveniently forgotten in this controversy is the fate of another segment of earlier generation of IDPs displaced since 1990. Even when the Eelam War IV began in 2006 there were 2,07,564 persons (66,623 families) who had become displaced from earlier bouts of fighting.[12] Of them only one-sixth were living in welfare centres and the rest stayed with relatives and friends. There have been no concerted efforts to resettle them either by local or international humanitarian organizations. Almost all IDPs were willing to leave the temporary shelters if they were offered suitable housing and sustainable living conditions elsewhere. Some initiatives taken by government agencies to relocate them in Vanni met with stiff resistance from the permanent local population. As they were civilians fleeing from the crossfire, and had not openly sided with LTTE, there was minimal security surveillance at the welfare centres. They could move out of the centres if they so desired, but the problem was that there was no place for them to go and start life all over again. As time passed by, they had settled for an existentialist lifestyle dependent on the weekly or monthly government handouts. The dependency syndrome had gripped even the camp supervisory staff who would have faced redundancy in the event of the camps being closed.

Not all persons displaced since 1990 were Tamils. Close upon 100,000 Muslims and Sinhalese living in Jaffna and Vanni districts had been forced out of these areas by LTTE as part of its ethnic cleansing programme. Coaxing them back to reoccupy their lands in the north and east presents more logistical problems than the issue of resettling Tamil IDPs. A person displaced as a result of being caught up in fighting may settle for clear signs of an end to such sporadic incidents as the minimum security needed to return, whereas the victim of ethnic cleansing would additionally look for convincing signs of change in behaviour on part of their former 'tormentors' as a precondition for return. The latter prospect could take many more years to crystallize.

(b) *The Externally Displaced in India*

After the anti-Tamil pogrom of 1983, the familiar trickle of Sri Lankan Tamils' flight to parts of south India that had in fact begun in the late 1950s became a flood. The Indian central government and Tamil Nadu state government did their best to accommodate the 'illegal immigrants' in camps hurriedly set up across the southern districts. To a dispassionate observer it looked as though India was making belated atonement, first for her role in fomenting anti-Sri Lanka uprising, and then engaging the same rebels and harassing the Tamil civilian population in general. 'During the IPKF period (1987 July-1990 March), there was massive displacement—1,00,000 families or 5,00,000 people, or 50 per cent of the peninsular population lost their dwellings' claimed the veteran conflict scholar, Rohan Gunaratne.[13] An unusually high percentage of Tamils fleeing to south India has been those of recent Indian origin who had migrated to Vanni from the Kandyan hill country tea estates in recent times. Many activists belonging to TELO, PLOTE and EPRLF, groups which had drifted out of LTTE control and sought succor from either IPKF or Indian authorities too had joined the stream of asylum seekers across the Palk Straits.

As any visitor to their camp sites would have observed, most of them were entertaining legitimate aspirations to return home, but recurring waves of fighting in the Vanni jungles held them in check for nearly two decades. Now that the threat of fighting has effectively been eliminated in the Vanni, it is the responsibility of Colombo-New Delhi-Chennai axis to give serious consideration to the possibility of reinitiating the process of repatriating these

EDPs on voluntary basis. Perhaps the reasoning behind the 1962 Sirimavo-Shastri agreement could be applied in reverse as the basis of this exercise, i.e. a section of the EDPS who are married to Indians, have found permanent employment in India, and have children admitted to educational or technical institutions in India may be considered for granting Indian citizenship, while the others applying for repatriation be provided with opportunities to start a fresh life in Sri Lanka. Given the administrative red-tape involved in processing repatriation applications, if the initiative begins in earnest now, the necessary groundwork for resettlement would be completed by the time the currently pressing issue of clearing the war-displaced off the Vanni camps would be brought to a close in the near future.

(d) *Tamil Diaspora*

Deriving from the Greek word *diaspeirein*, meaning dispersed or scattered, and initially used for dispersed Jews, the term 'diaspora' is currently being employed to denote international identities sharing common language, religion, customs and collective memory. Real or imagined political discrimination, better economic prospects and kinship connections usually intermingle in the motivation for diasporic movement away from their native countries. Post-Schneiderian thinking places more emphasis on existing practice of political persecution than structures based on familial structures as the main motivational force.[14] In Sri Lanka Tamil diasporic consciousness was constantly being fed by a series of legislations and practices favouring the majority Sinhalese community. Until 1983 the flow to the West was hardly noticeable and many of those who left returned home from time to time or on permanent basis. The major flow began after the anti-Tamil riots of July 1983, and gathered momentum with each armed confrontation, culminating in the 2006-9 Ealam War IV period. As of 2009, the rough estimates are: Canada 200,000, UK 120,000, Germany 60,000, France 50,000, Switzerland 52,000, US 35,000, Italy 24,000, Malaysia 25,000, the Netherlands 20,000, Norway 10,000, Denmark 9000.[15]

Canada hosts the largest Tamil population outside of Sri Lanka. Toronto has become the largest city with Sri Lankan Tamils in the world, relegating Jaffna into the second place. In France, a 'Little Jaffna' has sprung to life in Rue du Faubourg Saint-Denis, while another 'Little Jaffna' has begun to flourish in Zurich, Switzerland. However, after the collapse of LTTE and arrest of its leading financial manager, Kumaran Padmanadan, the Sri Lankan Tamil diaspora, numbering over one million, is in a state of bewilderment and disarray. Since the objective of creating a separate state in the areas earmarked by LTTE is no longer a viable proposition now, Tamil diaspora front organizations abroad are unlikely to pose as much a lethal threat to the Sri Lankan state as they had been in the past. The future configuration of its relationship *vis-à-vis* the 'mother country' will depend to a large extent on the attitude of the present leadership in Sri Lanka.

No international organization will be so impudent as to dispute the Sri Lankan government's legitimate right to probe into Tamil diaspora's past involvement in augmenting the LTTE's offensive capability. After all, Tamil diaspora formed the economic backbone of LTTE by way of contributing as much as 60 per cent of its procurement budget as early as 1996.[16] But in a context in which the Tamil diaspora is now left with no cause to fight for, it would be judicious for the government to adopt a conciliatory attitude toward the Tamils living abroad, and to create an atmosphere conducive for them to return either on temporary or permanent basis. In this connection, it is worth quoting verbatim the concluding paragraph of a report published by a panel of experts on this issue:

> Involve the Tamil, Sinhalese and Muslim men and women of the diaspora in a meaningful way in the reconstruction and development of the war-affected areas in Sri Lanka. Accept that the majority of the dispora will not return, but rather will participate in this process on the basis of *circulation*. It is unlikely that most members of the diaspora will return to the homeland in a permanent basis; rather they will circulate between both their host and home country. To support their involvement, the host countries as well as the Sri Lankan state should reformulate their citizenship, migration and development policies in the direction of dual citizenship; grant legal status to non-resident Sri Lankans; improve consular services; and establish a comprehensive infrastructure for mobilizing the skills and investment potential of the diaspora.[17]

Inside Sri Lanka, its security forces' recent victory at the battlefront has laid to rest the belief long-held by military experts all over the world that the LTTE could not be defeated militarily. Likewise the recent capture of its leading financier, Kumaran Padmanadan has proven fallacious the view that diaspora elites are not amenable to military reprisals because they live beyond the territorial jurisdiction of a state. Presumably, what is not feasible is to end solely by military means is the diasporic consciousness shared by them individually and collectively. This is a state of mind persisting and re-emerging *in tandem* with the perceived threat to an individual's or a community's almost universal desire for recognition—*thymos*—and socio-economic well-being.

A government can direct its physical prowess against individuals who have been identified as its enemies, but not against a body of consciousness spurring them into action. Diasporas spread across the world have provided enough testimony to the fact this consciousness cannot be totally eliminated by coercive state action—it is inane and self-defeating to wage a war against 'anger', or for that matter, 'terror'. However, there are examples closer at home, such as in Maldives, Bhutan and Nepal, to show that diaspora's hard stances tend to mellow with each liberal measure adopted by governments to reassure them of receiving equitable treatment back home. Although living abroad, they keep their lines of communications constantly open with their nuclear communities, and only when they are self-assured that their fraternal communities back at home lead safe and normal lives would their attitudes change in favour of opting out of the collision course with the government concerned.

This is not to say that all constituent individuals among diaspora communities will opt to return when conditions at the country of origin improve substantially. Be that as it may, in a rapidly globalizing world, nurturing a common loyalty towards both the country of origin and the country of settlement is not as contradictory an option as it may appear at first sight. As a matter of fact, there are thousands of people in the present-day world with 'homes' in two countries, showing amazing socio-cultural adaptability to fit themselves into the local ambience and contributing to the well being of both countries.

(e) *The War-displaced after 1996*

The issue that calls for immediate government attention is to screen the 2,00,000 odd war-displaced persons presently in over 30 camps in Vanni districts for security purposes, and to rehabilitate, resettle and finally reintegrate into society. The situation thus came into being is unmistakably a humanitarian crisis for those who ended up in camps, while it presented a security nightmare for the government authorities. The main difficulty has been to separate the innocent civilians among them from the LTTE ex-combatants.

When Eelam War IV began in earnest, the majority of Tamils in the north had come round to believe that LTTE represented their needs and aspirations. After all, the *de facto* LTTE rule held sway and scepter in most areas of the north and had in the process done much to restore the self-esteem and dignity of the Tamil population as a whole. The Tamil civilians, in turn, came to heed the LTTE *dictates* in their day-to-day activities. This had created a fuzzy state of affairs in which funding for all public works and welfare services came from the central government in the south, but the manner in which they were to be utilized came under the direction of LTTE. Naturally, the civil population did not bother to ponder over where the money came from but placed their loyalty at the feet of those who disbursed them. As a result, a symbiotic relationship developed between the Tamil civilian population and the Tigers—the civilians becoming the exoskeleton for the LTTE's underground existence and LTTE in turn assuming the role of protectors of Tamil civilians.

In the process, ordinary Tamil civilians became indistinguishable from the committed Tiger combatants, as much indistinct as the line between 'active' and 'passive' support for the insurgency. In the heat of intensified fighting, the 'bond' between them became something to be taken for granted and LTTE took maximum advantage of the situation to use civilians as a human shield, and a rigid external covering for soliciting international protection. When the 'human shield' was dismantled at the edge of LTTE's defeat, the civilians in it were either accosted or voluntarily trekked to the shelters that the government hurriedly set up in Vanni. It was humanly impossible to identify on sight active LTTE cadres from the non-partisan civilians as successive waves of evacuees drove thousands each day and night to the *cordon sanitaire*.

Having trounced the LTTE at the battle front, the euphoric government and security personnel are now saddled with the equally formidable task of screening the inmates so as to determine who could be allowed to leave and who should be kept back in the camps under a phased out release programme. Compounding the problem is the difficulty in distinguishing the still active LTTE activists from ex-combatants who have now resigned to accept the government writ over their localities. A substantial number of hardliners, having discarded their fatigues and their tell-tale-cyanide capsules, continue to mingle with the civilians in the camps. The process of screening each and every one of them is tedious at best. Amidst such confusion, it is inevitable that military necessity would become the basic principle of the law operative in the camps.

According to the secretary of defence, when the screening process comes to an end, 'the total number of terrorists in government custody could go up to 15,000, or as high as 20,000'.[18] Only those with specialized knowledge and experience are able to separate the ex-guerrilla cadres from ordinary civilians and mainly the government armed forces are equipped with such expertise. Besides, the Sri Lankan military, in contrast to a highly politicized police force and administrative personnel, have a reputation for not easily yielding to pressure exerted by politicians and other interested groups.

The challenge before the security forces-led Vanni camp administration is to pave the way for the release and arrange resettlement for their charges within a brief period of time—a task that the government bureaucracy in charge of the welfare centres established since 1990 could not accomplish in eighteen years. Rehabilitating the displaced is a daily, weekly and monthly process, gradually preparing the released to accept the new reality of restored government writ effective in their residential areas, slowly eroding old psychological barriers, and reintegrating into societies badly shaken by the recently ended war.

While 'return' is generally conceived as the process of moving back to one's home or area of former residence, the term 'resettlement' connotes responsibility in, as well as, outside the return process.

The ex-displaced may be deemed to have resettled for purposes of official recording, but may not be receiving adequate protection and assistance to restart a normal lifestyle. Then there are those who do not have homes or land to return to who would eventually have to be 'relocated' in new areas. Such uprooted individuals and families willy-nilly become 'aliens' in the new surroundings for years and perhaps decades on end.

A significant segment of those retained in Vanni Camps do not belong to the category of those caught in the crossfire of fighting, but have moved, or subjected to be mobilized, with LTTE fighting cadres as a human shield to cover its operations. The only law applicable for them is the law of the land, but as may be seen all over the world, it cannot be applied straight forward to IDPs, because of the difficulty in determining the degree of complicity in aiding and abetting the insurgency. This could involve lengthy legal proceedings, but it is in the national interest to initiate this process rather than to summarily condemn them as terrorists who helped wage war on the state.

As Sri Lankan government has now succeeded in removing the rebel challenge, the stage is already set for an ambitious rehabilitation programme. The first step in this direction is de-mining, involving huge sums of money and technical expertise. The UN requires a 99.6 per cent clearance rate before resettling people and the process costs 1-2 million USD per square kilometre. Highlighting the gravity of the problem, President Rajapaksa told the Indian newspaper *The Hindu*, 'Every square centimeter (of Vanni) has been mined by the LTTE. If something happens (to the resettled persons), I am responsible'. Indeed, in a highly convoluted situation such as this, much of the credibility of the political administration depends on the manner in which it discharges its responsibility toward the persons under its custody. With almost certainty it can be said that all those who are now clamouring for the speedy release of persons currently being kept in camps will raise another hue and cry if a single person thus released gets killed by a landmine on his return home.

Alongside the physical resettlement of IDPs there should be a collective and individual healing process whereby traumas and memories of war-related incidents can be contained within a reasonable level.

Addressing Political Apprehensions

This requires taking a hard look at the root causes of the conflict, the lethal confluence of which finally resulted in a process of polarization between the southern Sinhalese and ethnic minorities, mainly the Tamils in the political process. Such sharply divergent streams of thought are not uncommon in South Asian societies on the way to popular democratic rule. What is markedly different is the rapid hardening of attitudes on both sides leaving little room for compromise on the key issues involved.

The unitary form of government inherited from the British has continued to receive something approaching religious sanctity among the majority of Sinhalese. The dissentient Tamil political stance quickly changed from 'achieving constituent status within undivided nation', to wresting federal status to 'non-negotiable' Thimpu principles of distinct Tamil nationality, traditional homeland and the right of self-determination. The Sinhalese political leaders' relatively tolerant attitude towards their Tamil counterpart took a sharp turn in the direction of Sinhalese chauvinism since 1956. Even the architect of the 1956 SLFP victory, S.W.R.D. Bandaranaike, belatedly realized that declaring 'Sinhala *only*' as the official language was a mistake and sought to mollify the minority resentment to it by making Tamil as a language of administration in the northern and eastern provinces and accommodating the federal demand in a scheme for the establishment of regional councils for various administrative districts. However, he was forced to abandon these proposals due to intense Sinhalese chauvinist pressure. The same fate befell the attempt to revive the proposals during the Dudley Senanayake regime.

Gradually both groups moved into hard-line positions—Tamils demanding separate administration of their own and Sinhalese opposing any deviation from the unitary state principle. Through pressure exerted by India, the Sinhalese-led parliament in the south grudgingly adopted legislation to devolve administrative powers to the provinces, including the north-east province, but there was not sufficient political will in the south to implement the devolutionary arrangement in the spirit it was embodied in the 1987 Accord. No sooner had the north-eastern provincial council been established than did it announce unilateral independence (UDI) for the area coming under its purview, confounding the worst fears of the Sinhalese that any measure designed to devolve powers on area basis will necessarily lead to dismantling the unitary state. 'Once bitten, twice shy', the southern Sinhalese thereafter have come to equate devolution with secession, or worst still, an irredentist design to amalgamate the Tamil-majority areas with Tamil Nadu. In particular, the latter presented a frightening prospect for the Sinhalese who have all along been a majority with a minority complex in the context of contrasting their numerical strength with the combined aggregate of the Tamil population in Sri Lanka and south India.

The government armed forces' triumph over the LTTE in May 2009 has resurrected the old political debate on restructuring the governing process so as to accommodate the aspirations of the minority communities or to further restrict their political leverage. The controversy has extended to several options: (1) amend the existing constitution: (a) in the direction of giving effect to provisions embodied in the 1987 Indo-Sri Lanka Accord; (b) in the direction of effecting more centralized administration by way of dispensing with the existing provincial councils structure. (2) abolish the existing constitution and promulgate a new constitution: (a) in the direction of establishing a federal form of government; (b) in the direction of setting up a strong unitary form of government.

One of the principal reasons behind the current wave of disenchantment of the present constitution is on account of its failure to provide adequate devolution of administrative powers to the outlying provinces. Commenting on this aspect, S.C. Chandrahasan claims:

> The concept of linguistic states successfully addressed the aspirations of different linguistic groups within the Union of India influenced the Indo-Lanka Accord. But since the Sri Lankan Constitution was rigidly unitary, constitutional changes had to be made to accommodate meaningful devolution of powers. This had to be done through a two-thirds majority in parliament followed by a referendum in order to make it work. Unfortunately, the then Jayawardena government, which had a five sixth majority in Parliament, did not take up the challenge of putting it before

the people at a referendum which would have made it workable. Having failed to bring about the necessary constitutional change, they made the great mistake of pressurizing the Indian Peace Keeping Force to disarm the LTTE on one side and clandestinely providing weapons and money to the LTTE to fight the IPKF.[19]

However, given the intense public opposition that arose against the constitutional amendment (the 13th Amendment) establishing provincial councils, it seems unlikely that a referendum would have succeeded in securing the desired effect. In any case, the north-eastern provincial council's egregious decision to announce unilateral declaration of independence not only put paid to the prospects for granting some measure of self-governing powers to the Tamil-dominated provinces but also provided a powerful argument against devolution of powers in general. In the end, the people residing in the north-eastern provinces, for whose benefit the provincial council system was crafted by Indian authorities had to watch idly by while provincial councils were established in the southern provinces which did not demand it.

Even in the south, the provincial council system has been a qualified failure—a 'white elephant' in popular parlance. A recent survey has shown that '75 per cent of the money voted by central government to provincial councils is being used for payment of personal emoluments such as salaries and wages, overtime and holiday payments and other allowances'.[20] In these circumstances, the utility of the provincial council system as a measure for developing the outlying provinces is doubtful. The crux of the problem is that Sri Lanka's nine provinces are too small in size to warrant a full measure of devolution of powers on them. As K.M. de Silva has pointed out, '. . . if the federal units in India were as small in size as the provinces in Sri Lanka, India would have 426 states!'.[21] Devolution of such vital functions such as maintaining a separate police force, land utilization and management of river waters to a group of hitherto interconnected provinces will undoubtedly lead to increasing, and not reducing, the ethnic tension that the island has been experiencing since Independence.

Against this background, it is reasonable to assume that only a power sharing arrangement between the provincial legislatures and central parliament could bring about a harmonious and productive link between the centre-periphery relationship in governance. Hypothetically, an equal number of representatives elected to each provincial council through proportional representation could be selected via an electoral college to the central parliament, while the remaining segment of parliamentary membership being filled by representatives elected under the first-past-the post system of voting from constituencies demarcated throughout the island on the basis of population. This scheme ensures that marginalized communities living in the outlying provinces will have adequate representation at the centre just as much as the densely populated urban areas in the south. The presence of a contingent of provincial council-elected members in parliament will serve as a check against possible irresponsible and fissiparous trends at the provincial level while enriching the centre with *acquis communitaire*—acquisition of competence from the provincial units.

However, it would require a complete overhaul of the existing system of governance to incorporate such a sea change of constitutional revision. The basic tenets of democracy demand that all shades of political opinions are consulted on this vitally important issue and then move on to deploy logistics necessary to achieve this objective. What is essential to carry this process to a successful conclusion is a strong commitment on the part of the country's political leadership to the model of power sharing between the central legislature and provincial councils as the best way to represent the interests and aspirations of all communities in all parts of the country within an inclusive framework of good governance.

In the meantime, Sri Lanka may do well to request the UN to appoint a special coordinator to oversee the post-war reconstruction phase. The coordinator's primary mandate would be to accelerate the transition from war-time exigencies to peace-time normalcy by way of assisting the resettlement process in particular, and in general to mobilize foreign aid and build national capacity. This would in turn go a long way to dispel international criticism on various aspects of the way that government agencies are handling the post-war situation, and strengthen the hand of the UN as the best placed multilateral organization to mobilize international expertise for a national recovery plan encompassing a broad range of activities from microcredit to post-trauma psychological recovery.

Notes

1. Ted Robert Gurr (1993), *Minorities at Risk: A Global View of Ethno-Political Conflicts*, Washington, D.C.: US Institute of Peace, pp. 3-4.
2. David A. Lake (1995), *Ethnic Conflict and International Intervention*, University of California, IGCC Policy Brief, Summary, March, p. 1.
3. Kousar J. Azam (2001), *Ethnicity, Identity and the State in South Asia* (Introduction), New Delhi: South Asian Publishers, p. 4.
4. I.K. Indrapala (2005), *The Evolution of Ethnic Identity: The Tamils of Sri Lanka*, Colombo: MV Publications, pp. VIII-X.
5. E.B. Denham (1912), *Ceylon at the Census of 1911*, Colombo, p. 197.
6. Urmila Phadnis (1990), 'Role of State in Sri Lanka's Ethnic Conflict', *Mainstream*, vol. 29, no. 5, November, p. 16.
7. P. Ramasamy (1987), *New Delhi and Sri Lanka: Four Decades of Political Diplomacy*, New Delhi: Allied Publishers, p. 215.
8. *Human Rights Watch*, March 2008.
9. EU Experts' Report entitled 'The Implications of Certain Human Rights Conventions in Sri Lanka', quoted in Mandana Ismail Abeywickrema, 'EU Rights on GSP+', *The Sunday Leader*, 4 October 2009.
10. The figures are cited by Asanga Welikala (2008), *A State of Permanent Crisis*, CPA Publication.
11. Article by V. Anandasangaree, 'The IDPs: Urgent Steps Needed for Their Welfare', *Sunday Island*, 11 October 2009, p. 14.
12. 'A Profile of the Internal Displacement Situation in Sri Lanka: Civilian Displacement by Conflict Facing Severe Humanitarian Crisis', *IDMC*, http://www.internal-displacement.org, p. 254.
13. Rohan Gunaratne (1998), 'Impact of the Mobilised Tamil Diaspora on the Protracted Conflict in Sri Lanka', in Kumar Rupasinghe (ed), *Negotiating Peace in Sri Lanka: Efforts, Failures and Lessons*, published by International Alert of London, pp. 305-6.
14. For further reading on Schneiderian theory, David M. Schneider (1984), *A Critique of the Study of Kinship*, Ann Arbor: University Michigan Press.

    For a discussion of 'diasporic consciousness' more as a construct of surrounding social and historical forces rather than kinship related outcome, read Mark P. Whitaker (2004), 'Sri Lankan Tamil Diaspora:

Three Tamil Family Narratives', *Ethnic Studies Report*, vol. XXI, no. 1, January, Colombo: International Centre for Ethnic Studies Publication, pp. 61-5.

15. *Sri Lankan Tamil Diaspora*, http//en.wikipedia.org.
16. *Jane's Intelligence Review*, October 1996, p. 473.
17. Tyrol Ferdinands et al. (eds) (2004), *The Sri Lanka Peace Process at Crossroads: Lessons, Opportunities and Ideas for Principled Negotiations and Conflict Transformation*, Colombo, p. VI.
18. Report by Shamindra Fernando in *Sunday Island*, 2 July 2009, 'Gota Warns of Efforts to Free Hard Core Tigers'.
19. S.C. Chandrahasan, interviewed by Stanley Samarasinghe, *The Nation*, 25 October 2009, p. 11. Chandrahasan is an eminent lawyer and the son of S.J.V. Chalvanayagam.
20. Survey report by Chandani Kirinde, *Sunday Times*, 25 October 2009, p. 12.
21. K.M. de Silva (1999), 'Sri Lanka: Ethnic Conflict and the Search for a Durable Peace, 1978-1999', *Ethnic Studies Report*, vol. XVII, no. 2, July.

13

Ethnicity and Human Rights

A Study of Aboriginal Australians

B. MALINI REDDY AND B.A. SHILPA DEEKSHITH

Indigenous people are a significant and important part of humanity. They have social, cultural, economic and political characteristics that are distinct from those of the dominant societies in which they live.[1] It is estimated that there are more than 370 million indigenous people spread across 70 countries worldwide. They are the descendants of those who inhabited a country or a geographical region at the time when people of different cultures or ethnic origins arrived.[2] Despite their cultural differences, the various groups of indigenous people around the world share common problems related to the protection of their rights as distinct people.[3]

Considering the diversity of indigenous people, an official definition of 'indigenous' has not been adopted by any institution of the UN-system. Instead, the system has developed a modern understanding of this term based on the following:[4]

- Self-identification as indigenous peoples at the individual level and acceptance by the community as their member
- Historical continuity with pre-colonial and/or pre-settler societies
- Strong link to territories and surrounding natural resources
- Distinct social, economic or political systems
- Distinct language, culture and beliefs
- Form non-dominant groups of society

- Resolve to maintain and reproduce their ancestral environments and systems as distinctive peoples and communities.

Indigenous people are arguably among the most disadvantaged and vulnerable groups of people in the world today. The international community now recognizes that special measures are required to protect the rights of the world's indigenous peoples.[5]

Among the indigenous peoples are those of the Americas (for example, the Lakota in the USA, the Mayas in Guatemala or the Aymaras in Bolivia), the Inuit and Aleutians of the circumpolar region, the Saami of northern Europe, the Aborigines and Torres Strait Islanders of Australia and the Maoris of New Zealand.[6] With evidence of occupation over 60,000 years, the Aboriginal Australians may be the world's oldest people in the world's oldest land.[7]

Aboriginal Australians

The Australian indigenous population is estimated at around 4,58,500 persons, or 2.4 per cent of the total population. Clearly identifiable differences exist between the indigenous and non-indigenous populations. The indigenous population is more likely to reside in areas classified as very remote and is disproportionately disadvantaged across health and socio-economic indicators (ABS 2002). The indigenous people of Australia comprise two separate groups, Australian Aborigines and people from the Torres Strait Islands. Of the indigenous population, Torres Strait Islander people make up about 10.6 per cent of the total (ABS 2001). The generally used Australian definition states that an indigenous person is one who:[8]

- Has Aboriginal or Torres Strait Islander descent;
- Identifies as an Aboriginal or Torres Strait Islander person;
- Is accepted as an Aboriginal or Torres Strait Islander by the community in which he or she lives.

This definition is widely accepted within government departments, statutory bodies and institutions.

History

> If an uninhabited country be discovered and planted by English subjects, all the English laws then in being, which are the birthright of every English subject, are immediately there in force.
>
> William Blackstone

Aboriginal religion is deep and complex. Their art and myths are rich and varied. What is of great significance was their strong and foolproof system of incest prohibition, their system of kinship, reciprocity, and child-rearing. Aborigines held their land in trust, collectively and in perpetuity. United by religious and totemic ties, within the various social units, kinship implied certain behaviour and reciprocal responsibilities. For aboriginals, patterns of social interaction were prescribed, cooperation within each group was high, and group sanctions, by way of punishment for breach of rules, were harsh.[9]

Land was and is central to aboriginal societies, cultures and religions. Traditionally, from an aboriginal standpoint, all land was, and is, sacred because the deities shaped it, humanized it and put within it the resources it now contains. The land and its environment was managed, nurtured, protected and respected by aboriginal people in a cyclical process of birth, death and renewal that is central to much of aboriginal philosophy. For aboriginal Australians the land is the core of all spirituality, identity and purpose.[10]

In 1788, the first European settlement was established in Australia. The next hundred years saw aboriginal people forced out of their country, dispossessed of habitable land, shot, poisoned and massacred as successive waves of British settlers sought land for building, agriculture, grazing and mining.[11] When the British occupied Australia they called the country *terra nullius*—belonging to no-one. They did so, because they deemed the nomadic aboriginals as uncivilized.[12] Removed from their land, deprived of their traditional bush food and devastated by disease, malnutrition, poverty, alcoholism, violence and despair, most aboriginal people existed on town fringes and pastoral properties or were herded onto reserves and missions.[13]

Stolen Generation

> In 1987, a sensational 'discovery' was made by a Sydney University team, led by Australia's most celebrated pre-historian, Professor D.J. Mulvaney. They reported that the Australian population in 1788 was 750,000 or three times the previous estimate. They concluded that more than 600,000 people had died as result of white settlement.
>
> John Pilger, *New Statesman*, 10 July 2000

The 'stolen generation' were some 100,000 aboriginal children who were taken from their families on the territories, and raised in homes or adopted by white families in an effort to 'civilize' them by assimilation into white society.[14] It is estimated that 10 per cent of indigenous Australian children were removed from their families and communities under state sanctioned policies and removal practices in Australia between 1910 and 1970. Today, most indigenous families continue to be affected in one or more generations by the forcible removal of children during this time.[15] The physical and emotional damage to those taken away was profound and lasting. Most grew up in a hostile environment without family ties or cultural identity. As adults, many suffered insecurity, lack of self-esteem, a feeling of worthlessness, depression, suicide, violence, delinquency, abuse of alcohol and drugs and inability to trust. Lacking a parental model, many had difficulty bringing up their own children.[16]

Stolen Wages

The term 'stolen wages' refers to wages, savings, entitlements and other monies that state and federal governments in Australia did not pay to Aboriginal and Torres Strait Islander people who were under their control between 1905 and 1972.[17] During this period, most aboriginal and Torres Strait Islander people were controlled by various 'Protection' Acts. These gave the governments almost unlimited rights to control their lives.[18]

The Australian Senate in June 2006 voted to hold an inquiry into the practice of state and territory governments withholding the wages of aboriginal and Torres Strait Islander workers.[19]

Social Indicators of Well-Being

Poverty is not just about a 'lack of'. It is also about discrimination and exclusion.[20] On all indicators of poverty—material and non-material, absolute and relative—Aboriginal people emerge as the most disadvantaged group in Australia.[21]

Estimates from the National Aboriginal and Torres Strait Islander Survey (NATSIS) conducted by the Australian Bureau of Statistics in 1994, show that 63 per cent of the aboriginal adult population cited income from government transfers as their principle income source in contrast to a rate of only 13 per cent for non-indigenous Australians. Employment rates also show a long-term downward trend among aboriginals and employment growth has not kept up with the rapidly expanding aboriginal working-age population.[22] The problems of poor educational outcomes, low rates of labour participation, low income and welfare dependence has prevented many indigenous individuals and families from accumulating capital, or making investments which in turn leads to inter-generational poverty.[23]

For those living in remote communities, there is no real labour market. The only option is often part-time work on the work-for-the-dole programme for aboriginal Australians, known as the Community Development Employment Projects (CDEP) scheme.[24] CDEP was created by the Fraser government in 1977 to establish work programmes on remote aboriginal communities and to foster economic and social benefits.[25] While CDEP never offered real jobs or aboriginal control, in some communities it had been the only means to establish small local economies and it offered supplementary income in areas where few genuine employment opportunities existed.[26] CDEP was scraped in 2007 as a consequence of the Federal government's emergency intervention to reduce spending on alcohol and gambling in the 73 aboriginal communities the commonwealth is taking over in the northern territory.[27]

Aboriginals also top the medical statistics for diseases like coronary disease, cancer, diabetes, respiratory infections. They are at the bottom of the life expectancy table at 50-5 years or less for males and around 55 years for females.[28]

Aboriginal Australians also continue to be overrepresented in the prison population. Aboriginal and Torres Strait Islander people represented 31.8 per cent of all persons held in custody by the police during August 1995. In 1995, the police custody rate for indigenous people was 2,228 per 100,000 compared to 83 per 100,000 for non-indigenous people. As a result, indigenous people were 27 times more likely to find themselves in police custody than non-indigenous people. The highest rate of indigenous incarceration in police custody was in South Australia (4,841).[29] According to the Australian Institute of Criminology, Aboriginal Australians represented 20 to 22 per cent of Australia's prison population in June of 2005. Aboriginal Australians are 13 times as likely to be incarcerated and twice as likely to be victims of violence or to be threatened with violence.[30]

Australia led the world in social legislation in the early years of the twentieth century. The new Commonwealth government guaranteed Australian citizens a range of fundamental rights: women's suffrage in 1902, minimum wage in 1907, pensions for the aged and invalid in 1909, and a maternity allowance in 1912. Aboriginal Australians were denied access to these rights. At the state level, discriminatory laws or practices were introduced which excluded many aboriginal children from public schools.[31]

The aboriginal and Torres Strait Islander Social Justice Commissioner in 2001 argued that even today indigenous people are unable to benefit equally from mainstream services because they are insufficiently accessible to the particular cultural needs of aboriginals.[32]

Political Rights

Hardly any changes took place with Britain's transfer of power to a Federal Australia in 1900/1 under the new Federal Constitution. Until the 1960s, aboriginal people did not have effective citizenship. They were rigidly controlled by State laws. Many were confined to reserves which they could not leave without a permit. Following a 1967 referendum, the Federal (Canberra) government gained powers to legislate on aboriginal matters. Legislation opposing racial discrimination was passed in 1975. In 1990, Aboriginal and Torres Strait Islander Commission (ATSIC) was set up.[33]

The Aboriginal and Torres Strait Islander Commission (1990-2005) was the Australian government body through which aboriginal Australians and Torres Strait Islanders were formally involved in the process of government. While ATSIC's existence was always subject to the whims of the government, who represented the whole of Australia, ATSIC was an elected body whose constituency was indigenous Australians.[34]

Reconciliation

Reconciliation is based on indigenous and non-indigenous Australians coming to an honest understanding of their shared history, a commitment to building cooperative partnerships based on trust and respect and a recognition of the distinctive rights of indigenous peoples.[35]

In 1991 the report of the Royal Commission into Aboriginal Deaths in Custody revealed a complex and devastating picture of the effects of dispossession, colonization and institutional racism on Aboriginal peoples. Partly in response to the findings of the Royal Commission, the federal parliament established the Council for Aboriginal Reconciliation which had as its goal the 'transformation of aboriginal and non-aboriginal relations in this country'. This was followed in 1992 by the High Court's decision in Mabo, which rejected the idea that Australia was *terra nullius* (land belonging to no one) at the time of European settlement. The court recognized the common law right of indigenous peoples to land, based on their continuing use and connection to land.[36]

A national inquiry was set up in 1995 to study the forcible removal of aboriginal children. Its 1997 report 'Bringing Them Home' contained harrowing evidence. The Human Rights Equal Opportunity Commission outlined 54 recommendations in the 1997 'Bringing Them Home' report. The report's recommendations are supported by international law which provides that where a person's human rights have been violated, they must have access to an 'effective remedy'. The Stolen Generations have a right to restitution, rehabilitation, guarantees against reparation and compensation. In October 1998, Prime Minister John Howard declared that his government is committed to vigorously pursuing the goal of 'practical reconciliation' to reduce indigenous material disadvantage in the areas of health, housing, education and employment (Altman 2004).[37] In February 2008 Prime Minister Rudd offered a national apology to the stolen generation.

The Australian government has also announced a National indigenous Languages Policy aimed at keeping indigenous languages alive and supporting indigenous Australians to connect with their language, culture and country. Over a period of more than 160 years, the remains of indigenous Australians were collected, usually without consent, by explorers, travellers and scientists and shipped off to museums and private collections across the world. Indigenous Australians believe those ancestral spirits cannot rest until they are returned to their home country. The government is committed to working with indigenous people, other countries, museums and private collectors to repatriate ancestral remains as quickly as possible.[38]

A new opinion poll in September 2009 has found that 70 per cent of Australians believe improving the living conditions of aboriginal and Torres Strait Islander people should be a high or very high priority for the Federal government. The survey highlighted that 58 per cent of all respondents believed that Australian politicians do not know enough about Aboriginal history and culture to develop effective policy for them. Fifty-two per cent believed that Australian politicians had not learned from past successes and failures in indigenous policy making, 57 per cent felt that the living condition of indigenous people is negatively affecting Australia's reputation overseas.[39]

Conclusion

In March 2009, the United Nations Committee for the Elimination of Racial Discrimination (CERD) expressed serious concern that the Australian government has suspended the Racial Discrimination Act 1975 to enact the Northern Territory Emergency Response (intervention) laws. In responding to the urgent complaint against the intervention brought by indigenous leaders, the committee urged the Australian government to report on the progress it has made to reinstate the Racial Discrimination Act and build new relationship with aboriginal Australians. In April 2009, the United Nations Human Rights Committee reported that Australia had breached a number of its obligations under the International Covenant on Civil and Political Rights. It drew attention to the failure to establish a national indigenous representative body, insufficient consultation with indigenous people in decisions affecting their rights, failure to grant reparations to the Stolen Generations and the discriminatory nature of the Northern Territory intervention.[40]

The history of the debate on indigenous policy can be characterized by the tension between two ideological camps: assimilation *versus* self-determination. The first camp views integration of indigenous people into the mainstream economy and Western culture as inevitable and ultimately the way to achieve equality between indigenous and non-indigenous Australians. The self-determination approach argues that traditional indigenous cultures have a value in their own right, and indigenous people should choose for themselves the balance between preserving elements of their traditional culture and engagement in the mainstream economy.[41]

The right to self-determination is based on the simple acknowledgment that indigenous people are Australia's first people. The loss of this right to live according to a set of common values and beliefs, and to have that right respected by others, is at the heart of the current disadvantage experienced by indigenous Australians. Without self-determination it is not possible for indigenous Australians to fully overcome the legacy of colonization and dispossession.[42]

NOTES

1. Australian Bureau of Statistics (ABS) 2002, Australian Demographic Statistics 2002, Canberra, Australia. www.abs.gov.au.
2. ABS 2001, Australian Demographic Statistics 2001, Canberra, Australia. www.abs.gov.au.
3. Altman (2004), 'Practical Reconciliation and the New Mainstreaming:

Will it Make a Difference to Indigenous Australians?', *Dialogue*, 23 (2): 35-46, 2004. www.assa.edu.au.

4. 'About UNPFII and a Brief History of Indigenous Peoples and the International System', United Nations Permanent Forum on indigenous Issues. http://www.un.org/esa/socdev/unpfii/en/history.html.
5. 'Who are Indigenous Peoples?' Factsheet, United Nations Permanent Forum on Indigenous Issues. http://www.wipce2008.com/enews/pdf/wipce_fact_sheet_21-10-07.pdf
6. 'About UNPFII and a Brief History of Indigenous Peoples and the International System', op. cit.
7. 'Who are Indigenous Peoples?', op. cit.
8. 'About UNPFII and a brief history of Indigenous Peoples and the International System', op. cit.
9. 'Who are Indigenous Peoples?', op. cit.
10. 'History and Heritage', European Network for Indigenous Australian Rights, http://www.eniar.org/history.html.
11. 'Primary Eligibility Criteria for ABSTUDY: Chapter 10—Aboriginality or Torres Strait Islander Status', Department of Education, Employment and Workplace Relations. Australian Government. http://www.dest.gov.au/sectors/indigenous_education/publications_resources/abstudy/primary_eligibility_criteria_for_abstudy.
12. 'Genocide in Australia' by Colin Tatz, Research Discussion Paper No. 8, 1999, Australian Institute of Aboriginal and Torres Straits Islander Studies, Canberra. http://www.aiatsis.gov.au/research/docs/dp/DP08.pdf.
13. 'Land Rights', Fact Sheet, November 2007, Reconciliation Network. http://reconciliaction.org.au/nsw/education-kit/land-rights.
14. 'History and Heritage', op. cit.
15. 'Land Rights and Native Title', European Network for Indigenous Australian Rights, http://www.eniar.org/nativetitle.html.
16. 'History and Heritage', op. cit.
17. Australia's 'Stolen Generation and the Extinction of Aboriginality' by Peter Reed, British Library, London, 6 November 2002. http://www.culturewars.org.uk/2002-12/stolengeneration.htm
18. 'Bringing Them Home', Report of the National Inquiry into the Separation of Aboriginal and Torres Strait Islander Children from Their Families, Human Rights and Equal Opportunity Commission, Sydney, 1997. http://www.hreoc.gov.au/social_justice/bth_report/report/index.html.

19. 'The Stolen Generations', European Network for Indigenous Australian Rights, http://www.eniar.org/stolengenerations.html.
20. 'Stolen Wages', Policies in Focus, Department of Indigenous Affairs, Government of Western Australia. http://www.dia.wa.gov.au/Policies-in-Focus/Stolen-Wages.
21. 'Stolen Wages', Australians for Native Title and Reconciliation, ANTaR. http://www.antar.org.au/issues_and_campaigns/stolenwages.
22. 'National Day of Action for Stolen Aboriginal Wages', Media Release, 7 December 2005, Australians for Native Title and Reconciliation, ANTaR. http://antarqld.org.au/03_news/mr071205stolenwages.pdf.
23. 'The UDHR—What it Means for Australia Today', Address by Claire Mallinson, National Director, Amnesty International Australia, 22 October 2008, ACT Legislative Assembly. http://www.amnesty.org.au/wiki/The_UDHR_- What_it_means_for_Australia_today/
24. 'Aboriginal Australians and Poverty: Issues of Measurement' by Janet Taylor, Australian Institute of Family Studies, No. 35, August 1993, pp. 46-7. http://www.aifs.gov.au/institute/pubs/fm1/fm35jt.html.
25. 'Beyond the Rhetoric: The Next Step for Indigenous Affairs Policy' by Anne Daly & Diane Smith, 11 February 2001, University of Sydney. http://unpan1.un.org/intradoc/groups/public/documents/APCITY/UNPAN002438.pdf.
26. 'Poverty in Australia: A Focus on Indigenous Poverty from an International Human Rights Perspective' by Janet Cechanski, Human Rights Defender, 2002. http://www.austlii.edu.au/au/journals/HRD/2002/25.html.
27. 'Beyond the Rhetoric: The Next Step for Indigenous Affairs Policy', op. cit.
28. 'Indigenous Communities Ponder Life after CDEP' by Mick McLaughlin, ABC news, 2 August 2007. http://www.abc.net.au/news/stories/2007/08/02/1994630.htm?section=australia
29. 'CDEP Under Attack from ALP' by Jess Moore, 17 January 2009, Green Left online. http://www.greenleft.org.au/2009/779/40169.
30. 'Indigenous Communities Ponder Life After CDEP' by Mick McLaughlin, ABC news, 2 August 2007. http://www.abc.net.au/news/stories/2007/08/02/1994630.htm?section=australia
31. 'Genocide in Australia' by Colin Tatz, Research Discussion Paper No. 8, 1999, Australian Institute of Aboriginal and Torres Straits Islander Studies, Canberra. http://www.aiatsis.gov.au/research/docs/dp/DP08.pdf.

32. 'Indigenous Imprisonment in Australia: An Unresolved Human Rights Issue', op. cit.
33. 'Colonial Ideology and Aboriginal Australians' by Ghali Hassan, *Axis of Logic Exclusive*, 1 September 2007. http://axisoflogic.com/artman/publish/Article_25187.shtml
34. 'Aboriginal Struggle for Citizenship' by Kate Cameron, *Discovering Democracy*, New South Wales Department of Education and Training. http://www.abc.net.au/civics/democracy/struggle.htm.
35. 'Poverty in Australia: A Focus on Indigenous Poverty from an International Human Rights Perspective' by Janet Cechanski, *Human Rights Defender*, 2002. http://www.austlii.edu.au/au/journals/HRD/2002/25.html.
36. 'History and Heritage', European Network for Indigenous Australian Rights, http://www.eniar.org/history.html.
37. 'Aboriginal and Torres Strait Islander Commission', Encyclopedia, NationMaster.com http://www.statemaster.com/encyclopedia/Aboriginal-and-Torres-Strait-Islander-Commission.
38. 'Social Justice and Human Rights for Aboriginal and Torres Straits Islander Peoples', Information Sheet, Australian Human Rights Commission. http://www.hreoc.gov.au/Social_Justice/info_sheet.html.
39. 'Social Justice and Human Rights for Aboriginal and Torres Straits Islander Peoples', Information Sheet, Developed by the Human Rights and Equal Opportunities Commission, 2003. http://www.humanrights.gov.au/Social_Justice/info_sheet.html.
40. 'Apology an Essential First Step', *Amnesty International*, 13 February 2008. http://www.amnesty.org.au/news/comments/9067.
41. Australian Statement on Indigenous Issues to UNGA64 Third Committee. www.un.org/esa/socdev/unpfii/documents/statement_2009_Australia.doc - 2009-10-20.
42. 'New Polls Delivers Scathing Verdict on Government's Handling of Indigenous Policy', *Amnesty International*, 2 September 2009, http://www.amnesty.org.au/news/comments/21626. See also 'Human Rights', European Network for Indigenous Australian Rights, http://www.eniar.org/humanrights.html. 'Assimilation *vs.* Self- Determination' by Mike Dockery, Australians for Native Title and Reconciliation, ANTaR, 19 February 2009. http://www.antar.org.au/assimilation_vs_self_determination. 'Social Justice and Human Rights for Aboriginal and Torres Straits Islander Peoples', Information Sheet, Developed by the Human Rights and Equal Opportunities Commission, 2003. http://www.humanrights.gov.au/Social_Justice/info_sheet.html.

14

National Identity as a Factor of Effective Global Organization

Olga Potapova

It is an obvious fact that the modern world is multipolar and globalizing. Globalization processes have penetrated into various spheres of social and even personal life. This often causes several problems between globalization, increasing communication and incorporation on the one hand and national sovereignty and national identity on the other.

This brief paper deals with this issue of national identity in the global world. It also includes alternatives to the contemporary international system.

National identity is understood here as self-identification of a nation. It is a process when a nation becomes itself; and through this process a person realizes his affiliation to a particular social community. National identity should be considered as one of the main features of a national group. Representatives of the nation should consider themselves as members of a particular united group, which has a common territory, history, traditions, culture, and social institutes. During the process of forming or transforming of national identity we can observe setting of such concepts as 'we' and 'they'; 'own' and 'alien'. This process of so-called 'negative identity' produces not only self-identification with a particular group, but also a strong intolerance to members of other groups.

We can speak about a direct relation between intensity of identity and necessity of its expression. In other words, a nation with a strong negative identity needs an isolation and even contradistinction to others.

Thus, formation of a national identity is a basis of right to self-determination, which is natural for every nation. In the modern world we often face a problem of correlation between this important right and the principle of territorial integrity.

Globalization, pointed above, is an integral part of the modern world. There is an undoubted tendency to collaborate between states and regions in the international arena. International relations in the twenty-first century have become more and more complicated: there are new types of actors (non-governmental organizations or sub-nations within national states) and new types of problems (as for example humanitarian interventions or global warming). It is not surprising that the current system of world organization cannot always effectively cope with these new challenges. So it needs to be transformed—but to do so we have to elaborate the basic principles which can determine the parameters of transformation.

International law cannot give us such principles because international law itself needs to be corrected under contemporary circumstances. Nor can the international political practice provide a guideline. Thus I suppose we can turn to principles of ethics and morality and use them in the international sphere. The first of these thesis that needs to be considered is justice.

Why do I take justice as the measure and starting point in regulating international relations? Effective organization means first of all a just world order.

Traditionally the international political arena has been regarded as an anarchical state of nature, where 'might is right'. A moral notion of international justice has been considered more or less irrelevant. Rather, justice has been conceived in realistic terms; as mutual advantage between sovereign States. But the end of the bi-polar power structure of the Cold War and the acceleration of globalization have promoted a sense of global community where there is a need for justice based on shared ethical values—both between states and between individuals worldwide.

There is reason to speak of a normative turn in international political discourse. Issues like world poverty, climate change, human rights and humanitarian intervention, global trade, global democracy, and the use of force in the fight against terrorism, are now discussed in terms of moral and legal legitimacy and not solely political feasibility.

Conventional concepts and theories have taken a state or a national political structure as a prerequisite for justice. 'Statist' perspectives of justice, have, however been challenged by various cosmopolitan theories arguing that a valid approach to justice must be global in scope. Moreover, scholars and practitioners alike increasingly recognize that issues of justice are at the heart of many new global threats. In this, philosophers have begun the project of extending their domestic analyses of justice into the international arena.

Thus the main principles of international justice can be worked out along with domestic theories of justice. First of all, we should realize, that international justice presupposes construction of relations between actors all over the world on the ground of particular basic principles, which are accepted and realized by each actor. There are as we have already defined not only the rules of international law, although these rules are undoubtedly an important part of just world order. Justice on the contrary is more general and applies to more grounded values. The most significant component of a just world is the security and liberty of an individual. Consequently just international institutions should protect human rights. International justice deals with such issues like war, distribution of resources, equality, and national self-identification. Thus one of the important component of a just world organization is *prima facie* equality of rights for all actors and common shared values, such as preservation and priority of human rights.

Now let's turn to our main question: Is a just and effective world organization possible and how can we reach it?

Our hypothesis will assume positive answer to this question. In the modern globalizing world all people can and should collaborate. Here arises a problem of national identity in a globalizing world, which we will consider. I suppose that national identity can be one of the main positive factors for constructing a just world system, when all main rights of nations are observed and basic principles of international relations are respected.

This idea of a just and effective international order has been the concern of many philosophers. We can recognize ideas which deal with just world order in the main works of philosophers such as Augustine, Hobbes, Grozij, Hume, Kant and many others. The main contemporary writer who devoted his works to this theme was John Rawls. He is known for his theory of justice, which he put on an international level in his recent monograph *The Law of Peoples* (1999).

For Rawls, international justice is possible when all nations (which he names *peoples*) are free and equal. Representatives of peoples elaborate principles of a just world order. The main condition for our sketch here is a veil of ignorance, which means that representatives do not even know whom they represent.

Rawls considers representation as the veil of ignorance of liberal societies.[1] In the first use of the original position, its function as a device of representation means that it models fair conditions for the parties, as representatives of free and equal citizens, to specify the terms of cooperation regulating the basic structure of their society. Since that position includes the veil of ignorance, it also models acceptable restrictions on reasons for adopting a political conception of justice.

Three conditions are essential: First, the original position represents the parties (or citizens) fairly, or reasonably; second, it represents them as rational; and third, it represents them as decision makers capable of making the right option. We check that these three conditions are satisfied by observing that citizens are indeed represented fairly, or reasonably, in virtue of the symmetry and equality of their representatives' situation in the original position. Next, citizens are represented as rational by virtue of the aim of their representatives to do the best they can for their essential interests as persons. Finally, they are represented as deciding for appropriate reasons: The veil of ignorance prevents their representatives from invoking reasons deemed unsuitable, given the aim of representing citizens as free and equal persons.

At the next level, when the original position is used to extend a liberal conception to the law of peoples, it is a device of representation because it models fair conditions under which the parties, this time as representatives of societies well-ordered by liberal conceptions of justice, are to specify the law of peoples and the fair terms of their cooperation.[2]

So we can see that Rawls suggested a way when representation is somehow faceless. We can conclude from the abstracts of Rawls' theory of international justice that representatives of actors on the world arena should undoubtedly remember about interests of those whom they represent but at the certain moment of the agreement on particular question they do not know the national affiliation of each other. National identity is hidden at this moment, as some other factors temporarily fall into the background. Of course, national interests, which should be mentioned in the process of decision-making or agreement, depend on national identity. May be one of the ways to conciliate national identity of all members and participants of the world political process is to put in order these national interests. Representatives should behave as they rely not on national interests of every people in the world but on hypothetical basic interests. These are first of all interests of individuals who live in a peaceful and effective organized world system. All peoples are supposed to adopt common values which are the basis for construction of common shared interests. So these very general and very basic interests can serve as guidelines for representatives of peoples when they need to elaborate a particular agreement or make a common decision in the international sphere.

Such approach we can transfer to the process of identity forming. Every people has its own identity and it is important to realize this. All peoples, who form national states and all ethnic minorities within states, have a right to consider themselves as members of particular national group. Thus they have right to have their own language, to develop their own culture and to choose their own way of social organization.

And also to have equality and priority if these rights are declared in the Charter of the United Nation as one of the main foundation of peaceful and secure world order. To develop friendly relations among nations based on respect for the principle of equal rights and self-determination of peoples is the purpose of the United Nations as the world's premier international organization.[3] One of the ways that the

UN uses in achievement of its main purpose is solving international problems of an economic, social, cultural, or humanitarian character, with respect for human rights and for fundamental freedoms for all persons without distinction as to race, sex, language, or religion; and being a centre for harmonizing the actions of nations in the attainment of these common ends.[4] We should emphasize that it no way means some kind of loss of national identity.

According to Charles Beitz, who considers the issue of self-determination in terms of a just world order, self-determination is one of the most important and most obscure principles of contemporary international law and practice. The principle, according to Beitz, has rapidly been accepted as a main principle of international law. Besides the fact that the concept, twice mentioned in the United Nations Charter, as we have already noted, is cited as authority for the General Assembly's call for 'the granting of independence to colonial countries and peoples' in its Resolution 1,514 (XX) of 14 December 1960. In the last fifteen years, the General Assembly has reaffirmed this call almost annually, each time citing the principle of self-determination as if it were a self-evident first principle.

As the diversity of appeals to self-determination suggests, the principle can be interpreted in a variety of ways. Indeed, it has become so flexible a rhetorical device that some might think it to have lost its moral content. Although, as Beitz shows, such a conclusion would be extreme, the principle as stated above is ambiguous in at least three important ways, all illustrated by the various appeals to it mentioned.[5] There are some important questions that we must answer to clear up the role of national identity in the process of self-determination. First, it is not clear whether the 'self' in 'self-determination' refers to the government or to the population of a group. Does the principle simply requires the creation of an independent government among a previously dependent group, or does it require, in addition, that the new government be 'self-government', i.e. institutionally responsible to its people? A second ambiguity concerns the identities of the groups eligible to claim the right of self-determination. Standard applications of the principle involve colonial populations with memberships that are, in some sense, already established; but why should the scope of the principle be so restricted? Finally, one might wonder what kind of 'independence' would satisfy the principle. Is the severing of legal bonds sufficient, or does the principle also require dissolution of the economic and social relationships that may permit foreigners to continue to exert influence inside the colonized area even after formal independence has been achieved?[6] It will be wrong to absolute the right of every nation to self-determination. For my mind in contemporary world international system is transformed in such a way that non-governmental actors will play more important role than it will be earlier. After Rawls I suggest to use the term 'peoples' instead of 'states', and speak about national identity of peoples instead of self-determination of states.

Thus we accept a fact of self-determination and a right of every national group to find its own features and relations. We also accept the right of every person in the world to have a national identity which means to associate itself with particular national group.

At the same time we cannot be fully independent within the international community. We always must remember that we are at the same time members of the international society and it has its rules and laws. And we must respect these laws and since we have some rights we must respect the same rights of other peoples. When we need to work out some common principles or to accept certain agreement we should act so as we have not any identity except our membership of the world society.

This does not mean the loss of national identity. It implies that peoples when they need to elaborate strategy of interaction in global world or solve global problems should act as parts of a single global system and not as only representatives of nations.

So we can make a half-way conclusion that category of national identity should be first of all applicable in the case when we consider individuals, not any other actors of the international system, such as states, governments and various so named classical actors. National identity can apply to a person's self-identification. Indeed it deals much more with the individual's identification process; I mean here an individual's affiliation to some national group. This approach to the nature of identity appreciably simplifies our research of the phenomenon of national identity. Most of our conclusions are made in strong connection with the individual's perception of identity.

There is a variety of identities in the modern world and belonging to majority doesn't mean loss of the individual's own identity. The process of self-identification should mean not contradiction but cooperation of the concepts 'we' and 'they'. Each person (as each nation) has its own identity, which consists of many components. And when we speak about global action we should be blind to our national identity. In this case we can bring out just principles of world organization.

This position is close to ideas of some post-modern writers. According to Michael Walzer, every person possesses more than one identity. He/she can have the identity of a citizen of a particular state, member of some local minority group, member of his own family, some other identities and finally a personal identity, which belongs to this person directly.[7] The solution, proposed by Walzer, is to concentrate attention on this personal identity. It means the basic role of the personal identity in a process of self-identification. All other identities are in some way derived, and can be accepted as parts of an integrated personal identity.

Another outstanding post-modern researcher, Julia Kristeva, adheres to a similar theory. Kristeva, who devoted a number of her works to problems connected with immigrant societies and national minorities within national states, paid a lot of attention to the demarcation between individual identity and social or national identity.[8]

An effective state national policy is important for every government and for the global world as a whole. National identity should be a fundamental factor for not only the domestic politic of a particular state or certain national group, but also for conducting foreign policy and interactions between actors in the world arena. So attention of leaders of states or nations to the national identity is of prime importance.

It is up to the leaders and governments to form a 'positive' kind of national identity and to make an accent on the individuality with respect to human rights and right to have a personal identity. Such a policy of toleration should be adopted by both leaders of national minorities and governments of states. To act in a just world, to observe rights of each other and rules of international order is in the own interest of every nation. National policy and identification process should be constructive, only then it will be acceptable.

Thus, in a modern multicultural world the most effective alternative is to accept the diversities of societies with their own identities. The only way to reconcile identities of national minorities, identities of citizenship, identities of immigrant societies, etc., is to turn to individual identity, which includes more or less all of the above-listed identities.

Notes

1. J. Rawls, *The Law of Peoples*, Cambridge: Harvard University Press, 1999, p. 53.
2. Ibid., pp. 53-4.
3. The UN Charter, Article 1.
4. Ibid., Article 2, Article 55.
5. C. Beitz (1973), 'Self-determination', in Charles Beitz, *Political Theory and International Relations*, Princeton: Princeton University Press, p. 92.
6. Ibid., pp. 94-5.
7. M. Walzer (1999), *On Toleration*, New Haven: Yale University Press, p. 79.
8. J. Kristeva (1993), 'What of Tomorrow's Nation', in *Nations without Nationalism*, tr. Leon S. Roudiez, New York: Columbia University Press.

15

The Black Heart of Brussels

The Categories of Ethnic Entrepreneurship in the African Neighbourhood of Matongé

CARMEN DE MICHELE

Introduction

Almost every European city has its own China Town, Little Istanbul, Matongé or 'Schinkenstrasse'. Migrants, specially those with a different cultural background, tend to concentrate in specific areas. In the United States, still the primary destination of immigrants from all over the world, ethnic districts can be found in many big cities. Some of them, like China Town in San Francisco even became tourist attractions, because, as a local tourist brochure puts it 'you get the best of Beijing, but with clean streets'.

This paper looks at the economic structure of ethnic districts within an urban context, taking the ethnic neighbourhood of Matongé in Brussels as a case study. Very specific business dynamics can be observed within those areas, that often have more similarities to the countries of their origin than to their new home. For many migrants, the formal (and sometimes also informal) economy of the ethnic district is their first stop after arriving in the host country. But these areas do not only cover the necessities of the immigrants, but are also essential for the rest of the city.

An ethnic neighbourhood is an enclave which retains some cultural distinction from a larger, surrounding area. Usually the district revolves around businesses that are run by the members of the community (ethnic entrepreneurs). Although entrepreneurs have a high political and cultural significance for their community, this paper will look at their economic function. Their economic significance lies in their independent contribution to the economic development of their neighbourhood and their own ethnic group (Knight 1921: 283).

Increasing immigration can tighten the local labour market, specially in the low-skills job sector. Self-employment seems to be the perfect solution of this problem. The argument goes that immigrants who start their own businesses can be better integrated into the host society. Self-employment reduces welfare dependency, unemployment and poverty within the ethnic community and serves as a role model for the successful integration of future immigrants.

Beyond that, it has a positive effect on the city and its inhabitants as well. Ethnic neighbourhoods in urban areas create new shopping and entertainment opportunities and revive the inner cities. Immigrants tend to settle in those areas of the city where rents are affordable and therefore they bring new entrepreneurial dynamics into run-down and crime-ridden neighbourhoods.

Ethnic entrepreneurship can even have a positive effect on the immigrant's country of origin. Remittances sent back to family and friends help to relieve poverty and to avoid the necessity of future immigration. Many entrepreneurs keep strong business ties with their home country, building up a transnational business network.

The present paper will first give a brief introduction on the economic dynamics behind ethnic entrepreneurship. There are certainly many factors that influence the decision of becoming self-employed, but this paper will only mention two which seem plausible in this setting: discrimination on the labour market and the dynamics of the ethnic neighbourhood as an economic enclave. The African neighbourhood of Matongé serves as an example for illustrating these economic processes. I will examine the different kinds of self-employed that co-exist in the neighbourhood and their mutual interaction.

The paper is based on 22 interviews collected in Matongé in the autumn of 2006. All the people interviewed had a non-European ethnic background and were either first or second generation immigrants. They all defined themselves as self-employed.

Statistics on the informal economy are very unreliable due to the nature of the subject. There are no specific data for Matongé, so my paper can only categorize different forms of informal economic activity and estimate their impact.

The Ethnic Entrepreneur

For some decades social scientists have lost interest in entrepreneurship and considered it only of interest for development research or historical sociology. 'In the early 1970s there were sound grounds for concluding that the decline of the small enterprises was a universal and continuing process', explains Boissevain (1984: 23). But in the 1980s several researchers recognized that small businesses and entrepreneurship are still too important to be ignored (Light and Rosenstein 1995: 12).

The theory of entrepreneurship distinguishes between entrepreneurs and self-employed. The main distinction is that the entrepreneur belongs to an innovative elite. Schumpeter (1991: 413) explained that only 'one man or a few men' had the vision to become entrepreneurs. Wilken (1979: 60) distinguishes them from self-employed by claiming that only entrepreneurs innovate. Drucker (1985: 21) follows that line of argument saying that 'not every new small business is entrepreneurial or represents entrepreneurship'. The entrepreneur 'always searches for change; responds to it, and exploits it as an opportunity' (Drucker 1985: 27).

Innovation is hard to measure. After all, even a pizza topping or a new style of haircut can be an innovation (Abrams: 1978). Archer (1991: 797) argues that entrepreneurs are the elite of three different categories of self-employed. The 'industrial/merchant elite' represents 21 per cent of all self-employed. The 'general merchants and proprietors' constitute the biggest share of all self-employed with 51 per cent. At the lowest level, 28 per cent are 'petty merchants and proprietors'. This present paper will focus only on the last two categories.

History has shown that the distinction between self-employed and entrepreneurs is fuzzy. Not every innovative business innovation was initiated by a great entrepreneur. Major innovations can be the product of an entrepreneurial movement whose single members are not known.[1] So the distinction between the two is still problematic. In this paper the terms 'entrepreneur' and 'self-employed' will be used as synonyms.

It has been shown that immigrants and ethnic minorities engage in self-employment in a much higher proportion than the native population. This contradicts the classical assumption that a capitalist society would recruit entrepreneurs equally from men and women as well as from all ethnic and religious groups (Aronson 1991: 8). Some groups seem to be more responsive to the demands of the labour market and some cultures are more entrepreneurial than others. In fact, the foreigners generally exceed the entrepreneurship of the natives, but some ethnic minorities show even higher rates of self-employment than other foreign born.[2] Cultural theory explains these disparities by the cultural endowments of immigrant minorities that in some cases translate better into entrepreneurship. When the culture of a group highly values motivations and skills that encourage business enterprise, these minorities will produce socialized adults that are more likely to prosper in business (Min 1984: 344). But this argument can only offer a limited explanation of why foreign born are more often self-employed than native born members of the same ethnic group. One reason can be that the disadvantage in the labour market drives some ethnic groups into self-employment, independently from cultural traditions.

Discrimination in the Labour Market

Like every working person, immigrants have to decide whether they want to work as an employee or if they prefer becoming self-employed.

Self-employment is an important alternative to the labour market. Immigrants from different ethnic backgrounds often face discrimination in their daily lives (Solomos and Wrench 1993). The argument that immigrants take away precious jobs from the native population, specially in the low-skilled labour segment, continues to put pressure on politicians not to accept immigrants in Western European countries (Solomos 1993). The so-called 'simple disadvantage hypothesis' states that expected disadvantages in the labour market encourage self-employment, independently of the available resources (Aurand 1983).

Disadvantage is the oldest explanation of entrepreneurship. Max Weber claimed that the religious ethic of protestants encouraged business behaviour. Material wealth was considered a sign of divine benevolence. But he also admitted that protestants chose entrepreneurship because they were excluded from the civil service and the military (Weber 1958: 38-9).

In contrast, Werner Sombart (1951) argues that the cultural background of the Jews made them most suitable for entrepreneurship. He also mentions that they were excluded from many professions since the middle ages, as membership in guilds was only open for Christians.

Weber and Sombart argue that both, religious affinity towards entrepreneurship and labour force disadvantage due to religious discrimination, encouraged religious minorities to get involved in business.

While most authors focus on the business dynamics of ethnic group itself, only few describe the active role of discrimination by the natives (Light 1972, Waldinger et al. 1990, Smith and Feagin 1995).

In the case of pre-war United States, successful minority entrepreneurship had been seen as a manifestation of 'cultural repertoires' (Light 1972: 43-4). Light also recognizes that disadvantages in the labour market had been as much a driving force as cultural explanations (Light 1979).

Waldinger et al. (1990) offer an interactive model, in which ethnic entrepreneurship is described as a combination of cultural heritage, socio-cultural factors, as well as political and economic determinants. Ownership, access to non-ethnic consumer market, government policies, etc., determine the market conditions for the ethnic group, that reacts to the given circumstances.

Most theories rely on the assumption that ethnic entrepreneurs are different from their native colleagues. They are part of a specific social and economic network that is only accessible to a member of the same ethnic group. This 'social embeddedness' allows them to smooth their business operations, acquire knowledge, establish business relationships with clients and suppliers, recruiting labour and capital, etc. This reduces transaction costs by avoiding formal contracts and costs of labour recruitment. Social embeddedness gives ethnic entrepreneurs privileged access to the economic resources of their neighbourhood and puts 'outsiders' in a disadvantage. Certainly some markets are more sensitive to this mechanism than others. Specially those segments that are highly regulated by the government, through licenses or quotas, do not allow to take advantage of 'social embeddedness'.

The concept of 'mixed embeddedness', proposed by Rath and Kloosterman (2001), states that ethnic entrepreneurs engage in their social networks and transactions within the wider political and economic structures of the country.

In more recent literature, cultural affinities towards entrepreneurship are mostly not covered. There is a strong stress on analysing the problems of particular labour markets that lead to disadvantages for certain minority groups. A strong emphasis lies on the ethnic background of the workers and some authors see labour market discrimination as a particular form of racial discrimination (Jones, Mc Evoy and Barrett 1994). Several case studies indicate that the lack of employment options and the constant fear of unemployment force immigrants to start their own business, often below their level of skill (Ladbury 1984, Lubin 1985, Phizacklea 1988). These studies would point towards a business cycle explanation of self-employment. This argument states that there is a positive correlation between high aggregate unemployment rates and self-employment, which declines when a high level of formal employment is reached. This intuitive argument was tested by Steinmetz and Wright (1989), who found that there is only a correlation if a time trend is included in the analysis. Obviously self-employment is not as elastic and entrepreneurs cannot adapt as quickly to new conditions as employees do. Furthermore, a rise in unemployment does not affect all workers equally. Empirical evidence shows that low-skilled and manual workers are less likely to engage in self-employment than skilled and non-manual workers (Johnson 1981).

The 'simple disadvantage hypothesis' relies on the strong assumption that the amount of available resources is not relevant. Light and Rosenstein (1995) offer an extended approach, the 'resource-constraint variant'. They argue that the disadvantaged also need resources to undertake and survive self-employment.

Workers can face two different kinds of disadvantages: resource disadvantages or labour market disadvantages.

Resource disadvantages often have their roots in the worker's past. Resources include all assets that increase the productivity of the employee, such as financial means, human capital, language skills, a good network of contacts, good health, a reliable work ethic, etc. If for some reason the worker has only a few resources, the expected market return of his human capital is low. Therefore his productivity and his income are low as well. Many immigrants suffer from resource disadvantages because of the poor situation and the lack of opportunities in their country of origin.

Labour market disadvantages occur when workers receive returns that are below the expected returns for their human capital for reasons that are not related to their productivity. Qualified workers might not get a job according to their level of education and qualification. Discrimination (against gender, religion, ethnic background, etc.) is the main reason for labour market disadvantages.

Resource disadvantage tends to be worse than labour market disadvantages, since those affected have no means to undertake self-employment. So they cannot respond to possible labour market disadvantages that are related to their lack of resources. Entrepreneurial resources and the option of self-employment protect workers from abuse, discrimination and exploitation (Light and Rosenstein 1995: 154).

Many immigrants suffer from both types of disadvantages. In most cases, coming from a developing country does not provide them with a stable financial background, high education, knowledge of European culture, etc. On top of that, they face discrimination because of their ethnic origin, their religion, etc. Entrepreneurship can provide them the chance to avoid unfair treatment in the labour market.

The Ethnic Neighbourhood as an Economic Enclave

Building up one's own business does not only protect immigrant workers from labour market discrimination by the native population, but can also win the respect from both, members of the ethnic group and natives.

Although the native society might look down on the ethnic minority, they cannot ignore their economic power, which is a source of recognition in Western societies. Their entrepreneurial success and their proven capacity of leadership guarantees them the respect of the other members of their ethnic group and also sends a signal to the natives that the entrepreneur is a worthy member of the society. The concept of 'reactive ethnicity' describes how ethnic groups and immigrants react against real or threatened loss of status by engaging in entrepreneurial activities (Auster and Aldrich 1984). It arises as a reaction to the alien status of the ethnic group and tries to increase the collective self-esteem of the group. Entrepreneurs want to prove that they and the others are worthy of respect. This enhances entrepreneurship by encouraging solidarity between the members of the group (Light and Rosenstein 1995: 19). Ethnic solidarity has its price: Entrepreneurs must be aware of their paternalistic position within the group. Therefore they support other members by employing them in their business, giving them training, mentoring or sponsorship which they would not provide to anyone from outside the group. This sponsorship gives members of the same ethnic group the chance to move forward into subsequent self-employment (Cobas, Aickin and Jardine 1993).

Within the neighbourhood, some ethnic groups tend to specialize in certain branches. Hechter (1976: 215) calls this kind of arrangement 'cultural division of labour'. That way they can get highly influential within their industry. This specialization enhances market power. Since they are more likely to cooperate solitarily with the members of their own group who work in the same branch, it is possible to create some kind of cartels within the neighbourhood.

They can control the prices in their enclave and prevent outsiders from entering the market.

Ethnic entrepreneurs use their ethnic group as a business network. The group can carry business-related information. Since many of them work in the same branch, they inform each other about innovations or new ways of increasing profits. This speeds up the economic progress. Entrepreneurs who must co-exist within a neighbourhood are often more willing to help their fellow business men with advantageous business arrangements, advice, preferential purchasing prices, credits, etc.

The entrepreneur depends on the trust of his clients. His ethnic group can enhance mutual trust in each others' businesses. Rotating credit associations that avoid costly 'scanning' within an ethnic community are just one example of how social trust can enhance business activities.

Mutual trust within the ethnic group reduces external transaction costs. These costs are highly dependent on the legal framework and its implementation in which the economic activities take place. If transaction costs are too high, because of a weak framework, entrepreneurs have to rely on more bureaucratization, e.g. cost of writing explicit contracts, control mechanisms that enforce contracts, etc. In inefficient markets, entrepreneurs cannot rely on market mechanisms but must count on costly bureaucratization. In case the ethnic entrepreneurs maintain a network of mutual trust, it is possible to minimize transaction costs within the ethnic economy. Social trust that is anchored in the social networks of the ethnic community, helps to transact business more cheaply. Since the transaction costs within the ethnic economy are lower than those in the general economy, ethnic entrepreneurs can compete successfully with businesses outside their enclave.

The spatial concentration of an ethnic group helps to create these favourable settings for entrepreneurship. Living together in a neighbourhood strengthens trust and ties the ethnic group stronger together. Ethnic minorities and immigrants can achieve a high economic growth by creating an economic enclave within their neighbourhood.

One example of successful ethnic entrepreneurship is the African neighbourhood of Matongé in Brussels.

Matongé, the 'Little Kinshasa' in the Heart of Brussels

The city of Brussels is not really a city in the administrative sense, but a conglomeration of nineteen districts. Each of them has its own mayor and a district council. There is no mayor for the whole city. Some of the bigger communities like Bruxelles/Brussels, Uccle/Ukkel and Anderlecht have their own fire department and emergency services. There is no common strategy of urban planning. The lack of a superimposed plan has proven to be one of the city's biggest problems in the last decades.

The neighbourhood of Matongé belongs to the district of Elsene/Ixelles, which extends south of the Boulevard Exterieur. The heart of Ixelles (and Matongé) is the Chaussée d'Ixelles, which stretches from the Porte de Namur down to the Place Fernand Coq. The southern part of the district Ixelles is a high-end residential area, famous for its exquisite Art Nouveau architecture, the well-kept park Bois de la Cambre and the lively student atmosphere around the Université Libre de Bruxelles.

Matongé itself is part of Ixelles. The area is defined as the streets around the Chaussée d'Ixelles and the Chaussée de Wavre. The Boulevard Waterloo and the Porte de Namur in the north, the Rue Malibran and the Place Flagey in the south, the Avenue Louise in the west and the Rue du Trône in the east can be defined as the boundaries of the neighbourhood. The heart of the district is located on the Waerenbergh Hill and compounds the Galerie d'Ixelles, the Quartier St.-Boniface and the Porte de Namur.

The name 'Matongé' already hints at the ethnic origin of its inhabitants. It is the name of an entertainment district formerly known as Camp Renkin in Kalamu, Kinshasa, in the Democratic Republic of Congo. Around 13,000 Congolese live in Brussels, most of them in St Josse and Molenbeek, but for many of them Matongé was their first stop after arriving in Belgium. About 6,650 people live in Matongé, 45 per cent of them are non-Belgian. It is important to note that a large number of Congolese living in Matongé have

Belgian citizenship. Africans dominate the streets and are the most visible ethnic group[3] (Vincke 2000).

In the past decades many immigrants of different nationalities discovered Matongé for themselves. Still mainly Africans feel attracted by the large number of shops and services offered primarily to them, but also Asians, mainly from Turkey, India, Pakistan and Bangladesh built up their businesses in the streets of Matongé. Therefore it is not so much the present Congolese residents living in Matongé that provide the neighbourhood with its special flair. The fact that many businesses in the area cater towards an African clientele attracts many visitors from other districts who come and spend their leisure time in Matongé. Since the nearby Belgian cities, such as Antwerp, Leuven or Ghent are well linked to the capital by public transport, many immigrants come to Matongé on the weekend to shop and spend time.

An Ethnic Neighbourhood or a Segregated Ghetto?

The enclave as a socio-economic space certainly has its downsides, as it encourages ethnic segregation. The population within the district develops a strong 'within-group' orientation and does not feel the need to follow the melting-pot model of integration. Within the European Union, Brussels (together with Antwerp and Rotterdam) shows one of the highest level of segregation (Musterd 2005: 335). Is Matongé an ethnic neighbourhood or has it become a ghetto of migrants who are unwilling (or unable) to integrate into the Belgian society?

In the past, the Belgian government has not made too many efforts to mix the population or to enforce integration. Similar to the German approach, Belgian politicians regarded their immigrants more like 'guest workers' who were not meant to stay in the country in the long run. Immigrants were not regarded as permanent citizens and therefore there was no need for an intercultural policy. Until recently, immigrants were not given any voting rights in Belgium, neither on a national nor on a local level.

Even though the country has a low level of economic inequality and a strong welfare state, comparable to Germany and the Netherlands, cities like Brussels and Antwerp show high levels of social and ethnic inequality (Musterd 2005: 342).

The housing market played an important role enhancing segregation in the city of Brussels. Due to the large number of high-skilled and well-paid workers who move to the city, the housing market is constantly tight and rents have been increasing steadily in the last decades. As Kesteloot and van der Haegen (1997) show, the functioning of the housing market has increased the level of segregation. Belgian cities have a rather small share of social housing, compared to other European cities. They do not provide immigrants with affordable housing within the cities. Therefore immigrants must settle for the lowest segment of the real-estate market or engage in illegal occupation of houses. The housing market has very few control mechanisms and is almost totally oriented towards the free market.

Besides the political components, historic legacies play an important role in understantding the patterns of an ethnic neighbourhood. The case of Matongé shows that the area had already been an intercultural point of encounter for many decades. More recent political decisions have even augmented this function.

History of the Neighbourhood

The neighbourhood now called Matongé had been developed by mid-nineteenth century. It was formerly seen as part of Ixelles and had therefore no name of its own. The area now called after the African district in Kinshasa was formerly known as Quartier St. Boniface. The church of St. Boniface had been built in 1845 and was the centre of a small community in the outskirts of the city. Most of the buildings in Matongé were built several decades later. Many of them that are still used today. They were constructed by the end of the nineteenth century and the beginning of the twentieth century. Several houses were designed by the renowned Art Nouveau architect Ernest Blérot. This artistic style has its cradle in Brussels and the floral forms and expressive ornamentation of the art-nouveau became fashionable all over Europe. The Quartier St. Boniface was planned at the peak of the movement in Belgium and was therefore a fashionable living area at that time.[4] A more elaborated art-nouveau architecture that can still be found in the streets between Boulevard Waterloo and the Flagey indicate that the former suburb has always been a residential area for the more affluent upper-middle classes. While the southern end of the district with the lush Étanges d'Ixelles became a more up-market neighbourhood, St. Boniface's proximity to the historic centre of Brussels and to the less sophisticated Quartier Leopold made it more attractive to the middle class.

The neighbourhood started to get its present character at the end of the 1950s. After King Leopold III abdicated the throne in favour of his son Baudouin in 1950, the city made several efforts to become the capital of Europe. The 'Atomium' constructed for the World Fair in 1958 symbolizes the spirit of the era. One year later, the colonial power became the home of the EEC and the EURATOM.

The 'Maison des Colonies' (Ministry of the Colonies) and the 'Union des Femmes Coloniales' (Union of the Colonial Women) were located nearby, in the rue de Stassart near the Porte de Namur. The Union prepared the wives of the colonialists for their future life in Congo. For many of them, their long journey to Africa was prepared in Matongé. The cafés near the Ministry, like the still existing 'Horloge du Sud' served as meeting points for Belgians who travelled or returned from the colonies. The little podium and picture gallery inside the café invited African artists to showcase their works. Matongé was already a place of cultural exchange during the colonial times.

The 'Maison Africaine' (African House), also called 'Maisaf', was established in 1958 in the Quartier St. Boniface. It was meant as a student dormitory for the few African students from Congo, who were invited to study in Brussels with a scholarship by the Belgian government. Soon it became the meeting point for the African immigrants living in the capital. At this time, the building itself was not designed to become a place for social gathering. So the nearby areas started to see the immigrants as a potential clientele for their products and services.

The independence of Congo in 1960 led to a large influx of immigrants to Brussels and they brought their consumption patterns with them. The streets of Matongé were full of African stores, restaurants and cafes. Special hair salons, beauty parlours, clothing stores and jewellery shops started to offer their services to the newly-arrived African women. They imported their goods and fashion-styles from Kinshasa. Matongé became highly fashionable among African immigrants, who visited the neighbourhood in order to meet their countrymen.

It was never a ghetto for African immigrants. Quite the opposite was true. Many newly-arrived immigrants wanted to move to this neighbourhood, which they considered to be the trendy heart of their new home-city. In addition, some Belgians felt attracted by the multicultural atmosphere and the low rents and moved in. While in the beginning the Congolese outnumbered all other nationalities, today 45 African nationalities live or work in the neighbourhood, together with Latin Americans and Asians. Also many Rwandans, Cameroonians, Moroccans, Malians, Nigerians and Senegalese came to live in Belgium, after their countries gained independence. For most of them, language was no barrier to move to Belgium and they considered the small country and its inhabitants more open towards immigrants than, for instance, France, Germany or Great Britain.

The construction works for 'Cité Administrative', that means the administrative offices of the European Parliament, the European Council and the European Commission started at Round-Point Schuman in 1959. The NATO moved from Paris to Brussels in 1967. Brussels finally became the capital of Europe and started to prosper. Low-skilled workers were needed for construction works and to cater to the 'Eurocrats', the highly-paid employees of the European Union institutions. The city offered a large number of jobs for low-skilled immigrants.

The 'Cité Administrative' and specially the enlargement of the European Union also had their downsides on the neighbourhood of Matongè. The architectonical landmark of the European Union, the Palais Berlaymont, was constructed between 1963 and 1968 at the site of an old cloister. While in the 1960s and 1970s most of the buildings related to the European Union agglomerated near the Round-Point Schuhman, the gradual enlargement made new administrative space necessary. The area south of the Rue de la Lois, the Quartier Leopold, was almost completely demolished in order to create new space for the European Parliament building. The gigantic, 72 m high glass-building was finished in 1993 and cuts the old train station, Gare Léopold, from the Parc Leopold. The construction of the 'Caprice de Dieux', as it is mockingly called because of its cheese-box shape, destroyed the beauty of the whole neighbourhood. As more countries joined the Union, more office space was needed and morc houses were demolished. The cost of the building (about 2 billion Euros) were mainly covered by the City of Brussels. Real estate speculation drove up prices in the neighbouring districts. Matongé suffered from this effect as well. Its proximity to the former Quartier Léopold increased shop rents drastically. At the same time, the city had no money to invest in the urgently needed restoration of Matongé's buildings. For many Africans it became too costly to live in the vicinity of the Quartier Européen, as the European Union area is also called. But the neighbourhood was too run down to be attractive for the European Union employees, who preferred to move to the outskirts or to more up-scale neighbourhoods.

As the lively Quartier Léopold started to disappear under the bulldozers, Matongé became a dangerous place to visit. The whole area east of the Rue du Trône is almost deserted in the evening after the employees of the European Union leave their offices. Since there is nothing but office space in the Quartier Européen, most people do not dare to walk the empty streets at night.

In the 1990, the image of Matongé suffered from the high crime rates reported within the neighbourhood. Frequent police interventions created an uneasy atmosphere of violence and danger. The situation grew worse over the years, as many naive Brusselese moved out of Matongé. This negative situation reached its peak in January 2001, when a young man was killed by a police officer during a series of riots.

The district authorities and the residents try to bring the neighbourhood back to its old grandeur. But a crisis in the real estate sector and the increasing shabbiness of the buildings do not help to improve the situation. Matongé is trapped between Quartier Européen, which will soon be in need of more office space and the luxurious Ave. Louise. The mayor of Ixelles has ambitious plans to 'gentrify' the area and investors can not wait for the crumbling neighbourhood to be torn down, same as the Quartier Léopold before.

Congolese, African or Multicultural? Matongé's Ethnic Identity

The neighbourhood's ethnic diversity is one of its biggest asset, but it comes with some problems. Is Matongé still the Congolese neighbourhood it was in the 1950s or has it become African? Or even more, multicultural? And if the latter is the case, what does it mean for those working in this area? Who is the target group for businesses and services?

The question of identity is important not only for its inhabitants, but also for those doing business, as it defines both the demand and the supply side. If Matongé is a Congolese neighbourhood, it will be important to attract natives of the West African country by selling goods imported from Congo and services targeted towards these consumers. In case that Matongé defines itself as 'multicultural', the range of goods and services must be much broader, but it risks to lose its historic and distinct character.

Some of the newly-arrived immigrants complain that the neighbourhood has become too diverse. Not only must they adapt to the culture of Belgium, their new home, but they are also confronted with the strange cultures from other nationals. For the casual European visitor it does not make much of a difference if Matongé is Congolese or African, since he has trouble distinguishing between the two. For Africans it is of great importance, as they bring ethnic rivalries and political conflicts with them from their country of origin. If there is no peace among the African countries, can African expatriates peacefully co-exist in an African neighbourhood in Europe?

The European component plays a crucial role for Matongé's notion of identity. Almost all buildings and shops are owned by Europeans. While the immigrants live and work there, they rarely own their apartments and shops. That gives them only limited power to decide what happens within their neighbourhood and makes them vulnerable to economic changes. Increasing rents drove many Africans out of Matongé. But what is an African neighbourhood without Africans? Visitors want to experience an 'authentic ethnic neighbourhood'. In parts of Matongé, specially the Chaussée d'Ixelles, international chain stores (Mango, Burger King, H&M, etc.) opened their doors, making it look like any other European shopping area. Furthermore, as Africans started to move out, Asians moved in. Pakistani wholesellers operate former African stores, employing Africans and selling African goods at much lower prices. Much of the profit made within Matongé goes into their pockets.

Neighbourhoods change, business changes and consumption pattern change. So from an economic point of view, there should be no problem as long as business keeps on going. But in the case of Matongé, transition from a Congolese to an multicultural neighbourhood is not as smooth. Matongé-Bruxelles is a mythical place for those back in Congo. They imagine it similar to their Matongé in Kinshasa, just without poverty and full of amusement and open possibilities. Affluent Congolese come as tourists directly from Kinshasa to Matongé to shop and go out. The neighbourhood has become famous among Congolese all over the world. For many of those living abroad, Matongé is almost a pilgrimage site, a place they must visit in order to remember their native Kinshasa.

The notion of identity of the neighbourhood has also a political dimension. The last few years, the atmosphere between the Congolese in Matongé and the Belgian authorities have been tense. Since 2001, the police has nervously kept an eye on the area, using their authority even in minor incidents in order to prevent large-scale riots. One famous incident involved Papa Wemba, a famous Congolese singer.[5] Several political and human rights organizations based in Matongé want to ease the political situation in Congo. They are frustrated because as they think that the Belgian government does not do enough to solve the violent conflicts in its former colony. Even more, many Congolese think that Belgium owes their country a lot. King Leopold II built his capital with the money he got out of his colony, killing and torturing hundreds of thousands of Congolese. They feel ignored by the Belgian government and argue that Belgium does nothing to compensate its past crimes. Even though the Congolese had such a visible impact on the neighbourhood, the district authorities of Ixelles do not provide them either with a cultural centre or an exhibition space, nor a concert venue, a theatre, etc. There is no public venue for them to express their cultural identity. The only way for them to show visibility in their neighbourhood is through their businesses.

Ethnic Entrepreneurs in Matongé

The Newcomers: Asian Entrepreneurs

Most immigrants in Matongé come from developing countries, where self-employment is more common than in the developed world. In Europe wage employment predominates.

In Matongé many businesses are operated by foreigners. It is important to note that those who operate the shops, restaurants, beauty parlours, etc., are in most cases not the owners. They rent the location and start their business. It is important to keep in mind that most of the buildings in Matongé are owned by native Belgians. Even though a shop may work profitably, a sudden increase in rent can drive the entrepreneur out of business.

Most entrepreneurs in Matongé are of African or Asian origin. While Africans have a longer tradition in the neighbourhood, Asians too have been very successful in establishing businesses. A large number of immigrants come directly from Asia with the idea of opening a business. Many had already been entrepreneurs in their home countries and they bring certain resources with them. Asians like to focus on certain branches such as food markets, call centres or stores selling all kinds of goods at the same price (mostly everything below one euro). Turkish immigrants specialize on selling fastfood. Most of them offer 'halal' meat. Pakistani, Indians and Bangladeshis have focused their businesses on call centers, internet cafes and food stores. There are two major wholesalers operating in Matongé, both owned by immigrants from Pakistan. Most of their products are imported directly from Asia. But some Asian shops also sell African goods. Even though they are run by Asians, the employees are all Africans. As Matongé attracts many African visitors, selling products from the Black Continent is good business. Africans seem reluctant to buy African products from Asians, who have often little knowledge about the goods they are selling. So it turned out to be a good strategy to hire Africans as employees.

Surprisingly there are relatively few Chinese entrepreneurs in Matongé. The few immigrants from China operate grocery stores or Chinese restaurants. There is one store, located conveniently on the Chaussee du Wavre, which sells all kinds of cheap goods imported from China at a very low price. The spectrum ranges from food to cleaning products to smell artefacts. Many inhabitants of the neighbourhood like to shop there for their daily goods, since the prices are very low compared to those against the supermarkets.

Another Asian specialty is the 24-hours shop. Those little shops are always open and sell mainly food and drinks. They make a convenient stop for party-hoppers who want a bite to eat or cheap alcohol in the early hours. Since shop employees do not need special skills, labour costs are low. Prices in the 24-hours stores tend to be a bit higher than in the ordinary shops in order to compensate the additional costs of labour, but they still make a good profit.

African Entrepreneurs in Matongé

Inside the Galerie D'Ixelles most businesses are operated by Congolese. Restaurants sell coffee and snacks, travel agencies offer cheap flight to almost all African capitals and beauty parlours specialize in wigs, rasta-curls and artificial nails. The vendors prefer to communicate with each other and their customers in Lingala or in Swahili. Congolese come to Matongé and its shops to hear and speak their mother tongue, to get the latest news from their home country, and to buy African movies and newspapers.

Many different dialects are spoken within Congo, so it is often not easy to understand fellow countrymen. But there is a much larger linguistic tolerance between those who now meet in Matongé than between the Congolese in their country of origin. Conflicts between the country's ethnic tribes are also visible in Matongé, but the Congolese pretend to stick together against other African nationalities. Africans prefer to meet with people from the same country. Coffee shops are named 'Grands Lacs' or 'Tanganyika', attracting customers from Rwanda or Burundi. But still clients like to switch places frequently, as long as they are able to communicate with the owner and other customers.

Africans imported their concept of 'cafe' to Brussels. Belgians do not feel very attracted to typical African-style cafes and restaurants in Matongé. These are normally not very well decorated, cheap, noisy and crowded. Africans come to Matongé to communicate with other Africans and to find a piece of home. Those who have managed to imitate the style and the food of the cafés and restaurants from back home in Africa are the most successful.

Belgians and other Western Europeans prefer something more stylish, but still 'authentic'. They come to Matongé because they want to get authentic African food, but prepared and served in a European way. The restaurants that cater to non-Africans put more attention on decoration, a friendly atmosphere, French and Flemish speaking staff and food that adapts to the European taste. The menu is a mix of different regional African cuisines. Those restaurants and cafés are often run by second generation immigrants or Belgians who hire an African manager. The customers are mainly Belgians and other Western Europeans or racially mixed couples and groups. It is part of Matongé's image to be an 'authentic' African neighbourhood. It functions as a tourist attraction and the place to go for those who want to get a real 'African experience'. Shop owners respond to this desire by selling a exotic and adventurous picture of Africa, using the pre-defined ideas Europeans have from the Black Continent in order to sell their products. They create an artificial 'authentic neighbourhood', which runs parallel to the Matongé of the African immigrants. They want to attract young and wealthy Europeans who are open to new experiences. Richard Florida calls them the 'creative class' (Florida 2002). Thanks to the large amount of jobs for highly qualified, mobile workers Brussels has to offer and to Matongés geographic vicinity to the European Union institutions, the so-called 'creative class' comes to shop and dine in the African neighbourhood.

Ethnic neighbourhoods have become an indispensable part not just for the natives themselves as places to spend their leisure time, they play a crucial role as a tourist attraction, as Jan Rath has shown by the example of Chinatowns. The tourism and leisure industry is growing fast and promises high rates of returns.[6] 'Creative Cities' do not only attract mobile high-skilled workers, but also holiday tourists (Hall 2000). The neighbourhood is part of a larger industry that attracts thousands of tourists to Brussels each year. Thanks to its proximity to the historic districts, it is easy for tourists to visit Matongé on their sight-seeing tours. In order to sell itself as an authentic ethnic neighbourhood, Matongé needs to use its ethnic diversity and its symbols of 'differentness' as a marketing asset.

The increasing demand for 'interesting landscapes' that have the potential to draw additional tourists to the city, can provide the neighbourhood with increasing economic growth. Zurkin (1998) looks at those 'symbolic economies' and their appeal to affluent costumers. Immigrant and minority culture is not only tolerated but encouraged within the ethnic neighbourhood. Not only constructed spaces of leisure such as Disneyland or Coney Island have the power to attract visitors, but also inner-city neighbourhoods have a high potential to contribute to the local economy.

In the case of Matongé, increasing tourism is seen with mixed feelings. Tourism is about creating interesting myths and fantasies, as Selwyn (1996) shows, but it always bears the danger of increasing stereotypes and voyeurism. Not all immigrants are positive about the transformation of 'their' neighbourhood into a tourist attraction. Shop owners moan that many tourists come to the neighbourhood to look at the exotic goods in their shops, but hardly ever buy anything. They prefer taking a walk around the neighbourhood, and dining at international fast-food restaurants. Furthermore, some shops had been established to cater to the needs of the ethnic groups within the neighbourhoods, and they do not want other customers. They are sometimes considered as undesirable. Even worse, certain shopowners report that they very often disrespect the ethnic groups' culture and values.

Specially African immigrants tend to be more sensitive when it comes to selling their cultural heritage to tourists, since many of the 'exotic' goods sold by them are religious symbols in their home country. But still, Africans are eager to establish themselves as businessmen. As already mentioned, most food stores are operated by Indians and Pakistanis who have commercial experience. Africans are trying to catch up with them and win back the stores in 'their' neighbourhood. They import food and drinks from their country of origin and sell them to Africans. As retail prices in the country of export tend to be lower than in Belgium, they can still sell their products at a reasonable price, even after including transport costs, taxes, fixed costs, etc. African food shops are mostly owned by native Africans or by Asians who employ Africans. The African customers are familiar with the exotic products and expect the seller to have a certain level of expertise concerning African brands. Many shops have their signs written in three languages: French and Flemish (the two official languages of the city) as well as in an African language. For many newly-arrived immigrants this is of great help, since they do not speak any French or Flemish. In many shops, French is used for communication with 'outsiders', meaning Europeans or other Africans from different countries.

European owners of shops selling African goods usually try and sell them to other Europeans. They try to communicate the exotic character of their goods, sometimes by using old stereotypes. A Belgian-owned shop on rue Longue Vie, 'Mama Adelu', shows a picture of a half-naked African woman peeling manioc. It is no surprise that some Africans dislike the use of colonialist clichés and prefer buying from stores run by Africans.

Ethnic entrepreneurs in Matongé often have a double function. Their primary business is their store. But besides that, many of those shops function as meeting places and information points for members of the ethnic community. Several people work in Matongé without having a formal workplace in the neighbourhood. These are mainly self-employed business people who have no fixed workplace and working hours. They are mostly involved in import-export deals with Africa. The owner of the shop functions as an agent. They are very familiar with other expatriates living in the neighbourhood. If a certain service is needed, the shopowners contact the businessmen and get some kind of commission. Those who want to strike deals with other Africans must often rely on word-of-mouth propaganda and a bad reputation can quickly drive them out of business.

A common branch for this kind of self-employment is exporting used cars and car parts to Africa. Africans buy used cars from Belgium and ship them to their country of origin. Since the shipment itself is costly, they are always looking for immigrants coming from the country of destination who want to send larger goods back home. The car is filled with their boxes and they pay part of the shipping cost. This way they can send large goods for a fraction of the price charged for ordinary ground mail by the Belgian postal service. This very efficient way of sending goods back to their home continent needs a lot of coordination. Shop owners are often well informed about who travels to Africa, so that he can bring the two parties together. Specially those who operate travel agencies specialized in trips to Africa have a little side-business in bringing these people together. Many times their clients can only carry a limited amount of baggage on the plane, so they offer to organize the transport of excessive luggage. Those working in the car business often rely on the contacts on the business people in Matongé in order to cut their costs of transportation.

Since the neighbourhood is the meeting point of the African diaspora in Brussels, immigrants from all other communities come to Ixelles to conduct business. By focusing on one area, the import-export business people have a larger pool of potential clients. Those who work in the branch often have good connections with business people back in Africa. Mostly they have not got enough resources to build-up a more formal business on their own and have to rely on casual export deals. They usually spend only limited time in one place and then move to another city. They do not see Europe as their new home, but as a good place to make some money and then return to Africa. These businessmen often use the money earned in Europe to buy a house or build-up a business in their native country. These are mostly young men who have come to Europe without bringing their family with them. That makes them very flexible, but it is difficult to build-up trust towards those who have just arrived in town. It is highly important for them to have a good reputation in Matongé. If they turn out to be unreliable, they won't be contacted anymore in the future. The shop owner ensures some kind of quality control through this reputation mechanism. A reputable shop owner would not recommend his clients to strike deals with someone who has proven to be a bad business partner, since he is risking his own reputation as well.

Having a little side business is not uncommon. Low-skilled immigrant workers sometimes have to engage in additional activities to make ends meet. They have a formal employment, but they do extra jobs after work or at home. Similar to the business people in the import-export business, they rely on word-of-mouth propaganda. Some of these second jobs are catered towards other Africans. One example is women who do manicure, hair-dressing, waxing, etc., at their homes after work. They normally have not got enough financial resources to open a beauty parlour. So they earn an additional income with these little extra services.

Most of these small services are performed for Belgians and other Europeans. Besides their regular work, immigrants take additional jobs: they babysit in the evenings, help with minor renovations in houses or when someone is moving out, etc. Some play in music bands, work as music instructors and perform in the evenings.

These odd jobs also go hand-in-hand with a small private retail business. There is not enough demand for certain goods to rent a shop and sell them regularly. One example is of African musical instruments. There is no shop selling them in Matongé, but there are informal ways of buying them.[7] There is a very wide variety of these small side-jobs and many offer their services on blackboards located in the shops in the neighbourhood.

Certainly this kind of side jobs are necessary for many to cover the high living costs. Some of these activities are considered illegal, as they are not reported and the income is not taxed. While some these people have a regular job, these additional side-jobs are part of the informal economic sector.

Informal Economy

The term 'informal economy' (or 'informal economic sector') refers to all economic activities that are carried out outside the formal economy regulated by economic and legal institutions. The income generated by the informal economy is 'unregulated by the institutions of society, in a legal and social environment in which similar activities are regulated' (Portes and Haller 2005). Those activities are not taxed and do not contribute to the Gross National Product (GNP).

Informal economic activity accounts for a large share of income within almost every economy. Similar to self-employment, it provides workers with an option to avoid discrimination in the labour market.

The informal economy is specially attractive to those who lack financial resources. It does not take much investment to engage in informal activities and they offer high rates of return (often to compensate the high risks involved).

Many people coming from developing countries have worked in the informal economic sector for all their lives. In most countries of the Third World, the formal economy plays only a side-role.

It comes as no surprise that some immigrants decide to engage in informal activities, at least for a while.

Also Matongé has its share of informal economy. Due to the illegal character of most informal economic activities, no official data exist. Its extent can only be estimated. But the informal economy must also rely on consumers and therefore there is a 'word-of-mouth' knowledge about who offers which kind of services.

The case of Matongé shows that formal and informal economy are closely linked, both within and outside the neighbourhood.

Several immigrants already came in contact with it while they are still in their home countries. Almost all newly-arrived immigrants hope to get a job in the labour market in Belgium. Specially the Congolese have developed an efficient network of contacts to place their countrymen into low-skilled jobs. It is common practice that they rely on the services of 'agents'. These agents already organize jobs before the immigrant arrives in Belgium. They work together with colleagues back in Kinshasa, Lubumbashi, etc., who recruit potential candidates in Congo. These agents charge a very high fee (up to 5,000 Euros) for their services and many immigrants find themselves trapped in low-wage jobs with high debts. The agents make their clients believe that a job as a kitchen helper or housekeeper in Belgium would bring them and their families back home prosperity. They often do not mention the high costs of living in Brussels, which swallow up a big share of their income. For many young women the services of these agents has been disastrous. They were promised employment as nannies, waitresses or housekeepers that turned out be informal jobs in the porn industry. Certainly the help of those agents is often at the edge of illegality. But those who have no friends or family in Brussels on which they can count, must rely on their help. Even though most African immigrants are aware of the dangers involved in contacting an agent, they appreciate their insider knowledge. Agents are very proficient when it comes to finding ways around administrative formalities, like speeding up or avoiding the immigration process, getting free health care, dealing with the police, etc. It is important to note that some immigrants are highly dependent on these agents, at least during the first weeks or months. Some of them arrive in Belgium with an illegal immigration status. The agents are the only ones they can depend upon. It is not unheard of that Africans throw away their documents after entering the country, so that they cannot be sent back to their native country. They apply for new documents, indicating a different nationality or a different age, in order to facilitate immigration or avoid criminal prosecution. The African agents in Brussels are then the only ones who know about their background and who can provide them with jobs. They often end up working in the informal sector.

The 'employers' of those low-skilled workers may be of different ethnic backgrounds. A large share of immigrants work for Belgians (or other Western Europeans) in their private households, e.g. as nanny, housekeepers, care for the elderly, etc. Wages are normally below the minimum wage. The low labour costs of immigrants is their competitive advantage. Belgians employ them because they demand less wage than native workers for the same job. While Belgian employees are more likely to ask their employers to register them, in order to get social security benefits, immigrants are more willing to work without formal registration.

The same goes for work within the businesses of Matongé. Some find employment in shops of the neighbourhood. They often work for an employer with the same ethnic background as themselves. One reason for this is that there is a stronger trust between the members of the same ethnic group. Furthermore business owners declare that their employee needs no formal registration because he is 'part of the family' and actually does not really work there, and is just helping out. If anyone comes for inspection, the owner can get away with this argument.

African immigrants without legal immigration status undertake self-employment in the informal sector, since working for someone always implies a certain risk of getting caught by the immigration authorities. The variety of services offered within this area is immense, ranging from beauty services such as hair-dressing or manicure to language classes to religious services. They mostly work and receive their customers in their homes. Due to the nature of their jobs, the clientele is mainly from the same ethnic origin. Specially women sometimes see these kind of activity as the only way to make some money. Sometimes they are not supposed to seek formal employment because of cultural reasons or because they have to take care of their small children. Working at home or offering side-services provides them with an additional income. Since they work in a private environment, they must almost totally rely on word-of-mouth propaganda.

Criminal Activities

Depending on the definition, criminal activities can be included within the informal economy. Informal economic activities are not regulated by the government or legal institutions and therefore may become criminal. But they have no regulated, i.e. formal counterpart against which they can be compared.

The bad image Matongé gained in the 1990s was mainly because it was considered a haven for illegal activities. It is known that a few immigrants engage in criminal activities, such as robbery or drug dealing. Certainly they are a very small minority among those immigrants who seek to make a living in Belgium. But violent incidents between the police and drug dealers have consequences for the whole neighbourhood. When an area is considered unsafe, people are reluctant to visit its bars, restaurants, cinemas and clubs at night. Without customers, these places are forced to close down, making the streets look even more deserted. Tenants are not willing to take the feeling of insecurity anymore and move out of the neighbourhood. The rents decrease and the buildings start to crumble. Shop owners lose their clients and must close their businesses. This vicious circle developed in Matongé in the 1990s, before the Community of Ixelles decided to invest in its infrastructure.

Certainly the streets of Matongé have become safer in the past years. But still many Brusselese consider it to be a dangerous place after dark. Part of this negative image comes from another informal economic sector, that is the erotic industry. Several table dance bars, game parlours with skimpily clad waitresses and brothels can be found in the neighbourhood. Even though it is not the number one red light district of the city, prostitution is visible on the streets. Most prostitutes in the bars and on the streets are women from Africa. They are sometimes recruited directly in their native country and brought to Belgium through 'agents'. The women mainly cater to white males. Some of them seek their clients in the more luxurious clubs at the nearby Avenues Louise or Toison d'Or, and bring them to their locations in Matongé. At night they attract a large number of visitors and thanks to their services many bars and clubs operate with high returns.

Some Congolese women earn their living in a different way. They are called 'Mammans Courages' and have been immortalized by many songs of Congolese singers (the famous Papa Wemba dedicated them several). The main activity is to steal in department stores during the day and sell the stolen goods at night in the streets of Matongé. Some of them even accept orders for certain goods and deliver them within just a few hours. Obviously their business is not favourable for the shopowners, who lose clients. But the 'Mammans' mainly specialize in expensive consumer goods produced in Europe or the US. Since most entrepreneurs in Matongé import their (mainly cheap) goods from Africa or China, there is no direct rivalry. So their work is tolerated by most business people of the neighbourhood.

Conclusion

The peaceful co-existence between the various groups in Matongé provides a fertile ground for successful ethnic entrepreneurship. Africans, specially Congolese, dominate the economic activities, but also Asian immigrants were able to integrate in the economy of the enclave. Tolerance towards other nationalities, mutual trust within the ethnic social network and the desire to win the respect of other community members make entrepreneurship in Matongé very prosperous. The neighbourhood's image as 'authentic African neighbourhood' in the heart of Brussels attracts many visitors and tourists.

The future of Matongé is uncertain. Its success is heavily dependent on the ethnic entrepreneurs. In the past years there had been attempts to make their life more difficult, by increasing rents, enforcing earlier closing hours, lowering noise levels for bars and clubs or infiltrating the neighbourhood with international chain stores and supermarkets, such as McDonald's or Lidl.

It will be crucial for Matongé's survival to keep up its identity as a unique ethnic neighbourhood. The city authorities must be convinced that it is worth preserving the 'Kinshasa of the North'.

Notes

1. Light and Rosenstein (1995: 4) mention the example of fast food restaurants and frozen foods. Ray Kroc and Harlan Sanders, founders of McDonald's and Kentucky Fried Chicken fast food chains respectively stand out as famous entrepreneurs. But they were not the inventors of fast-food. They responded to the demand of the American public and became the leaders of a larger social movement that transformed the eating habits of the US citizens.
2. Just to name a few examples, Langlois and Razin (1989: 345) have shown that Canadians of German or Dutch origin are more frequently self-employed than other immigrants. Portes, Clark and Lopez (1981: 18) found that 20 per cent of the Cubans in Miami were self-employed and another 30 per cent worked in Cuban-owned enterprises. The corresponding rates for Mexicans were much lower.
3. On voit dans ses rues ce qu'on attend y voir. Il y a des Congolais, bien visibles. La majorité des passants sont néanmoins Belges de souche, même si sur quelques arpents se concentrent des Africains. C'est le cas de l'entrée des Galeries de Matonge, où l'on rencontre des groupes de jeunes Congolais, lingalaphones et Kinois, bien 'sapés', et qui semblent perpétuellement à cheval entre Ici et Là-bas. Porte de Namur, on remarque durant la journée, de pimpantes adolescentes congolaises, habillées dernier cri, conscientes de leur corps. [In the streets we see what we expected to see. There are Congolese, very visible. However, the

majority of pedestrians are native Belgians, even if Africans focus on a few acres.

This is the case at the entry to the 'Galleries Matonge', where we meet groups of young Congolese, 'lingala phones' and people from Kinshasa, very elegantly dressed and who seem perpetually straddling between Here and There. Porte de Namur, as we can appreciate during the day, elegant Congolese girls, dressed to the latest fashion, aware of their bodies]—Édouard Vincke, 2000: 7.

4. Some of the first art-nouveau buildings by the most important architects of the movements were built in the proximity to the Quartier Boniface. The Ave. Louise/Rue Defacqz shows one of the first art-nouveau buildings of the city designed by Paul Hanker and Hotel Solvay (1894) built by the most famous architect of his time, Victor Horta.
5. Papa Wemba came to Matongé before one of his concerts. A large number of fans waited for him in the streets and a fight broke out. The police tried to control the crowd using force and declared Papa Wemba *persona non grata* in Matongé. The authorities justified their decision by saying that the musician used his popularity to influence the Congolese in Belgium on who to vote for the elections in Congo in July 2006. He used his visit to Brussels to show his political protégés back home in Kinshasa that he still has the power to control the Congolese diaspora.
6. The European Union generates a large amount of the global tourist revenues. According to the World Travel and Tourism Council (2001), by 2011, Europe's share is expected to grow up to 32 per cent of the global total. In 2001, travel and tourism contributed 4.8 per cent of the European Unions GDP and provides jobs for 12.3 per cent of the workforce.
7. Rue Longue Vie, on a pu voir une blonde Flamande et sa jeune fille s'enquérir d'une boutique de djembés. Un Black, boucle à l'oreille et outils de plombier à la main, leur explique qu'il n'y a pas de telles boutiques à Matonge. Il leur refile des adresses de circuit informel. A l'enseigne des 'Tambours Sacrés ', c'est chez Doudou, biologiste moléculaire. [Logue Vie Street, we could see a blone Flemish woman with her daughter ask for a shop for *djembes.* A Black, ear loop and plumber tools in hand, explains that there is no such shop in Matonge. He tells them some informal addresses. At the sign of the 'Second Drums' there is Doudou, a molecular biologist]—Édouard Vincke, 2000: 8.

References

Abrams, J.J. (1978), 'Determining Consumer Demand and Marketing Opportunities for Nutritional Products', *Food Technology* 32: 79-85.

Archer, Melanie (1991), 'Self-Employment and Occupational Structure in an Industrializing City: Detroit, 1880', *Social Forces* 69: 785-809.

Aronson, Robert L. (1991), *Self-Employment: A Labor Market Perspective*, Ithaca, NY: ILR Press.

Aurand, Harold (1983), 'Self-Employment Last Resort of the Unemployed', *International Social Science Review* 58: 7-11.

Auster, Ellen and Howard Aldrich (1984), 'Small Business Vulnerability, Ethnic Enclaves, and the Ethnic Enterprise', in Robin Ward and Richard Jenkins (eds.), *Ethnic Communities in Business*, Cambridge: Cambridge University Press.

Boissevain, Jeremy (1984), 'Small Entrepreneurs in Contemporary Europe', in Robin Ward and Richard Jenkins (eds.), *Ethnic Communities in Business*, New York: Cambridge University Press, pp. 20-38.

Cobas, Jose, Mikel Aikin and Douglas S. Jardine (1993), 'Industrial Segmentation, The Ethnic Economy, and Job Mobility: The Case of Cuban Exiles in Florida', *Quality and Quantity* 27: 249-70.

Drucker, Peter F. (1985), *Innovation and Entrepreneurship: Practices and Principles*, New York: Harper & Row.

Florida, Richard (2002), *The Rise of the Creative Class and How Its Transforming Work, Leisure, Community and Everyday Life*, New York: Basis Books.

Hall, P. (2000), 'Creative Cities and Economic Development', *Urban Studies*, 37.4: 639-49.

Hechter, Michael (1976), 'Ethnicity and Industrialization: On Proliferation of the Cultural Division of Labour', *Ethnicity* 3: 214-24.

Johnson, Peter (1981), 'Unemployment and Self-Employment: A Survey', *Industrial Relations Journal* 12: 5-15.

Jones, Trevor, David McEvoy and Gilles Barrett (1994), 'Labour Intensive Practices in the Ethnic Minority Firm', in J. Atkinson and D. Storey (eds.), *Employment, the Small Firm and the Labour Market*, London: Routledge.

Kesteloot, C. and H. van der Haegen (1997), 'Foreigners in Brussels 1981-1991: Spatial Continuity and Social Change', *Tijdschrift voor Economische en Sociale Geografie* 88.2: 99-104.

Kloosterman, R. and J. Rath (2001), 'Immigrant Entrepreneurs in Advanced Economies: Mixed Embeddedness Further Explored', in

R. Kloosterman and J. Rath (eds), *Journal of Ethnic and Migration Studies*, Special issue on 'Immigrant Entrepreneurship', 27.2: 189-202.

Knight, Frank (1921), *Risk, Uncertainty, and Profit,* Boston: Houghton Mifflin.

Ladbury, Sarah (1984), 'Choice, Chance or No Alternative? Turkish Cypriots in Business in London', in Robin Ward and Richard Jenkins (eds.), *Ethnic Communities in Business,* Cambridge: Cambridge University Press.

Langlois, Andre and Eran Razin (1989), 'Self-Employment among Ethnic Minorities in Canadian Metropolitan Areas', *Canadian Journal of Regional Science,* 12: 335-54.

Light, Ivan (1972), *Ethnic Enterprise in America,* Berkeley CA: University of California Press.

——— (1979), 'Disadvantaged Minorities in Self-Employment', *International Journal of Comparative Sociology* 20: 31-45.

Light, Ivan and Carolyn Rosenstein (1995), *Race, Ethnicity and the Entrepreneurship in Urban America,* New York: De Gruyter.

Lubin, Nancy (1995), 'Small Business Owners', in Rita J. Simon (ed.), *New Lives: The Adjustment of Soviet and Jewish Immigrants in the U.S. and Israel,* Lexington, MA: Lexington Books.

Min, Pyong Gap (1984), 'From White Collar Occupations to Small Business: Korean Immigrants' Occupational Adjustment', *The Sociological Quarterly* 25: 333-52.

Musterd, Sako (2005), 'Social and Ethnic Segregation in Europe: Levels, Causes and Effects', *Journal of Urban Affairs,* vol. 27, no. 2: 331-48.

Phizacklea, Annie (1988), 'Entrepreneurship, Ethnicity and Gender,' in Sallie Westwood and Parminder Bhachu (eds), *Enterprising Women,* London: Routledge.

Portes, Alejandro, Juan M. Clark and Manuel M. López (1981), 'Six Years Later: The Process of Incorporation of Cuban Exiles in the United States: 1973-1979', *Cuban Studies* 11/12: 140-68.

Portes, Alejandro and William Haller (2005), 'The Informal Economy', in N. Smelser and R. Swedberg (eds.) *Handbook of Economic Sociology,* 2nd edn, Russell Sage Foundation.

Schumpeter, Joseph (1991), 'Comments on a Plan for the Study of Entrepreneurship', in Richard Swedberg (ed.), *Joseph A. Schumpeter: The Economics and Sociology of Capitalism,* Princeton: Princeton University Press.

Selwyn, T. (ed.) (1996), *The Tourist Image: Myths and Myth Making in Tourism*, Chichester: John Wiley and Sons.

Smith, Michael Peter and Joe R. Feagin (eds.) (1995), *The Bubbling Cauldron: Race, Ethnicity, and the Urban Crisis*, Minneapolis: University of Minnesota Press.

Solomos, J. (1993), *Race and Racism in Britain*, 2nd edn., London: Macmillan.

Solomos, J. and J. Wrench (eds.) (1993), *Racism and Migration in Western Europe*, Oxford: Berg.

Sombart, Werner (1951), *The Jews and Modern Capitalism*, Glencoe IL: Free Press.

Steinmetz, George and Erik Olin Wright (1989), 'The Fall and Rise of the Petty Bourgeoisie: Changing Pattern of Self-Employment in the Postwar United States', *American Journal of Sociology* 94: 973-1018.

Vincke, Édouard (2000), *Longue vie à Matongue*, Agenda Culturel 11. Brussels, 7-8.

Waldinger, Roger et al. (1990), *Ethnic Entrepreneurs: Immigrant Business in Industrial Societies*, Newberry Park CA: Sage.

Weber, Max (1958), *The Protestant Ethic and Spirit of Capitalism*, New York: Scribner's.

Wilken, James (1979), *Entrepreneurship: A Comparative and Historical Study*, Norwood NJ: Ablex.

World Travel and Tourism Council (2001), *Tourism Satellite Accounting Research Year 2001*, London: European Union.

Zurkin, S. et al. (1998), 'Urban Lifestyles: Diversity and Standardization in Spaces of Consumption', *Urban Studies* 35.5-6: 825-39.

16

Coercive Semblance

Imperial Construction of 'Japaneseness' in the Early Twentieth Century

YOSHIYA MAKITA

Since the Meiji Restoration in 1868, the Japanese government had urgently promoted Western-style modernization of its social organization. While Japan went on to reorganize the society under the influence of European countries and the United States, Japanese colonial expansion over East Asia complicated its task of nation state building. This paper examines the delineation process of 'Japanese' ethnic identity in the early twentieth century by focusing on the ideological reinterpretation of 'Japaneseness' through the process of colonial expansion. In the late nineteenth century, Japan gradually extended its imperial rule to its southern and northern peripheries. In 1871, Japan forced the Kingdom of Ryuku, an independent kingdom ruling the small islands south of the Kyushu area, into the Japanese jurisdiction of Kagoshima prefecture under the central government, and the king of Ryuku became a regional domain lord in Japan a year later. After Japan formally annexed Ryukyu and replaced it with Okinawa prefecture in 1879, people in the region came to face the oppressive assimilation policy of the central government in which Japanese officials attempted to coerce Ryuku people to speak 'standard' Japanese language and transplant the feelings of loyalty to the Japanese emperor in their mind. In the north, the Japanese government applied the similar assimilation policy to control the Ainu people, an ethnic minority group living in the northern region of Japan. Since the Japanese government embarked on the enterprise of developing its northern area in 1869, Japanese officials had directly and indirectly devastated the social, economic, and political system of Ainu people. In 1899, the Japanese national legislature passed an Act to protect natives in Hokkaido which prescribed impoundment of land previously possessed by Ainu people, forced their changes to Japanese names, and banned their traditional culture.

These early annexation experiences set the basis of administrative policy of the Japanese colonial enterprises at the turn of the twentieth century when Japan further expanded its territory overseas. As a gain of the Sino-Japanese War in 1894-5, Japan acquired Taiwan by the Treaty of Shimonoseki and began its colonial rule over the island. Throughout the period of the Japanese colonial rule by 1945, ethnic policy in Taiwan fluctuated between two opposite directions of economic inclusion of Taiwanese into Japanese industrial organization and political exclusion of them from legal rights as Japanese. Yet the Japanese government always stated the total assimilation of Taiwanese into Japanese at least as its final goal of colonial rule although Japanese officials at the same time deliberately added that the adaptation process would be slow and time-consuming. While implementing colonial policy in the similar ambiguity between inclusion and exclusion, the Japanese rule in Korea was more inclined to the assimilation of Korean people. After leasing Kwantung Territory in the north-eastern region of China as a result of the Russo-Japanese War in 1904-5, Japan then annexed Korea in 1910. The Japanese governor-general of Korea forced Korean people to use Japanese language and tried to implant loyalty to imperial Japan through their Japanization although officials denied basic rights of Japanese to these colonized people as in Taiwan. When Japan seized the right of mandatory administration of the Micronesian islands from the League of Nations after the First World War, the colonial expansion of Japanese empire reached its apex. Through these territorial expansions, imperial Japan came to include diverse ethnic groups under its banner of Empire. Until the end of the Second World War, the population of minority groups under Japanese rule, or those who had not been considered as 'Japanese', increased and occupied nearly one-third of the total population of the Empire. Until the end of the Second World War, Japan had been a multi-ethnic empire.

The existence of diverse ethnic groups under its rule, however, generated a difficult task for Japanese officials to construct a modern nation state which was, in theory, conditioned by the homogeneity of a nation. In contrast to colonial enterprises of most European countries which in many cases established indirect rule over their colonial territories and made clear distinction between colonizers and the colonized in ethnic identity, imperial Japan set the assimilation of people in colonized areas to 'Japanese' as its goal of colonization at least in the formal statement of the government. Oguma Eiji, a Japanese historian, insisted that the Japanese colonial policy put the national identity of the colonized under imperial rule of Japan in an ambiguous status between 'Japanese' and 'non-Japanese' and Japanese officials intentionally appropriated this ambiguity. Japanese officials mobilized colonized people into the industrial workforce as 'Japanese' while the government denied the suffrage of the colonized as 'non-Japanese'.

Yet the principle, or logic for justification, which Japanese officials utilized to construct a multi-ethnic empire at the same time building homogeneous nation state still remains unclear. Different from European countries which had their long tradition of nation state building since the early nineteenth century, Japan had to deal with the two tasks of colonial enterprise and nation state building concurrently. This paper argues that, relying on the discourse of the standard of civilization to justify their colonial rule over various Asian groups, Japanese officials rendered hierarchical reordering of Japanese ethnicity behind the territorial expansion of Japan and reintegrated different groups in the population by introducing the concept of pan-Asianism. Imperial Japan attempted to enlarge the ideological limit of Japaneseness through the advocacy of ethnic similarity among Asian nations which assured the potential of colonized Asian people to be assimilated into Japanese. Still, Japanese officials also insisted that difference existed at present among ethnic groups in the attainment level of modern civilization, and thus subdivided the population within the imperial hierarchy. Based on their estimation of the degree of civilization, Japanese officials entitled those who lived in the main islands of Japan to the category of first-class Japanese, while people in the colonized areas came to be differentiated as the second-class Japanese.

Throughout their colonial rules, Japanese officials repeatedly emphasized the level of social infrastructure of medicine and hygiene as particular one of the criteria to judge the degree of civilization in the colonized areas. The relief activities of the Red Cross Society of Japan during the wars reveal the ways in which Japanese officials focused on the level of medical practices to differentiate themselves from colonized people. The international Red Cross movement formally began in 1863 when Henry Dunant and other Swiss citizens organized the International Committee for Relief to the War Wounded, which was later renamed the International Committee of the Red Cross (ICRC). The international Red Cross movement promoted humanitarianism as a moral standard of civilization at least in a normative sense through its advocacy of humane assistance to the war wounded on both sides of the belligerent countries. At the turn of the twentieth century, admission of a national organization to the ICRC came to signify the nation's legitimation as a 'civilized' member of the international society. For Japan, still a small country in the Far East struggling to elevate its international status, membership to the ICRC provided diplomatic leverage to acquire its position as a world power as well as an ideological device to differentiate itself from other Asian countries by utilizing the distinction between the 'civilized' and the 'uncivilized'. The Red Cross movement in Japan started in 1877 when a Japanese statesman Sano Tsunetami established Hakuaisha (the Society of Benevolence). After the Japanese government acceded to the Geneva Convention in 1886, Hakuaisha changed its title to the Red Cross Society of Japan (RCSJ) and became the first Asian member of the International Committee of the Red Cross the following year.

As the only Asian country with an organization admitted to the ICRC, Japan strengthened her international position as a 'civilized' country by holding onto the Red Cross ideal of humanitarianism during the wars and at the same time distancing herself from other Asian countries. One official history of the RCSJ published in 1910 reflected the relief activities during the Sino-Japanese War as humane aid to the 'backward' country, stating that Japan 'tolerated the stupidity and obstinateness of this country [China] by unbounded magnanimity and, with the spirit of benevolence, did not blame her for the reckless deed' and thus 'showed the virtue of our country known by her righteousness and revealed the brightness and modest character of our nation before the eyes of the world public'. While faithfully implementing humanitarian aid on the battlefields, the RCSJ disapproved of moves to establish Chinese and Korean Red Cross societies which burgeoned during the war in 1894-5 and again in 1904-5. Although Korea joined the Geneva Convention in 1903 and set-up her own Red Cross organization, the RCSJ established its regional committee in Korea after the Russo-Japanese War and forcibly absorbed the Korean national society in 1909. Medical activities of the RCSJ in north-eastern China in the Russo-Japanese War ideologically reinforced the power relationship between Japan and China. During and after the war, the RCSJ deployed a large number of its medical workers in the north-eastern region of China. A physician detached to the Dagushan army hospital by the RCSJ soon realized the steady increase in the number of native patients at the hospital. 'The attitude of *dojin* (barbarians) to our hospital is quite favorable', reported the physician in 1904, 'for they are enjoying the benefit of reliable medical care for the first time in their life at our hospital and our treatment is effective and free'. Propagation of Western-style medicine among the native people was a 'civilizing' task for the physician and his only complaint stemmed from the high frequency with which 'patients abandon the treatment before complete therapy once they make a partial recovery, although we are earnestly encouraging these patients to visit the hospital continuously to ensure the complete cure and thus to reveal miraculous effects of our medical treatment to them'. Medicine and hygiene functioned as criteria to estimate the level of civilization and justified Japanese colonial rule over the region.

When Japan annexed Korea in 1910, Japanese officials introduced the same logic of civilization. While the imperial government emphasized that the Japanese and the Korean shared a common ancestor in ancient times and thus Koreans could be assimilated into Japan, officials alleged that the full assimilation of Koreans to

Japanese would take a long time due to the long separation since the Middle Ages. Officials thought of the contemporary differences of the two groups as difference in the level of civilization or in the flexibility of mind to accept modern civilization. Until the time when Korean people caught up with the Japanese standard of civilization and thus fully became assimilated with Japanese, declared Japanese administration in Korea, Japan would 'instruct' Korean people as second-class Japanese. The Japanese government tactfully appropriated the cultural similarity and difference of Asian people for their colonial enterprises and reasoned multi-ethnic situation within Japanese imperial order by utilizing discourses on the standard of civilization. The principle of civilization justified differentiation of 'Japanese' from colonized people at the same time hierarchically incorporating diverse ethnic groups into the single mould of a 'Japanese' empire. Japanese officials insisted the 'coidentity in race and culture' of Asian people and assumed potential ability of Asian people to be assimilated into Japanese. This assimilationism gradually grew into the vehement advocacy of pan-Asianism and its conceptual elaboration in Japan during the 1910s and 1920s and later gave ideological basis for Japanese invasion into Asian countries after the 1930s.

The consequences of the Russo-Japanese War in 1904-5 stimulated the independence movements among Asian countries under colonial rule of the European powers. The military victories of the Japanese army over the Russian troops in the north-eastern region of China provoked a growing sense of Asian power in the mind of Asian activists by squashing the myth of European superiority to Asia. In India, many political activists saw the war as a conflict between the West and the East and exalted Japanese victories. Jawaharlal Nehru regained his confidence in the potentiality of Asian people for overcoming European rule by this Japanese example and Bal Gangadhar Tilak praised the efficiency of the Japanese army and emphasized the Japanese spirit of self-sacrifice and self-devotion. Some Indian radicals dreamed of an Asian alliance against the European powers and visited Japan to import weapons for their struggle in India and to gain Japanese support for their activities. Rash Behari Bose was one of these Indian radicals who came to Japan. Born as a son of a clerk of the Bengal government in Subaldaha, Burdwan in 1886, Bose grew up in Chandannagar. While working as a head clerk at the Forest Research Institute in Dehradun, Bose gradually committed himself to radical activities for the Independence of India. Since the administrative partition of Bengal Province by British Viceroy George Nathaniel Curzon in 1905, terrorist attacks against British officials had intermittently stormed eastern India. With his knowledge and skill of handling bombs, Bose became one of the leading figures in these attacks. When the British colonial government thwarted the plan of mutiny by Indian soldiers in Lahore on February 1915, however, Bose was forced to flee to Japan.

In Japan, Rash Behari Bose scrambled to find Japanese financial sponsors for their radical activities and expected Japanese national support for the Independence of India. Yet the Japanese diplomatic policy of international cooperation with the Western powers constituted the basis for international action of Japan in the 1910s and the early 1920s, and therefore many of the Japanese politicians hesitated to openly help Indian activists. The Anglo-Japanese Alliance provided that Japan allowed for the British colonial order in India in return for British tolerance for Japanese rule in Korea. When the Ghadar Party instigated mutiny among the Indian soldiers stationed in Singapore during the First World War, the Japanese army jumped into the suppression of the rebellion under this alliance with Britain. But the attitude of the Japanese political leaders to the activities of Indian radicals was ambivalent. While the government promised Britain to arrest Indian radicals including Bose, Japanese officials in fact shielded Bose from extradition and finally rescinded the order of his deportation. To make a breakthrough against obstacles of international politics, Bose approached a group of Japanese radical nationalists who insisted that Japanese should express opposition to Western imperial expansion in Asia. In October 1915, Bose met Okawa Shumei in Tokyo, a Japanese radical intellectual who had currently studied colonial politics in India and advocated liberation of India through Japanese cooperation under the banner of pan-Asianism. With Okawa and other Japanese radical nationalists, Bose came to join the pan-Asian movement in Japan.

Absorbing knowledge on the contemporary colonial situation of Asian countries from Bose and other Asian radicals, Okawa formulated his idea of pan-Asianism. According to the philosophical explanation of Okawa, Asians, especially Indian people in the past, had put too much emphasis on the spiritual side of their life and thus failed to integrate their spirituality with social life. The separation of the inner individual life from the external social life had degenerated social institutions which 'devils of whitemen' appropriated for their greed. Okawa insisted that Asians should regenerate themselves by integrating modern social institutions with Asian spiritual tradition and cooperate with each other to overthrow Western colonial order. The advocacy of pan-Asianism by Okawa and other Japanese radical intellectuals attracted many Asian revolutionaries. Still, there was a critical difference between Okawa and Bose in their understanding of pan-Asianism. While Bose and many other Asian radicals expected the realization of pan-Asianism to be an alliance with Japan and other Asian countries on an equal standing, Okawa planned to extend hierarchical order which imperial Japan imposed on colonized Asian groups within its territory to other Asian countries, and thought of the propagation of the Japanese cause of imperialism, under which Asian countries should be federated against the menace of the Western powers, as 'the burden of our empire to the world'. For Okawa, the relation of Japan with other Asian countries should be that of father and son and alliance of Asian countries should be under the instruction of imperial Japan at least temporarily until other Asians caught up with Japan in the level of civilization. The Japanese leadership over other Asian countries was justified and differentiated from European colonial order by assuming 'coidentity in culture and race'. This reproduction of hierarchical ethnic order of imperial Japan in the idea of pan-Asianism advocated by Okawa and other radicals steadily enhanced its influence in Japan. Since the late nineteenth century, Japanese officials gradually extended the ideological reach of 'Japanese' through their handlings of colonial enterprises. Appropriating the discourses of the standard of civilization as a norm of modern international society, the Japanese government constructed a hierarchical order of 'Japanese' within the population. Pan-Asianism from the late 1910s embodied this imperial project of (re)constructing the concept of Japaneseness and in its extreme form led Japan to the path of military invasion of Asian countries during the Second World War.

* In the main text of this paper, names of Japanese appear by family name, last name in order.

References

Asano, Toyomi (2008), *Teikoku-Nihon no Shokuminchi Housei: Houiki-Tougou to Teikoku-Chitsujo*, Nagoya: Nagoyadaigaku-Shuppankai.

Boissier, Pierre (1985), *From Solferino to Tsushima: History of the International Committee of the Red Cross*, Geneva: Henry Dunant Institute.

Duara, Prasenjit (2001), 'The Discourse of Civilization and Pan-Asianism', *Journal of World History* 12, no. 1: 99-130.

Forsythe, David P. (2005), *The Humanitarians: The International Committee of the Red Cross*, New York: Cambridge University Press.

Gong, Gerrit W. (1984), *The Standard of 'Civilization' in International Society*, Oxford: Clarendon Press.

Hutchinson, John F. (1996), *Champions of Charity: War and the Rise of the Red Cross*, Boulder: Westview Press.

Kawamata, Keiichi (1906), *Nichiro Sensou Shi* (The History of the Russo-Japanese War), Tokyo: Shobunsha.

——— (1910), *Nihon-Sekijujisha Hattatsushi*, Tokyo: Nihon-Sekijujisha Hattatsushi Hakkoujo.

Matsumoto, Kenichi (2004), *Okawa Shumei*, Tokyo: Iwanami-Shoten.

Nagasaki, Nobuko (1978), 'Okawa Shumei no Shoki Indo Kenkyu: Nichi-In Kankei no Ichisokumen', *Rekishi to Bunka* 7 (March): 122.

——— (1983), 'Rashu Bihari Bosu Kou', in *Nihon Gunsei to Ajia no Minzoku-Undou*, ed. Hiroshi Tanaka, Tokyo: Ajia-Keizai Shuppankai, pp. 135-65.

Nakajima, Takeshi (2005), *Nakamuraya no Bosu: Indo Dokuritsu-Undou to Kindai Nihon no Ajia-Shugi*, Tokyo: Hakusuisha.

Oguma, Eiji (1998), *'Nihonjin' no Kyokai: Okinawa, Ainu, Taiwan, Chosen, Shokuminchi Shihai kara Hukki-Undou made*, Tokyo: Shinyousha.

——— (1995), *Tanitsu-Minzoku Shinwa no Kigen: 'Nihonjin' no Jigazou no Keihu*, Tokyo: Shinyousha.

Okawa, Shumei (1995), 'Rasu Bihari Bosu kun no Omoide', in Kuromitsu Soma, Yasuo Soma, and Tadanao Nakayama (eds.), *Ajia no Mezame: Indo-Shishi Bihari Bosu to Nihon*, Tokyo: Ozorasha [1942]), 233-7.

Okawa-Shumei Zenshu Kankoukai (ed) (1962), *Okawa Shumei Zenshu* 2, Tokyo: Iwasaki-Shoten.

Otsuka, Takehiko (2009), *Okawa Shumei: Aru Hukko-Kakushinshugisha no Shisou,* Tokyo: Koudansha.

The Red Cross Society of Japan (1915), *Humanity and Patriotism,* a pamphlet presented at the Panama Pacific International Exposition at San Francisco.

Reeves, Caroline (2005), 'From Red Crosses to Golden Arches: China, the Red Cross, and The Hague Peace Conference, 1899-1900', in *Interactions: Transregional Perspectives on World History,* ed. Jerry H. Bentley, Renate Bridenthal and Anand A. Yang, Honolulu: University of Hawai'i Press, 64-93.

Rikugun Shou (1917), *Meiji Sanju-Shichi-Hachi-Nen Seneki Manshu Gunsei Shi* 2-2, Tokyo: Rikugun Shou.

Sakai, Kazuomi (2009), *Kindai Nihon Gaikou to Ajia Taiheiyou Chitsujo,* Kyoto: Showadou.

Sareen, Tilak Raj (2005), 'Indo to Nichiro-Sensou', in *Nichiro-Sensou Kenkyu no Shinshiten,* ed. Nichiro-Sensou Kenkyukai, Yokohama: Seibunsha, pp. 292-302.

Shashi Hensan Iinkai (ed.) (1911), *Nihon-Sekijuji Shashi-Kou,* Tokyo: Nihon-Sekijujisha.

Shinohara, Toru (2001), *Kindai Nihon no Tashazou to Jigazou,* Tokyo: Kashiwashobou.

Tachikawa, Kyoichi and Haruhiko Shuku (2008), 'Seihu oyobi Gun to ICRC tou tono Kankei: Nisshin Sensou kara Taiheiyou Sensou made', *Bouei-Kenkyujo Kiyou,* vol. 11, no. 1 (November): 69-125.

Willemin, Georges and Roger Heacock under the direction of Jacques Freymond (1984), *The International Committee of the Red Cross,* Boston: Martinus Nijhoff Publishers.

17

The Dilemma of a People

Interrogating Identity Crisis in Igboland

VICTOR UKAOGO

Introduction

There is no better way to preface this paper than to share a little encounter I had with my students in a classroom. While teaching a course in Nigerian history at Igbinedion University some years back, a student ostensibly from the north took me by surprise, by asking whether it was appropriate for 'a Yoruba man' to head AREWA, the influential socio-political grouping in northern Nigeria. I tried for several minutes to convince him albeit the class that there exist several unresolved identity questions in several parts of the country including the south-west especially given the conflictual history of Ilorin anchored on the rebellion of Afonja. In the north, it is difficult to properly identify who the real Nigerians are as Nigerians, Chadians, Malians, etc., all claim to be Nigerians once they cross the border into Nigeria. Of course, several stories exist about how such people with questionable Nigerian identity had even tasted power in parts of the country. I could not place if the young man was satisfied with my reply but almost immediately another student in the class raised his hands to ask why a very prominent Nigerian diplomat of 'Yoruba' extraction would relate with his kith and kin in the daytime only to fraternize with northern power brokers at night on account of being a 'northerner'. This attitude according to the young man had given the diplomat (with dual citizenship) much more juicy diplomatic postings and opportunities than any other 'Yoruba man'. This intro would seem important here because the two questions above suggests the crisis of identity in Nigeria. What these students raised in the south-west are all too visible in all parts of the country including the south-east and parts of the south-south where Igbos are domiciled.

However, there is a prevailing identity crisis in parts of delta and rivers state where Igbos and Igbo-speaking people have ceaselessly denied their Igbo ancestry, the most recent being the widely publicized recant of Emeka Amadi, the accomplished literary icon of Igbo extraction in rivers state. He is not alone. A preponderant number of Igbos in these two states deny their Igboness and speak against the Igbos with despicable bitterness. They also blame the Igbos for any real or imagined problem they encounter in the Nigerian public space. For instance Emeka Esogbue acknowleged the identity dilemma of western Igbos and proceeded to blame 'core Igbos' for the ongoing crisis. Accordingly, he opined that:

> The first major issue of dilemma confronting this region is the problem of ethnic identity, the present state of the region weakened by abandonment and lack of vision has again raised the question on whether Anioma people are Igbos or not. This question has generated a lot of debate in the past and present, and will continue to do so even as it hampers growth and development in this region and presents us with nothing but pauperization. I make bold to comment that the attitude of the Igbo of South East to their Anioma counterparts have not really justified that Anioma are Igbo except on paper, and that if ever the people (of) South East deem this necessary, they have always relied and ended such only with historical support and not more, however actions have failed to justify this.[1]

It is indeed difficult if not pathetic to discuss the identity crisis in Igboland or any part of the country. For the Igbos, it is all too worrisome because a combination of self-inflicted injuries and externally generated conditions have created a debilitating social construct that has torn the Igbo nation into shreds. But suffice it to affirm the undiluted Igboness of all Igbos within and without the artificially created political confines of south-east Nigeria. There is no fake Igbo nor an artificial Igbo.[2] There is no better evidence to support this than a fatherly intellectual discourse I had with

M.A Onwujiogwu, one of Nigeria's most celebrated political anthropologists and sociologists in Okada town shortly before his transition. He told me that: 'I am an Ibusa man but from my long years of researching Igbo history, I have been able to trace my roots to a village very near to Awka in Anambra State. Same applies to many and several other Igbos in western Igboland.'[3]

In Rivers state, several Igbo settlements and communities have had cause to change or alter their names and names of their communities on account of the need to cover or distort the Igboness in them. It is therefore common to see several Igbo names deliberately misspelt to distort the meaning. In these names, alphabet such as 'R', 'H' are smuggled in to confuse a whole lot of people on the real meaning of the words. In some others, certain alphabet are removed such as 'N' in Nneka (Neka), all for the same purpose. These alphabet were deliberately inserted or extracted to either give new meaning to the names involved or distort the meanings. It would seem quite plausible to opine that externally generated conditions have done more harm to the identity crisis in Igboland than the reason of self-inflicted pain. This can be evidenced from two interrelated perspectives. First, curious and injurious boundary adjustment and state/region creation intrigues may have kickstarted the crisis in western Igboland when the Igbos of Anioma extraction were forcefully put in the Benin province with loud protests which were ignored. Their situation was not in any way remedied when it was further carved into the defunct Bendel state, again with greater resentment. The final inclusion of these Igbos into the present Delta state certainly worsened the identity crisis of the period. We shall come back to this.

Igbo Identity Crisis and Controversies

> . . . our region can and should only be correctly referred to as 'Anioma', and not 'Western Igbo, 'Ika-Igbo' all of which presage nothing but 'fake Igbos' . . . these derogatory references are threateningly tending to overshadow and send our prestigious name, Anioma to its early grave. . . .[4]

Prefacing this section with this quote signposts the depth of the crisis contained in the denial of the Igboness of western Igbos. Expectedly, enough controversy trail the disposition of Igbos in delta and rivers especially their denial of their ancestral interconnectedness with Igbos of the south-east. But Ephraim Adinlofu, a delta Igbo recently said that the issue is beyond the 'question of whether the people of Agbor or Ndokwa are disclaiming their Igboness' but the need to show concrete affinity between the 'core Igbos and Igbos in other lands'.[5] The on-going controversy concerning the change of title of the paramount ruler of Agbor from the 'Obi' of Agbor to 'Dein' of Agbor would seem very insightful, controversial and symbolic. In obvious disagreement with the change above, one of the subjects of the Agbor throne Adinlofu observed that:

> 'Obi' as the title designate, is an undiluted Igbo nomenclature. It is not an Hausa, Bini, Yoruba, Ishan or Fulani terminology. Apart from the differences in Igbo dialects and historical variances in origin, the other common variable for research revolves around this and title of 'Obi'.[6]

This change in nomenclature may mean much but in the opinion of Ogaranya Uju Nkwucha Afuleze, ethnicity is directly linked to divinity but it has been argued that:

> . . . it is not up to them to say what they are and what they are not. When God created them, He did not ask them who they wanted to be. He just created them Igbo. The only way you'll know who belongs to what ethnic group in Nigeria is the name and what language the name comes from. Anybody whose name is Amadi or Onyeri or Eke, or Odili, Wanodi (Nwanodi) does not need to tell you who he is. He is Igbo, his politics notwithstanding.[7]

All the traditional rulers of Delta Igbo communities bear the title of 'Obi'. They do not bear 'Oba' or any other related title but perhaps the strong wave of denials of Igbo link by several individuals and groups may have informed the young Obi's change of title. But the question must be asked why Igbos would want to deny their ancestry and heritage. Indeed Scott Iwuji writing in an article posted on the internet on 10 July 2008 felt puzzled why groups would keep abandoning or disowning the Igbo ethnic group as theirs. Put more aptly, why do groups keep dropping out of the bigger confederacy of the Igbo nation? Three theoretical and analytical explanation suffices.

(a) *The Survival-Political Imperative*

The Nigerian civil war which lasted between 1967 and 1970 had several adverse outcomes and consequences especially for the Igbos and more so for the Igbos outside the present south-east configuration. We must remember that the 1966 coup severely lampooned and held as the major cause of the civil war was led by an Igbo of Delta extraction, Major Chukwuma Kaduna Nzeogwu from Okpanam community. It is, however, intriguing how and why Asaba and its environs became a fertile ground for genocidal experiments by the federal forces. Perhaps further researches would reveal why the Asaba axis (with close proximity to Okpanam) became the theatre of genocidal eruptions and reprisals by the federal forces during the war. And as observed by a scholar:

> For the Igbos, the verifiable genocide conducted against their kith and kin in western Igboland by the federal forces headed by Major-General Ibrahim Haruna at the twilight of the war especially the passion, zest and zeal with which millions were killed notably children, women and able-bodied men would suggest a pre-meditated agenda to derace or de-populate the Igbos.[8]

In tandem to the above, Herbert Ekwe-Ekwe reveals that: '...during the course of four months in 1966, 80,000 Igbo and other Eastern Nigerians were hunted down and killed in several Northern towns and cities and elsewhere in the federation'.[9]

The famous Asaba massacres and those that took place around Asaba would seem to be a brutal retaliatory onslaught against Nzeogwu's kith and kin. Was the Asaba genocide[10] meant to hit back at Nzeogwu's immediate constituency or was it a mere coincidence? This was the situation immediately during the war and it compelled the Igbos of delta extraction (Ika-Igbo) to redefine themselves as non-Igbos. There was therefore palpable fear and tension on how to survive. On the strength of this Eghosa Osaghae affirms that the so-called minority Igbos had no choice but to redefine their origin in order to survive. It is this redefinition that manifested into the denial of Igbo ancestry by Igbos themselves. The Osaghae theory of racial redefinition holds for instance that: 'The Ikwerre of Rivers who had all along been regarded as an Igbo sub-group were forced to redefine themselves as non-Igbos.'[11]

In the confusion that followed, half truths were ingeniously crafted to intimidate the sub-groups in the delta who in the face of threatened survival, decided to deny their identity. Moreover, it was also believed that the Igbos maltreated minorities in the east,[12] a situation that created anti-Igbo sentiments as evidenced in the 'abandoned property' saga.

In the prevailing circumstance, an unwritten policy defining the relationship between Igbos and other components of the Nigerian federation was articulated by the federal government. One such policy includes the minoritization of the Igbos by sundry policies. In this direction, making the Igbos minorities became an ongoing project pursued with relentless vigour. It has, however, had catastrophic outcomes and consequences for the Igbos. For instance, the hurried balkanization of Nigeria by Gowon into 12 states was ostensibly done not only to break the Biafran solidarity and resistance but to ensure that the Igbos become a certain minority by all means. All successive governments have used state creation strategy to get back at the Igbos. To achieve this, a large chunk of Igbo-speaking people were excised from Igboland and put in states where they constitute mere minorities. This explains why western Igboland is in present day delta state while an innumerable number of Igbo communities are lumped in rivers state. Instead of allowing them to be with their kith and kin, they are separated and indoctrinated on why they must distance themselves from the so-called 'core-Igbos'. It has given rise to an ethnic crisis in Igboland where Igbos in these two Igbo-minority-states consistently deny their Igbo ancestry.[13] Consider the laughable act of excising three (3) communities from Egbema ancient Kingdom in Imo state and putting them in rivers state in a dubious state creation and boundary adjustment exercise. The current Inspector General of Police of the Federation (IGP) is of Egbema extraction incorporated into the rivers state from Imo state. He is still the Agunechemba 1 of Egbema in rivers state. Today, the ethnic identity of the IGP is not openly discussed and so nobody can say he is from Ndoni or Egbema or any other place. It is a secret. This is no surprise because the Igbos of rivers extraction have been indoctrinated to affirm that they have no ancestry in Igboland.[14] In Abia state, several oil communities in Ukwa axis of the state including Obigbo are today in rivers state. A curious trend in these equally curious exercises remains that all the excised communities in Igboland are oil producing enclaves. In the calculation of the government at the centre, oil proceeds from these communities would enrich the Igbos and give them certain strength that is not required of them. Orji Uzor Kalu, former governor of Abia state battled his arch enemy, ex-President Olusegun Obasanjo to the bitterest end on the need to return over 40 Abia oil wells credited to rivers state. The most convenient way to avoid the envisaged prolonged anti-Igbo policies was for the western Igbos to navigate away from the core Igbos while keeping a safe distance from them.

(b) *Historico-Analytical Framework*

Solomon Omojie[15] had argued that so long two languages Ika and Ozarra are spoken in Agbor, it will be difficult to insist that an Agbor man is purely an Igboman. This is because, there still exist several enduring Bini influences in Agbor as evidenced in names such as Agbontaen, Obaigbena, Ovia, Osahon, Osaigbovo, Osagie, etc. Moreover several cultural practices in Agbor like new year festivities, chieftaincy titles, marriage ceremonies, cultural and traditional dressing have deep Bini influences, totally different from the Igbo variation. On this, Agbor could not be entirely an Igbo settlement. To Solomon, both Igbos and Binis may have migrated into Agbor to settle and thereafter have influences in the town. While Emeka Esogbue[16] held the view that western Igbos are not Igbos but 'Anioma', Gabriel Nwanze[17] also of delta Igbo extraction held a contrary opinion. However, the intellectual exchanges between Solomon Omojie and Gabriel Nwanze on the origin and identity of Agbor people remain most insightful and illuminating.

However, M.A. Onwujeogwu's scholarly researches have shown from where the majority of delta Igbos came from. He told me personally at Okada that the Ibusa people actually migrated to their present abode from an Anambra town called Igbouzo (Anglicized to Ibusa). This was properly documented and compiled into a book as far back as 1972.[18] The variations in historical explanation which has become a controversy of sorts encouraged diverse individuals within the delta Igbo enclave to pitch their camp wherever it suited their persuasion and sensibilities. This explains the divergent opinion of individuals on the matter. But it would seem that the denials have gained ascendancy and has trickled down to the younger generation who know next to nothing on why an Emeka or Chukwuka could not expressly affirm his Igboness.

(c) *Unresolved Prejudices and Primordial Inclinations*

On a general note, there exist a multitude of other reasons why several western Igbos have navigated away from their Igbo heritage. A summary detail of several unresolved assumptions contains core grievances of western Igbos against eastern Igbos. This naturally includes the opinion of notable individuals. This includes:

- Emma Okocha's allegation challenging the Igbos to account for what happened to Major Kaduna Nzeogwu at the battlefront;
- Odimegwu Ojukwu's alleged oversight of not including western Igbo in the Biafran map;
- The abandonement of Ika-Igbo officers who fought at Biafra and have either not received pension till date or had died on account of poverty;
- The inability or refusal of Eastern Igbos to condole delta Igbos on the massacre of their people on account of their being Igbos and by extension 'Biafrans'.
- The seeming unwillingness of Ohaneze Ndi Igbo to support the creation of Anioma state;
- The dissimilar treatment given to Orji Uzor Kalu and Pat Utomi by Ohaneze Ndi Igbo when both vied for the presidency of the country;
- The abandonment of Anioma people by core Igbos, etc.

What is to be Done

From all indications, the prevailing angst of western Igbos against their own across the Niger which has informed the large-scale disclaimer against the Igbo nation could be addressed at least to ensure that a semblance of unity returns to the people. But there must be a deliberate show of willingness by all to achieve this. Several methods exists that could probably engender ethnic harmony amongst the Igbos irrespective of which state they live in. This will include but not limited to:

- A deliberate and conscious policy of giving all Igbos a feeling of belonging no matter where they come from. It has been observed that the Igbos of delta and rivers extraction feel alienated and abandoned by the Igbos of the south-east. They must be cultivated and given a sense of belonging through sundry means. The Ohaneze Ndi Igbo can do something in this direction especially now that it is headed by an 'Anioma' man;
- The apex Igbo organization must purge itself of hypocrisy and double standards in order to champion the renaissance and resurgence of Igbo relevance;
- The Igbos should strive to attain power at the centre in a democratic manner through a clearly defined collaboration and alliance with other ethnic nationalities. This is imperative in order to invalidate several anti-Igbo policies that hamper the progress of the Igbos. The conspiratorial and selfish attitude of certain Igbo politicians must be checked if the above is to be realized;
- More importantly, the negatively used republicanist philosophy of the Igbos anchored on the '*Igbo enwe Eze*' syndrome is archaic and defeatist. A more progressive philosophy that will bind all Igbos together is preferred to the duplicitious engagements which has yielded no dividend whatsoever. The Igbo needs a leader, a spokesman in the mould of Awolowo, Adesanya who can articulate properly the needs of the generality of Igbos in the country;
- There must be a concious policy by the Eastern Igbos to support by all means possible the creation of an Anioma state for western Igbos or any other in rivers state that have remained minorities and cannot come near power in their present place of abode. This is important if the containment policy orchestrated at the centre and which the Igbos complained about at the Oputa panel is to be upturned;

- The Igbos could also work towards ensuring that all Igbos are put in the same geo-political zone such as the south-east. This will put an end to all the squabbles on alleged alienation, negligence and abandonement. Indeed, it will ensure the return of Igbo oil wells now in other states' jurisdictions;
- There is need for a re-orientation of the Igbos especially in the area of negative commerce, internet fraud and naive politics. The uncontrolled attitude of some Igbo politicians who ride on the back of the Igbos to attain power and push no Igbo agenda at the top must be addressed by Ohaneze that can provide more visionary leadership and articulate practicable methods of sanctioning such 'black sheep' in our midst.

Conclusion

It is not enough to continually cry over situations or conditions that can be helped. The identity crisis in Igboland is not beyond the Igbos themselves to handle. They have done nothing, rather many have intensified their sterile search for solutions in places where there is none. There is no better way of addressing this matter than the Igbos themselves embracing their brothers across the Niger. They must show concern about their welfare, they must show understanding to their pains, anguish and aspirations. They must be helped to attain whatever task they have set for themselves. For instance, a Yoruba man remains Yoruba whether in Brazil, Benin or in Togo, same for the Hausa/Fulani in Niger, Chad or elsewhere. The governors of the south-east and Ohaneze must conciously develop a policy aimed at bringing Igbos in other zones together and in the process cultivate and visit them, collaborate with them and generally show them that they are needed as brothers and sisters. This really will halt this spate of disengagement from the Igbo nation.

Notes

1. Emeka Esogbue, 'Anioma: Igbo, Ijaw,Itsekiri, Urhobo, Isoko: Leave Us Alone' article posted on the internet on 20 May 2008 (accessed on 12 April 2009).
2. Interview with M.A. Onwuejeogwu, 11 June 2006.

3. Interview with M.A. Onwuejeogwu, Igbinedion University, Okada, 11 June 2006.
4. Esogbue, op. cit.
5. Ephraim Adinlofu, ' Igbos of Delta State and the Crisis of Identity' (Conclusion), posted on the Internet on the on 9 May 2008 (accessed on the 12 May 2009).
6. Ibid.
7. Ogaranya Uju Nkwucha Afuleze, quoted without source by Emeka Esogbue, 20 May 2008.
8. Victor Ukaogo, 'Gowon–Obasanjo 'Pact' and the *De-Igbonization* Project, 1966-2007', accepted for Publication, *Journal of Igbo Studies*, vol. 1, no.1, 2009.
9. Herbert Ekwe-Ekwe, 'Obasanjo's Obsession with Biafra Versus Facts of History', USAfricaonline.com and CLASS Magazine, posted on the internet on 23 May 2001 (accessed on 19 May 2009).
10. Lawrence Chinedu Nwobu, 'Remembering Murtala Muhammed: The Butcher of Asaba', posted on the internet on 19 February 2009 (accessed on 13 April 2009).
11. E.E. Osaghae, 'Social Movements and Rights' Claims in the Niger-Delta', working document, Department of Political Science, Igbinedion University, Okada, 2007.
12. Willink Minority Report, cited from Victor Ukaogo, 'From Palm Oil to Crude Oil: The Impact of International Trade on Niger–Delta Communities, 1895-1995,' Ph.D thesis submitted to School of Post Graduate Studies, University of Lagos, 2008, p. 265.
13. Osaghae, op. cit.
14. Victor Ukaogo, 'From Palm Oil to Crude Oil: The Impact of International Trade on Niger–Delta Communities, 1895-1995', Ph.D thesis submitted to School of Post Graduate Studies, University of Lagos, 2008, p. 269.
15. Solomon Omojie, 'Bini Influences in Agbor', Response to Ephraim Adinloju's Igbos of Delta State and the Crisis of Identity' (Conclusion), posted on the internet on the 3 November 2008.
16. Emeka Esogbue, 'Response to Ephraim Adinloju's Igbos of Delta State and the Crisis of Identity' (Conclusion), posted on the internet on 20 November 2008 (accessed on 13 April 2009).
17. Gabriel Nwanze, 'Response to Ephraim Adinloju's Igbos of Delta State and the Crisis of Identity' (Conclusion), posted on the internet on 19 January 2009 (accessed on 13 April 2009).
18. M.A Onwuejeogwu, 'The Traditional Political System of Ibusa', 1972.

Contributors

JAVEED ALAM is Former Chairman, Indian Council of Social Science and Research, New Delhi.

R.A. ARIYARATNE is Director, Regional Centre for Strategic Studies, Colombo, Sri Lanka.

KOUSAR J. AZAM is Professor and former Head, Department of Political Science, Osmania University, Hyderabad.

B.A. SHILPA DEEKSHITH is Lecturer, Department of Political Science, St. Ann's College for Women, Mehdipatnam, Hyderabad.

KRISHNA HACHHETHU is Academic Coordinator, Centre for Nepal & Area Studies, Tribhuvan University, Kirtipur, Kathmandu, Nepal.

ADEEL KHAN is at the School of Humanities, Faculty of Arts and Science, University of New England, Armidale, New South Wales, Australia.

ASHUTOSH KUMAR is Reader in Indian Politics, Department of Political Science, Panjab University, Chandigarh.

YOSHIYA MAKITA is Research Scholar, Graduate School of Social Sciences, Hitotsubashi University, Chiyoda-ku, Tokyo, Japan.

B. MALINI REDDY is Head of the Department of Political Science, St. Ann's College for Women, Mehdipatnam, Hyderabad.

EMANUELA MANGIAROTTI is a PhD scholar, BSIS (University of Kent) United Kingdom.

CARMEN DE MICHELE is Academic Assistant, Institute of Economics, University Ludwig-Maximilians, Munich, Germany.

SAJAL NAG is Chair, Department of History, Assam University, Silchar, Assam.

M.S. PRABHAKARA is an eminent Journalist from Guwahati, Assam.

OLGA POTAPOVA is at the Faculty of Philosophy, School of Economics, Moscow, Russia.

P.K. RYNGNGA is Assistant Professor, Northeastern Hill University, Shillong, Assam.

D.R. SAHU is Associate Professor, Department of Sociology, University of Lucknow, Lucknow.

K.R. SHARMA is Centenary Professor and former Dean of Social Sciences, Department of Social Sciences, University of Delhi.

VALLABU SRILATHA is Assistant Professor at Centre for Indian Ocean Studies, Osmania University, Hyderabad.

VICTOR UKAOGO is at the Department of History and International Relations, Redeemer's University, Redemption City, Ognu State, Nigeria.

Index